Great Issues
in American
History:

*

*From Settlement
to Revolution,
1584–1776*

GREAT ISSUES IN AMERICAN HISTORY:

From Settlement to Revolution, 1584–1776

EDITED BY

Clarence L. Ver Steeg and Richard Hofstadter

VINTAGE BOOKS

A DIVISION OF RANDOM HOUSE

New York

Preface

THESE documentary selections are intended to provide a generous sampling from the major political controversies in the colonial period of American history. We hope that the general introductions, together with the headnotes supplied for each selection, will serve to set the documents in their historical context in such a way as to make it possible for a reader with a modest knowledge of American history to read them profitably and without further supplement. This volume, together with its companion volumes, has been planned with special concern for the interests and needs of undergraduates who will have occasion to use them in connection with a textbook or a general survey of American history.

With this in mind, we have not tried to make the general introductions into a collective history of American politics, nor even into histories of the particular issues selected. They are intended to provide a brief setting for issues of central importance. The introductions will serve their purpose if they refresh the memory of the general reader and assist the student in establishing the links between these sources and his other readings.

It has been our purpose to concentrate on political controversy. Texts of statutes are generally not included. They are available in reference books and are usually well summarized for the student's purposes in general books. Neither have we—except in the cases of a few documents whose special importance seemed to demand their inclusion—reprinted purely illustrative materials. Almost everything in these volumes can be described as argumentative. These documents reproduce the words of major actors of American political history—whether judges, statesmen, legislative bodies, or private individuals of influence—engaged in debating issues of central importance. Moreover, it is our conviction that social, economic, and even intellectual conflict is reflected in political issues and that often the best way to analyze these deep-seated divisions is by taking their measure through political disputes. In these volumes it has not been possible to include all the historical issues that may be considered important. To achieve such inclusiveness seems less desirable than that every issue selected should be discussed in some depth in the chosen documents, and that opposing views should be adequately represented.

Of necessity, the documents have been edited, and the ellipses indicate omitted portions. But we have tried to avoid snippets. Where a limited segment from a larger text has been selected, enough has been included in each case to provide a coherent sample of the original argument at the point at which the author was stating the novel or essential portions of his case. Some small amount of modernization has been imposed on most documents but without any change in their meaning, character, or flavor.

The original edition of *Great Issues* was two volumes, covering the period 1765–1957. In this edition, it has been expanded to three volumes: The first volume, *From Settlement to Revolution, 1584–1776,* is by Clarence L. Ver Steeg and Richard Hofstadter; the second, *From the Revolution to the Civil War, 1765–1865,* by Richard Hofstadter; and the final volume, *From Reconstruction to the Present Day, 1864–1969,* by Richard Hofstadter. To offer added adaptability Part VII of the present volume is repeated in the next volume on the years 1765 to 1865. Teachers wishing to use this volume to conform with a colonial course ending with the Revolution, or its successor for a course beginning with the Revolution and concluding with the Civil War, will be able to satisfy their respective needs. The last volume covering the years from Reconstruction to the present day has been updated to include major issues of the 1960s.

R. H.
C. VS.

Contents

PART I: THE COLONIZING IMPULSE

PART II: THE ESTABLISHMENT OF SELF-GOVERNMENT

PART III: THE ECONOMIC REGULATION OF THE EMPIRE

PART IV: THE POLITICS OF INTERNAL CONTROVERSY

PART V: CONSTITUTIONAL CONTEST BETWEEN COLONY AND CROWN

PART VI: THE POLITICS OF INTERNATIONAL RIVALRY

Great Issues
in American
History:
*
*From Settlement
to Revolution,
1584–1776*

✷ PART I ✷

The Colonizing Impulse

THE colonizing impulse grew out of a search by the nations of Western Europe for new sea routes to the fabulous East, source of silver, gold, precious gems, spices, perfumes, and other exotic products. Because of their strategic location in the Mediterranean, between 1100 and 1500 the Italian cities and their merchants monopolized this trade. Portugal led the way in breaking this monopoly by exploring Africa, combining the search for an all-water route to the East with the aim of Christianizing Africa and trading. Later, other European nations joined in this competition. In 1498 Vasco da Gama, sailing under the Portuguese flag, rounded the southern tip of Africa and made port at Calicut, India, thereby achieving a goal set more than a century and a half earlier.

Spain competed with Portugal by financing a desperate scheme, proposed by Christopher Columbus, to reach the East by sailing west. Columbus' discovery of the New World marked a watershed in history by making the Atlantic instead of the Mediterranean one of the principal highways of the known world and by planting outposts of western civilization in the Americas which, in modern times, became independent and powerful nations. Within two years Spain founded its first colony in the New World, and within thirty years Spanish conquistadores had imposed Spanish rule on Mexico and Latin America, bringing back undreamed-of American treasure in gold and silver.

The effect in Europe was dramatic. The theory took root that no nation could be great and powerful unless it possessed colonies in the New World, and their establishment became a national goal. Colonies were expected to produce raw materials, particularly those not grown in the parent country, to be processed at home for sale in the world market as finished goods. Hopes were also raised that precious metals would be discovered in every American colony and that a water route through the continental barrier would be found.

Every dimension of life in Western Europe interacted with the New World colonies, but in the political, diplomatic, and economic spheres the relationship became critical. Each nation of Western Europe asked itself how it could best compete in colonizing the New World. The success of one was viewed by the others as a threat to their national interests. Once a colony was founded, each nation followed the policies peculiar to itself to strengthen and improve its position.

England joined in the competition for New World territory in 1497 when John Cabot, commanding the *Matthew,* sailed for the American continent, reached Newfoundland, and returned. In a second voyage in 1498, of which little is known, Cabot apparently followed the contours of the Atlantic coastline of North America. But no English settlement was established for more than a hundred years, not until Jamestown, Virginia in 1607.

In this interval of a century England was transformed. The Italian and German merchant ties of 1500 were sharply reduced, and a merchant class in England gained prominence. Joint-stock trading companies, unknown in 1500 but numbering in the hundreds by 1600, became a corporate device to exploit commercial exchanges with the ports of Europe and Asia. In 1500 England was a Catholic country, but by 1600, stirred by the religious revolution of the Protestant Reformation, it had severed ties with Rome and formed a national church. In the process many Englishmen divided into dissenting religious groups, and, subsequently, a legacy of differing sects was transplanted to the English colonies in America. Between 1500 and 1600 the Tudor line of English monarchs consolidated their hold on the throne and the country by enlisting the support of local governments and Parliament. The concept of a people with a voice in government and a king with limited power was also transplanted to the English colonies.

Although the immediate significance of colonization of the New World was recognized, an evaluation of it as a factor in the developing history of mankind awaited a more dispassionate appraisal by Adam Smith in 1776 (Document 1) when the American Declaration of Independence signaled unmistakably that the history of colonization had reached a crisis. The recommendations of Christopher Columbus regarding the role of colonies in relation to the mother country represent a beginning in the history of American colonization (Document 2). His observations were directed to the Spanish Crown as a guide for public policy.

In 1493 a Spanish settlement was established in Hispaniola, present-day Haiti. Additional settlements in the Caribbean became staging bases for Balboa's discovery of the Pacific (1513) and Hernando Cortes' conquest of Mexico (1519). Francisco Pizarro's conquest of Peru (1532) was launched from the Isthmus of Panama. Each expedition fulfilled earlier hopes of profitable colonizing ventures. The wealth found in Mexico and Peru, particularly the discovery of precious metals, made Spain rich. Each country of Western Europe visualized Spain as the model upon which to pattern itself if it, too, were to become rich and powerful.

France sent Jacques Cartier to the New World in 1534; his name became famous but he failed to establish a colony. French efforts to plant settlements in South America and in territory immediately north of Florida also failed. More than a half-century later, Samuel de Champlain (Document 3) succeeded where his predecessors had failed by founding Quebec in 1608.

England made no serious attempt to follow up on Cabot's voyages of 1497 to 1498. Domestic upheaval prevented full concentration on overseas expansion. King Henry VII and his son, Henry VIII, the father of Queen Elizabeth, directed their energies to the unification of England and the establishment of a Tudor dynasty. The colonizing impulse, however, gradually gained fervency in England. One of its most articulate advocates was Richard Hakluyt (Document 4) who saw in colonization the appropriate expression of England's greatness and the foundation for a glorious English future.

England's first attempts at settlements in America were initiated under the auspices of landed proprietors, Sir Humphrey Gilbert and later Sir Walter Raleigh, who were granted large domains in the New World by the king in return for establishing English colonies. These men did not have singly the financial resources to sustain a settlement until it grew roots sufficient to maintain itself. Thus Gilbert's attempts failed (1578, 1583), as did those of Raleigh (1585, 1587)—although it should be noted that Raleigh faced the unusual handicap in his final effort of a protracted war with Spain in which the English fleet defeated the Spanish Armada (1588).

Only when England, as a matter of national policy, matched its colonizing impulse with one of its developing economic strengths, the joint-stock company, did English colonization succeed. The first of these efforts was, of course, Virginia. The instructions sent with the expedition detailed the procedure to be followed, including management of the sensitive problem of possible Spanish intruders (Document 5). The founding of Virginia profoundly disturbed Spain (Document 6), but, despite the political-diplomatic confrontation, Virginia set the pattern for successful English colonization.

The colonizing impulses of individuals often differed sharply from stated public policy. One of the most eloquent and humanizing discussions of why men and women wished to find their destinies in a strange, new land is given by William Bradford, the governor of Plymouth Colony (Document 7), which was settled in 1620. Companies are also composed of people; the individuals composing the Virginia Company disagreed on the proper course to follow in advancing the welfare of the colony (Document 8). Because of the broad authority of the Virginia Company, each decision was essentially a political one.

The desire of people to find a better life and the desire of government to strengthen its national and international position led to policy decisions in which both hoped to benefit. Social discontent arising from the displacement of families from the land, a difference of religious views growing out of the sweeping intellectual and religious revolution of the Protestant Reformation, and the economic strength found in the rise of merchants along with the creation of companies to extend their enterprising spirit are molded together in a fascinating semi-propagandizing pamphlet by the Reverend John White, an earthy, realistic English Puritan divine who argues for the establishment of Massachusetts Bay (Document 9).

Massachusetts Bay received its charter in 1629, and in 1630 a "Great Migration" of about 700 men, women, and children, together with their household goods, livestock, and other supplies, sailed for New England to join the 400 hardy souls who had preceded them. From 1635 to 1636 Thomas Hooker and others migrated from Massachusetts Bay to found towns on the Connecticut River. Offshoots from Massachusetts Bay also sprang up when it banished leaders like Roger Williams, founder of Rhode Island, and Anne Hutchinson because of their differing political and religious views. Reports that Massachusetts Bay ignored English rule and enforced political practices and religious conformity unacceptable in England invited governmental inquiry. Steps were taken, unsuccessfully as it turned out, to rescind the charter of Massachusetts Bay (Document 10). A grievance, but of a very different kind, emanated from Chesapeake Bay (Document 11) where Virginia wished to block the impending proprietary grant of Maryland to Lord Baltimore. Virginia's protest failed.

By 1633 the full sweep of the English colonizing impulse had revealed itself—the role of international competition, the importance of national public policy, the direction of private economic interests, and the driving force of religious convictions. Each emerged out of debate and argument and, in turn, produced further debate and argument. Each was reflected in political issues, broadly conceived.

DOCUMENT 1

ADAM SMITH, "OF COLONIES," FROM *THE WEALTH OF NATIONS,* 1776

Adam Smith, a brilliant eighteenth-century English political economist, had the advantage of judging the significance of colonies by a rigorous examination based on the colonial experience of 300 years. His overview has a built-in bias: he strongly disapproved of excessive regulation of colonial trade by parent countries. But his analysis is rich with insight and remarkably dispassionate in its argument. Adam Smith recognized that the discovery of the New World not only brought wealth and prosperity to the Old World, but that it also marked a divide in the history of mankind. The passage that follows is the work of this economic theorist who discusses problems in a language readily understandable by everyone.

Of the advantages which Europe has derived from the discovery of America. . . .

Those advantages may be divided, first, into the general advantages which Europe, considered as one great country, has derived from those great events; and, secondly, into the particular advantages which each colonizing country has derived from the colonies which particularly belong to it, in consequence of the authority or dominion which it exercises over them.

The general advantages which Europe, considered as one great country, has derived from the discovery and colonization of America, consist, first, in the increase of its enjoyments; and, secondly, in the augmentation of its industry.

The surplus produce of America, imported into Europe, furnishes the inhabitants of this great continent with a variety of commodities which they could not otherwise have possessed, some for conveniency and use, some for pleasure, and some for ornament, and thereby contributes to increase their enjoyments.

The discovery and colonization of America, it will readily be allowed, have contributed to augment the industry, first, of all the countries which trade to it directly; such as Spain, Portugal, France, and England; and, secondly, of all those which, without trading to it directly, send, through the medium of other countries, goods to it of their own produce; such as Austrian Flanders, and some provinces of Germany, which, through the medium of the countries before mentioned, send to it a considerable quantity of linen and other goods. All such countries have evidently gained a more extensive market for their surplus produce, and must consequently have been encouraged to increase its quantity.

But, that those great events should likewise have contributed to encourage the industry of countries, such as Hungary and Poland, which may never, perhaps, have sent a single commodity of their own produce to America, is not, perhaps, altogether so evident. That those events have done so, however, cannot be doubted. Some part of the produce of America is consumed in Hungary and Poland, and there is some demand there for the sugar, chocolate, and tobacco, of that new quarter of the world. But those commodities must be purchased with something which is either the produce of the industry of Hungary and Poland, or with something which had been purchased with some part of that produce. Those commodities of America are new values, new equivalents, introduced into Hungary and Poland to be exchanged there for the surplus produce of those countries. By being carried thither they create a new and more extensive market for that surplus produce. They raise its value, and thereby contribute to encourage its increase. Though no part of it may ever be carried to America, it may be carried to other countries which purchase it with a part of their share of the surplus produce of America; and it may find a market by means of the circulation of that trade which was originally put into motion by the surplus produce of America.

Those great events may even have contributed to increase the enjoyments, and to augment the industry of countries which not only never sent any commodities to America, but never received any from it. Even such countries may have received a greater abundance if other commodities from countries of which the surplus produce had been augmented by means of the American trade. This greater abundance, as it must necessarily have increased their enjoyments, so it must likewise have augmented their industry. A greater number of new equivalents of some kind or other must have been presented to them to be exchanged for the surplus produce of that industry. A more extensive market must have been created for that surplus produce, so as to raise its value, and thereby encourage its increase. The mass of commodities annually thrown into the great circle of European commerce, and by its various revolutions annually distributed among all the different nations comprehended within it, must have been augmented by the whole surplus produce of America. A greater share of this greater mass, therefore, is likely to have fallen to each of those nations, to have increased their enjoyments, and augmented their industry. . . .

The particular advantages which each colonizing country derives from the colonies which particularly belong to it, are of two different kinds; first, those common advantages which every empire derives from the provinces subject to its dominion; and, secondly, those peculiar advantages which are supposed to result from provinces of so very peculiar a nature as the European colonies of America. . . .

The discovery of America, and that of a passage to the East Indies by the Cape of Good Hope, are the two greatest and most important events recorded in the history of mankind. Their consequences have already been very great: but, in the short period of between two and three centuries which has elapsed since these discoveries were made, it is impossible that the whole extent of their consequences can have been seen. What benefits, or what misfortunes to mankind may hereafter result from those great events, no human wisdom can foresee. By uniting, in some measure, the most distant parts of the world, by enabling them to relieve one another's wants, to increase one another's enjoyments, and to encourage one another's industry, their general tendency would seem to be beneficial. . . .

In the mean time, one of the principal effects of those discoveries has been to raise the mercantile system to a degree of splendour and glory which it could never otherwise have attained to. It is the object of that system to enrich a great nation rather by trade and manufactures than by the improvement and cultivation of land, rather by the industry of the towns than by that of the country. But, in consequence of those discoveries, the commercial towns of Europe, instead of being the manufacturers and carriers for but a very small part of the world (that part of Europe which is washed by the Atlantic ocean, and the countries which lie round the Baltic and Mediterranean seas), have now become the manufacturers for the numerous and thriving cultivators of America, and the carriers, and in some respects the manufacturers too, for almost all the different nations of Asia, Africa, and America. Two new worlds have been opened to their industry, each of them much greater and more extensive than the old one, and the market of one of them growing still greater and greater every day. . . .

DOCUMENT 2

CHRISTOPHER COLUMBUS, LETTER TO THE KING AND QUEEN OF SPAIN,
(UNDATED, PROBABLY 1694)

Christopher Columbus' daring needs no introduction, but one is often pleasantly surprised at the fine quality of mind of this self-taught, red-haired, handsome, talented, and ambitious man. Within two years after the discovery of America, before he fell under the cloud of the king's disfavor, Columbus advocated the establishment of a Spanish colony in the New World, closely regulated and directed by the Crown. That he should sense the direction of future events testifies to his perception. Spain acted upon Columbus' advice

*and quickly planted a colony in Hispaniola (Haiti)
that became the stepping stone for further Spanish
incursions into the Americas. In a larger sense, the
Spanish settlement at Hispaniola served as the foun-
tainhead of a mainstream in the evolution of the New
World, the European colonization of the Western
Hemisphere.*

Most High and Mighty Sovereigns,

In obedience to your Highnesses' commands, and with
submission to superior judgment, I will say whatever occurs
to me in reference to the colonization and commerce of
the Island of Espanola, and of the other islands, both those
already discovered and those that may be discovered hereafter.

In the first place, as regards the Island of Espanola:
Inasmuch as the number of colonists who desire to go
thither amounts to two thousand, owing to the land being
safer and better for farming and trading, and because it
will serve as a place to which they can return and from
which they can carry on trade with the neighboring islands:

Item. That in the said island there shall be founded
three or four towns, situated in the most convenient places,
and that the settlers who are there be assigned to the aforesaid places and towns.

Item. That for the better and more speedy colonization
of the said island, no one shall have liberty to collect gold
in it except those who have taken out colonists' papers,
and have built houses for their abode, in the town in which
they are, that they may live united and in greater safety.

Item. That each town shall have its alcalde [Mayor]
. . . and its notary public, as is the use and custom in
Castile.

Item. That there shall be a church, and parish priests
or friars to administer the sacraments, to perform divine
worship, and for the conversion of the Indians.

Item. That none of the colonists shall go to seek gold
without a license from the governor or alcalde of the town

where he lives; and that he must first take oath to return to the place whence he sets out, for the purpose of registering faithfully all the gold he may have found, and to return once a month, or once a week, as the time may have been set for him, to render account and show the quantity of said gold; and that this shall be written down by the notary before the alcalde, or, if it seems better, that a friar or priest, deputed for the purpose, shall be also present.

Item. That all the gold thus brought in shall be smelted immediately, and stamped with some mark that shall distinguish each town; and that the portion which belongs to your Highnesses shall be weighed, and given and consigned to each alcalde in his own town, and registered by the above-mentioned priest or friar, so that it shall not pass through the hands of only one person, and there shall be no opportunity to conceal the truth.

Item. That all gold that may be found without the mark of one of the said towns in the possession of any one who has once registered in accordance with the above order shall be taken as forfeited, and that the accuser shall have one portion of it and your Highnesses the other.

Item. That one per centum of all the gold that may be found shall be set aside for building churches and adorning the same, and for the support of the priests or friars belonging to them; and, if it should be thought proper to pay any thing to the alcaldes or notaries for their services, or for ensuring the faithful performance of their duties, that this amount shall be sent to the governor or treasurer who may be appointed there by your Highnesses.

Item. As regards the division of the gold, and the share that ought to be reserved for your Highnesses, this, in my opinion, must be left to the aforesaid governor and treasurer, because it will have to be greater or less according to the quantity of gold that may be found. Or, should it seem preferable, your Highnesses might, for the space of one year, take one half, and the collector the other, and a better arrangement for the division be made afterward.

Item. That if the said alcaldes or notaries shall commit or be privy to any fraud, punishment shall be provided, and the same for the colonists who shall not have declared all the gold they have.

Item. That in the said island there shall be a treasurer, with a clerk to assist him, who shall receive all the gold belonging to your Highnesses, and the alcaldes and notaries of the towns shall each keep a record of what they deliver to the said treasurer.

Item. As, in the eagerness to get gold, every one will wish, naturally, to engage in its search in preference to any other employment, it seems to me that the privilege of going to look for gold ought to be withheld during some portion of each year, that there may be opportunity to have the other business necessary for the island performed.

Item. In regard to the discovery of new countries, I think permission should be granted to all that wish to go, and more liberality used in the matter of the fifth, making the tax easier, in some fair way, in order that many may be disposed to go on voyages.

I will now give my opinion about ships going to the said Island of Espanola, and the order that should be maintained; and that is, that the said ships should only be allowed to discharge in one or two ports designated for the purpose, and should register there whatever cargo they bring or unload; and when the time for their departure comes, that they should sail from these same ports, and register all the cargo they take in, that nothing may be concealed.

Item. In reference to the transportation of gold from the island to Castile, that all of it should be taken on board the ship, both that belonging to your Highnesses and the property of every one else; that it should all be placed in one chest with two locks, with their keys, and that the master of the vessel keep one key and some person selected by the governor and treasurer the other; that there should come with the gold, for a testimony, a list of all that has been put into the said chest, properly marked, so that each owner may receive his own; and that, for the faithful performance of this duty, if any gold whatsoever is found outside of the said chest in any way, be it little or much, it shall be forfeited to your Highnesses.

Item. That all the ships that come from the said island shall be obliged to make their proper discharge in the port of Cadiz, and that no person shall disembark or other person be permitted to go on board until the ship has been visited by the person or persons deputed for that purpose, in the said city, by your Highnesses, to whom the master shall show all that he carries, and exhibit the manifest of all the cargo, it may be seen and examined if the said ship brings any thing hidden and not known at the time of lading.

Item. That the chest in which the said gold has been carried shall be opened in the presence of the magistrates of the said city of Cadiz, and of the person deputed for that purpose by your Highnesses, and his own property be given to each owner.—I beg your Highnesses to hold me in your protection; and I remain, praying our Lord God for your Highnesses' lives and the increase of much greater States.

DOCUMENT 3

SAMUEL DE CHAMPLAIN, VOYAGES, 1604

France, together with Portugal, Holland, Sweden, and England, followed the lead of Spain. Each nation envied the growing wealth and power of Spain that were derived from its possessions in the New World. Each nation, therefore, saw its future position as dependent upon New World colonies.

The first French voyager of note was Jacques Cartier, who began his explorations of North America in 1534. But Samuel de Champlain was responsible for a series of French explorations into North America in the late sixteenth and early seventeenth centuries that resulted in the founding of the first successful French colony at Quebec in 1608. In the following passage taken from Champlain's writings, the sense of European competition, particularly with Spain, for the New World is well-developed.

The inclinations of men differ according to their varied dispositions; and each one in his calling has his particular end in view. Some aim at gain, some at glory, some at the public weal. The greater number are engaged in trade, and especially that which is transacted on the sea. Hence arise the principal support of the people, the opulence and honor of states. This is what raised ancient Rome to the sovereignty and mastery over the entire world, and the Venetians to a grandeur equal to that of powerful kings. It has in all times caused maritime towns to abound in riches, among which Alexandria and Tyre are distinguished, and numerous others, which fill up the regions of the interior with the objects of beauty and rarity obtained from foreign nations. For this reason, many princes have striven to find a northerly route to China, in order to facilitate commerce with the Orientals, in the belief that this route would be shorter and less dangerous.

In the year 1496, the king of England commissioned John Cabot and his son Sebastian to engage in this search. About the same time, Don Emanuel, king of Portugal, despatched on the same errand Gaspar Cortereal, who returned without attaining his object. Resuming his journeys the year after, he died in the undertaking; as did also his brother Michel, who was prosecuting it perseveringly. In the years 1534 and 1535, Jacques Cartier received a like commission from King Francis I, but was arrested in his course. Six years after, Sieur de Roberval, having renewed it, sent Jean Alfonse of Saintonge farther northward along the coast of Labrador; but he returned as wise as the others. In the years 1576, 1577, and 1578, Sir Martin Frobisher, an Englishman, made three voyages along the northern coasts. Seven years later, Humphrey Gilbert, also an Englishman, set out with five ships, but suffered shipwreck on Sable Island, where three of his vessels were lost. In the same and two following years, John Davis, an Englishman, made three voyages for the same object; penetrating to the 72d degree, as far as a strait which is called at the present day by his name. After him, Captain Georges made also a voyage in 1590, but in consequence of the ice was compelled to return without having made any discovery. The Hollanders, on their part, had no more precise knowledge in the direction of Nova Zembla.

So many voyages and discoveries without result, and attended with so much hardship and expense, have caused us French in late years to attempt a permanent settlement in those lands which we call New France, in the hope of thus realizing more easily this object; since the voyage in search of the desired passage commences on the other side of the ocean, and is made along the coast of this region. These considerations had induced the Marquis de la Roche, in 1598, to take a commission from the king for making a settlement in the above region. With this object, he landed men and supplies on Sable Island; but, as the conditions which had been accorded to him by his Majesty were not fulfilled, he was obliged to abandon his undertaking, and leave his men there. A year after, Captain Chauvin accepted another commission to transport settlers to the same region; but, as this was shortly after revoked, he prosecuted the matter no farther.

After the above, notwithstanding all these accidents and disappointments, Sieur de Monts desired to attempt what had been given up in despair, and requested a commission for this purpose of his Majesty, being satisfied that the previous enterprises had failed because the undertakers of them had not received assistance, who had not succeeded, in one nor even two years' time, in making the acquaintance of the regions and people there, nor in finding harbors adapted for a settlement. He proposed to his Majesty a means for covering these expenses, without drawing any thing from the royal revenues; viz., by granting to him the monopoly of the fur-trade in this land. This having been granted to him, he made great and excessive outlays, and carried out with him a large number of men of various vocations. Upon his arrival, he caused the necessary number of habitations for his followers to be constructed. This expenditure he continued for three consecutive years, after which, in consequence of the jealousy and annoyance of certain Basque merchants, together with some from Brittany, the monopoly which had been granted to him was revoked by the Council to the great injury and loss of Sieur de Monts, who, in consequence of this revocation, was compelled to abandon his entire undertaking, sacrificing his labors and the outfit for his settlement.

But since a report had been made to the king on the fertility of the soil by him, and by me on the feasibility of discovering the passage to China, without the inconveniences of the ice of the north or the heats of the torrid zone, through which our sailors pass twice in going and twice in returning, with inconceivable hardships and risks, his Majesty directed Sieur de Monts to make a new outfit, and send men to continue what he had commenced. This he did. And, in view of the uncertainty of his commission, he chose a new spot for his settlement, in order to deprive jealous persons of any such distrust as they had previously conceived. He was also influenced by the hope of greater advantages in case of settling in the interior, where the people are civilized, and where it is easier to plant the Christian faith and establish such order as is necessary for the protection of a country, than along the sea-shore, where the savages generally dwell. From this course, he believed the king would derive an inestimable profit; for it is easy to suppose that Europeans will seek out this advantage rather than those of a jealous and intractable disposition to be found on the shores, and the barbarous tribes.

DOCUMENT 4

RICHARD HAKLUYT, *DISCOURSE OF WESTERN PLANTING,* 1584

Richard Hakluyt devoted his life to recording every piece of evidence that could contribute to English participation in the colonization of the New World.

He listened to the tales of returning voyagers and re-
peated them for a broad reading audience. He sup-
ported the adventures of Sir Humphrey Gilbert and
Sir Walter Raleigh; he urged England to confront
Spain and claim the great rewards of "raysing trades"
and other profits that England could have if it ap-
plied itself with zeal and purposefulness to coloniza-
tion. Stern anti-Catholic arguments of Protestant Eng-
land—the Spanish flinging overboard English prayer
books and the like—complemented the political and
economic arguments for planting English colonies in
the New World.

**A particuler discourse concerninge the greate necessitie
and manifolde comodyties that are like to growe to this
Realme of Englande by the Westerne discoveries lately
attempted, Written in the yere 1584 by Richarde Hack-
luyt of Oxforde at the requeste and direction of the righte
worshipfull Mr. Walter Raghly [Raleigh] nowe Knight,
before the comynge home of his Twoo Barkes: and is de-
vided into xxi chapiters, the Titles whereof followe in the
nexte leafe.**

1. That this westerne discoverie will be greately for
the inlargement of the gospell of Christe whereunto the
Princes of the refourmed relligion are chefely bounde
amongest whome her Majestie is principall.

2. That all other englishe Trades are growen beggerly
or daungerous, especially in all the kinge of Spaine his
Domynions, where our men are dryven to flinge their
Bibles and prayer Bokes into the sea, and to forsweare
and renownce their relligion and conscience and consequently theyr obedience to her Majestie.

3. That this westerne voyadge will yelde unto us all
the commodities of Europe, Affrica, and Asia, as far as
wee were wonte to travell, and supply the wantes of all
our decayed trades.

4. That this enterprise will be for the manifolde im-
ploymente of nombers of idle men, and for bredinge of
many sufficient, and for utterance of the greate quantitie
of the commodities of our Realme.

5. That this voyage will be a great bridle to the

Indies of the kinge of Spaine and a means that wee may arreste at our pleasure for the space of tenne weekes or three monethes every yere, one or twoo hundred saile of his subjectes shippes at the fysshinge in Newfounde lande.

6. That the mischefe that the Indian Threasure wrought in time of Charles the late Emperor father to the Spanishe kinge, is to be had in consideracion of the Q. moste excellent Majestie, leaste the contynuall commynge of the like threasure from thence to his sonne, worke the unrecoverable annoye of this Realme, whereof already wee have had very dangerous experience.

7. What speciall meanes may bringe kinge Phillippe from his high Throne, and make him equal to the Princes his neighbours, wherewithall is shewed his weakenes in the west Indies.

8. That the limites of the kinge of Spaines domynions in the west Indies be nothinge so large as is generally imagined and surmised, neither those partes which he holdeth be of any such forces as is falsely geven oute by the popishe Clergye and others his suitors, to terrifie the Princes of the Relligion and to abuse and blinde them.

9. The Names of the riche Townes lienge alonge the sea coaste on the northe side from the equinoctiall of the mayne lande of America under the kinge of Spaine.

10. A Brefe declaracion of the chefe Ilands in the Bay of Mexico beinge under the kinge of Spaine, with their havens and fortes, and what commodities they yelde.

11. That the Spaniardes have executed most outragious and more then Turkishe cruelties in all the west Indies, whereby they are every where there, become moste odious unto them, whoe woulde joyne with us or any other moste willingly to shake of their moste intollerable yoke, and have begonne to doo it already in dyvers places where they were Lordes heretofore.

12. That the passage in this voyadge is easie and shorte, that it cutteth not nere the trade of any other mightie Princes, nor nere their Contries, that it is to be perfourmed at all tymes of the yere, and nedeth but one kinde of winde, that Ireland beinge full of goodd havens on the southe and west sides, is the nerest parte of Europe

to it, which by this trade shall be in more securitie, and the sooner drawen to more Civilitie.

13. That hereby the Revenewes and customes of her Majestie bothe outwardes and inwardes shall mightely be inlarged by the toll, excises, and other dueties which without oppression may be raised.

14. That this action will be greately for the increase, mayneteynaunce and safetie of our Navye, and especially of greate shippinge which is the strengthe of our Realme, and for the supportation of all those occupacions that depende upon the same.

15. That spedie plantinge in divers fitt places is moste necessarie upon these luckye westerne discoveries for feare of the daunger of being prevented by other nations which have the like intentions, with the order thereof and other reasons therewithall alleaged.

16. Meanes to kepe this enterprise from overthrowe and the enterprisers from shame and dishonor.

17. That by these Colonies the Northwest passage to Cathaio and China may easely quickly and perfectly be searched oute aswell by river and overlande, as by sea, for proofe whereof here are quoted and alleaged divers rare Testymonies oute of the three volumes of voyadges gathered by Ramusius and other grave authors.

18. That the Queene of Englande title to all the west Indies, or at the leaste to as moche as is from Florida to the Circle articke, is more lawfull and righte then the Spaniardes or any other Christian Princes.

19. An aunswer to the Bull of the Donacion of all the west Indies graunted to the kinges of Spaine by Pope Alexander the VI whoe was himselfe a Spaniarde borne.

20. A brefe collection of certaine reasons to induce her Majestie and the state to take in hande the westerne voyadge and the plantinge there.

21. A note of some thinges to be prepared for the voyadge which is sett downe rather to drawe the takers of the voyadge in hande to the presente consideracion then for any other reason for that divers thinges require preparation longe before the voyadge, without which the voyadge is maymed.

DOCUMENT 5

INSTRUCTIONS FOR THE VIRGINIA COLONY, 1606

The moment arrived in the first decade of the seventeenth century when England began a second round of colonizing attempts, this time using joint-stock companies as the vehicle to plant settlements rather than giving extensive grants to a landed proprietor such as Gilbert or Raleigh, whose attempts at colonization in the 1570s and 1580s had failed. The founding of Virginia marked the beginning of a twenty-five year period in which every colony in the New World was established by means of a joint-stock company. A variety of motives intensified the colonizing impulse—international rivalry, propagation of religion, enlarged opportunity for individual men—but none exceeded that of trade and profit. The companies were created to make a profit; their investments in the colonies were based on this assumption. Early in the 1630s merchants and investors discovered that they could employ their money in other more rewarding enterprises. After 1631, therefore, no colony was founded by mercantile enterprise, but by that date the enterprisers had left a legacy of colonization that was to endure.

In these instructions for the Virginia Company, the power of Spain and the fear derived from past failures invade every line. The detail and precision of the instructions reflect the work of experienced men; Richard Hakluyt, the younger, for example, probably had a hand in writing them.

As we doubt not but you will have especial care to observe the ordinances set down by the King's Majesty and delivered unto you under the Privy Seal; so for your better directions upon your first landing we have thought good to

recommend unto your care these instructions and articles
following.

When it shall please God to send you on the coast of
Virginia, you shall do your best endeavour to find out a
safe port in the entrance of some navigable river, making
choice of such a one as runneth farthest into the land,
and if you happen to discover divers portable rivers, and
amongst them any one that hath two main branches, if the
difference be not great, make choice of that which bendeth
most toward the North-West for that way you shall soon-
est find the other sea.

When you have made choice of the river on which you
mean to settle, be not hasty in landing your victuals and
munitions; but first let Captain Newport discover how far
that river may be found navigable, that you make election
of the strongest, most wholesome and fertile place; for if
you make many removes, besides the loss of time, you
shall greatly spoil your victuals and your caske, and with
great pain transport it in small boats.

But if you choose your place so far up as a bark of fifty
tuns will float, then you may lay all your provisions ashore
with ease, and the better receive the trade of all the countries about you in the land; and such a place you may
perchance find a hundred miles from the river's mouth,
and the further up the better. For if you sit down near the
entrance, except it be in some island that is strong by
nature, an enemy that may approach you on even ground,
may easily pull you out; and if he be driven to seek you
a hundred miles [in] the land in boats, you shall from
both sides of the river where it is narrowest, so beat them
with your muskets as they shall never be able to prevail
against you.

And to the end that you be not surprized as the French
were in Florida by Melindus, and the Spaniard in the same
place by the French, you shall do well to make this double
provision. First, erect a little stoure at the mouth of the
river that may lodge some ten men; with whom you shall
leave a light boat, that when any fleet shall be in sight,
they may come with speed to give you warning. Secondly,
you must in no case suffer any of the native people of the

country to inhabit between you and the sea coast; for you cannot carry yourselves so towards them, but they will grow discontented with your habitation, and be ready to guide and assist any nation that shall come to invade you; and if you neglect this, you neglect your safety.

When you have discovered as far up the river as you mean to plant yourselves, and landed your victuals and munitions; to the end that every man may know his charge, you shall do well to divide your six score men into three parts; whereof one party of them you may appoint to fortifie and build, of which your first work must be your storehouse for victuals; the other you may imploy in preparing your ground and sowing your corn and roots; the other ten of these forty you must leave as centinel at the haven's mouth. The other forty you may imploy for two months in discovery of the river above you, and on the country about you; which charge Captain Newport and Captain Gosnold may undertake of these forty discoverers. When they do espie any high lands or hills, Captain Gosnold may take twenty of the company to cross over the lands, and carrying a half dozen pickaxes to try if they can find any minerals. The other twenty may go on by river, and pitch up boughs upon the bank's side, by which the other boats shall follow them by the same turnings. You may also take with them a wherry, such as is used here in the Thames; by which you may send back to the President for supply of munition or any other want, that you may not be driven to return for every small defect.

You must observe if you can, whether the river on which you plant doth spring out of mountains or out of lakes. If it be out of any lake, the passage to the other sea will be more easy, and [it] is like enough, that out of the same lake you shall find some spring which run[s] the contrary way towards the East India Sea; for the great and famous rivers of Volga, Tan[a]is and Dwina have three heads near joynd; and yet the one falleth into the Caspian Sea, the other into the Euxine Sea, and the third into the Paelonian Sea.

In all your passages you must have great care not to offend the naturals [natives], if you can eschew it; and imploy some few of your company to trade with them for corn and all other . . . victuals if you have any; and this you must do before that they perceive you mean to plant among them; for not being sure how your own seed corn will prosper the first year, to avoid the danger of famine, use and endeavour to store yourselves of the country corn.

Your discoverers that pass over land with hired guides, must look well to them that they slip not from them: and for more assurance, let them take a compass with them, and write down how far they go upon every point of the compass; for that country having no way nor path, if that your guides run from you in the great woods or desert, you shall hardly ever find a passage back.

And how weary soever your soldiers be, let them never trust the country people with the carriage of their weapons; for if they run from you with your shott, which they only fear, they will easily kill them all with their arrows. And whensoever any of yours shoots before them, be sure they may be chosen out of your best marksmen; for if they see your learners miss what they aim at, they will think the weapon not so terrible, and thereby will be bould to assault you.

Above all things, do not advertize the killing of any of your men, that the country people may know it; if they perceive that they are but common men, and that with the loss of many of theirs they diminish any part of yours, they will make many adventures upon you. If the country be populous, you shall do well also, not to let them see or know of your sick men, if you have any; which may also encourage them to many enterprizes.

You must take especial care that you choose a seat for habitation that shall not be over burthened with woods near your town; for all the men you have, shall not be able to cleanse twenty acres a year; besides that it may serve for a covert for your enemies round about.

Neither must you plant in a low or moist place, because it will prove unhealthfull. You shall judge of the good air by the people; for some part of that coast where the lands are low, have their people blear eyed, and with swollen bellies and legs; but if the naturals be strong and clean made, it is a true sign of a wholesome soil.

You must take order to draw up the pinnace that is

left with you, under the fort: and take her sails and anchors ashore, all but a small kedge to ride by; least some ill-dispositioned persons slip away with her.

You must take care that your marriners that go for wages, do not mar your trade; for those that mind not to inhabite, for a little gain will debase the estimation of exchange, and hinder the trade for ever after; and therefore you shall not admit or suffer any person whatsoever, other than such as shall be appointed by the President and Counsel there, to buy any merchandizes or other things whatsoever.

It were necessary that all your carpenters and other such like workmen about building do first build your storehouse and those other rooms of publick and necessary use before any house be set up for any private person: and though the workman may belong to any private persons yet let them all work together first for the company and then for private men.

And seeing order is at the same price with confusion, it shall be adviseably done to set your houses even and by a line, that your street may have a good breadth, and be carried square about your market place and every street's end opening into it; that from thence, with a few field pieces, you may command every street throughout; which market place you may also fortify if you think it needfull.

You shall do well to send a perfect relation by Captaine Newport of all that is done, what height you are seated, how far into the land, what commodities you find, what soil, woods and their several kinds, and so of all other things else to advertise particularly; and to suffer no man to return but by pasport from the President and Counsel, nor to write any letter of anything that may discourage others.

Lastly and chiefly the way to prosper and achieve good success is to make yourselves all of one mind for the good of your country and your own, and to serve and fear God the Giver of all Goodness, for every plantation which our Heavenly Father hath not planted shall be rooted out.

DOCUMENT 6

LETTERS FROM DON PEDRO DE ZUNIGA, THE SPANISH AMBASSADOR TO ENGLAND, TO THE KING OF SPAIN,
1607

The interplay among the nations of Europe for positions of power in the New World is often best revealed in the reports of an ambassador to his sovereign. In this case, Don Pedro de Zuniga, the Spanish ambassador to England, hastened to inform his king of the English venture in Virginia. He evaluates the significance of that enterprise in relation to Spanish territorial claims and interests. The measured response of King James I of England, which gives the impression that nothing whatever is afoot, acts out a ploy commonly used by men of power in the seventeenth century—and, for that matter, every other century.

September 22 Sire:

I have reported to your Majesty how there had come to Plymouth one of the vessels that went to Virginia, and afterwards there came in another, which vessels are still here. Captain Newport makes haste to return with some people—and there have combined merchants and other persons who desire to establish themselves there; because it appears to them the most suitable place that they have discovered for privateering and making attacks upon the merchant fleets of Your Majesty. Your Majesty will command to see whether they will be allowed to remain there. On account of this report I sent to ask an audience of the King at Salisbury, and God was so pleased that from that day I have not been able to rise from my bed. Whereupon I have repeated my request stating the reason why I did not go on the day which had been designated to me. He has sent me to be visited very graciously and in the same way, the Queen; and I desire nothing more than to have health to fulfil what Y. M. [Your Majesty] has commanded me to see in what manner they take up that business, which I fear, he will say is not his businesse; and that he will order it to be set right—and in the meantime they will make every effort they can. It is very desirable Y. M. should command that such a bad project should be uprooted now while it can be done so easily. I hope to God I shall be able to speake to the King within eight days; because at that time he will come nearer to this place.

I have found a confidential person, through whom I shall find out what shall be done in the Council (which they call Council of Virginia). They are in a great state of excitement about that place and very much afraid lest Your Majesty should drive them out of it. They go about with a plan that if this be not done, they will make this King take the business in his own hands. And there are so many who here, and in other parts of the Kingdom, speak already of sending people to that country, that it is advisable not to be too slow; because they will soon be found there with large numbers of people, whereupon it will be much more difficult to drive them out than now, etc.

May Our Lord preserve and guard the Catholic Person of Y. M. as all christendom needeth. . . .

October 5 Sire:

When the King came to Hampton Court, which was on the 22d of last month, I sent to ask an audience, and he sent me word, that it pleased him to wait 'till he should return there; because he was leaving the next day to hunt, on the other side of London . . . Day before yesterday he returned, and I sent again begging an audience. He was sick with fever that day and he replied that this, and his waiting for the Members of his Council, prevented his doing what I wished and that he would let me know when he was so disposed. In this way I have not been able to say anything to the King about Virginia; but I understand that a ship is sailing there and a tender with about 120 men and from all who go they require an oath of allegiance. A man has told me to-day, a man who usually tells me the truth, that these men are complaining of what the King does for the Scotch who may go there, and that he favors them more than themselves. They are in the greatest fear, that Y. M. will give orders to have them stopped; because all see that their sending there can no longer be approved, as Y. M. takes it. It appears clearly to me now that it is not their intention to plant colonies, but to send out pirates from there, since they do not take women, but only men. I have not wished to detain this courier, because the King might be one of these days in bad health. I understood that he writes to Y. M. desiring much to strengthen the bonds of Friendship. I believe that there are some things that have to be done for the service of God and of Y. M., etc.—as for myself, a cloud has disappeared from my heart, because now I see a door is opening for free speech in religion. May God open it in such a manner that His sacred service may be entirely fulfilled, and may He protect, etc.

October 8 Sire:

Saturday night I had a message from the Chamberlain in which he told me that the King would give me an audience, yesterday, Sunday, at 2.

He received me as usual very courteously, and after we had seated ourselves, I told him how your Majesties had grieved over the death of his daughter.

He replied to this with much gratefulness. Then I told him that Y. M. had ordered me to represent to him how contrary to good friendship and brotherly feeling it was, that his subjects should dare wish to colonize Virginia, when that was a part of the Spanish Indies, and that he must look upon this boldness as very obnoxious.

He answered that he had not particularly known what was going on; that as to the navigation to Virginia he had never understood that Y. M. had any right to it; but that it was a very distant country where Spaniards lived, and that in the Treaties of Peace with him and with France it was not stipulated that his subjects should not go there,

except to the Indies, and that as Y. M.'s people had discovered new regions, so it seemed to him, that his own
people might do likewise. I replied to him that it was a
condition of the Treaty of Peace, that in no way should
they go to the Indies. The King said to me that those
who went, did it at their own risk and that if they came
upon them in those parts there would be no complaint
should they be punished. I told him that to punish them
was all right, but that it would be better for the closer
union between Y. M.'s subjects and his own, and that this
invention of going to Virginia for colonising purposes was
seen in the wretched zeal with which it was done, since the
soil is very sterile, and that hence there can be no other
purpose connected with that place than that it appears to
them good for pirates, and that this could not be allowed.
He told me in reply that he had never known Y. M. was
interested in this, but since I assured him it was so, and
that they might send pirates out from there, he would
seek information about it all, and would give orders that
satisfaction should be given to me by the Council, and
that he was inclined to think as I did, having heard it
said that the soil was very sterile and that those have been
sadly deceived who had hoped to find there great riches—
that no advantage from it all came to him, and that if
his subjects went where they ought not to go, and were
punished for it, neither he nor they could complain. I said
in reply that the difficulties were such as must be considered and the best remedy was to prevent and cut it
short from here, since it was publicly known, that two
vessels had sailed from a port of this kingdom for the
Indies, and that two others were being laden here to go.
The King told me they were terrible people and that he
desired to correct the matter. I represented to him how
well his subjects would always be treated in all parts of
Y. M. dominions *to which they can go,* and with how
much good will Y. M. commands it so. He told me, he
saw now perfectly well how certain everything was that I
told him, because in the last Parliament there had been so
much excitement about the two ships seized in the Indies. . . .

October 16 Sire:

I have written to Y. M. and reported the audience which I had concerning the Virginia affair. I sent to Hampton Court to remind the Council of the answer due me, as the King had told me, and Count Salisbury tells me that having discussed it with the King, he replied to him nearly what he told me: If the English go where they may not go, let them be punished—and having looked carefully into the matter, it seems to him that they may not go to Virginia—and that thus, if evil befalls them, it will not be on his account, since to him this will not appear as being contrary to friendship and peaceful disposition. He says, he does not wish to do what *he has been asked to do, in preventing their going and commanding those who are out there to return,* and the reason of this is, because that would be acknowledging that Your Majesty is Lord of all the Indies.

Those who are urging the colonization of Virginia, become every day more eager to send people, because it looked to them as if this business was falling to sleep after all that has been done for it, and before Nativity there will sail from here and from Plymouth five or six ships. *It will be serving God and Y. M. to drive these villains out from there, hanging them in time which is short enough for the purpose.* They have been told that the Earl of Tyrone has reached Coruña and that he has been very well received there. They are now anxious to see what will be done to him, and they are afraid Y. M. may perhaps in the name of His Holiness send him with some Italian forces to Ireland, so as to stir up there some rebellion, and they say, that if this should be so, they would openly declare war, but that, if not, they will faithfully keep the peace with Y. M. This is, therefore, finally to tell me that they are not in favor of war, and I have replied to them, that Y. M. has always faithfully observed the Treaties of Peace, and that he will do so now. . . .

DOCUMENT 7

WILLIAM BRADFORD, *OF PLYMOUTH PLANTATION,* 1630–1650

William Bradford, who left Holland with the small band of Pilgrims to found Plymouth Colony, became its governor and historian. Bradford's manuscript remained unpublished until the nineteenth century, although earlier chronicler-historians had pirated large segments of it, passing the results off as their own findings. Bradford's Of Plymouth Plantation *not only compares favorably with the best writing of his time but its essential dignity and simplicity of spirit, not to mention its dispassionate tone, also make it a literary as well as a historical work. The passage that follows is a departure from the documents that precede it, because for Bradford the colonizing impulse is projected in terms of people and their everyday wishes for self-fulfillment rather than as some grandiose scheme for national greatness or immoderate personal profit.*

Showing the Reasons and Causes of Their Removal

After they had lived in this city about some eleven or twelve years (which is the more observable being the whole time of that famous truce between that state and the Spaniards) and sundry of them were taken away by death and many others began to be well stricken in years (the grave mistress of Experience having taught them many things), those prudent governors with sundry of the sagest members began both deeply to apprehend their present dangers and wisely to foresee the future and think of timely remedy. In the agitation of their thoughts, and much discourse of things hereabout, at length they began to incline to this conclusion: of removal to some other place. Not out of any newfangledness or other such like giddy humor by which men are oftentimes transported to their great hurt and danger, but for sundry weighty and solid reasons, some of the chief of which I will here briefly touch.

And first, they saw and found by experience the hardness of the place and country to be such as few in comparison would come to them, and fewer that would bide it out and continue with them. For many that came to them, and many more that desired to be with them, could not endure that great labour and hard fare, with other inconveniences which they underwent and were contented with. But though they loved their persons, approved their cause and honoured their sufferings, yet they left them as it were weeping, as Orpah did her mother-in-law Naomi, or as those Romans did Cato in Utica who desired to be excused and borne with, though they could not all be Catos. For many, though they desired to enjoy the ordinances of God in their purity and the liberty of the gospel with them, yet (alas) they admitted of bondage with danger of conscience, rather than to endure these hardships. Yea, some preferred and chose the prisons in England rather than this liberty in Holland with these afflictions. But it was thought that if a better and easier place of living could be had, it would draw many and take away these discouragements. Yea, their pastor would often say that many of those who both wrote and preached now against them, if they were in a place where they might have liberty and live comfortably, they would then practice as they did.

Secondly. They saw that though the people generally bore all these difficulties very cheerfully and with a resolute courage, being in the best and strength of their years; yet old age began to steal on many of them; and their great and continual labours, with other crosses and sorrows, hastened it before the time. So as it was not only probably thought, but apparently seen, that within a few years more they would be in danger to scatter, by necessities pressing them, or sink under their burdens, or both. And therefore according to the divine proverb, that a wise man seeth the plague when it cometh, and hideth himself, Proverbs xxii:3, so they like skillful and beaten soldiers were fearful either to be entrapped or surrounded by their enemies so as they should neither be able to fight nor fly. And therefore thought it better to dislodge betimes to some place of better advantage and less danger, if any such could be found.

Thirdly. As necessity was a taskmaster over them so they were forced to be such, not only to their servants but in a sort to their dearest children, the which as it did not a little wound the tender hearts of many a loving father and mother, so it produced likewise sundry sad and sorrowful effects. For many of their children that were of best dispositions and gracious inclinations, having learned to bear the yoke in their youth and willing to bear part of their parents' burden, were oftentimes so oppressed with their heavy labours that though their minds were free and willing, yet their bodies bowed under the weight of the same, and became decrepit in their early youth, the vigour of nature being consumed in the very bud as it were. But that which was more lamentable, and of all sorrows most heavy to be borne, was that many of their children, by these occasions and the great licentiousness of youth in that country, and the manifold temptations of the place, were drawn away by evil examples into extravagant and dangerous courses, getting the reins off their necks and departing from their parents. Some became soldiers, others took upon them far voyages by sea, and others some worse courses tending to dissoluteness and the danger of their souls, to the great grief of their parents and dishonour of God. So that they saw their posterity would be in danger to degenerate and be corrupted.

Lastly (and which was not least), a great hope and inward zeal they had of laying some good foundation, or at least to make some way thereunto, for the propagating and advancing the gospel of the kingdom of Christ in those remote parts of the world; yea, though they should be but even as stepping-stones unto others for the performing of so great a work.

These and some other like reasons moved them to undertake this resolution of their removal; the which they afterward prosecuted with so great difficulties, as by the sequel will appear.

The place they had thoughts on was some of those vast and unpeopled countries of America, which are fruitful and fit for habitation, being devoid of all civil inhabitants, where there are only savage and brutish men which range up and down, little otherwise than the wild beasts of the same. This proposition being made public and coming to the scanning of all, it raised many variable opinions amongst men and caused many fears and doubts amongst themselves. Some, from their reasons and hopes conceived, laboured to stir up and encourage the rest to undertake and prosecute the same; others again, out of their fears, objected against it and sought to divert from it; alleging many things, and those neither unreasonable nor unprobable; as that it was a great design and subject to many unconceivable perils and dangers; as, besides the casualties of the sea (which none can be freed from), the length of the voyage was such as the weak bodies of women and other persons worn out with age and travail (as many of them were) could never be able to endure. And yet if they should, the miseries of the land which they should be exposed unto, would be too hard to be borne and likely, some or all of them together, to consume and utterly to ruinate them. For there they should be liable to famine and nakedness and the want, in a manner, of all things. The change of air, diet and drinking of water would infect their bodies with sore sicknesses and grievous diseases. And also those which should escape or overcome these difficulties should yet be in continual danger of the savage people, who are cruel, barbarous and most treacherous, being most furious in their rage and merciless where they overcome; not being content only to kill and take away life, but delight to torment men in the most bloody manner that may be; flaying some alive with the shells of fishes, cutting off the members and joints of others by piecemeal and broiling on the coals, eat the collops of their flesh in their sight whilst they live, with other cruelties horrible to be related.

And surely it could not be thought but the very hearing of these things could not but move the very bowels of men to grate within them and make the weak to quake and tremble. It was further objected that it would require greater sums of money to furnish such a voyage and to fit them with necessaries, than their consumed estates would amount to; and yet they must as well look to be seconded with supplies as presently to be transported. Also many precedents of ill success and lamentable miseries befallen others in the like designs were easy to be found, and not forgotten to be alleged; besides their own experience, in their former troubles and hardships in their removal into Holland, and how hard a thing it was for them to live in that strange place, though it was a neighbour country and a civil and rich commonwealth.

It was answered, that all great and honourable actions are accompanied with great difficulties and must be both enterprised and overcome with answerable courages. It was granted the dangers were great, but not desperate. The difficulties were many, but not invincible. For though there were many of them likely, yet they were not certain. It might be sundry of the things feared might never befall; others by provident care and the use of good means might in a great measure be prevented; and all of them, through the help of God, by fortitude and patience, might either be borne or overcome. True it was that such attempts were not to be made and undertaken without good ground and reason, not rashly or lightly as many have done for curiosity or hope of gain, etc. But their condition was not ordinary, their ends were good and honourable, their calling lawful and urgent; and therefore they might expect the blessing of God in their proceeding. Yea, though they should lose their lives in this action, yet might they have comfort in the same and their endeavours would be honourable. They lived here but as men in exile and in a poor condition, and as great miseries might possibly befall them in this place; for the twelve years of truce were now out and there was nothing but beating of drums and preparing for war, the events whereof are always uncertain. The Spaniard might prove as cruel as the savages of America, and the famine and pestilence as sore here as there, and their liberty less to look out for remedy.

After many other particular things answered and alleged on both sides, it was fully concluded by the major part to put this design in execution and to prosecute it by the best means they could.

DOCUMENT 8

DISAGREEMENTS WITHIN THE VIRGINIA COMPANY, 1623

*When each colony was founded, those who adminis-
tered its day-to-day policy frequently disagreed not
only on what this policy should be but also on
whether it accomplished the object for which it was
designed. Virginia was no exception. In the first years
of the colony, Captain John Smith disagreed vigorously with his fellow councillors on how the infant
settlement should be run. By 1611, Sir Thomas Dale
and later Sir Thomas Gates invoked rigorous and
perhaps necessary regulations for Virginia from which
no divergence was permitted. Disputes took place
among members of the Virginia Company in London.
Merchants with international connections disagreed
on the merits of tobacco planting and its prospective
market as well as on the degree of self-government
to allow settlers in Virginia. They also disagreed over
which economic developments should be encouraged.
When a decision was necessary, the members of the
company required fresh intelligence from Virginia to
arrive at a judgment. This requirement invited the
submission of different viewpoints. In the following
document the wisdom of company policy and decisions is vigorously debated.*

April, 1623

The Lord Cavendish acquainted the Company, that
divers ancient Planters, masters of Shipps, Marriners, and
sundry other persons that have Lived Long in Virgina, and
have beene many tymes there, had presented the great

Comittee with an answere unto Capt Butlers Information, concerning the Colony in Virginia; wherein they did directly contrary the most mayne pointe of his Information, proving them to be false and scandalous; which was by erection of hande ordered to be read, being this which followeth.

The Answers of divers Planters that have long lived in Virginia as alsoe of sundry Marriners and other persons that have bene often at Virginia unto a paper intituled The Unmasked face of our Colony in Virginia as it was in the Winter of the yeare—1622

1. I founde the Plantations generally seated uppon meere Salt marishes full of infectious Boggs and muddy Creekes, and Lakes, and therby subjected to all those inconveniences and diseases which are soe commonly found in the most Unsounde and most Unhealthy parts of England wherof everie Country and Clymate hath some.

Answere. Wee say that there is no place inhabited but is conveniently habitable. And for the first Plantation which is Kiccoutan against which (if any be) most exception may be made, itt is every way soe well disposed that in that place well governed men may enjoy their healths and live as plentifully as in any parte of England or other his Majesties Dominions, yett that there are Marishes in some places wee acknowledge; Butt soe as they are more Comodious for divers good respects and uses then if they were wantinge. As for Boggs wee knowe of none in all the Country and for the rest of the Plantations as Newporte News, Blunt poynt, Wariscoyake, Martins Hundred, Paspahey and all the Plantations right over against James Citty, and all the Plantations above these which are many they are verie fruitfull and pleasant Seates, free from Salt Marishes beinge all on the fresh River and they are all verie healthfull and high Land except James Citty which is yett as high as Debtforde or Radclyffe.

2. I founde the shores and sides of those parte of the Mayne River wher our Plantations are setled every wher soe shallow as noe Boates can approach the shores soe that besides the difficulty daunger and spoile of goods in the Landinge of them, the people are forced to a Continuall wadinge and wettinge of themselves and that in the prime of winter when the Shipps commonly arrive, and therby gett such vyolent surfetts of colde uppon colde as seldome leave them untill they leave to live.

Answere. That generally for the Plantations att all times from halfe floud to halfe ebb any Boate that drawes betwixt three and 4 foote water may safely com in and Land their Goods dry on Shore without wadinge and for further Cleeringe of these [this] false objections the Seamen there doe att all times deliver the goods they bringe to the Owners dry on Shore, wherby itt plainely appears not any of the Country people there inhabitinge are by this means in daunger of their lives, [And] at a great many of Plantations belowe James Citty and allmost all above they may att all times Land dry.

3. The new people that are yearly sent over which arrive here for the most part very Unseasonably in Winter, finde neither Guest house Inne, nor any the like place to shroud themselves in at their arrivall, noe not soe much as a stroake given towards any such charitable worke soe that many of them by want hereof are not onely seen dyinge under hedges and in the woods but beinge dead ly some of them for many dayes Unregarded and Unburied.

Answere. To the first they Answere that the winter is the most healthfull time and season for arrivall of new Commers. True itt is that as yett theris noe Guesthouse or place of interteynment of [for] Strangers. Butt wee averr that itt was a late intent and had by this time been putt in practise to make a generall gatheringe for the buildinge of such a Convenient house which by this time had been in good forwardnes had itt not pleased God to suffer this Disaster to fall out by the Indians. But although there be no publique Guesthouse yett are new Commers entertayned and lodged and provided for by the Governor in pryvate houses; And for any dyinge in the feilds (through this defecte) and lyinge unburied, wee are altogether ignorant, yett that many dy suddenly by the hand of God, wee often see itt to fall out even in this flourishinge and plentifull Citty in the middest of our streets, as for dyinge under hedges theris noe hedge in all Virginia.

4. The Colony was this winter in much distress of victuall soe that English meale was soulde at the rate of thirtie shillings a bushell their owne native Corne called Maize at ten and fifteen shillings the bushell, The which howsoever itt lay heavy uppon the shoulders of the Generallytie it may be suspected not to be unaffected by some of the cheife, for they only haveinge the means in these extremities to trade for Corne with the Natives doe herby ingrosse [all] into their hands and soe sell that abrode at their owne prices, and my selfe have heard from the mouth of a prime one amongst them that hee would never wish that their owne Corne should be cheaper among them then eight shillings the bushell.

Answere. True itt is that English meale hath of late since the Massacre been sould for Tenn pounds of Tobacco the bushell which no understandinge man can there value above fifteen shillings sterlinge and here wee finde (without a Massacre) by the judgment of God for our ~~murringe~~ [murmuring] att plentie Wheat hath this yeare been sould and still is in many places at three times the rate itt hath borne within two or three years last past: And againe Indian Corne hath heretofore commonly been sould after the rate of five shillings the bushell, And farther meale bore so high a price this year as itt cost redy mony in England together with the fraight and other charges neer uppon twelve shilling soe that if itt were sould att Tenn pounds of Tobacco ther will not be gayned twenty in the hundred.

5. Ther Howses are generally the worst that ever I sawe the meanest Cottages in England beinge every way equall (if not superior) with the moste of the best, And besides soe improvidently and scattringly are they seated one from an other as partly by their distance but especially by the interposition of Creeks and Swamps as they call them they offer all advantages to their savadge enimys and are utterly deprived of all suddaine recollection of themselves uppon any tearmes whatsoever.

Answere. First that the houses there were most built for use and not for ornament and are soe farr from beinge soe meane as they are reported that throughout his Majesties Dominions here, all labouringe mens houses (which wee cheifly professe our selvs to be) are in no wise generally for goodnes to be compared unto them And for the houses of men of better Ranke and quallety they are soe much better and convenyent that noe man of quallety without blushinge can make exception against them; Againe for the Creeks and Swamps every man ther that cannott goe by Land hath either a Boate or a Conoa for the Conveyinge and speedy passage to his neighbors house. As for Cottages ther are none in Virginia that they knowe.

6. I found not the least peec of fortification, Three Peeces of Ordinance onely mounted at James Citty and one at Flowerdue Hundred but never a one of them serviceable Soe that itt is most certaine that a smale Barke of one hundred Tunns may take its time to pass up the River in spite of them and comminge to an Anchor before the Towne may beate all their houses downe aboute their eares, and so forceinge them to retreat into the Woods may land under the favour of their Ordinance, and rifle the Towne at pleasure.

Answere. Itt is true theris as yett no other artificiall fortifications then Pallisadoes wherof allmoste everie Plantation hath one, and divers of them hath Trenches, And this last yeare Captain Eache was sent for that purpose. As for great Ordinance there are fower peeces mounted att James Citty and all serviceable, ther are six Mounted at Flowerdue Hundred all of them likewise serviceable, And three mounted att Kiccoutan and all of them serviceable, there are likewise att Newporte Newes three all of them serviceable ther are likewise att Henrico seaven peeces and att Charles hundred two, and in other places, besides fowlers and Murders att divers places.

7. Expectinge accordinge to their printed Books a great forwardnes of divers and sundry Commodities, At myne arrivall I found not any one of them so much as in any

towardnes of being for the Iron workes were utterly wasted, and the men dead, The furnaces for Glass and Pots at a stay, and in a smale hope, As for the rest they were had in a generall derision even amongst themselves, and the Pamphlets that had published there beinge sent thither by Hundreds wer laughed to scorne, and every base fellow boldly gave them the Lye in divers perticulers, Soe that Tobacco onely was the buisines and for ought that I coulde here every man madded uppon that and lyttle thought or looked for ~~else~~ any thinge else.

Answere. That the Country yeilds divers usefull and rich Commodities which by reason of the Infancie of the Plantation, and this unexpected Massacre, cannot yett be brought to perfection and is no lesse hindred by the emulous and envious reports of ill willers whose pryvate ends by time wilbe discovered and by God recompenced. And wee doe further answer that this Country is a moste fruitfull Country, and doth certainly produce divers rich Commodities. Itt is true that the Ironworks are wasted and the men dead, but that was by the Massacre which if itt had not happened ther had been a good proofe of that Commodity, for the works wer in a very great forwardnes. As for Vines likewise ther were divers Vineyeards planted in sundry places butt all of them putt back by the Massacre, but for [the] peoples derydinge of these Commodities or [the] books sent by the Company wee have never heard of any such scoffinge or derisions butt as the Governor and Counsell ther are very desirous and have sett forth Proclamations to cause all men to sett both Vines and Mulbery Trees, so the people generally are very desyrous and forward to rayse those former Commodities of Wine and Silke, and likewise divers other good Commodities.

8. I found the Antient Plantations of Henrico, and Charles Citty wholly quitted and lefte to the spoile of the Indians who not onely burned the houses saide to be once the best of all others, but fell Uppon the Poultry, Hoggs, Cowes, Goates, and Horses wherof they killed great numbers to the great greife as well as ruine ~~to~~ [of] ye Olde Inhabitants, whoe stick not to affirme that these were not onely the best and healthiest parts of all others but might

allsoe by their naturall strength of scituation have been the most easefully preserved of all ~~others~~ [the rest].

9. Wheras accordinge to his Majesties gratious Letters Patents his People in Virginia are as neer as possibly may be to be governed after the excellent Lawes and Customes of Englande. I founde in the Government there not onely ignorant and enforced strayings in diver particulers but willfull and intended ones; Insomuch as some who urged due conformity were [have] in contempt been tearmed men of Lawe, and ~~were~~ excluded from those rights which by orderly proceedings they were elected and sworne unto here.

10. There havinge been as it is thought not fewer then Tenn thousand soules transported thither ther are not through the afore named abuses and neglects above Two thousand of them at the present to be found alive, many of them alsoe in a sickly and desperate estate: Soe that itt may undoubtedly be expected, that unless the Confusions and pryvate ends of some of the Company here, and the bad executions in secondinge them by their Agents there be redressed with speed, by some divine and supreame hand, that in steed of a Plantation it will shortly gett the name of a Slaughterhouse, and soe justly become both odious to our selves and contemptible to all the worlde.

Answere. All these wee leave to be answered by the Governor and Company some of them beinge unfitt to be determyned of by us. And for the last wee being ignorant how many have been transported or are now lyvinge there.

Wee whose names are hereunder and hereafter writt^n have uppon mature deliberation and after full examination and consideration of the premises drawne upp these answers beinge such as wee finde in our consyencies to be true, and shall att all times justifie them uppon our oathes In wittnes wherof wee have hereunder sett our hands.

I William Mease Mynister haveinge lived tenn years in Virginia [and] affirme all the answeres above except that of the Ordinance and Pallisadoes.

William Mease.

I Marmaduke Raynor have gone 3 severall times Master of Ships to Virginia and lived 16 monneths there together and affirme all the answers above.

Marmaduke Rayner.

I John Procter have lived 14 Years in Virginia and doe affirme all the answers above except that of the Ordinance and Pallysadoes but I knowe ther are [is] neer uppon 20 peeces of Ordinance.

John Procter.

I William Ewens have gone Master of Ships to Virginia 4 severall times and lived one wholl year ther or ther aboutes, and affirme all the answers above except that of the Ordinance and Pallisadoes.

William Ewens.

I James Carter Master of the Truelove doe affirme all the answers within written butt that I have not seen the Ordnance att Henrico and Charles Citty butt all the rest I have.

James Carter.

I Gregory Pearle having been Maistersmate and lived in Virginia 16 monneths doe affirme all the answers within written save that I have not seen the Ordinance att Henrico and Charles Citty.

Gregory Pearle.

I William Green beinge Chirurgion [Surgeon] in the Temperance haveinge lived 17 monneths in Virginia doe affirme all the answers within written except that I have not seen the Ordnance att Henryco.

William Green [Surgeon].

I Henry Hitch Chirurgion of the James haveinge been 2 severall times in Virginia and lived att one time there about 5 monneths doe affirme all the Answers within written save that I know not of the Matters about James Citty.

Henry Hitch.

I Edward Sanders haveinge lived 3 years in Virginia doe affirme all the answers within written except that of the

Ordinance and Pallysadoes and other matters that above Paspahay.

The marke of E. S. Edward Sanders.

I John Dennis Master of the Marmaduk affirme all the answers within written except that of the Guesthouse the Ordinance, and the Palisadoes.

John Dennis.

I Tobias Felgate have gone Master and Mate of Ships 5 times to Virginia and affirme all the Answers [above] except that of the Ordinance onely.

Tobias Felgate.

I Samuell Mole have lived 3 years or ther aboutes in Virginia beinge a Chirurgion and affirme all the Answers within written save that I have not sene the Ordinance att Henrico and Charles Citty nor have been in Henrico.

Samuell: Mole.

I Thomas Prosser have gone 3 times Masters Mate to Virginia and have lived att one time above 3 quarters of a year there and affirme all the answers within written ~~save that I have not seen~~ [except of that of] the Ordnance and Pallysadoes.

Thomas Prosser.

I Robert Dodson haveinge been twice in Virginia [do] affirme all the answers within written for all matters from James Citty Downeward saveinge that I doe not knowe of the Proclamations for Vines.

Robert Dodson.

I Maurice Thompson have lived 6 years in Virginia doe affirme all the answers within written save that I know not ~~any thing~~ of the Ordinance att flowerdue hundred nor att Henrico and Charles Citty.

Maurice Tompson.

I John Snoade haveinge lived 3 years and halfe in Virginia doe affirme all the answers within written ~~except~~ [savinge] that I [have not seen] the Ordnance ~~and Pallysadoes and~~

~~other matters above Paspahay~~ att Flowerdue Hundred [and] Henrico and Charles Citty.

[John Snoad.]

DOCUMENT 9

JOHN WHITE, *THE PLANTERS' PLEA,*
1630

During the decade of the 1620s, the Reverend John White worked to establish an English colony in New England. Living in Dorchester, England, White witnessed first-hand the result of the land enclosures that forced tenants to move to villages and towns that lacked opportunities for employment and housing. The social problems of seventeenth-century England, therefore, intruded into White's everyday life and action. In 1623 he became a stockholder and promoter of the Dorchester Company, whose object was to plant a settlement that would offer fishermen from England a New World base.

John White also witnessed and participated in the great religious ferment in England in which the Puritans within the Anglican Church slowly gained adherents and power. He recognized that the founding of a colony in New England might relieve the contemporary distress in English social and religious life. Although White never migrated to America, he is considered by the earliest historians of Massachusetts as "under God, one of the chief founders of Massachusetts Bay in New England."

That New-England is a fit Country for the seating of an English Colonie, for the propagation of Religion.

1. Argument or occasion, trade into the countrey. Not onely our acquaintance with the soil and Natives there, but more especially our opportunity of trading thither for Furres and fish, perswade this truth, if other things be answerable. It is well knowne, before our breach with Spaine,

we usually sent out to New-England, yearely forty or fifty
saile of ships of reasonable good burthen for fishing onely.
And howsoever it fals out that our New-found-land voyages prove more beneficiall to the Merchants; yet it is as
true, these to New-England are found farre more profitable
to poore Fishermen; so that by that time all reckonings are
cast up, these voyages come not farre behind the other in
advantage to the State.

2. *The fitnesse of the countrey for our health and
maintenance.* No Countrey yeelds a more propitious ayre
for our temper, then New-England, as experience hath made
manifest, by all relations: manie of our people that have
found themselves alway weake and sickly at home, have
become strong, and healthy there: perhaps by the dry-
nesse of the ayre and constant temper of it, which seldome
varies suddenly from cold to heate, as it doth with us: So
that Rheumes are very rare among our English there;
Neyther are the Natives at any time troubled with paine of
teeth, sorenesse of eyes, or ache in their limbes. It may bee
the nature of the water conduceth somewhat this way;
which all affirme to keepe the body alwaies temperately
soluble, and consequently helps much to the preventing, and
curing of the Gout, and Stone, as some have found by experience. As for provisions for life: The Corne of the
Country (which it produceth in good proportion with reasonable labour) is apt for nourishment, and agrees, although not so well with our taste at first; yet very well with
our health; nay, is held by some Physitians, to be restora-
tive. If wee like not that, wee may make use of our owne
Graines, which agree well with that soil, and so doe our
Cattle: nay, they grow unto a greater bulke of body there,
then with us in England. Unto which if wee adde the fish,
fowle, and Venison, which that Country yeelds in great
abundance, it cannot be questioned but that soil may assure sufficient provision for food. And being naturally apt
for Hempe and Flax especially, may promise us Linnen
sufficient with our labour, and woollen too if it may be
thought fit to store it with sheepe.

3. *Argument from the emptinesse of the Land.* The
Land affords void ground enough to receive more people

then this State can spare, and that not onely wood grounds, and others, which are unfit for present use: but, in many places, much cleared ground for tillage, and large marshes for hay and feeding of cattle, which comes to passe by the desolation hapning through a three yeeres Plague, about twelve or sixteene yeeres past, which swept away most of the Inhabitants all along the Sea coast, and in some places utterly consumed man, woman and childe, so that there is no person left to lay claime to the soil which they possessed; In most of the rest, the Contagion hath scarce left alive one person of an hundred. And which is remarkable, such a Plague hath not been knowne, or remembred in any age past; nor then raged above twenty or thirty miles up into the Land, nor seized upon any other but the Natives, the English in the heate of the Sicknesse commercing with them without hurt or danger. Besides, the Natives invite us to sit downe by them, and offer us what ground wee will: so that eyther want of possession by others, or the possessors gift, and sale, may assure our right: we neede not feare a cleare title to the soil.

4. *Argument from the usefulnesse of that Colony to this State.* In all Colonies it is to bee desired that the daughter may answer something backe by way of retribution to the mother that gave her being. Nature hath as much force, and founds as strong a relation betweene people and people, as betweene person and person: So that a Colonie denying due respect to the State from whose bowels it issued, is as great a monster, as an unnaturall childe. Now, a Colonie planted in New-England may be many wayes usefull to this State.

As first, in furthering our Fishing-voyages (one of the most honest, and every way profitable imployment that the Nation undertakes) It must needs be a great advantage unto our men after so long a voyage to be furnished with fresh victuall there; and that supplyed out of that Land, without spending the provisions of our owne countrey. But there is hope besides, that the Colonie shall not onely furnish our Fisher-men with Victuall, but with Salt too, unlesse mens expectation and conjectures much deceive them: and so quit unto them a great part of the charge of their voyage, beside the hazard of adventure.

Next, how serviceable this Country must needs be for provisions for shipping, is sufficiently knowne already: At present it may yeeld Planks, Masts, Oares, Pitch, Tarre, and Iron; and hereafter (by the aptnesse of the Soil for Hempe) if the Colonie increase, Sailes and Cordage. What other commodities it may afford besides for trade, time will discover. Of Wines among the rest, there can be no doubt; the ground yeelding naturall Vines in great abundance and varietie; and of these, some as good as any are found in France by humane culture. But in the possibilitie of the serviceablenesse of the Colonie to this State, the judgement of the Dutch may somewhat confirme us, who have planted in the same soil, and make great account of their Colonie there.

5. *Argument from the benefit of such a Colony to the Natives.* But the greatest advantage must needes come unto the Natives themselves, whom wee shall teach providence and industry, for want whereof they perish oftentimes, while they make short provisions for the present, by reason of their idlenesse, and that they have, they spend and wast unnecessarily, without having respect to times to come. Withall, commerce and example of our course of living, cannot but in time breed civility among them, and that by Gods blessing may make way for religion consequently, and for the saving of their soules. Unto all which may bee added, the safety and protection of the persons of the Natives, which are secured by our Colonies. In times past the Tarentines (who dwell from those of Mattachusets bay, neere which our men are seated; about fifty or sixty leagues to the North-East) inhabiting a soil unfit to produce that Countrey graine, being the more hardy people, were accustomed yeerely at harvest to come down in their Canoes, and reape their fields, and carry away their Corne, and destroy their people, which wonderfully weakened, and kept them low in times past: from this evill our neighbourhood hath wholy freed them, and consequently secured their persons and estates; which makes the Natives there so glad of our company.

Objection 1. But if we have any spare people, Ireland is a fitter place to receive them then New-England. Being 1,

Nearer. 2, Our owne. 3, Void in some parts. 4, Fruitfull. 5, Of importance for the securing of our owne Land. 6, Needing our helpe for their recovery out of blindnesse and superstition.

Answer. Ireland is well-nigh sufficiently peopled already, or will be in the next age. Besides, this worke needs not hinder that, no more then the plantation in Virginia, Bermudas, S. Christophers, Barbados, which are all of them approved, and incouraged as this is. As for religion, it hath reasonable footing in Ireland already, and may easily be propagated further, if wee bee not wanting to our selves. This Countrey of New-England is destitute of all helpes, and meanes, by which the people might come out of the snare of Satan. Now although it be true, that I should regard my sonne more then my servant; yet I must rather provide a Coate for my servant that goes naked, then give my sonne another, who hath reasonable clothing already.

Objection 2. But New-England hath divers discommodities, the Snow and coldnesse of the winter, which our English bodies can hardly brooke: and the annoyance of men by Muskitoes, and Serpents: and of Cattle, and Corne, by wild beasts.

Answer. The cold of Winter is tolerable, as experience hath, and doth manifest, and is remedied by the abundance of fuell. The Snow lyes indeed about a foot thicke for ten weekes or there about; but where it lies thicker, and a month longer as in many parts of Germany, men finde a very comfortable dwelling. As for the Serpents, it is true, there are some, and these larger then our Adders; but in ten yeares experience no man was ever indangered by them; and as the countrey is better stored with people, they will be found fewer, and as rare as among us here. As for the wilde beasts, they are no more, nor so much dangerous or hurtfull here, as in Germany and other parts of the world. The Muskitoes indeed infest the planters, about foure moneths in the heat of Summer; but after one yeares acquaintance, men make light account of them; some sleight defence for the hands and face, smoake, and a close house may keepe them off. Neither are they much more noysome then in Spaine, Germany, and other parts; nay, then the fennish parts of Essex, and Lincolne-shire. Besides, it is credibly reported, that twenty miles inward into the Countrey they are not found: but this is certaine, and tried by experience, after foure or five yeares habitation they waxe very thinne: It may be the hollownesse of the ground breeds them, which the treading of the earth by men and cattle doth remedy in time.

Objection 3. But if the propagation of religion bee the scope of the plantation, New-England which is so naked of inhabitants, is the unfittest of any place for a Colony; it would more further that worke to set downe in some well-peopled countrey, that might afford many subjects to worke upon, and win to the knowledge of the truth.

Answer. But how shall we get footing there? the Virginian Colony may bee our precedent; where our men have beene entertained with continuall broyles by the Natives, and by that meanes shut out from all hope of working any reformation upon them, from which, their hearts must needes be utterly averse by reason of the hatred which they beare unto our persons: whereas, New-England yeelds this advantage, that it affords us a cleare title to our possessions there; and good correspondence with the Natives; whether out of their peaceable disposition, or out of their inability to make resistance, or out of the safety which they finde by our neighbourhood, it skills not much; this is certaine, it yeelds a faire way to work them to that tractablenesse which will never bee found in the Virginians: Neither have wee any cause to complaine for want of men to worke upon; the in-land parts are indifferently populous, and Naraganset-bay and river, which borders upon us, is full of Inhabitants, who are quiet with us, and Trade with us willingly, while wee are their neighbours, but are very jealous of receiving either us or the Dutch into the bowells of their Country, for feare wee should become their Lords.

Besides, in probabilitie, it will be more advantagious to this worke to beginne with a place not so populous: For as the resistance will be lesse, so by them having once received the Gospell, it may be more easily and successefully spread to the places better peopled, who will more easily receive it from the commendation of their owne Countrie-men, then from strangers, and flocke to it as Doves to the windowes.

Though in the place where they plant, there are not many Natives, yet they have an opportunitie, by way of trafficke and commerce (which at least is generally once a yeare) with the Natives in a large compasse, though farre distant from them, by which meanes they grow into acquaintance with them, and may take many advantages of convaying to them the knowledge of Christ, though they live not with them.

Objection 4. But the Countrey wants meanes of wealth that might invite men to desire it; for there is nothing to bee expected in New-England but competency to live on at the best, and that must bee purchased with hard labour, whereas divers other parts of the West-Indies offer a richer soil, which easily allures Inhabitants, by the tender of a better condition then they live in at present.

Answer. As unanswerable argument, to such as make the advancement of their estates, the scope of their undertaking; but no way a discouragement to such as aime at the propagation of the Gospell, which can never bee advanced but by the preservation of Piety in those that carry it to strangers; Now wee know nothing sorts better with Piety than Competency; a truth which Agur hath determined long agoe, Proverbs 30:8. Nay, Heathen men by the light of Nature were directed so farre as to discover the overflowing of riches to be enemie to labour, sobriety, justice, love and magnanimity: and the nurse of pride, wantonnesse, and contention; and therefore laboured by all meanes to keepe out the love and desire of them from their wellordered States, and observed and professed the comming in and admiration of them to have beene the foundation of their ruine. If men desire to have a people degenerate speedily, and to corrupt their mindes and bodies too, and besides to toll in theeves and spoilers from abroad; let them seeke a rich soil, that brings in much with little labour; but if they desire that Piety and godlinesse should prosper; accompanied with sobriety, justice and love, let them choose a Countrey such as this is; even like France, or England, which may yeeld sufficiency with hard labour and industry:

the truth is, there is more cause to feare wealth then poverty in that soil.

DOCUMENT 10

COMPLAINTS AGAINST NEW ENGLAND, 1632–1638

Reports reached England that Connecticut and Massachusetts Bay in particular disregarded English policy. Both enforced a strict religious conformity while at the same time encouraging religious dissenters in England of like beliefs to join them. In its trade relationships New England pursued a course of self-interest and ignored governance by the mother country. This document includes some of the complaints lodged against New England, Winthrop's response, and finally the decision of the king's commissioners not to take action.

At Whitehall, April 4th, 1638.

Present

Lord Archbishop of Canterbury	Earl of Holland
Lord Keeper	Lord Cottington
Lord Treasurer	Mr. Treasurer
Lord Privy Seal	Mr. Comptroller
Earl Marshal	Mr. Secretary Cooke
Earl of Dorset	Mr. Secretary Windebank

This day the Lords Commissioners for foreign plantations, taking into consideration that the petitions and complaints of his Majesty's subjects, planters and traders in New England, grow more frequent than heretofore, for want of a settled and orderly government in those parts; and calling to mind that they had formerly given order, about two or three years since, to Mr. Cradock, a member of the plantation, to cause the grant, or letters patent for that plantation (alleged by him to be there remaining, in the hands of Mr. Winthrop,) to be sent over hither; and that notwithstanding the same, the said letters patent were not, as yet, brought over: and their lordships being now informed by Mr. Attorney General, that a *quo warranto* had been taken by him brought according to former order, against the said patent, and the same was proceeded to judgment against so many as had appeared, and that they which had not appeared were outlawed:

Their lordships, well approving of Mr. Attorney's care and proceeding therein, did now resolve and order, that Mr. Meawtes, clerk of the council, attendant upon the said commissioners for foreign plantations, should, in a letter from himself to Mr. Winthrop, inclose and convey this order unto him. And their lordships hereby, in his Majesty's name, and according to his express will and pleasure, strictly require and enjoin the said Winthrop, or any other in whose power or custody the said letters patents are, that they fail not to transmit the said patent hither by the return of the ship, in which the order is conveyed to them; it being resolved that in case of any further neglect or contempt by them shewed therein, their lordships will cause a strict course to be taken against them, and will move his Majesty to reassume into his hands the whole plantation.

To the Right Honourable, the Lords Commissioners for Foreign Plantations.

The humble petition of the Massachusetts, in New England, in the general court there assembled, the 6th day of September, in the fourteenth year of the reign of our Sovereign Lord, King Charles.

Whereas, it hath pleased your Lordships, by order of the 4th of April last, to require our patent to be sent unto you; we do here humbly and sincerely profess, that we are ready to yield all due obedience to our Sovereign Lord the King's Majesty, and to your Lordships under him, and in this mind we left our native country, and according thereunto hath been our practice ever since; so as we are much grieved that your Lordships should call in our patent, there being no cause known to us for that purpose, our government being settled according to his Majesty's grant, and we not answerable for any defect in other plantations. This is that which his Majesty's subjects do believe and profess, and therefore we are all humble suitors to your Lordships, that you would be pleased to take into further consideration our condition, and to afford unto us the liberties of subjects, that we may know what is laid to our charge, and have leave and time to answer for ourselves before we be condemned as a people unworthy of his Majesty's favour or protection. As for the *quo warranto* mentioned in the said order, we do assure your Lordships, that we were never called to make answer to it, and if we had, we doubt not but we have a sufficient plea to put in.

It is not unknown to your Lordships that we came into these remote parts with his Majesty's license and encouragement, under his great seal of England, and in the confidence we had of the great assurance of his favour, we have transported our families and estates, and here have we built and planted, to the great enlargement and securing of his Majesty's dominions in these parts, so as if our patent should be now taken from us, we should be looked at as runagates and outlaws, and shall be enforced either to remove to some other place, or to return to our native country again, either of which will put us to insuperable extremities; and these evils (among others,) will necessarily follow:

1. Many thousand souls will be exposed to ruin, being laid open to the injuries of all men.

2. If we be forced to desert the place, the rest of the plantations about us (being too weak to subsist alone,) will for the most part dissolve and go along with us, and then will this whole country fall into the hands of French or Dutch, who would speedily embrace such an opportunity.

3. If we should lose all our labour and cost, and be deprived of those liberties which his Majesty hath granted us, and nothing laid to our charge, nor any failing to be found in us in point of allegiance (which all our countrymen do take notice of, and we justify our faithfulness in this behalf,) it will discourage all men hereafter from the like undertakings upon confidence of his Majesty's royal grant.

4. Lastly, if our patent be taken from us (whereby we suppose we may claim interest in his Majesty's favour and protection,) the common people here will conceive that his Majesty hath cast them off, and that nereby they are freed from their allegiance and subjection, and thereupon will be ready to confederate themselves under a new government, for their necessary safety and subsistence, which will be of dangerous example unto other plantations, and perilous to ourselves, of incurring his Majesty's displeasure, which we would by all means avoid. Upon these considerations we are bold to renew our humble supplication to your Lordships, that we may be suffered to live here in this wilderness, and that this poor plantation, which hath found more favour with God than many other, may not find less favour from your Lordships, that our liberties should be restrained, when others are enlarged; that the door should be kept shut upon us, while it stands open to all other plantations; that men of ability should be debarred from us, while they have encouragement to other colonies. We do not question your Lordships' proceedings, we only desire to open our griefs where the remedy is to be expected. If in any thing we have offended his Majesty and your Lordships, we humbly prostrate ourselves at the footstool of supreme authority.

Let us be made the objects of his Majesty's clemency, and not cut off in our first appeal from all hope of favour. Thus with our earnest prayers unto the King of kings for long life and prosperity to his sacred Majesty, and his royal family, and for all honour and welfare to your Lordships, we humbly take leave.

This is a true copy, compared with the original on file, as attests

Edward Rawson, Secretary.

The Lords Commissioners, to whom the letter above written from Mr. Winthrop was directed, either rested satisfied in what was therein alleged, and so made no further demand of returning the patent; or otherwise, which some think more probable, concernments of an higher nature intervening in that juncture of time, gave a supersedeas to that design and intendment. . . . Nothing more was done therein during the former king's reign; and his Majesty now reigning, since his coronation, confirmed the charter of the Massachusetts anew, in one of his letters.

DOCUMENT 11

THE KING OVERRIDES VIRGINIA'S OBJECTIONS TO THE GRANT GIVEN LORD BALTIMORE, 1629–1633

In 1632 Charles I granted Lord Baltimore, a Catholic, the right to establish a proprietary colony north of Virginia. Baltimore's powers were almost unqualified. He had the right to set up a government, complete control of the distribution of land, and he held a monopoly of all the trade of the colony. In short, Lord Baltimore's word was law. Virginia objected strongly to the grant given Lord Baltimore. In this document, Virginia's objections are set out. Virginia was unsuccessful in its opposition, and it was instructed by the king to assist the settlers of Maryland when they arrived. The proprietary grant to Baltimore marked a turning point in the English colonizing impulse as joint-stock companies disappeared and proprietary colonies reappeared to become the principal pattern of colonization for the remainder of the seventeenth century.

Order of the Lords Commissioners for Foreign Plantation.

3 July 1633.

At the Starre Chamber the thirde of July 1633.

Present

Lord Keeper	Earl of Danby
Lord Privy Seale	Lord Viscount Wentworth
Lord High Chamberlain	Lord Viscount Falkland
Earl of Dorset	Lord Cottington
Earl of Bridgewater	Mr. Secretary Windebanck

Whereas an humble Petition of the Planters in Virginia was presented to his Majesty, in which they remonstrate that some Grants have lately been obteined of a great proportion of Lands and Territorys within the lymitts of the Colonie there being the places of their Traffique, and so near to their habitations, as will give a generall disheartning to the Planters if they be divided into severall Governments, and a Barre to that Trade, which they have long exercised towards their Supportation and reliefe under the confidence of his Majesty's royall and gracious intentions towards them, as by the said Petition more largely appeareth; for as much as his Majesty was pleased on the twelveth of May last to refer to the Boarde the consideration of this Petition, that upon the advice and report of their Lordshipps, such order might be taken, as to his Majesty's wisdom should seeme best. It was thereupon ordered on the 4th of June last, that the Business should be heard the seconde Friday in this Terme, which was the 28th of the last Month, and that all parties interested should then attend, which was accordingly performed, and their Lordshipps having heard the Cause, did then order that the Lord Baltimore being one of the parties, and the Adventurers and Planters of Virginia aforesaid should meet together between that tyme and this day and accommodate their controversy in friendly manner if it might be, and likewise sett downe in wryting the propositions made by either partie, with their severall answers and reasons, to be presented to the Boarde this day, which was likewise accordingly done. Now their Lordshipps having heard and maturely considered the sayde propositions, answers and reasons, and whatsover else was alleaged on either parte, did think fit to leave the Lord Baltimore to his Patent and the other Partie to the course of Lawe according to their desire; but for the preventing of further questions their Lordshipps did also think fit and order that things standing as they doe, the Planters on either side shall have free traffique and commerce each with other, and that neither parte shall receive any fugitive persons belonging to the other, nor doe any Act which may drawe a warre from the Natives upon either of them; and lastly that they shall sincerely enterteine all good correspondence and assist each other on all occasions, in such manner as becometh fellow-subjects and members of the same state.

The King to the Governor and Council of Virginia.

12 July 1633.

Trustie and Welbeloved wee greete you well. Whereas wee have lately receaved a Petition from your Lordshipp's government and the rest of the Planters in Virginia which we referred to the Lords of our Counsell who upon sundry deliberate hearings of the Lord Baltimore and those of your side did order that for so much as concerneth the Lord Baltimore there should be a mutuall correspondence betweene him and you, and you should agree in anything that may concerne the good and advancement of that plantation, which order our pleasure is shall be duly observed on both sides.

Now forasmuch as the said Lord Baltimore intends to transport to that part called Maryland, which wee have given him, a good number of our subjects who upon their arrivall and during the infancy of his plantation may perhaps have occasion to use the friendly helpe and assistance of you, and the rest of the old Planters there, in many occasions, for theire better support in that remote part of our dominions wee therefore well approving his good endevors, and intending the furtherance of his undertaking, doe hereby will and require you to use the said Lord Baltimore as well with that Courtesie and respect, that belong to a person of his rank and qualitie, and departed from hence with our speciall licence and in our very good grace and favour as also to suffer his servants and Planters to buy and transport such Cattell and other commodities to their Colony, as you may conveniently spare at reasonable rates and in all other things to hold that good correspondence with him and his planters, and to give them from tyme to tyme such lawfull assistance, as may conduce to both your safeties and the advancement of the plantation of those Countries, wherein wee require you

and the rest of our subjects there to joyne unanimously together and to use your best care and diligence. Given under our Signett.

✳ PART II ✳

The Establishment
of Self-Government

A discussion and analysis of political issues must begin
with the establishment of the institutions of self-government, for it is within this framework that issues develop.
Englishmen coming to America carried the seeds of self-
government with them: it was a unique bequest, unrealized
by the colonial establishments of the other nations of Western Europe. The English had enjoyed the privileges of local
government at home for centuries, so that they fully accepted the practice if not the theory that the power of the
sovereign was limited. The most obvious practical indication of this conviction is the power exercised by Parliament after the sixteenth century.

The operation of trading companies reinforced the
pattern found in English government. In order for an English trading company to conduct business in any area of
the world, it required a charter from the Crown, because
each company in effect represented an extension of England in a political as well as commercial sense. The charters
authorized these companies to govern themselves, always,
of course, with the provision that the decisions made and
the actions taken did not contravene the goals of the nation as expressed by the sovereign.

The third Virginia Charter of 1612 (Document 1)
reflects precisely this practice and experience. The Virginia

Company had the right to govern itself, and this governing authority extended to its New World colony. For the first few years the company appointed councillors who resided in the colony, one of whom was Captain John Smith. But divided authority among those appointed generated so many troubles that eventually the company agreed to select a governor, specifically Lord Delaware, with absolute authority. After the colony began to take root, the principal men in the company, especially Sir Edwin Sandys, promoted the practice of allowing the settlers residing in Virginia to participate in governing the colony. The result was the establishment of the House of Burgesses in 1619 (Document 2).

The first colony in New England, Plymouth colony, was also a joint-stock venture, whose stockholders remained in England. Too poor to invest in the enterprise, the Pilgrims of Plymouth invested themselves instead, each man being counted as one share of stock. The origin of self-government in Plymouth arose from decidedly different conditions from those of Virginia. The Pilgrims sailed to the New World secure in the knowledge that they had been awarded a land patent in Virginia. They landed instead on Cape Cod, whether by accident or by design is still debated. In any case, the Pilgrims disembarked outside of the authorized jurisdiction of any other colony. Because they feared the rule of those outside their membership, the Mayflower Compact (Document 3) was signed, thus becoming the foundation of self-government in that colony. The Pilgrims clearly represented the ultimate view of the Protestant Reformation, namely, that a group of men could form their own church, a religious conviction complementing the idea that men could assemble to form their own government. The political authority of the Plymouth Plantation was never secure, however, and eventually in 1691 Plymouth was incorporated into Massachusetts Bay.

The Massachusetts Bay Charter (Document 4) represented still another way in which self-government developed in the American colonies. In this case, the governing powers granted by the king in the charter were transferred to the New World. What had been intended as a grant of authority to a joint-stock trading organization was transformed by the ruling group within the Massachusetts Bay Company into a self-governing commonwealth. Yet another basis for self-government is found in the action of towns in Connecticut which mutually agreed in the Fundamental Orders (Document 5) to establish a colony. These towns had no authority to make this move; they possessed no charter from the English Crown. Only after they had lived under this self-imposed "constitution" for two decades were they able to receive official approval from the Crown, which then granted Connecticut a royal charter.

Each of the preceding documents became the foundation for colonial self-government; but another and equally important level of government, the institutions of local government, was also developed. Local government in America was modeled upon the practice in England. The shire or county in England had its colonial counterpart (Document 6). The county sheriff, the county clerk, the county justices of the peace, are all derived from the English model. Some county offices in England were not reproduced in America because their functions were fulfilled in other ways. An example is the lord-lieutenant in England whose duties were assumed by the colonial governor. In most colonies outside of New England, the county was the local political unit represented in the colonial assembly. Officials of the county government settled conflicting land titles, conducted county courts, and supervised elections. Local problems or issues of larger consequence were advanced to the colonial legislature or the colonial court. County officials enforced colonial legislation. In New England this role was played by the towns. In all colonies the legal system, so important a part of civil liberty, operated through a system of county courts.

Important as the establishment of self-governing institutions is, its vitality can be judged only when tested. In almost every colony, testing took place during the entire seventeenth century, but two especially important episodes are Bacon's Rebellion in Virginia in 1676 and the response of Massachusetts Bay to the revocation of its charter in 1684.

Bacon's Rebellion, the result of seething unrest in Virginia, is well-described by Robert Beverley, a seventeenth-century planter turned historian (Document 7). Governor Berkeley's views of the causes of the uprising (Document 8) differ sharply from those of his opponent, Nathaniel Bacon, who claimed he represented the people (Document 9). Bacon died, and with him the rebellion. But this did not prevent the royal commissioners sent from England to investigate the uprising from recommending certain reforms within the colonial government (Document 10), although they soundly assailed the actions of Bacon. Because of Bacon's actions, no Virginia governor after William Berkeley possessed the power he had exercised.

The test in Massachusetts Bay took a different form. In 1661, the colony re-stated its allegiance to the English Crown and reaffirmed its right of self-government (Document 11). But this did not prevent Edward Randolph, the Crown's Surveyor General of Customs, from severely criticizing the practices of Massachusetts Bay (Document 12). There was enough truth in Randolph's reports, not only about Massachusetts Bay but also about most of the other colonies, to encourage the Lords of Trade to embark upon a vast experiment in colonial government. The Massachusetts Bay Charter was rescinded in 1684. In its place, the Lords of Trade established in 1686 the Dominion of New England whose territory extended from Massachusetts Bay through New Jersey.

The Dominion of New England did not provide for a colonial assembly. Therefore, the legislatures of New York and New Jersey as well as those of other New England colonies were eliminated. Sir Edmund Andros was appointed governor of this new political creation, with Francis Nicholson, who resided in New York, as his deputy. The Dominion provided for a council whose membership was controlled by Andros. Not only were the preceding governmental institutions challenged by the creation of the Dominion, but other fundamental practices were also under siege including the validation of land titles and the right of colonials to tax themselves. If the Dominion had had an opportunity to develop, it would have changed the history of the American colonies and affected dramatically the evolution of American political institutions.

Events in England killed the Dominion experiment.

In 1688, two years after it had been instituted, King James II was overthrown by a bloodless revolution. William and Mary of Holland (Mary was the daughter of James II) ascended the throne after cautious and deliberative negotiations with leading members of Parliament. New England took advantage of this opportunity to overthrow Governor Andros as the representative of a discredited monarch. The New England colonists, to regain their former standing, identified their efforts with those of fellow Englishmen at home. An anonymous pamphleteer argues cogently for this identity of interest (Document 13).

The New England colonies regained their former charters, except for Massachusetts Bay, which received a new charter in 1691, to the accompaniment of an expansive and articulate pamphlet entitled "The Revolution of New England Justified." These experiences opened the way for a much deeper inquiry into the nature of self-government in America. The Reverend John Wise, a native of New England and the son of an indentured servant, explored the foundation for self-government in a semi-philosophical treatise, *The Vindication of the New England Churches* (Document 14).

Self-government in America underwent a long and troublesome history during its first century, but the solidity of its base was no longer in dispute by 1700. In the eighteenth century a new series of political issues arose, focusing on the question: Where does the authority of England end and the authority of each colony begin?

DOCUMENT 1

THE THIRD VIRGINIA CHARTER,
1612

Virginia received three charters, one in 1606, another in 1609, and the third in 1612. The differences among the three charters lie primarily in the territorial jurisdiction of the company, not in the right to govern the colony. In 1609, the "sea to sea" provision was inserted, and in 1612 jurisdiction was extended east-

ward from the Virginia shores to include islands, such as Bermuda, in the Atlantic.

From the outset the Virginia Company was granted the authority to govern its own colony. A ruling council in England, composed of members of the joint-stock company who were usually merchants of great distinction, was formed immediately after King James I granted the charter of 1606. The councillors were appointed ostensibly by the king, but in reality were nominated by the membership, or more often, by the inner executive group of the company. The council in England issued instructions to the first settlers appointing a colonial council to make daily decisions. This group proved ineffective, and a governor, Lord Delaware, was eventually appointed. Acting under the council in England, the governor had absolute power. The authority to establish or alter a government in Virginia was based upon the charter granted by the king; in this sense, the king delegated some of his power to others.

James, by the Grace of God, King of England, Scotland, France, and Ireland, Defender of the Faith; To all to whom these Presents shall come, Greeting. Whereas at the humble Suit of divers and sundry our loving Subjects, as well Adventurers as Planters of the first Colony in Virginia, and for the Propagation of Christian Religion, and Reclaiming of People barbarous, to Civility and Humanity, We have, by our Letters-Patents, bearing Date at Westminster, the three-and-twentieth Day of May, in the seventh Year of our Reign of England, France, and Ireland, and the two-and-fortieth of Scotland, Given and Granted unto them that they and all such and so many of our loving Subjects as should from time to time, for ever after, be joined with them as Planters or Adventurers in the said Plantation, and their Successors, for ever, should be one Body politick, incorporated by the Name of The Treasurer and Company of Adventurers and Planters of the City of London for the first Colony in Virginia;

And whereas also for the greater Good and Benefit of the said Company, and for the better Furtherance, Strengthening, and Establishing of the said Plantation, we

did further Give, Grant and Confirm, by our Letters-
Patents unto the said Company and their Successors, for
ever, all those Lands, Countries or Territories, situate, lying and being in that Part of America called Virginia, from
the Point of Land called Cape or Point Comfort all along
the Sea Coasts to the Northward two hundred Miles; and
from the said Point of Cape Comfort all along the Sea
Coast to the Southward two hundred Miles; and all that
Space and Circuit of Land lying from the Sea Coast of
the Precinct aforesaid, up into the Land throughout from
Sea to Sea West and North-west; and also all the Islands
lying within one hundred Miles along the Coast of both
the Seas of the Precinct aforesaid; with divers other Grants,
Liberties, Franchises and Preheminences, Privileges, Profits,
Benefits, and Commodities granted in and by our said
Letters-patents to the said Treasurer and Company and
their Successors for ever.

Now forasmuch as we are given to understand, that in
those Seas adjoining to the said Coasts of Virginia, and
without the Compass of those two hundred Miles by Us
so granted unto the said Treasurer and Company as aforesaid, and yet not far distant from the said Colony in
Virginia, there are or may be divers Islands lying desolate
and uninhabited, some of which are already made known
and discovered by the Industry, Travel, and Expences of
the said Company, and others also are supposed to be and
remain as yet unknown and undiscovered, all and every
of which it may import the said Colony both in Safety and
Policy of Trade to populate and plant; in Regard whereof,
as well for the preventing of Peril, as for the better Commodity of the said Colony, they have been humble suitors
unto Us, that We would be pleased to grant unto them an
Enlargement of our said former Letters-patents. . . . all
and singular those Islands whatsoever situate and being
in any Part of the Ocean Seas bordering upon the Coast
of our said first Colony in Virginia, and being within
three Hundred Leagues of any of the Parts heretofore
granted to the said Treasurer and Company in our said
former Letters-Patents as aforesaid. . . . To have and to
hold, possess and enjoy, all and singular the said Islands
in the said Ocean Seas so lying and bordering upon the

Coast and Coasts of the Territories of the said first Colony in Virginia, as aforesaid. With all and singular the said Soils, Lands, Grounds, and all and singular other the Premises heretofore by these Presents granted or mentioned to be granted to them. . . .

And We are further pleased, and We do by these Presents grant and confirm, that Philip Earl of Montgomery, William Lord Paget, sir John Starrington, Knight etc., whom the said Treasurer and Company have since the said last Letters-Patents nominated and set down as worthy and discreet Persons fit to serve Us as Counsellors, to be of our Council for the said Plantation, shall be reputed, deemed, and taken as Persons of our said Council for the said first Colony, in such Manner and Sort, to all Intents and Purposes, as those who have been formerly elected and nominated as our Counsellors for that Colony, and whose Names have been, or are inserted and expressed in our said former Letters-Patents.

And we do hereby ordain and grant by these Presents, that the said Treasurer and Company of Adventurers and Planters aforesaid, shall and may, once every week, or oftener, at their Pleasure, hold, and keep a Court and Assembly for the better Order and Government of the said Plantation, and such Things as shall concern the same; And that any five Persons of our Council for the said first Colony in Virginia, for the Time being, of which Company the Treasurer, or his Deputy, to be always one, and the Number of fifteen others, at the least, of the Generality of the said Company, assembled together in such Manner, as is and hath been heretofore used and accustomed, shall be said, taken, held, and reputed to be, and shall be a sufficient Court of the said Company, for the handling and ordering, and dispatching of all such casual and particular Occurrences, and accidental Matters, of less Consequence and Weight, as shall from Time to Time happen, touching and concerning the said Plantation.

And that nevertheless, for the handling, ordering, and disposing of Matters and Affairs of greater Weight and Importance, and such as shall or may, in any Sort, concern the Weal Publick and general Good of the said Company and Plantation, as namely, the Manner of Government from Time to Time to be used, the ordering and Disposing of the Lands and Possessions, and the settling and establishing of a Trade there, or such like, there shall be held and kept every Year, upon the last Wednesday, save one, of Hillary Term, Easter, Trinity, and Michaelmas Terms, for ever, one great, general, and solemn Assembly, which four Assemblies shall be stiled and called, The four Great and General Courts of the Council and Company of Adventurers for Virginia; In all and every of which said Great and General Courts, so assembled, our Will and Pleasure is, and we do, for Us, our Heirs and Successors, for ever, Give and Grant to the said Treasurer and Company, and their Successors for ever, by these Presents, that they, the said Treasurer and Company, or the greater Number of them, so assembled, shall and may have full Power and Authority, from Time to Time, and at all Times hereafter, to elect and chuse discreet Persons, to be of our said Council for the said first Colony in Virginia, and to nominate and appoint such Officers as they shall think fit and requisite, for the Government, managing, ordering, and dispatching of the Affairs of the said Company; And shall likewise have full Power and Authority, to ordain and make such Laws and Ordinances, for the Good and Welfare of the said Plantation, as to them from Time to Time, shall be thought requisite and meet: So always, as the same be not contrary to the Laws and Statutes of this our Realm of England. . . .

DOCUMENT 2

AN ORDINANCE AND CONSTITUTION OF THE VIRGINIA COMPANY IN ENGLAND FOR A COUNCIL OF STATE AND GENERAL ASSEMBLY, 24 JULY 1621

The first specific instance of genuine self-government in the English colonies was the meeting of the first House of Burgesses in Virginia in 1619. It convened in "James City" on July 30, 1619 and was dissolved on August 4, 1619. Twenty-two men were present, representing eleven geographic constituencies, together with the governor, Sir George Yeardley. They met at the church, organized themselves into an effective legislative body, and passed acts to regulate Indian trade, to govern personal conduct, to encourage silk production and a storage minimum of corn for each person, to discourage enticement of tenants and servants away from their masters, to establish a public "magazine," or warehouse, for tobacco, and other like measures affecting the daily life of the settlers.

The precedent set by the establishment of a self-governing assembly in colonial Virginia was one of the most important and enduring political actions in American history. The instructions from the council in England authorizing the meeting are missing, but historians believe that the instructions reissued in 1621 were based upon the original instructions sent in 1619.

An Ordinance and Constitution of the Treasurer Council, and Company in England, for a Council of State and General Assembly.

I. To all people, to whom these presents shall come, be seen, or heard, the treasurer, council, and company of adventurers and planters for the city of London for the first colony of Virginia, send greeting. Know ye, that we, the said treasurer, council, and company, taking into our careful consideration the present state of the said colony of Virginia, and intending by the divine assistance, to settle such a form of government there, as may be to the greatest benefit and comfort of the people, and whereby all injustice, grievances, and oppression may be prevented and kept off as much as possible, from the said colony, have thought fit to make our entrance, by ordering and establishing such supreme councils, as may not only be assisting to the governor for the time being, in the administration of justice, and the executing of other duties to this office belonging, but also, by their vigilant care and prudence, may provide, as well for a remedy of all inconveniences, growing from time to time, as also for advancing of increase, strength, stability, and prosperity of the said colony:

II We therefore, the said treasurer, council, and company, by authority directed to us from his majesty under the great seal, upon mature deliberation, do hereby order and declare, that, from hence forward, there shall be two supreme councils in Virginia, for the better government of the said colony aforesaid.

III. The one of which councils, to be called the council of state (and whose office shall chiefly be assisting, with their care, advice, and circumspection, to the said governor) shall be chosen, nominated, placed, and displaced, from time to time, by us the said treasurer, council and company, and our successors: which council of state shall consist, for the present only of these persons, as are here inserted, viz., sir Francis Wyatt, governor of Virginia, captain Francis West, sir George Yeardley, knight, sir William Neuce, knight, marshal of Virginia, Mr. George Sandys, treasurer, Mr. George Thorpe, deputy of the college, captain Thomas Neuce, deputy for the company, Mr. Powlet, Mr. Leech, captain Nathaniel Powel, Mr. Christopher Davidson, secretary, Doctor Potts, physician to the company, Mr. Roger Smith, Mr. John Berkeley, Mr. John Rolfe, Mr. Ralph Hamer, Mr. John Pountis, Mr. Michael Lapworth, Mr. Harwood, Mr. Samuel Macock. Which said counsellors and council we earnestly pray and desire, and in his majesty's name strictly charge and command, that (all factions, partialities, and sinister respect laid aside) they bend their care and endeavours to assist the said governor; first and principally, in the advancement of the honour and service of God, and the enlargement of his kingdom against the heathen people; and next, in erecting of the said colony in due obedience to his majesty, and all lawful authority from his majesty's directions; and lastly, in maintaining the said people in justice and christian conversation amongst themselves, and in strength and ability to withstand their enemies. And this council, to be always, or for the most part, residing about or near the governor.

IV. The other council, more generally to be called by the governor, once yearly, and no oftener, but for very extraordinary and important occasions, shall consist for the present, of the said council of state, and of two burgesses out of every town, hundred, or other particular plantation, to be respectively chosen by the inhabitants: which council shall be called The General Assembly, wherein (as also in the said council of state) all matters shall be decided, determined, and ordered by the greater part of the voices then present; reserving to the governor always a negative voice. And this general assembly shall have free power, to treat, consult, and conclude, as well of all emergent occasions concerning the publick weal of the said colony and every part thereof, as also to make, ordain, and enact such general laws and orders, for the behoof of the said colony, and the good government thereof, as shall, from time to time, appear necessary or requisite;

V. Whereas in all other things, we require the said general assembly, as also the said council of state, to imitate and follow the policy of the form of government, laws, customs, and manner of trial, and other administration of justice, used in the realm of England, as near as may be even as ourselves, by his majesty's letters patent, are required.

VI. Provided, that no law or ordinance, made in the said general assembly, shall be or continue in force or validity, unless the same shall be solemnly ratified and confirmed, in a general quarter court of the said company here in England, and so ratified, be returned to them under our seal; it being our intent to afford the like measure also unto the said colony, that after the government of the said colony shall once have been well framed, and settled accordingly, which is to be done by us, as by authority derived from his majesty, and the same shall have been so by us declared, no orders of court afterwards, shall bind the said colony, unless they be ratified in like manner in the general assemblies. In witness whereof we have hereunto set our common seal the 24th of July, 1621. . . .

DOCUMENT 3

THE MAYFLOWER COMPACT,
11 NOVEMBER 1620

Whereas self-government in Virginia was granted deliberately by the company, self-government in Plymouth grew out of an emergency. The Pilgrims left England with the authority to settle in northern Virginia, having received a patent for a grant of land there. When the Pilgrims landed on Cape Cod in New England, they were outside the jurisdiction of any official English governmental authority. The Pilgrims of the Leyden Congregation from Holland constituted only one-third of the people on board the Mayflower. *Part of the remaining two-thirds were sympathetic to their religious convictions. But because these Pilgrims were a minority, they feared that actions might be taken contrary to their self-interest. The Mayflower Compact encouraged everyone aboard the ship to abide by regulations adopted by the self-constituted "Civil Body Politick," in which the Leyden Congregation leaders predominated.*

In the Name of God, Amen. We, whose names are underwritten, the Loyal Subjects of our dread Sovereign Lord King James, by the Grace of God, of Great Britain, France, and Ireland, King, Defender of the Faith, etc. Having undertaken for the Glory of God, and Advancement of the Christian Faith, and the Honour of our King and Country, a Voyage to plant the first Colony in the northern Parts of Virginia; Do by these Presents, solemnly and mutually, in the Presence of God and one another, covenant and combine ourselves together into a civil Body Politick, for our better Ordering and Preservation, and Furtherance of the Ends aforesaid: And by Virtue hereof do enact, constitute, and frame, such just and equal Laws, Ordinances, Acts, Constitutions, and Officers, from time to time, as shall be thought most meet and convenient for the general Good of the Colony; unto which we promise all due Submission and Obedience. In Witness whereof we have hereunto subscribed our names at Cape-Cod the eleventh of November, in the Reign of our Sovereign Lord King James, of England, France, and Ireland, the eighteenth, and of Scotland, the fifty-fourth, Anno Domini, 1620.

Mr. John Carver	Mr. Samuel	Peter Brown
Mr. William	Fuller	Richard
Bradford	Mr. Christopher	Britteridge
Mr. Edward	Martin	George Soule
Winslow	Mr. William	Edward Tilly
Mr. William	Mullins	John Tilly
Brewster	Mr. William	Francis Cooke
Isaac Allerton	White	Thomas Rogers
Myles Standish	Mr. Richard	Thomas Tinker
John Alden	Warren	John Ridgdale
John Turner	John Howland	Edward Fuller
Francis Eaton	Mr. Steven	Richard Clark
James Chilton	Hopkins	Richard Gardiner
John Craxton	Digery Priest	Mr. John Allerton
John Billington	Thomas Williams	Thomas English
Joses Fletcher	Gilbert Winslow	Edward Doten
John Goodman	Edmund	Edward Liester
	Margesson	

DOCUMENT 4

CHARTER OF MASSACHUSETTS BAY,
1629

The charter of Massachusetts Bay represents still another way in which self-government was established in the English colonies of North America. In this case, the Massachusetts Bay Company, a joint-stock company resident in England, whose membership included merchants and landed gentry, received a charter from the Crown. The government of the com-

*pany and the extent of its authority were clearly
stated in the charter, with an unstated premise that
the management of the company and thus the charter
itself would remain in England.*

*However, a group of Puritans within the Massa-
chusetts Bay Company adopted a pledge known as
the Cambridge Agreement, in which they stipulated
that they would not only migrate to the New World
but also carry the charter with them. This last step
was taken to assure those Puritans in the company
who settled in New England that they would retain
control of company management. By bringing the
charter to America, the Puritans took the first step
in transforming Massachusetts Bay from a trading
company into a commonwealth, because the charter
became the constitution of the colony.*

And further, That the said Governour and Companye,
and their Successors, maie have forever one comon Seale,
to be used in all Causes and Occasions of the said Company, and the same Seale may alter, chaunge, breake, and
newe make, from tyme to tyme, at their pleasures. And
our Will and Pleasure is, and Wee doe hereby for Us, our
Heires and Successors, ordeyne and graunte, That from
henceforth for ever, there shalbe one Governor, one
Deputy Governor, and eighteene Assistants of the same
Company, to be from tyme to tyme constituted, elected
and chosen out of the Freemen of the saide Company, for
the twyme being, in such Manner and Forme as hereafter
in theis Presents is expressed, which said Officers shall
applie themselves to take Care for the best disposeing and
ordering of the generall buysines and Affaires of, for, and
concerning the said Landes and Premisses hereby mentioned, to be graunted, and the Plantation thereof, and
the Government of the People there. And for the better
Execution of our Royall Pleasure and Graunte in this Behalf, Wee doe, by theis presents, for Us, our Heires and
Successors, nominate, ordeyne, make, and constitute; our
welbeloved the saide Mathewe Cradocke, to be the first
and present Governor of the said Company, and the saide
Thomas Goffe, to be Deputy Governor of the saide Com-

pany, and the saide Sir Richard Saltonstall, Isaack Johnson, Samuell Aldersey, John Ven, John Humfrey, John
Endecott, Simon Whetcombe, Increase Noell, Richard
Pery, Nathaniell Wright, Samuell Vassall, Theophilus
Eaton, Thomas Adams, Thomas Hutchins, John Browne,
George Foxcrofte, William Vassall, and William Pinchion,
to be the present Assistants of the saide Company, to continue in the saide several Offices respectivelie for such
tyme, and in such manner, as in and by theis Presents is
hereafter declared and appointed.

And further, Wee will, and by theis Presents, for Us,
our Heires and Successors, doe ordeyne and graunte, That
the Governor of the saide Company for the tyme being, or
in his Absence by Occasion of Sicknes or otherwise, the
Deputie Governor for the tyme being, shall have Authoritie from tyme to tyme upon all Occasions, to give order
for the assembling of the saide Company, and calling them
together to consult and advise of the Bussinesses and
Affaires of the saide Company, and that the said Governor, Deputie Governor, and Assistants of the saide Company, for the tyme being, shall or maie once every Moneth,
or oftener at their Pleasures, assemble and houlde and
keepe a Courte or Assemblie of themselves, for the better
ordering and directing of their Affaires, and that any
seaven or more persons of the Assistants, togither with the
Governor, or Deputie Governor soe assembled, shalbe
saide, taken, held, and reputed to be, and shalbe a full and
sufficient Courte or Assemblie of the said Company, for
the handling, ordering, and dispatching of all such Buysi-
nesses and Occurrents as shall from tyme to tyme happen,
touching or concerning the said Company or Plantation;
and that there shall or maie be held and kept by the Governor, or Deputie Governor of the said Company, and
seaven or more of the said Assistants for the tyme being,
upon every last Wednesday in Hillary, Easter, Trinity, and
Michas Termes respectivelie forever, one greate generall
and solemne assemblie, which foure generall assemblies
shalbe stiled and called the foure great and generall Courts
of the saide Company.

In all and every, or any of which saide greate and
generall Courts soe assembled, Wee doe for Us, our Heires

and Successors, give and graunte to the said Governor and
Company, and their Successors, That the Governor, or in
his absence, the Deputie Governor of the saide Company
for the tyme being, and such of the Assistants and Freeman of the saide Company as shalbe present, or the greater
nomber of them so assembled, whereof the Governor or
Deputie Governor and six of the Assistants at the least
to be seaven, shall have full Power and authoritie to choose,
nominate, and appointe, such and soe many others as they
shall thinke fitt, and that shall be willing to accept the
same, to be free of the said Company and Body, and
them into the same to admitt; and to elect and constitute
such Officers as they shall thinke fitt and requisite, for
the ordering, mannaging, and dispatching of the Affaires
of the saide Governor and Company, and their Successors;
And to make Lawes and Ordinances for the Good and
Welfare of the saide Company, and for the Government
and ordering of the saide Landes and Plantation, and the
People inhabiting and to inhabite the same, as to them
from tyme to tyme shalbe thought meete, soe as such
Lawes and Ordinances be not contrarie or repugnant to
the Lawes and Statuts of this our Realme of England.

And, our Will and Pleasure is, and Wee doe hereby
for Us, our Heires and Successors, establish and ordeyne,
That yearely once in the yeare, for ever hereafter, namely,
the last Wednesday in Easter Tearme, yearely, the Governor, Deputy-Governor, and Assistants of the saide Company and all other officers of the saide Company shalbe
in the Generall Court or Assembly to be held for that Day
or Tyme, newly chosen for the Yeare ensueing by such
greater parte of the said Company, for the Tyme being,
then and there present, as is aforesaide. And, if it shall
happen the present governor, Deputy Governor, and assistants, by theis presents appointed, or such as shall hereafter be newly chosen into their Roomes, or any of them,
or any other of the officers to be appointed for the said
Company, to dye, or to be removed from his or their
severall Offices or Places before the saide generall Day of
Election (whome Wee doe hereby declare for any Mis-
demeanor or Defect to be removeable by the Governor,
Deputie Governor, Assistants, and Company, or such

greater Parte of them in any of the publique Courts to be
assembled as is aforesaid) That then, and in every such
Case, it shall and maie be lawfull, to and for the Governor, Deputie Governor, Assistants, and Company aforesaide, or such greater Parte of them soe to be assembled
as is aforesaide, in any of their Assemblies, to proceade
to a new Election of one or more others of their Company in the Roome or Place, Roomes or Places of such
Officer or Officers soe dyeing or removed according to
their Discretions, And, immediately upon and after such
Election and Elections made of such Governor, Deputie
Governor, Assistant or Assistants, or any other officer of
the saide Company, in Manner and Forme aforesaid, the
Authoritie, Office, and Power, before given to the former
Governor, Deputie Governor, or other Officer and Officers
soe removed, in whose Steade and Place newe shalbe soe
chosen, shall as to him and them, and everie of them,
cease and determine

Provided alsoe, and our Will and Pleasure is, That
aswell such as are by theis Presents appointed to be the
present Governor, Deputie Governor, and Assistants of
the said Company, as those that shall succeed them, and
all other Officers to be appointed and chosen as aforesaid,
shall, before they undertake the Execution of their saide
Offices and Places respectivelie, take their Corporal Oathes
for the due and faithfull Performance of their Duties in
their severall Offices and Places, before such Person or
Persons as are by theis Presents hereunder appointed to
take and receive the same. . . .

And, further our Will and Pleasure is, and Wee doe
hereby for Us, our Heires and Successors, ordeyne and
declare, and graunte to the saide Governor and Company,
and their Successors, That all and every the Subjects of
Us, our Heires or Successors, which shall goe to and inhabite within the saide Landes and Premisses hereby mentioned to be graunted, and every of their Children which
shall happen to be borne there, or on the Seas in goeing
thither, or retorning from thence, shall have and enjoy
all liberties and Immunities of free and naturall Subjects
within any of the Domynions of Us, our Heires or Successors, to all Intents, Constructions, and Purposes what-

soever, as if they and everie of them were borne within
the Realme of England. And that the Governor and Deputie Governor of the said Company for the Tyme being, or
either of them, and any two or more of such of the saide
Assistants as shalbe thereunto appointed by the saide Governor and Company at any of their Courts or Assemblies
to be held as aforesaide, shall and maie at all Tymes, and
from tyme to tyme hereafter, have full Power and Authoritie to minister and give the Oathe and Oathes of
Supremacie and Allegiance, or either of them, to all and
everie Person and Persons, which shall at any Tyme or
Tymes hereafter goe or passe to the Landes and Premisses
hereby mentioned to be graunted to inhabite in the same.

And, Wee doe of our further Grace, certen Knowledg
and meere Motion, give and graunte to the saide Governor
and Company, and their Successors, That it shall and maie
be lawfull, to and for the Governor or Deputie Governor,
and such of the Assistants and Freemen of the said Company for the Tyme being as shalbe assembled in any of
their generall Courts aforesaide, or in any other Courtes
to be specially sumoned and assembled for that Purpose,
or the greater Parte of them (whereof the Governor or
Deputie Governor, and six of the Assistants to be alwaies
seaven) from tyme to tyme, to make, ordeine, and estab-
lishe all Manner of wholesome and reasonable Orders,
Lawes, Statutes, and Ordinances, Directions, and Instructions, not contrairie to the Lawes of this our Realme of
England, aswell for setling of the Formes and Ceremonies
of Government and Magistracy, fitt and necessary for the
said Plantation, and the Inhabitants there, and for nameing
and setting of all sorts of Officers, both superior and inferior, which they shall finde needefull for that Governement and Plantation, and the distinguishing and setting
forth of the severall duties, Powers, and Lymytts of every
such Office and Place, and the Formes of such Oathes
warrantable by the Lawes and Statutes of this our Realme
of England, as shalbe respectivelie ministred unto them
for the Execution of the said severall Offices and Places;
as also, for the disposing and ordering of the Elections of
such of the said Officers as shalbe annuall, and of such
others as shalbe to succeede in Case of Death or Removeall,

and ministring the said Oathes to the newe elected Officers, and for Impositions of lawfull Fynes, Mulcts, Imprisonment, or other lawfull Correction, according to the Course of other Corporations in this our Realme of England, and for the directing, ruling, and disposeing of all other Matters and Thinges, whereby our said People, Inhabitants there, may be soe religiously, peaceablie, and civilly governed, as their good Life and orderlie Conversation, maie wynn and incite the Natives of Country, to the Knowledg and Obedience of the onlie true God and Savior of Mankinde, and the Christian Fayth, which in our Royall Intention, and the Adventurers free Profession, is the principall Ende of this Plantation.

Willing, commaunding, and requiring, and by theis Presents for Us, our Heires, and Successors, ordeyning and appointing, that all such Orders, Lawes, Statuts and Ordinances, Instructions and Directions, as shalbe soe made by the Governor, or Deputie Governor of the said Company, and such of the Assistants and Freemen as aforesaide, and published in Writing, under their common Seale, shalbe carefullie and dulie observed, kept, performed, and putt in Execution, according to the true Intent and Meaning of the same; and theis our Letters-patents, or the Duplicate or exemplification thereof, shalbe to all and everie such Officers, superior and inferior, from Tyme to Tyme, for the putting of the same Orders, Lawes, Statutes, and Ordinances, Instructions, and Directions, in due Execution against Us, our Heires and Successors, a sufficient Warrant and Discharge.

And Wee doe further, for Us, our Heires and Successors, give and graunt to the said Governor and Company, and their Successors by theis Presents, that all and everie such Chiefe Comaunders, Captaines, Governors, and other Officers and Ministers, as by the said Orders, Lawes, Statuts, Ordinances, Instructions, or Directions of the said Governor and Company for the Tyme being, shalbe from Tyme to Tyme hereafter imploied either in the Government of the saide Inhabitants and Plantation, or in the Waye by Sea thither, or from thence, according to the Natures and Lymitts of their Offices and Places respectively, shall from Tyme to Tyme hereafter for ever, within the

Precincts and Partes of Newe England hereby mentioned
to be graunted and confirmed, or in the Waie by Sea
thither, or from thence, have full and Absolute Power and
Authoritie to correct, punishe, pardon, governe, and rule
all such the Subjects of Us, our Heires and Successors,
as shall from Tyme to Tyme adventure themselves in any
Voyadge thither or from thence, or that shall at any Tyme
hereafter, inhabite within the Precincts and Partes of Newe
England aforasaid, according to the Orders, Lawes, Ordinances, Instructions, and Directions aforesaid, not being
repugnant to the Lawes and Statutes of our Realme of
England as aforesaid. . . .

DOCUMENT 5

FUNDAMENTAL ORDERS OF CONNECTICUT, 14 JANUARY 1638

*The Fundamental Orders of Connecticut represent
still another way in which self-government gained a
strong foothold in the American colonies. The towns
of Hartford, Windsor, and Wethersfield had grown up
around the Connecticut Valley, each town being, in
a sense, an offshoot of Massachusetts Bay. Because
of their common interests, religious and secular, these
towns decided to combine into a colony, Connecticut.
Connecticut finally received a royal charter in 1663,
but self-government preceded official recognition.*

Forasmuch as it hath pleased the Allmighty God by
the wise disposition of his divyne providence so to Order
and dispose of things that we the Inhabitants and Resi-
dents of Windsor, Harteford and Wethersfield are now
cohabiting and dwelling in and uppon the River of Con-
ectecotte and the Lands thereunto adjoyneing; And well
knowing where a people are gathered togather the word
of God requires that to mayntayne the peace and union
of such a people there should be an orderly and decent
Government established according to God, to order and

dispose of the affayres of the people at all seasons as occation shall require; doe therefore assotiate and conjoyne our selves to be as one Publike State or Commonwelth; and doe, for our selves and our Successors and such as shall be adjoyned to us att any tyme hereafter, enter into Combination and Confederation togather, to mayntayne and preserve the liberty and purity of the gospell of our Lord Jesus which we now professe, as also the disciplyne of the Churches, which according to the truth of the said gospell is now practised amongst us; As also in our Civell Affaires to be guided and governed according to such Lawes, Rules, Orders and decrees as shall be made, ordered and decreed, as followeth:

1. It is Ordered, sentenced and decreed, that there shall be yerely two generall Assemblies or Courts, the one the second thursday in Aprill, the other the second thursday in September, following; the first shall be called the Courte of Election, wherein shall be yerely Chosen from tyme to tyme soe many Magestrats and other publike Officers as shall be found requisitte: Whereof one to be chosen Governor for the yeare ensueing and untill another be chosen, and noe other Magestrate to be chosen for more then one yeare; provided allwayes there be six chosen besids the Governor; which being chosen and sworne according to an Oath recorded for that purpose shall have power to administer justice according to the Lawes here established, and for want thereof according to the rule of the word of God; which choise shall be made by all that are admitted freemen and have taken the Oath of Fidellity, and doe cohabitte within this Jurisdiction (having beene admitted Inhabitants by the major part of the Towne wherein they live,) or the major parte of such as shall be then present.

2. It is Ordered, sentenced and decreed, that the Election of the aforesaid Magestrats shall be on this manner: every person present and quallified for choise shall bring in (to the persons deputed to receave them) one single paper with the name of him written in it whom he desires to have Governor, and he that hath the greatest number of papers shall be Governor for that yeare. And the rest of the Magestrats or publike Officers to be chosen in this

manner: The Secretary for the tyme being shall first read the names of all that are to be put to choise and then shall severally nominate them distinctly, and every one that would have the person nominated to be chosen shall bring in one single paper written uppon, and he that would not have him chosen shall bring in a blanke: and every one that hath more written papers than blanks shall be a Magistrat for that yeare; which papers shall be receaved and told by one or more that shall be then chosen by the court and sworne to be faithfull therein; but in case there should not be six chosen as aforesaid, besids the Governor, out of those which are nominated, then he or they which have the most written papers shall be a Magestrate or Magestrats for the ensueing yeare, to make up the aforesaid number.

3. It is Ordered, sentenced and decreed, that the Secretary shall not nominate any person nor shall any person be chosen newly into the Magestracy which was not propownded in some Generall Courte before, to be nominated the next Election; and to that end it shall be lawfull for ech of the Townes aforesaid by their deputyes to nominate any two whom they conceave fitte to be put to election; and the Courte may ad so many more as they judge requisitt.

4. It is Ordered, sentenced and decreed that noe person be chosen Governor above once in two yeares, and that the Governor be always a member of some approved congregation, and formerly of the Magestracy within this Jurisdiction; and all the Magestrats Freemen of this Commonwelth: and that no Magestrate or other publike officer shall execute any parte of his or their Office before they are severally sworne, which shall be done in the face of the Courte if they be present, and in case of absence by some deputed for that purpose.

5. It is Ordered, sentenced and decreed, that to the aforesaid Courte of Election the severall Townes shall send their deputyes, and when the Elections are ended they may proceed in any publike searvice as at other Courts. Also the other Generall Courte in September shall be for makeing of lawes, and any other publike occasion, which conserns the good of the Commonwelth.

6. It is Ordered, sentenced and decreed, that the Governor shall, ether by himselfe or by the secretary, send out summons to the Constables of every Towne for the cauleing of these two standing Courts, one month at least before their severall tymes: And also if the Governor and the gretest parte of the Magestrats see cause uppon any spetiall occation to call a generall Courte, they may give order to the secretary soe to doe within fowerteene dayes warneing; and if urgent necessity so require, uppon a shorter notice, giveing sufficient grownds for it to the deputyes when they meete, or els be questioned for the same; And if the Governor and Major parte of Magestrats shall ether neglect or refuse to call the two Generall standing Courts or ether of them, as also at other tymes when the occations of the Commonwelth require, the Freemen thereof, or the Major parte of them, shall petition to them soe to doe; if then it be ether denyed or neglected the said Freemen or the Major parte of them shall have power to give order to the Constables of the severall Townes to doe the same, and so may meete togather, and chuse to themselves a Moderator, and may proceed to do any Acte of power, which any other Generall Courte may.

7. It is Ordered, sentenced and decreed that after there are warrants given out for any of the said Generall Courts, the Constable or Constables of ech Towne shall forthwith give notice distinctly to the inhabitants of the same, in some Publike Assembly or by goeing or sending from howse to howse, that at a place and tyme by him or them lymited and sett, they meet and assemble them selves togather to elect and chuse certen deputyes to be att the Generall Courte then following to agitate the afayres of the commonwelth; which said Deputyes shall be chosen by all that are admitted Inhabitants in the severall Townes and have taken the oath of fidellity; provided that non be chosen a Deputy for any Generall Courte which is not a Freeman of this Commonwelth.

The a-foresaid deputyes shall be chosen in manner following: every person that is present and quallified as before expressed, shall bring the names of such, written in severall papers as they desire to have chosen for that Imployment, and these 3 or 4, more or lesse, being the number agreed on to be chosen for that tyme, that have greatest number of papers written for them shall be deputyes for that Courte; whose names shall be endorsed on the backe side of the warrant and returned into the Courte, with the Constable or Constables hand unto the same.

8. It is Ordered, sentenced and decreed, that Wyndsor, Hartford and Wethersfield shall have power, ech Towne, to send fower of their freemen as deputyes to every Generall Courte; and whatsoever other Townes shall be hereafter added to this Jurisdiction, they shall send so many deputyes as the Courte shall judge meete, a resonable proportion to the number of Freemen that are in the said Townes being to be attended therein; which deputyes shall have the power of the whole Towne to give their voats and alowance to all such lawes and orders as may be for the publike good, and unto which the said Townes are to be bownd.

9. It is ordered and decreed, that the deputyes thus chosen shall have power and liberty to appoynt a tyme and a place of meeting togather before any Generall Courte to advise and consult of all such things as may concerne the good of the publike, as also to examine their owne Elections, whether according to the order, and if they or the gretest parte of them find any election to be illegall they may seclud such for present from their meeting, and returne the same and their resons to the Courte; and if it prove true, the Courte may fyne the party or partyes so intruding and the Towne, if they see cause, and give out a warrant to goe to a newe election in a legall way, either in whole or in parte. Also the said deputyes shall have power to fyne any that shall be disorderly at their meetings, or for not coming in due tyme or place according to appoyntment; and they may returne the said fynes into the Courte if it be refused to be paid, and the tresurer to take notice of it, and to . . . levy the same as he doth other fynes.

10. It is Ordered, sentenced and decreed, that every Generall Courte, except such as through neglecte of the Governor and the greatest parte of Magestrats the Freemen themselves doe call, shall consist of the Governor, or some one chosen to moderate the Court, and 4 other

Magestrats at least, with the major parte of the deputyes of the severall Townes legally chosen; and in case the Freemen or major parte of them through neglect or refusall of the Governor and major parte of the magestrats, shall call a Courte, that it shall consist of the major parte of Freemen that are present or their deputyes, with a Moderator chosen by them: In which said Generall Courts shall consist the supreme power of the Commonwelth, and they only shall have power to make laws or repeale them, to graunt levyes, to admitt of Freemen, dispose of lands undisposed of, to severall Townes or persons, and also shall have power to call ether Courte or Magestrate or any other person whatsoever into question for any misdemeanour, and may for just causes displace or deale otherwise according to the nature of the offence; and also may deale in any other matter that concerns the good of this common welth, excepte election of Magestrats, which shall be done by the whole boddy of Freemen: In which Courte the Governor or Moderator shall have power to order the Courte to give liberty of spech, and silence unceasonable and disorderly speakeings, to put all things to vote, and in case the vote be equall to have the casting voice. But non of the Courts shall be adjorned or dissolved without the consent of the major parte of the Court.

11. It is ordered, sentenced and decreed, that when any Generall Courte upon the occations of the Commonwelth have agreed uppon any summe or somes of mony to be levyed uppon the severall Townes within this Jurisdiction, that a Committee be chosen to sett out and appoynt what shall be the proportion of every Towne to pay of the said levy, provided the Committees be made up of an equall number out of each Towne.

14th January, 1638, the 11 Orders abovesaid are voted.

THE EARLY ESTABLISHMENT OF LOCAL GOVERNMENT: COUNTY, TOWN, LEGAL SYSTEM, SEVENTEENTH CENTURY

The establishment of colonial governments, composed normally of a governor, a council, and a legislative assembly elected by the freemen of the colony, comprised one vital sector of self-government. A second sector, equally important but less emphasized, was the gradual evolution of local government. Every colony was eventually divided into "shires," meaning counties. A county represented the base of the legal system for the colony; it also served as the "government of record," recording the ownership of land, wills, inventories of the estates of deceased persons, and the like. In most southern and middle colonies, the county was also the basic unit of representation to the legislative assembly. In New England, the township rather than the county served this purpose.

The law as enacted by the colonial legislatures operated upon the people through the county government and its officials. Cases arising from civil disputes or criminal cases originated at the local level and were settled mostly in the county courts. If a civil case involved a large sum of money—the precise figure differed from colony to colony—or a criminal action involved the loss of life, it was appealed to a higher colonial court, customarily consisting of the governor and the colonial council. In every colony, political jurisdiction and thus political issues fell within one of three levels of government—the king and Parliament, the colonial government, or the local government.

The document which follows includes official enactments in Virginia and Massachusetts Bay, and a description of the courts in operation in Virginia by three contemporary observers, Henry Hartwell, James Blair, and Edward Chilton.

[Virginia, 1634]

In 1634. The country divided into 8 shires, which are to be governed as the shires in England.

The Names of the Shires are:

James City	Warwick River
Henrico	Warrosquyoake
Charles Citty	Charles River
Elizabeth Citty	Accawmack

And Lieutenants to be appointed the same as in England, and in a more especial manner to take care of the warr against Indians. And as in England sheriffs shall be elected to have the same power as there; and sergeants, and bailiffs where need requires.

Commissioners, instead of £5 causes, may determine £10 causes and one of the council to have notice to attend and assist in each court of shire.

[Virginia, 1643, Jurisdiction]

Whereas it was enacted at an Assembly in June 1642 that the comissioners of the severall counties respectively should have power and authoritie to hear and determine all debts and differences under the summe of sixteen hundred pounds of tobacco or the valew thereof, Where also, It was enacted at the said Assembly that everie monthly court respectively should keep their courts monthly upon the severall days therein mentioned (vizt.)

Henrico on the first of everie month	
Charles Citty the	3d
James County the	6th
Isle of Wight the	9th
Upper Norfolk the	12th
Lower Norfolk the	15th

Elizabeth County the	18th
Warwick County the	21st
York County the	24th
Northampton the	28th of everie month.

Be it enacted this present Grand Assembly that the said monthly courts be reduced to the number of six yearly, the daies to be ascertained as formerly, And in stead of monthly courts to call countie courts, and the comissioners to be stiled comissioners of the countie courts, And for the prevention of many chargeable suits tending to the molestation and ruine of divers poor men for pettie and triviall debts, It is thought fitt and enacted by this Grand Assembly, that no court of justice within the collony shall proceed to determine or adjudge or at all take cognisance of any suite hereafter to be comenced for or concerning any debt under the value of 20 shillings sterling or two hundred pounds of tobaccoe, but in such case, the next adjoyning comissioner to the creditor to sumon the debtor or defendant by warrant before him upon complaint to him made and to determine the same by order in writing under his hand which order shall be binding, And in case of non-performance, The said comissioner is authorised to comitt to prison the person who shall be refractory to such order as aforesaid.

[Virginia, 1643, Trial by Jury]

Whereas it was enacted at an Assembly in June 1642, That if either plaintiff or defendant shall desire the verdict of a jury for the determining of any suite depending within any of the courts of this collony, he or they shall signifie therein their desire by petition under his or their hands unto the said courts, before the said cause had any hearing, upon the day of tryall, if it be the desire of the plaintiff. And their petitions to be fyled in the Secretary's office, and with the clerke of the monthly court, And if the defendant shall desire it, he or they shall signifie the same upon the entry of his appearance in the Secretary's office. . . .

[Massachusetts, 1635/36, Jurisdiction]

Att the Generall Court, holden att Newe Towne, March 3, 1635/36.

Whereas particular townes have many things which concerne onely themselves, and the ordering of their owne affaires, and disposeing of businesses in their owne towne, it is therefore ordered, that the freemen of every towne, or the major parte of them, shall onely have power to dispose of their owne lands, and woods, with all the previlidges and appurtenances of the said townes, to graunt lotts, and make such orders as may concerne the well ordering of their owne townes, not repugnant to the lawes and orders here established by the Generall Court; as also to lay mulks and penaltyes for the breach of theis orders, and to levy and distreine the same, not exceedeing the somme of twenty shillings; also to chuse their owne particular officers, as constables, surveyors for the high wayes, and the like; and because much busines is like to ensue to the constables of severall townes, by reason they are to make distresses, and gather fynes, therefore that every towne shall have two constables, where there is neede, that soe their office may not be a burthen unto them, and they may attend more carefully upon the discharge of their office, for which they shalbe lyeable to give their accompts to this Court when they shalbe called thereunto.

[Hartwell, *et al.*, *The Present State of Virginia, 1697*,]

Concerning the Administration
of Justice in Virginia

The Courts of Justice are not distinct as in England, but Causes belonging to Chancery, King's Bench, Common Pleas, Exchequer, Admiralty, and Spirituality, are decided altogether in one and the same Court: And if any one that apprehends himself to be injured at Common Law, would appeal to Chancery, he only desires an Injunction in Chancery, and has another Hearing, but before the same Men still.

For deciding of all Causes there are two Sorts of Courts in the Country, viz., the County Court, and the General Court.

There is a County Court in every County; which consists of eight or ten Gentlemen of the Inhabitants of that County, to whom the Governor gives a Commission during Pleasure to be the Justices of the Peace for that County; he renews that Commission commonly every Year, for that brings new Fees, and likewise gives him an Opportunity to admit into it new Favourites, and exclude others that have not been so zealous in his Service. These Justices take the Oath of a Judge, with the other Oaths of Allegiance, etc. They hold a Court once a Month, or if there be but little Business, once in two Months, and have a Power of deciding all Sorts of Causes in their several Counties above 20 shillings or two hundred Pounds of Tobacco, Value, except such as reach to the Loss of Life or Limb, which are reserved to the General Court, to which also Appeals lye from these County Courts.

These County Courts having always been held by Country Gentlemen, who had no Education in the Law, it was no Wonder if both the Sense of the Law was mistaken, and the Form and Method of Proceedings was often very irregular; but of late the Insufficiency of these Courts has been much more perceived and felt than in former Times, while the first stock of Virginia Gentlemen lasted, who having had their Education in England, were a great deal better accomplished in the Law, and Knowledge of the World, that their Children and Grandchildren, who have been born in Virginia, and have had generally no Opportunity of Improvement by good Education, further than that they learned to read, write, and cast Accompts, and that but very indifferently.

The General Court so called because it trys the Causes of the whole Country, is held twice a Year by the Governor and Council, as Judges, at James Town, viz., in the Months of April and October. It is strange that they never had a Commission for holding of this Court, nor never took the Oath of Judges, perhaps it was not designed by the Crown that they should hold it, since besides that they are unskilful in the Law, it is thought an inconvenient thing in all Governments, that the Justice and Policy of the Government should be lodged in the same Persons, who ought indeed to be a Check upon one another; and therefore the Governor had Power, by the Advice of the Council, to set up Courts of Judicature; but that they should make themselves the supreme Court, proceeds either from the same Spirit of ingrossing all Power into their own Hands, of which are discovered so many Instances before, or perhaps rather from the Poverty of the Country in its Infancy, which was not able to go to the Charge of maintaining Judges well skilled in the Law, for this we must acknowledge is of an elder Date than the other Usurpations, which generally had their Original but of late Years, to wit, about the time of the Lord Culpepper's Government, when the Government of Virginia, which before had been a Business of Care and Danger, came now to be a Business of Gain and Advantage. However it is, it is certain that it is a continual heavy Grievance in that Country; that if a Man be injured in Point of Law or Equity, there is no Superior there to whom he can make his Complaint, nor no possible way of Redress without an infinite Charge in bringing the Matter to Whitehall, which few in that Country have Purse and Skill to manage. And indeed, we are so much the more confirmed in the Opinion that it was never designed by them, whosoever they were that had the first modelling of the Virginia Government, but has proceeded from some of the above-mentioned Causes, because we perceive in all other English as well as foreign Plantations, Judges were established in distinct Persons from the Governor and Council, who had the Administration of the Policy and Government.

Any Cause may commence in the general Court, that exceeds the Value of 16 pounds Sterling or 16 Hundred Pounds of Tobacco, and by Appeal, any Cause whatsoever may be brought thither. This Court takes Cognizance of all Causes in Chancery, the King's Bench, the Common Pleas, the Exchequer, the Admiralty and Spirituality.

There lies no Appeal from this Court at present, but to the King in Council, and that only where the Value exceeds 300 pounds Sterling and where good Security to pay the Principal with all Costs and Damages is given.

The Forms of Proceeding in this Court are, almost

in every Thing, disagreeable to the Laws of England, and very irregular. Original and judicial Writs run not in the Name of the King, but resemble Warrants made by Justices of the Peace. There are no formal Declarations there, Petitions are made use of in their stead; neither is there any Method observed in Pleading. There are not above four several original Writs allowed of, i.e., such as they made use of. No Writ of Error is allowed of, Appeals are made use of in their Place, and, by a Rule made in the general Court, no new Matter is to be moved upon an Appeal. By a Law of that Country, the respective Sheriffs are obliged to make Returns that the Writs, which they received, are executed, and this Return must be three Days before the Day of Hearing in the County Court, otherwise they are to be fined, notwithstanding this Law, in all the Time that we were there, we could never hear that any Writs issued from the County Court, but the Sheriff's *Colore Officii* made Arrests without them, which has been the Occasion of great Troubles, and as yet never rectifyed.

No *Venire* issues there for summoning Juries, but in criminal Cases only, and then but six are returned from the Vicinage. The Sheriff does return Juries summoned without any Warrant or Authority, and they are not out of the Vicinage, but oftentimes from the remotest Parts of the County, from the Place where the Fact arises, and many Times Inhabitants of other Countys are of the Jury, nay sometimes the whole Jury. There is no Pannel returned into the Office. The Sheriff, when the Jury are to appear, calls over their Names, which he knows by his Pocket-Book, or by a little Scrip of Paper which he holds in his Hand.

Coroners are not there elected by the County, but receive their Authority by a Commission from the Governor.

The Granting of Probates and Administrations is by Law lodged solely in the County Courts, yet the general Court often grants them. As this is against Law, so it may be of ill Consequence. Notwithstanding the County Courts grant the Administrations and Probars yet the Governor signs them or appoints other Persons to do it. Sometimes Administrations and Probates are granted by a County Court, and yet no Part of the Estate lies in that County.

DOCUMENT 7

ROBERT BEVERLEY ON BACON'S REBELLION, 1704

Bacon's Rebellion in 1676 tested self-government in Virginia. One of Virginia's earliest historians, Robert Beverley, a contemporary of Nathaniel Bacon who led the rebellion, described the origin and contours of the uprising in his History and Present State of Virginia, *published almost thirty years after the event. Beverley sided with Governor Berkeley during the course of the dispute, and, although his recounting of the events is not wholly dispassionate, Beverley was still a shrewd and thoughtful observer, whose account is as perceptive as any ever published.*

The occasion of this rebellion is not easy to be discovered: but 'tis certain there were many things that concurred towards it. For it cannot be imagined, that upon the instigation of two or three traders only, who aimed at a monopoly of the Indian trade, as some pretend to say, the whole country would have fallen into so much distraction; in which people did not only hazard their necks by rebellion, but endeavored to ruin a governor, whom they all entirely loved, and had unanimously chosen; a gentleman who had devoted his whole life and estate to the service of the country, and against whom in thirty-five years experience there had never been one single complaint. Neither can it be supposed, that upon so slight grounds, they would make choice of a leader they hardly knew, to oppose a gentleman that had been so long and so deservedly the darling of the people. So that in all probability there was something else in the wind, without which the body of the country had never been engaged in that insurrection.

Four things may be reckoned to have been the main ingredients towards this intestine commotion, viz., First, The extreme low price of tobacco, and the ill usage of the planters in the exchange of goods for it, which the country, with all their earnest endeavors, could not remedy. Secondly, The splitting the colony into proprieties, contrary to the original charters; and the extravagant taxes they were forced to undergo, to relieve themselves from those grants. Thirdly, The heavy restraints and burdens laid upon their trade by act of Parliament in England. Fourthly, The disturbance given by the Indians. Of all which in their order.

First, Of the low price of tobacco, and the disappointment of all sort of remedy, I have spoken sufficiently before. Secondly, Of splitting the country into proprieties.

King Charles the Second, to gratify some nobles about him, made two great grants out of that country. These grants were not of the uncultivated wood land only, but also of plantations, which for many years had been seated and improved, under the encouragement of several charters granted by his royal ancestors to that colony. Those grants were distinguished by the names of the Northern and Southern grants of Virginia, and the same men were concerned in both. They were kept dormant some years after they were made, and in the year 1674 begun to be put in execution. As soon as ever the country came to know this, they remonstrated against them; and the assembly drew up an humble address to his majesty, complaining of the said grants, as derogatory to the previous charters and privileges granted to that colony, by his majesty and his royal progenitors. They sent to England Mr. Secretary Ludwell and Colonel Park, as their agents to address the king, to vacate those grants. And the better to defray that charge, they laid a tax of fifty pounds of tobacco per poll, for two years together, over and above all other taxes, which was an excessive burden. They likewise laid amercements of seventy, fifty, or thirty pounds of tobacco, as the cause was on every law case tried throughout the country. Besides all this, they applied the balance, remaining due upon account of the two shilling per hogshead, and fort duties, to this use. Which taxes and amercements fell heaviest on the poor people, the effect of whose labor would not clothe their wives and children. This made them desperately uneasy, especially when, after a whole year's patience under all these pressures, they had no encouragement from their agents in England, to hope for remedy; nor any certainty when they should be eased of those heavy impositions.

Thirdly, Upon the back of all these misfortunes came out the act of 25 Car. II. for better securing the plantation trade. By this act several duties were laid on the trade from one plantation to another. This was a new hardship, and the rather, because the revenue arising by this act was not applied to the use of the plantations wherein it was raised: but given clear away; nay, in that country it seemed to be of no other use, but to burden the trade, or create a good income to the officers; for the collector had half, the comptroller a quarter, and the remaining quarter was subdivided into salaries; till it was lost.

By the same act also very great duties were laid on the fisheries of the plantations, if manufactured by the English inhabitants there; while the people of England were absolutely free from all customs. Nay, though the oil, blubber and whale bone, which were made by the inhabitants of the plantations, were carried to England by Englishmen, and in English built ships, yet it was held to a considerable duty, more than the inhabitants of England paid.

These were the afflictions that country labored under when the fourth accident happened, viz., the disturbance offered by the Indians to the frontiers. . . .

This addition of mischief to minds already full of discontent, made people ready to vent all their resentment against the poor Indians. There was nothing to be got by tobacco; neither could they turn any other manufacture to advantage; so that most of the poorer sort were willing to quit their unprofitable employments, and go volunteers against the Indians.

At first they flocked together tumultuously, running in troops from one plantation to another without a head,

till at last the seditious humor of Colonel Nathaniel Bacon
led him to be of the party. This gentleman had been
brought up at one of the Inns of court in England, and
had a moderate fortune. He was young, bold, active, of
an inviting aspect, and powerful elocution. In a word, he
was every way qualified to head a giddy and unthinking
multitude. Before he had been three years in the country,
he was, for his extraordinary qualifications, made one of
the council, and in great honor and esteem among the
people. For this reason he no sooner gave countenance to
this riotous mob, but they all presently fixed their eyes
upon him for their general, and accordingly made their
addresses to him. As soon as he found this, he harangued
them publicly. He aggravated the Indian mischiefs, complaining that they were occasioned for want of a due regulation of their trade. He recounted particularly the other
grievances and pressures they lay under, and pretended
that he accepted of their command with no other intention
but to do them and the country service, in which he was
willing to encounter the greatest difficulties and dangers.
He farther assured them he would never lay down his arms
till he had revenged their sufferings upon the Indians, and
redressed all their other grievances.

By these insinuations he wrought his men into so perfect an unanimity, that they were one and all at his devotion. He took care to exasperate them to the utmost, by
representing all their misfortunes. After he had begun to
muster them, he dispatched a messenger to the governor,
by whom he aggravated the mischiefs done by the Indians,
and desired a commission of general to go out against
them. This gentleman was in so great esteem at that time
with the council, that the governor did not think fit to
give him a flat refusal; but sent him word he would consult the council, and return him a farther answer.

In the mean time Bacon was expeditious in his preparations, and having all things in readiness, began his march,
depending on the authority the people had given him. He
would not lose so much time as to stay for his commission;
but dispatched several messengers to the governor to
hasten it. On the other hand, the governor, instead of a
commission, sent positive orders to him to disperse his

men and come down in person to him, upon pain of being declared a rebel.

This unexpected order was a great surprise to Bacon, and not a little trouble to his men. However, he was resolved to prosecute his first intentions, depending upon his strength and interest with the people. Nevertheless, he intended to wait upon the governor, but not altogether defenceless. Pursuant to this resolution, he took about forty of his men down with him in a sloop to Jamestown, where the governor was with his council.

Matters did not succeed there to Mr. Bacon's satisfaction, wherefore he expressed himself a little too freely. For which, being suspended from the council, he went away again in a huff with his sloop and followers. The governor filled a long boat with men, and pursued the sloop so close, that Colonel Bacon moved into his boat to make more haste. But the governor had sent up by land to the ships at Sandy Point, where he was stopped and sent down again. Upon his return he was kindly received by the governor, who, knowing he had gone a step beyond his instructions in having suspended him, was glad to admit him again of the council; after which he hoped all things might be pacified.

Notwithstanding this, Colonel Bacon still insisted upon a commission to be general of the volunteers, and to go out against the Indians; from which the governor endeavored to dissuade him, but to no purpose, because he had some secret project in view. He had the luck to be countenanced in his importunities, by the news of fresh murder and robberies committed by the Indians. However, not being able to accomplish his ends by fair means, he stole privately out of town; and having put himself at the head of six hundred volunteers, marched directly to Jamestown, where the assembly was then sitting. He presented himself before the assembly, and drew up his men in battalia before the house wherein they sat. He urged to them his preparations; and alledged that if the commission had not been delayed so long, the war against the Indians might have been finished.

The governor resented this insolent usage worst of all, and now obstinately refused to grant him anything, offering his naked breast against the presented arms of his followers. But the assembly, fearing the fatal consequences of provoking a discontented multitude ready armed, who had the governor, council and assembly entirely in their power, addressed the governor to grant Bacon his request. They prepared themselves the commission, constituting him general of the forces of Virginia, and brought it to the governor to be signed.

With much reluctancy the governor signed it, and thereby put the power of war and peace into Bacon's hands. Upon this he marched away immediately, having gained his end, which was in effect a power to secure a monopoly of the Indian trade to himself and his friends.

As soon as General Bacon had marched to such a convenient distance from Jamestown that the assembly thought they might deliberate with safety, the governor, by their advice, issued a proclamation of rebellion against him, commanding his followers to surrender him, and forthwith disperse themselves, giving orders at the same time for raising the militia of the country against him.

The people being much exasperated, and General Bacon by his address and eloquence having gained an absolute dominion over their hearts, they unanimously resolved that not a hair of his head should be touched, much less that they should surrender him as a rebel. Therefore they kept to their arms, and instead of proceeding against the Indians they marched back to Jamestown, directing their fury against such of their friends and countrymen as should dare to oppose them. . . .

By this time the governor had got together a small party to side with him. These he furnished with sloops, arms and ammunition, under command of Major Robert Beverley, in order to cross the bay and oppose the malcontents. By this means there happened some skirmishes, in which several were killed, and others taken prisoners. Thus they were going on by a civil war to destroy one another, and lay waste their infant country, when it pleased God, after some months' confusion, to put an end to their misfortunes, as well as to Bacon's designs, by his natural death. He died at Dr. Green's in Gloucester county. But where he was buried was never yet discovered, though afterward there was great inquiry made, with design to expose his bones to public infamy.

In the meanwhile those disorders occasioned a general neglect of husbandry, and a great destruction of the stocks of cattle, so that people had a dreadful prospect of want and famine. But the malcontents being thus disunited by the loss of their general, in whom they all confided, they began to squabble among themselves, and every man's business was, how to make the best terms he could for himself.

Lieutenant General Ingram (whose true name was Johnson) and Major General Walklate, surrendered, on condition of pardon for themselves and their followers, though they were both forced to submit to an incapacity of bearing office in that country for the future.

Peace being thus restored, Sir William Berkeley returned to his former seat of government, and every man to his several habitation. . . .

When this storm, occasioned by Bacon, was blown over, and all things quiet again, Sir William Berkeley called an assembly, for settling the affairs of the country, and for making reparation to such as had been oppressed. After which a regiment of soldiers arrived from England, which were sent to suppress the insurrection; but they, coming after the business was over, had no occasion to exercise their courage. . . .

With the regiment above mentioned arrived commissioners, to enquire into the occasion and authors of this rebellion; and Sir William Berkeley came to England: where from the time of his arrival, his sickness obliged him to keep his chamber till he died; so that he had no opportunity of kissing the king's hand. But his majesty declared himself well satisfied with his conduct in Virginia, and was very kind to him during his sickness, often enquiring after his health, and commanding him not to hazard it by too early an endeavor to come to court.

DOCUMENT 8

GOVERNOR WILLIAM BERKELEY ON BACON'S REBELLION, 19 MAY 1676

When Bacon's Rebellion erupted with surprising and stunning swiftness, William Berkeley had been governor of Virginia for more than thirty years. During the early years of his administration, Berkeley was considered a stalwart and reliable friend of the planters. Through the years he introduced more rigidity in the use of power while, at the same time, aging deprived him of a recognition of the economic, political, and social transition that Virginia, as well as other settled colonies, was undergoing. Berkeley saw Bacon's action as a direct challenge to his own authority—which it was. Bacon, in the governor's opinion, was guilty of treason.

The declaration and Remonstrance of Sir William Berkeley his most sacred Majesties Governor and Captain Generall of Virginia.

Sheweth That about the yeare 1660 Coll. Mathews the then Governor dyed and then in consideration of the service I had don the Country, in defending them from, and destroying great numbers of the Indians, without the loss of three men, in all the time that warr lasted, and in contemplation of the equall and uncorrupt Justice I had distributed to all men, Not onely the Assembly but the unanimous votes of all the Country, concurred to make me Governor in a time, when if the Rebells in England had prevailed, I had certainly dyed for accepting itt, 'twas Gentlemen an unfortunate Love, shewed to me, for to shew myselfe gratefull for this, I was willing to accept of this Governement againe, when by my gracious Kings favour I might have had other places much more proffitable, and lesse toylesome then this hath beene. Since that time that I returned into the Country, I call the great God, Judge of all things in heaven and earth to wittness, that I doe not know of any thing relateive to this Country, wherein I have acted unjustly, corruptly, or negligently, in distributeing equall Justice to all men, and takeing all possible care to preserve their proprietys, and defend them from their barbarous enimies.

But for all this, perhapps I have erred in things I know not of, if I have I am soe conscious of humane frailty, and my owne defects, that I will not onely acknowledge them, but repent of, and amend them, and not like the Rebell Bacon persist in an error, onely because I have comitted itt, and tells me in diverse of his Letters that itt is not for his honnor to confess a fault, but I am of opinion that itt is onely for divells to be incorrigable, and men of principles like the worst of divells, and these he hath, if truth be reported to me, of diverse of his expressions of Atheisme, tending to take away all Religion and Laws.

And now I will state the Question betwixt me as a Governor and Mr. Bacon, and say that if any enimies should invade England, any Councellor Justice of peace, or other inferiour officer, might raise what forces they could to protect his Majesties subjects, But I say againe, if after the Kings knowledge of this invasion, any the greatest peere of England, should raise forces against the kings prohibition this would be now, and ever was in all ages and Nations accompted treason. Nay I will goe further, that though this peere was truly zealous for the preservation of his King, and subjects, and had better and greater abillitys then all the rest of his fellow subjects, to doe his King and Country service, yett if the King (though by false information) should suspect the contrary, itt were treason in this Noble peere to proceed after the King's prohibition, and for the truth of this I appeale to all the laws of England, and the Laws and constitutions of all other Nations in the world, And yett further itt is declaired by this Parliament that the takeing up Armes for the King and Parliament is treason, for the event shewed that what ever the pretence was to seduce ignorant and well affected people, yett the end was ruinous both to

King and people, as this will be if not prevented, I doe therefore againe declair that Bacon proceedeing against all Laws of all Nations modern and ancient, is Rebell to his sacred Majesty and this Country, nor will I insist upon the sweareing of men to live and dye togeather, which is treason by the very words of the Law.

Now my friends I have lived 34 yeares amongst you, as uncorrupt and dilligent as ever Governor was, Bacon is a man of two yeares amongst you, his person and qualities unknowne to most of you, and to all men else, by any vertuous action that ever I heard of, And that very action which he boasts of, was sickly and fooleishly, and as I am informed treacherously carried to the dishonnor of the English Nation, yett in itt, he lost more men then I did in three yeares Warr, and by the grace of God will putt myselfe to the same daingers and troubles againe when I have brought Bacon to acknowledge the Laws are above him, and I doubt not but by God's assistance to have better success then Bacon hath had, the reason of my hopes are, that I will take Councell of wiser men then my selfe, but Mr. Bacon hath none about him, but the lowest of the people.

Yett I must further enlarge, that I cannot without your helpe, doe any thinge in this but dye in defence of my King, his laws, and subjects, which I will cheerefully doe, though alone I doe itt, and considering my poore fortunes, I can not leave my poore Wife and friends a better legacy then by dyeing for my King and you: for his sacred Majesty will easeily distinguish betweene Mr. Bacons actions and myne, and Kinges have long Armes, either to reward or punish.

Now after all this, if Mr. Bacon can shew one precedent or example where such actings in any Nation what ever, was approved of, I will mediate with the King and you for a pardon, and excuce for him, but I can shew him an hundred examples where brave and great men have beene putt to death for gaineing Victorys against the Comand of their Superiors.

Lastly my most assured friends I would have preserved those Indians that I knew were howerly att our mercy, to have beene our spyes and intelligence, to finde out our bloody enimies, but as soone as I had the least intelligence that they alsoe were trecherous enimies, I gave out Commissions to distroy them all as the Commissions themselves will speake itt.

To conclude, I have don what was possible both to friend and enimy, have granted Mr. Bacon three pardons, which he hath scornefully rejected, suppoaseing himselfe stronger to subvert then I and you to maineteyne the Laws, by which onely and Gods assisting grace and mercy, all men must hope for peace and safety. I will add noe more though much more is still remaineing to Justifie me and condemne Mr. Bacon, but to desier that this declaration may be read in every County Court in the Country, and that a Court be presently called to doe itt, before the Assembly meet, That your approbation or dissattisfaction of this declaration may be knowne to all the Country, and the Kings Councell to whose most revered Judgments itt is submitted, Given the xxixth day of May, a happy day in the xxviiith yeare of his most sacred Majesties Reigne, Charles the second, who God grant long and prosperously to Reigne, and lett all his good subjects say Amen.

DOCUMENT 9

BACON'S DECLARATION IN THE NAME OF THE PEOPLE, 30 JULY 1676

Like many men who challenge authorized government, Bacon quickly took the position that he truly represented the people. His signature, "General by Consent of the People," is an interesting commentary, and his Declaration in the Name of the People *lays the blame for Virginia's failures directly upon the Governor, "who hath traiterously . . . injured his Majesties interest here. . . ." Historians have debated whether Bacon did, in fact, have the backing of the rank and file in Virginia. Those who argue that he did note the 600 men who rallied to his cause, of whom some seventy were black. Those who argue against Bacon note that he issued the Declaration without consulting others, and that he assumed the title of "General by Consent of the People."*

The Declaracon of the People.

1. For haveing upon specious pretences of publiqe works raised greate unjust taxes upon the Comonality for the advancement of private favorites and other sinister ends, but noe visible effects in any measure adequate, For not haveing dureing this long time of his Gouvernement in any measure advanced this hopefull Colony either by fortificacons Townes or Trade.

2. For haveing abused and rendred contemptable the Magistrates of Justice, by advanceing to places of Judicature, scandalous and Ignorant favorites.

3. For haveing wronged his Majesties prerogative and interest, by assumeing Monopoly of the Beaver trade, and for haveing in that unjust gaine betrayed and sold his Majesties Country and the lives of his loyall subjects, to the barbarous heathen.

4. For haveing, protected, favoured, and Imboldned the Indians against his Majesties loyall subjects, never contriveing, requireing, or appointing any due or proper meanes of sattisfaction for theire many Invasions, robberies, and murthers comitted upon us.

5. For haveing when the Army of English, was just upon the track of those Indians, who now in all places burne, spoyle, murther and when we might with ease have distroyed them: who then were in open hostillity, for then haveing expressly countermanded, and sent back our Army, by passing his word for the peaceable demeanour of the said Indians, who imediately prosecuted theire evill intentions, comitting horred murthers and robberies in all places, being protected by the said ingagement and word past of him the said Sir William Berkeley, haveing ruined and laid desolate a greate part of his Majesties Country, and have now drawne themselves into such obscure and remote places, and are by theire success soe imboldned and confirmed, by theire confederacy soe strengthned that the cryes of blood are in all places, and the terror, and

constirnation of the people soe great, are now become, not onely a difficult, but a very formidable enimy, who might att first with ease have beene distroyed.

6. And lately when upon the loud outcryes of blood the Assembly had with all care raised and framed an Army for the preventing of further mischeife and safe-guard of this his Majesties Colony.

7. For haveing with onely the privacy of some few favorites, without acquainting the people, onely by the alteracon of a figure, forged a Comission, by we know not what hand, not onely without, but even against the consent of the people, for the raiseing and effecting civill warr and distruction, which being happily and without blood shed prevented, for haveing the second time attempted the same, thereby calling downe our forces from the defence of the fronteeres and most weekely exposed places.

8. For the prevencon of civill mischeife and ruin amongst ourselves, whilst the barbarous enimy in all places did invade, murther and spoyle us, his majesties most faithfull subjects.

Of this and the aforesaid Articles we accuse Sir William Berkeley as guilty of each and every one of the same, and as one who hath traiterously attempted, violated and Injured his Majesties interest here, by a loss of a greate part of this his Colony and many of his faithfull loyall subjects, by him betrayed and in a barbarous and shamefull manner exposed to the Incursions and murther of the heathen, And we doe further declare these the en-sueing persons in this list, to have beene his wicked and pernicious councellours Confederates, aiders, and assisters against the Comonality in these our Civill comotions.

Sir Henry Chichley	William Claiburne Junior
Lieut. Coll. Christopher Wormeley	Thomas Hawkins
	William Sherwood
Phillip Ludwell	John Page Clerke
Robert Beverley	John Cluffe Clerke
Richard Lee	John West
Thomas Ballard	Hubert Farrell
William Cole	Thomas Reade
Richard Whitacre	Matthew Kempe
Nicholas Spencer	
Joseph Bridger	

And we doe further demand that the said Sir William Berkeley with all the persons in this list be forthwith delivered up or surrender themselves within fower days after the notice hereof, Or otherwise we declare as followeth.

That in whatsoever place, howse, or ship, any of the said persons shall reside, be hidd, or protected, we declaire the owners, Masters or Inhabitants of the said places, to be confederates and trayters to the people and the estates of them is alsoe of all the aforesaid persons to be confiscated, and this we the Comons of Virginia doe declare, desiering a firme union amongst our selves that we may joyntly and with one accord defend our selves against the common Enimy, and lett not the faults of the guilty be the reproach of the inocent, or the faults or crimes of the oppressours devide and separate us who have suffered by theire oppressions.

These are therefore in his majesties name to command you forthwith to seize the persons above mentioned as Trayters to the King and Country and them to bring to Midle plantacon, and there to secure them untill further order, and in case of opposition, if you want any further assistance you are forthwith to demand itt in the name of the people in all the Counties of Virginia.

Nathaniel Bacon
Generall by Consent of the people.

DOCUMENT 10

ROYAL COMMISSION IN VIRGINIA ON BACON'S REBELLION,
27 FEBRUARY 1677

When news of Bacon's Rebellion reached England, a Royal Commission was established to discover the causes of the disturbance and report them to the king. The Royal Commission was accompanied to Virginia by several hundred soldiers. By the time the expedition from England reached Virginia, Bacon was dead, the rebellion had been quelled, and Governor Berkeley was once again in control.

> *Although the commission was authorized only to report to the king, it exceeded its authority by making specific recommendations to the governor, the council, and the assembly. The report to the authorities in England was much less specific, and it closed, at least officially, the incident of Bacon's Rebellion. The unofficial effect of the rebellion was of great significance: no future governor of Virginia, however powerful, could exercise the arbitrary authority available to Berkeley.*

Gentlemen:

There is another thing which wee must alsoe recommend to your consideration (i.e.), the Reduceing of the great Sallary of the members of the Assembly to such moderate rates as may render them less grevious and burthensome to the Countrie, And this wee cannot but earnestlest offer to you for that his Majestie hath bin pleased to shew Himselfe soe signally concerned herein, as appeares by his Royall Proclamations and his Private instructions to us.

In order to immediate Redress whereof wee offer to you our joynt opinion as followeth.

1. That an Act of Assembly may pass for the future calling of a New Assembly to be elected and chosen every two yeares (under the quallifications, which the Right honourable Governour can declare you from his Majesties late instructions sent him over by us) whereby to make those of the present Assembly more ready to Comply with his Majesties Royall Commands for the Retrenching of their former salaries; Whereas by reason of their constant sitting, they receive onely and pay not, which this alterations will well remedy, and make the charge and expence equall by alternate Receipts and Payments, and consequently alleviate the present Pressure which the people seem soe much concerned in.

2. Wee are of opinion that for the future noe Salary be payd received, or continued to any member of Assembly for any longer time then he or they shall there personally sitt and shall cease dureing the travelling time of there Comeing and returning to and from the said Assembly.

3. That from henceforth there be noe accounts or Reckonings demanded paid, or allowed for Liquors dranke

by any members at Committees there.

4. That every Chairman of the severall Committees of Assembly doe for time to come draw their owne reports themselves, whereby to save the Country that great Charge of Clerks purposely imployed and paid for writeing the Same: some haveing (as wee are informed) 4000 pounds weight of tobacco for scarce twentie Lines writeing.

5. That the people of the severall Counties for which you serve as Burgesses may noe longer complaine of the largeness of your Salaries, nor yourselves of the lessening and retrenching of the same, Wee alsoe Commend to your present care the Regulation and abatement of the excessive and unreasonable rates sett by Ordinary keepers upon all sorts of Liquors, especially in an about James-Towne at Assembly times which seems to us the true reason that the Members of Assembly cannot finde there account, or be content with a Reasonable salary because of such excessive rates and prices, which the Ordinary keepers doe arbitrarily and at their owne pleasure and libertie impose upon liquors and the people. . . .

As to such other greivances as are of publique concernment (as often as they shall come to our knowledge and examination) Wee shall prepare to transmitt them home to his Majestie for his Royall Redress; And for all others that relate onelie to the private interest of partie and partie, we shall returne such to you of the Assembly to consider of (as improper for our inspection) and Leave them to the Remedie of your lawes already provided, and hereafter to bee made for their just Releife therein. . . .

Wee can onely add that Wee are upon all occasions most reddy to manifest ourselves for our Royall Masters, and this his Countryes Service.

> Most Honoured Friends
> Your most Faithfull
> Humble Servants
> Herbert Jeffreys
> John Berry
> Francis Morrison.

DOCUMENT 11

MASSACHUSETTS BAY ASSERTS ITS RIGHT TO GOVERN, 10 JUNE 1661

As in Virginia, self-government in New England was also tested. In 1661, after the Stuart monarchy had been restored to the English throne following the period of the Puritan Rebellion and the Puritan Commonwealth, Massachusetts, at a session of the General Court, its legislative assembly, reaffirmed its allegiance to the Crown, but at the same time restated what it regarded as its "liberties." This definition focused upon its right to self-government rather than upon civil liberties.

The Court mett at the time appointed. The answers of the committee unto the matters proposed to theire consideration by the honnored Generall Court—

Concerning our liberties.

1. Wee conceive the pattent (under God) to be the first and maine foundation of our civil politye here, by a Gouvernour and Company, according as is therein exprest.

2. The Gouvernour and Company are, by the pattent, a body politicke, in fact and name.

3. This body politicke is vested with power to make freemen.

4. These freemen have power to choose annually a Gouvernour, Deputy Gouvernour, Asistants, and theire select representatives or deputies.

5. This gouvernment hath also to sett up all sortes of officers, as well superior as inferior, and point out theire power and places.

6. The Gouvernour, Deputy Gouvernour, Asistants, and select representatives or deputies have full power and authoritie, both legislative and execcutive, for the gouvern-

ment of all the people heere, whither inhabitants or strain-
gers, both concerning eclesiasticks and in civils, without
appeale, excepting lawe or lawes repugnant to the lawes of
England.

7. The gouvernment is priviledged by all fitting meanes
(yea, and if neede be, by force of armes) to defend themselves, both by land and sea, against all such person or
persons as shall at any time attempt or enterprise the destruction, invasion, dettriment, or annoyance of this plantation, or the inhabitants therein, besides other priviledges
mentioned in the pattent, not heere expressed.

8. Wee conceive any imposition prejudiciall to the
country contrary to any just lawe of ours, not repugnant to
the lawes of England, to be an infringement of our right.

Concerning our duties of alleagiance to our soveraigne lord the king.

1. Wee ought to uphold and to our power mainteine
this place, as of right belonging to our soveraigne lord the
king, as holden of his majesties mannour of East Green-
wich, and not to subject the same to any forreigne prince
or potentate whatsoever.

2. Wee ought to endeavour the preservation of his
majesties royall person, realmes, and dominions, and so
farre as lieth in us, to dicover and prevent all plotts and
conspiracies against the same.

3. Wee ought to seeke the peace and prosperitie of
our king and nation, by a faith full discharge in the gouv-
erning of this people committed to our care—

   a. By punishing all such crimes (being breaches of the
   first or second table) as are committed against the
   peace of our soveraigne lord the king, his royall croune
   and dignity.

   b. In propogating the gospell, defending and upholding
   the true Christian or Protestant religion according
   to the faith given by our Lord Christ in his word;
   our dread soveraigne being stiled "defender of the
   faith."

The promisses considered, it may well stand with the
loyalty and obedience of such subjects as are thus priviledged by theire rightfull souveraigne (for himself, his

heires, and successours for ever), as cause shall require, to pleade with theire prince against all such as shall at any time endeavor the violation of theire priviledges.

Wee further judge that the warrant and letter from the kings majesty, for the apprehending of Col. Whalley and Col. Goffe, ought to be diligently and faithfully executed by the authority of this country.

And also, that the Generall Court may doe safely to declare, that in case (for the future) any legally obnoxious, and flying from the civil justice of the state of England, shall come over to these partes, they may not heere expect shelter.

Boston, 10 April, 1661. By the order and consent of the committee.

DOCUMENT 12

EDWARD RANDOLPH CONDEMNS MASSACHUSETTS BAY BEFORE THE LORDS OF TRADE, 12 JUNE 1683

Edward Randolph was appointed Surveyor General of Customs in the American colonies. A man more often moved by bias than by conviction, Randolph prepared voluminous reports condemning practices in the colonies. He accused them of evading the Navigation Acts, of failing to heed the king's instructions to the governors, of developing their own legal systems, and of curbing, especially in New England, the Church of England. Randolph wished to eliminate all proprietary colonies, to reduce the power of the assemblies, and to improve enforcement of acts of Parliament by increasing the number of royal officials resident in the colonies. Randolph's reports had a factual basis but were usually inflated accounts. Nonetheless, his reports spurred a growing movement among English officials aimed at curtailing self-government in the colonies. This document represents the type of report submitted by Randolph.

12 June 1683

Articles of high misdemeanour exhibited against the Governor and Company of Massachusetts by Edward Randolph. 1. They execute the powers in their charter otherwise than as directed, and exceed them. 2. They have made laws repugnant to the laws of England, and have not repealed those objected to by Sir William Jones and Sir Francis Winnington as they promised. 3. They continue to raise money from non-freemen, contrary to the opinion of Sir Robert Sawyer. 4. They continue to exact an oath of fidelity to themselves, notwithstanding the King's orders to the contrary, and make such oath essential to the tenure of office and even freedom of the Company. 5. They have refused to the King's subjects the benefit of juries in trial of civil causes, and denied to such as were not of their persuasion copies of records to enable them to appeal to the King. 6. They have obstructed the execution of the Acts of Trade and Navigation, and refused to recognise many of them. They award executions against the King's officers in causes under appeal to the King, obstruct his officers in the discharge of their duty, refuse appeals to the King, and set up their own naval office in opposition to his. They have made in October 1680 an arbitrary order compelling the King's officers to deposit security in Court for a special Court, contrary to law and royal order, and have refused to repay such deposits when ordered by the King. 7. They impose customs on goods imported from England, though this was judged by Sir Robert Sawyer to be illegal. They have found against the King in all causes for seizure of ships in the face of clear evidence. 8. They opposed the King's Commissioners in 1664, notwithstanding their protestations of loyalty, proclaimed the General Court the supreme judicature of the Colony, received Goffe and Wha'ley, the regicides, with honour, and protected them. 9. They have not administered the oath of allegiance to the King to the inhabitants, though required by law and by their charter. 10. They have invaded the rights of the Duke of York, Lord High Admiral, by erecting an Admiralty Court of their own. 11. They discountenance and discourage members of the Church of England, forcing them under penalties to attend their meetings, and accounting all others unlawful assemblies. 12. They coin money, which their own Agent admitted to be a high crime, and, though pretending to beg the King's pardon for it, persisted therein. 13. They have committed divers other high crimes in contempt of the King and to the oppression of his subjects. Whereupon their Lordships, finding the Agents not duly impowred by their Commission to consent to such regulation of their Government as shall bee thought fit according to His Majesty's directions, Doe agree to Report that Mr. Attorney bee Ordered to bring a Quo Warranto against the Privileges of their Charter, And that such Papers and Evidencies as shall bee needful in this Case bee sent to Mr. Attorney for his better information therein.

DOCUMENT 13

THE GLORIOUS REVOLUTION IN NEW ENGLAND, 18 APRIL 1689

In 1684, the colonial charters of New England were revoked and replaced by a new government framed in England known as the Dominion of New England. Under its provisions jurisdiction extended from Massachusetts Bay to New Jersey. Sir Edmund Andros, residing in Boston, was appointed governor with Sir Francis Nicholson, who resided in New York, named as his deputy.

The establishment of the Dominion eliminated the respective colonial legislatures in New England. Governor Andros was provided with a council, but in practice, if not in theory, he controlled its appointments. As a result, self-government in New England was seriously jeopardized. At this juncture in 1688, the so-called Glorious Revolution in England took place. James II abandoned the throne, and King William and Queen Mary of Holland, with the consent of Parliament, ascended it.

When news of the Glorious Revolution reached New England, its leaders imprisoned Andros who, they asserted, was appointed by a regime that had now been discredited. This document indicates how quickly the men of Massachusetts Bay moved to identify their action with that of the new sovereigns and Parliament. The ultimate aim of the New England leaders was to restore the degree of self-government that they enjoyed before the imposition of the Dominion of New England. The leaders of Boston met in the council room of the Town-House on April 18, 1689, and out of this meeting came the following "Declaration" which makes a case against the legality of the Dominion.

I. We have seen more than a decad of Years rolled away, since the English World had the Discovery of an horrid Popish Plot; wherein the bloody Devotoes of Rome had in their Design and Prospect no less than the extinction of the Protestant Religion: which mighty work they called the utter subduing of a Pestilent Heresy; wherein (they said) there never were such hopes of Success since the Death of Queen Mary, as now in our days. And we were of all men the most insensible, if we should apprehend a Countrey so remarkable for the true Profession and pure Exercise of the Protestant Religion as New-England is, wholly unconcerned in the Infamous Plot. To crush and break a Countrey so entirely and signally made up of Reformed Churches, and at length to involve it in the miseries of an utter Extirpation, must needs carry even a Supererogation of merit with it among such as were intoxicated with a Bigotry inspired into them by the great Scarlet Whore.

II. To get us within the reach of the desolation desired for us, it was no improper thing that we should first have our Charter Vacated, and the hedge which kept us from the wild Beasts of the field, effectually broken down. The accomplishment of this was hastened by the unwearied sollicitations, and slanderous accusations of a man, for his Malice and Falshood, well known unto us all. Our Charter was with a most injurious pretence (and scarce that) of Law, condemned before it was possible for us to appear at

Westminster in the legal defence of it; and without a fair leave to answer for our selves, concerning the Crimes falsly laid to our charge, we were put under a President and Council, without any liberty for an Assembly, which the other American Plantations have, by a Commission from His Majesty.

III. The Commission was as Illegal for the form of it, as the way of obtaining it was Malicious and unreasonable: yet we made no Resistance thereunto as we could easily have done; but chose to give all Mankind a Demonstration of our being a people sufficiently dutiful and loyal to our King: and this with yet more Satisfaction, because we took pains to make our selves believe as much as ever we could of the Whedle then offered unto us; That his Magesty's desire was no other than the happy encrease and advance of these Provinces by their more immediate Dependance on the Crown of England. And we were convinced of it by the courses immediately taken to damp and spoyl our Trade; whereof decayes and complaints presently filled all the Country; while in the mean time neither the Honour nor the Treasure of the King was at all advanced by this new Model of our Affairs, but a considerable Charge added unto the Crown.

IV. In little more than half a Year we saw this Commission superseded by another, yet more Absolute and Arbitrary, with which Sir Edmond Andross arrived as our Governour: who besides his Power, with the Advice and Consent of his Council, to make Laws and raise Taxes as he pleased; had also Authority by himself to Muster and Imploy all Persons residing in the Territory as occasion shall serve; and to transfer such Forces to any English Plantation in America, as occasion shall require. And several Companies of Souldiers were now brought from Europe, to support what was to be imposed upon us, not without repeated Menaces that some hundreds more were intented for us.

V. The Government was no sooner in these Hands, but care was taken to load Preferments principally upon such Men as were strangers to, and haters of the People: and every ones Observation hath noted, what Qualifications recommended a Man to publick Offices and Employments, only here and there a *good Man* was used, where others could not easily be had; the Governour himself, with Assertions now and then falling from him, made us jealous that it would be thought for his Majesties Interest, if this People were removed and another succeeded in their room: And his far-fetched Instruments that were growing rich among us, would gravely inform us, that it was not for his Majesties Interest that we should thrive. But of all our oppressors we were chiefly squeezed by a crew of abject Persons, fetched from New-York, to be the Tools of the Adversary, standing at our right hand; by these were extraordinary and intollerable Fees extorted from every one upon all occasions, without any Rules but those of their own insatiable Avarice and Beggary; and even the probate of a Will must now cost as many Pounds perhaps as it did Shillings heretofore; nor could a small Volume contain the other Illegalities done by these Horse-Leeches in the two or three Years that they have been sucking of us; and what Laws they made it was as impossible for us to know, as dangerous for us to break; but we shall leave the Men of Ipswich and of Plimouth (among others) to tell the story of the kindness which has been shown them upon this account. Doubtless a Land so ruled as once New-England was, has not without many fears and sighs beheld the wicked walking on every side, and the vilest Men exalted.

VI. It was now plainly affirmed, both by some in open Council, and by the same in private converse, that the people in New-England were all Slaves, and the only difference between them and Slaves is their not being bought and sold; and it was a maxim delivered in open Court unto us by one of the Council, *that we must not think the Priviledges of Englishmen would follow us to the end of the World*: Accordingly we have been treated with multiplied contradictions to Magna Charta, the rights of which we laid claim unto. Persons who did but peaceably object against the raising of Taxes without an Assembly, have been for it fined, some twenty, some thirty, and others fifty Pounds. Packt and pickt Juries have been very common things among us, when, under a pretended form of Law, the trouble of some honest and worthy Men has been aimed at: but when some of this Gang have been brought upon the Stage, for the most detestable Enormities that ever the Sun beheld, all Men have with Admiration seen what methods have been taken that they might not be treated according to their Crimes. Without a Verdict, yea, without a Jury sometimes have People been fined most unrighteously; and some not of the meanest Quality have been kept in long and close Imprisonment without any the least Information appearing against them, or an Habeas Corpus allowed unto them. In short, when our Oppressors have been a little out of Mony, 'twas but pretending some Offence to be enquired into, and the most innocent of Men were continually put into no small Expence to answer the Demands of the Officers, who must have Mony of them, or a prison for them tho none could accuse them of any Misdemeanour.

VII. To plunge the poor People every where into deeper Incapacities, there was one very comprehensive Abuse given to us; Multitudes of pious and sober Men through the Land, scrupled the Mode of Swearing on the Book, desiring that they might Swear with an uplifted Hand, agreeable to the ancient Custom of the Colony; and though we think we can prove that the Common Law amongst us (as well as in some other places under the English Crown) not only indulges, but even commands and enjoins the Rite of lifting the Hand in Swearing; yet they that had this Doubt, were still put by from serving upon any Juries; and many of them were most unaccountably Fined and Imprisoned. Thus one Grievance is a Trojan Horse, in the Belly of which it is not easy to recount how many insufferable Vexations have been contained.

VIII. Because these things could not make us miserable fast enough, there was a notable Discovery made of we know not what flaw in all our Titles to our Lands; and, though besides our purchase of them from the Natives; and, besides our actual peaceable unquestioned possession of them for near threescore Years, and besides the Promise of K. Charles II. in his Proclamation sent over to us in the Year 1683, That no Man here shall receive any Prejudice in his Free-hold or Estate: We had the Grant of our Lands, under the Seal of the Council of Plimouth: which Grant was Renewed and Confirmed unto us by King Charles I. under the Great Seal of England; and the General Court which consisted of the Patentees and their Associates, had made particular Grants hereof to the several Towns (though 'twas now denyed by the Governour, that there was any such Thing as a Town) among us; to all which Grants the General Court annexed for the further securing of them, *A General Act,* published under the Seal of the Colony, in the Year 1684. Yet we were every day told, That no man was owner of a Foot of Land in all the Colony. Accordingly, Writs of Intrusion began every where to be served on People, that after all their Sweat and their Cost upon their formerly purchased Lands, thought themselves Freeholders of what they had. And the Governor caused the Lands pertaining to these and those particular Men, to be measured out for his Creatures to take possession of; and the Right Owners, for pulling up the Stakes, have passed through Molestations enough to tire all the patience in the World. They are more than a few, that were by Terrors driven to take Patents for their Lands at excessive rates, to save them from the next that might petition for them: and we fear that the forcing of the People at the Eastward hereunto, gave too much Rise to the late unhappy Invasion made by the Indians on them. Blanck Patents were got ready for the rest of us, to be sold at a Price, that all the Mony and Moveables in the Territory could scarce have paid. And several Towns in the Country had their Commons begged by Persons (even by some of the Council themselves) who have been privately encouraged thereunto, by those that sought for Occasions to impoverish a Land already Peeled, Meeted out and Trodden down.

IX. All the Council were not ingaged in these ill Actions, but those of them which were true Lovers of their Country, were seldom admitted to, and seldomer consulted at the Debates which produced these unrighteous Things: Care was taken to keep them under Disadvantages; and the Governor, with five or six more, did what they would. We bore all these, and many more such Things, without making any attempt for any Relief; only Mr. Mather, purely out of respect unto the Good of his Afflicted Country, undertook a Voyage into England; which when these Men suspected him to be preparing for, they used all manner of Craft and Rage, not only to interrupt his Voyage, but to ruin his Person too. God having through many Difficulties given him to arrive at White-hall, the King, more than once or twice, promised him a certain Magna Charta for a speedy Redress of many things which we were groaning under: and in the mean time said, That our Governor should be written unto, to forbear the Measures that he was upon. However, after this, we were injured in those very Things which were complained of; and besides what Wrong hath been done in our Civil Concerns, we suppose the Ministers, and the Churches every where have seen our Sacred Concerns apace going after them: How they have been Discountenanced, has had a room in the reflections of every man, that is not a stranger in our Israel.

X. And yet that our Calamity might not be terminated here, we are again Briared in the Perplexities of another Indian War; how, or why, is a mystery too deep for us to unfold. And tho' 'tis judged that our Indian Enemies are not above 100 in number, yet an Army of One Thousand English hath been raised for the Conquering of them; which Army of our poor Friends and Brethren now under Popish Commanders (for in the Army as well as in the Council, Papists are in Commission) has been under such a conduct, that not one Indian hath been killed, but more English are supposed to have died through sickness and hardship, than we have adversaries there alive; and the whole War hath been so managed, that we cannot but suspect in it, a branch of the Plot to bring us low; which we leave to be further enquired into in due time.

XI. We did nothing against these Proceedings, but only cry to our God; they have caused the cry of the Poor to come unto him, and he hears the cry of the Afflicted. We have been quiet hitherto, and so still we should have been, had not the Great God at this time laid us under a double engagement to do something for our security: besides, what we have in the strangely unanimous inclination, which our Countrymen by extreamest necessities are driven unto. For first, we are informed that the rest of the English America is Alarmed with just and great fears, that they may be attaqu'd by the French, who have lately ('tis said) already treated many of the English with worse then Turkish Cruelties; and while we are in equal danger of being surprised by them, it is high time we should be better guarded, than we are like to be while the Government remains in the hands by which it hath been held of late. Moreover, we have understood (though the Governour has taken all imaginable care to keep us all ignorant thereof) that the Almighty God hath been pleased to prosper the noble undertaking of the Prince of Orange, to preserve the three Kingdoms from the horrible brinks of Popery and Slavery, and to bring to a Condign punishment those worst of men, by whom English Liberties have been destroyed; in compliance with which Glorious Action, we ought surely to follow the Patterns which the Nobility, Gentry and Commonalty in several parts of those Kingdoms have set before us, though they therein chiefly proposed to prevent what we already endure.

XII. We do therefore seize upon the Persons of those few Ill men which have been (next to our Sins) the grand Authors of our Miseries; resolving to secure them, for what Justice, Orders from his Highness, with the English Parliament shall direct, lest, ere we are aware, we find (what we may fear, being on all sides in danger) our selves to be by them given away to a Forreign Power, before such Orders can reach unto us; for which Orders we now humbly wait. In the mean time firmly believing, that we have endeavoured nothing but what meer Duty to God and our Country calls for at our Hands: We commit our Enterprise unto the Blessing of Him, who hears the cry of the Oppressed, and advise all our Neighbours, for whom we have thus ventured our selves, to joyn with us in Prayers and all just Actions, for the Defence of the Land.

DOCUMENT 14

JOHN WISE, *VINDICATION OF THE GOVERNMENT OF THE NEW ENGLAND CHURCHES,* 1717

John Wise, an earthy, robust clergyman of Ipswich, New England, was almost as well known among his

contemporaries for physical prowess as for intellec-
tual influence. He wrote a number of pamphlets dur-
ing his career on the right of self-government, but
none more important than the Vindication. *The issue*
he intended to address was the government of New
England churches, but the direction of his inquiry led
him to theorize on the roots and rationale of the right
of people to govern themselves. The result is a philo-
sophical argument for self-government based upon the
experience of a man born and raised in the colonies.
In the work of John Wise, self-government in Amer-
ica is elevated from practice to theory.

I shall disclose several principles of natural knowledge, plainly discovering the law of nature, or the true sentiments of natural reason, with respect to man's being and government. And in this essay I shall peculiarly confine the discourse to two heads, namely, of the natural (in distinction from the civil), and then, of the civil being of man. And I shall principally take Baron Puffendorff for my chief guide and spokesman.

1. I shall consider man in a state of natural being, as a free-born subject under the crown of heaven, and owing homage to none but God himself. It is certain civil government in general is a very admirable result of providence, and an incomparable benefit to mankind, yet must needs be acknowledged to be the effect of human free-compacts and not of divine institution; it is the produce of man's reason, of human and rational combinations, and not from any direct orders of infinite wisdom, in any positive law wherein is drawn up this or that scheme of civil government. Government (says Lord Warrington) is necessary . . . in that no society of men can subsist without it; and that particular form of government is necessary which best suits the temper and inclination of a people. Nothing can be God's ordinance, but what he has particularly declared to be such; there is no particular form of civil government described in God's word, neither does nature prompt it. . . .

The prime immunity in man's state, is that he is most properly the subject of the law of nature. He is the favorite animal on earth; in that this part of God's image, namely, reason, is congenate with his nature, wherein by a law immutable, enstamped upon his frame, God has provided a rule for men in all their actions, obliging each one to the performance of that which is right, not only as to justice, but likewise as to all other moral virtues, the which is nothing but the dictate of right reason founded in the soul of man. That which is to be drawn from man's reason, flowing from the true current of that faculty, when unperverted, may be said to be the law of nature, on which account, the Holy Scriptures declare it written on men's hearts. For being endowed with a soul, you may know from yourself, how, and what you ought to act (Rom. 2:14). These having not a law, are a law to themselves. So that the meaning is, when we acknowledge the law of nature to be the dictate of right reason, we must mean that the understanding of man is endowed with such a power, as to be able, from the contemplation of human condition to discover a necessity of living agreeably with this law; and likewise to find out some principle, by which the precepts of it, may be clearly and solidly demonstrated. The way to discover the law of nature in our own state, is by a narrow watch, and accurate contemplation of our natural condition and propensions. . . .

The second great immunity of man is an original liberty enstamped upon his rational nature. He that intrudes upon this liberty, violates the law of nature. In this discourse I shall waive the consideration of man's moral turpitude, but shall view him physically as a creature which God has made and furnished essentially with many ennobling immunities, which render him the most august animal in the world, and still, whatever has happened since his creation, he remains at the upper end of nature, and as such is a creature of a very noble character. For as to his dominion, the whole frame of the lower part of the universe is devoted to his use, and at his command; and his liberty under the conduct of right reason is equal with his trust. Which liberty may be briefly considered, internally as to his mind, and externally as to his person.

(1) The native liberty of man's nature implies, a faculty of doing or omitting things according to the

direction of his judgment. But in a more special meaning, this liberty does not consist in a loose and ungov-
ernable freedom, or in an unbounded license of acting.
Such license is disagreeing with the condition and
dignity of man, and would make man of a lower and
meaner constitution than brute creatures, who in all
their liberties are kept under a better and more rational
government by their instincts. Therefore, as Plutarch
says: Those persons only who live in obedience to reason, are worthy to be accounted free: they alone live
as they will, who have learned what they ought to will.
So that the true natural liberty of man, such as really
and truly agrees to him must be understood, as he is
guided and restrained by the ties of reason and laws of
nature; all the rest is brutal, if not worse.

(2) Man's external personal, natural liberty, ante-
cedent to all human parts or alliances, must also be
considered. And so every man must be conceived to be
perfectly in his own power and disposal, and not to
be controlled by the authority of any other. And thus
every man must be acknowledged equal to every man,
since all subjection and all command are equally banished on both sides; and considering all men thus at
liberty, every man has a prerogative to judge for himself, namely, what shall be most for his behoof, happiness, and well-being.

The third capital immunity belonging to man's nature,
is an equality amongst men; which is not to be denied by
the law of nature, till man has resigned himself with all
his rights for the sake of a civil state, and then his personal
liberty and equality is to be cherished and preserved to the
highest degree, as will consist with all just distinctions
amongst men of honor, and shall be agreeable with the
public good. For man has a high valuation of himself, and
the passion seems to lay its first foundation (not in pride,
but) really in the high and admirable frame and constitution of human nature. . . .

2. To consider man in a civil state of being, wherein
we shall observe the great difference between a natural
and political state; for in the latter state many great dispro-

portions appear, or at least many obvious distinctions are soon made amongst men, which doctrine is to be laid open under a few heads.

(1) Every man, considered in a natural state, must be allowed to be free and at his own disposal; yet to suit man's inclinations to society, and in a peculiar manner to gratify the necessity he is in of public rule and order, he is impelled to enter into a civil community, and divests himself of his natural freedom, and puts himself under government, which, amongst other things, comprehends the power of life and death over him, together with authority to enjoin him some things to which he has an utter aversion, and to prohibit him other things for which he may have as strong an inclination—so that he may be often, under this authority, obliged to sacrifice his private for the public good; so that though man is inclined to society, yet he is driven to a combination by great necessity. For that the true and leading cause of forming governments and yielding up natural liberty, and throwing man's equality into a common pile to be new cast by the rules of fellowship, was really and truly to guard themselves against the injuries men were liable to interchangeably; for none so good to man as man, and yet none a greater enemy. So that,

(2) The first human subject and original of civil power is the people; for as they have a power every man over himself in a natural state, so upon a combination they can and do bequeathe this power unto others, and settle it according as their united discretion shall determine. For that this is very plain, that when the subject of sovereign power is quite extinct, that power returns to the people again. And when they are free, they may set up what species of government they please; or if they rather incline to it, they may subside into a state of natural being, if it be plainly for the best. . . .

(3) The formal reason of government is the will of a community yielded up and surrendered to some other subject, either of one particular person or more, conveyed in the following manner.

Let us conceive in our mind a multitude of men, all naturally free and equal, going about voluntarily to erect themselves into a new commonwealth. Now their condition being such, to bring themselves into a politic body they must needs enter into divers covenants.

1. They must interchangeably each man covenant to join in one lasting society, that they may be capable to concert the measures of their safety, by a public vote.

2. A vote or decree must then nextly pass to set up some particular species of government over them. And if they are joined in their first compact upon absolute terms to stand to the decision of the first vote concerning the species of government, then all are bound by the majority to acquiesce in that particular form thereby settled, though their own private opinions incline them to some other model.

3. After a decree has specified the particular form of government, then there will be need of a new covenant, whereby those on whom sovereignty is conferred engage to take care of the common peace and welfare; and the subjects, on the other hand, to yield them faithful obedience; in which covenant is included that submission and union of wills by which a state may be conceived to be but one person. So that the most proper definition of a civil state is this, namely: A civil state is a compound moral person, whose will (united by those covenants before passed) is the will of all, to the end it may use and apply the strength and riches of private persons towards maintaining the common peace, security, and well-being of all, which may be conceived as though the whole state was now become but one man; in which the aforesaid covenants may be supposed, under God's providence, to be the divine fiat pronounced by God, "Let us make man." And by way of resemblance the aforesaid being may be thus anatomized.

(1) The sovereign power is the soul infused, giving life and motion to the whole body.

(2) Subordinate officers are the joints by which the body moves.

(3) Wealth and riches are the strength.

(4) Equity and laws are the reason.

(5) Counsellors the memory.

(6) *Salus Populi,* or the happiness of the people is the end of its being, or main business to be attended and done.

(7) Concord amongst the members and all estates, is the health.

(8) Sedition is sickness, and civil war death.

4. The parts of sovereignty may be considered thus—

(1) As it prescribes the rule of action, it is rightly termed legislative power.

(2) As it determines the controversies of subjects by the standard of those rules, so is it justly termed judiciary power.

(3) As it arms the subjects against foreigners, or forbids hostility, so it is called the power of peace and war.

(4) As it takes in ministers for the discharge of business, so it is called the right of appointing magistrates. So that all great officers and public servants must needs owe their original to the creating power of sovereignty; so that those whose right it is to create may dissolve the being of those who are created, unless they cast them into an immortal frame, and yet must needs be dissoluble if they justly forfeit their being to their creators.

(5) The chief end of civil communities is, that men thus conjoined may be secured against the injuries they are liable to from their own kind; for if every man could secure himself singly, it would be great folly for him to renounce his natural liberty, in which every man is his own king and protector.

(6) The sovereign authority, besides that it inheres in every state as in a common and general subject, so further according as it resides in some one person, or in a council (consisting of some select persons, or of all the members of a community) as in a proper and particular subject, so it produceth different forms of commonwealths, namely, such as are either simple and regular, or mixed.

The forms of a regular state are three only, which forms arise from the proper and particular subject in which the supreme power resides. As,

1. A democracy, which is when the sovereign power is lodged in a council consisting of all the members, and where every member has the privilege of a vote. This form of government appears in the greatest part of the world to have been the most ancient. For that reason seems to show it to be most probable, that when men (being originally in a condition of natural freedom and equality) had thoughts of joining in a civil body, would without question be inclined to administer their common affairs by their common judgment, and so must necessarily, to gratify that inclination, establish a democracy; neither can it be rationally imagined that fathers of families, being yet free and independent, should in a moment or little time take off their long delight in governing their own affairs, and devolve all upon some single sovereign commander; for that it seems to have been thought more equitable that what belonged to all should be managed by all, when all had entered by compact into one community. . . .

A democracy is then erected, when a number of free persons do assemble together in order to enter into a covenant for uniting themselves in a body; and such a preparative assembly hath some appearance already of a democracy; it is a democracy in embryo, properly in this respect, that every man hath the privilege freely to deliver his opinion concerning the common affairs. Yet he who dissents from the vote of the majority is not in the least obliged by what they determine, till by a second covenant a popular form be actually established; for not before then can we call it a democratical government, namely, till the right of determining all matters relating to the public safety is actually placed in a general assembly of the whole people; or by their own compact and mutual agreement, determine themselves the proper subject for the exercise of sovereign power. And to complete this state, and render it capable to exert its power to answer the end of a civil state, these conditions are necessary.

(1) That a certain time and place be assigned for assembling.

(2) That when the assembly be orderly met, as to time and place, that then the vote of the majority must pass for the vote of the whole body.

(3) That magistrates be appointed to exercise the authority of the whole for the better despatch of business of every day's occurrence, who also may, with more mature diligence, search into more important affairs; and if in case any thing happens of greater consequence, may report it to the assembly, and be peculiarly serviceable in putting all public decrees into execution, because a large body of people is almost useless in respect of the last service, and of many others as to the more particular application and exercise of power. Therefore it is most agreeable with the law of nature, that they institute their officers to act in their name and stead.

2. The second species of regular government is an aristocracy, and this is said then to be constituted when the people or assembly, united by a first covenant, and having thereby cast themselves into the first rudiments of a state, do then by common decree devolve the sovereign power on a council consisting of some select members; and these having accepted of the designation, are then properly invested with sovereign command, and then an aristocracy is formed.

3. The third species of a regular government is a monarchy, which is settled when the sovereign power is conferred on some one worthy person. It differs from the former, because a monarch, who is but one person in natural as well as in moral account, and so is furnished with an immediate power of exercising sovereign command in all instances of government; but the forenamed must needs have particular time and place assigned, but the power and authority is equal in each.

Mixed governments, which are various and of divers kinds (not now to be enumerated), yet possibly the fairest in the world is that which has a regular monarchy, settled upon a noble democracy as its basis; and each part of the government is so adjusted by pacts and laws that render the whole constitution in elysium. It is said of the British empire, that it is such a monarchy as that, by the necessary subordinate concurrence of the lords and commons in the making and repealing all statutes or acts of parliament, it hath the main advantages of an aristocracy and of a democracy, and yet free from the disadvantages and evils of either. It is such a monarchy as, by most admirable temperament, affords very much to the industry, liberty, and happiness of the subject, and reserves enough for the majesty and prerogative of any king who will own his people as subjects, not as slaves. It is a kingdom that, of all the kingdoms of the world, is most like to the kingdom of Jesus Christ, whose yoke is easy and burden light. . . . Thus having drawn up this brief scheme concerning man, and the nature of civil government he is become sole subject of, I shall proceed to make improvements of the premises to accommodate the main subject under our consideration.

PART III

The Economic Regulation of the Empire

THE search for a new all-water route to Asia by the countries of Western Europe led to the discovery of North and South America and colonization. Colonization, in turn, led to the formulation of policies, political and economic in substance, to determine the precise relationship of the New World settlements to the country that had established them. The purpose of these formulations was to strengthen the authority and effectiveness of the mother country. The concepts underlying such policies are called mercantilism, a term unknown in the sixteenth and seventeenth centuries but coined later to describe the goals embraced by these policies and the system of achieving them.

Under mercantilism the political authority of the nation was used to establish economic priorities and regulations to strengthen the state. Today we take the existence of nations for granted. But between 1450 and 1700, a nation was a relatively new phenomenon, and its authority was often fragile.

Although every nation accepted mercantilism, the forms of mercantilism varied from country to country, depending upon the natural resources of each. Because gold and silver poured into Spain from its colonies, the emphasis there was on bullionism, a national preoccupation with money. France attempted to eliminate internal tariff barriers to create a free national market. The French government also encouraged the production of luxury goods, usually by providing subsidies. The Dutch emphasized international trade by encouraging the building of ships and training of seamen to enlarge Holland's role as a middleman.

In the context of mercantilism, colonies were founded to serve the vital interests of the mother country by producing commodities unavailable at home, and all colonial trade was regulated so as to benefit the mother country. In the broadest sense, the colonizing impulse was a significant political means to an end, namely, that of nation-building.

English economic policy resembled that of other mercantilist nations of Western Europe. Woolen producers were subsidized, thus providing incentives to diminish dependence upon Flemish weavers. The Statute of Artificers and Apprentices regulated labor so that the labor force would not be idle or work in enterprises considered antithetical to the larger national goal of a vigorous, strong state. In the ensuing debates on policy, the language was that of economics whereas the issue, at bottom, was political.

The prevailing political view was that a nation grew stronger at the expense of other nations. From this perspective, for example, the international trade of the world was conceived of as fixed. A particular nation's share of the world's trade could only be increased by the reduction of another's share. To obtain a larger portion, a nation needed to regulate its trade to improve its commercial position in relation to other nations. Often internal regulation was also required to achieve this end, subsidizing desirable manufactures, encouraging the production of specific commodities, or fixing prices. Management of the economic life of the colonies was the external side of this pattern of regulation and control, with one special twist: the colonies were considered subordinate to the mother country and were to exist entirely for its benefit. This point of view had extremely important constitutional repercussions (see Part V) concerning colonial rights, but it was equally significant in the economic life of the colony.

Could the English prohibit a colony from engaging in manufacturing? Could they limit the issuance of paper money?

English thinking about the role of the colonial economy and the importance of trade for the national welfare is analyzed by a number of English political economists. Among these is Josiah Child (Document 1), who discussed the shortcomings as well as the merits of the English Navigation Acts, but who proclaimed the Enumeration Act of 1660 as one of the best ever adopted. The Enumeration Act reenacted the English regulation that goods sent to or from the colonies must come in English bottoms and further specified that certain staples—tobacco, indigo, ginger, sugar, and so forth—produced in the English colonies could only be marketed through the mother country. Because tobacco was "enumerated," the Chesapeake Bay colonies of Virginia and Maryland were seriously affected. Normally, they sent part of their tobacco crop, often in Dutch ships, to European markets. John Bland, representing the Chesapeake planters, protested vigorously against the policy of enumeration (Document 2), but to no avail.

After 1660, Parliament strengthened its regulation by adopting a series of enactments: the Staple Act of 1663, which stated that the importation of European goods into the colonies must come through England; the Plantation Duty Act of 1673, which required a ship carrying enumerated commodities to post a bond before leaving the American port of origination; and, finally, the Act of 1696, which created Admiralty Courts in America to enforce the Navigation Acts. These measures did channel Chesapeake trade through England—but at a cost to the American producer—and force colonial imports into an artificial trade channel. The Navigation Acts were strictly enforced; there is little evidence of smuggling.

In 1733, the enactment of the Molasses Act intruded seriously upon well-established lines of colonial trade, especially those between the French colonies in the West Indies and New England. During the debate over the Molasses Act pamphlets criticizing the impending legislation were published, which stated that the English colonies on the North American continent would be ruined if the act were to pass (Document 3). When the Molasses Act was adopted over these objections, the American colonies managed to evade it. The defiance of the Molasses Act, in contrast with the obedience accorded previous Navigation Laws, marked the growing commercial power of the colonies, a signal that they were becoming important enough to avoid being entirely subordinated by Britain when economic realities or vital interests dictated a different course.

Another mark of the economic maturity of the colonies is the issue of colonial manufactures. Joshua Gee, whose analytical essays on British policy found a receptive audience at home, comes out squarely in favor of the suppression of colonial manufactures (Document 4). The first attempt at regulation was the Woolen Act of 1699, which was directed against Ireland more than the American colonies, but this act was in reality a harbinger of future British policy. The Hat Act of 1732 was designed to eliminate competition between colonial hat makers and English hat makers by severely restricting the colonial operation. The Iron Act of 1750 must be classified in yet another category. It encouraged the production of pig and bar iron and prohibited the erection of slitting mills to manufacture finished iron goods. This act hurt some English producers (Document 5) while helping others (Document 6). The colonials vigorously opposed the act (Document 7). Thus far, British regulatory legislation began with trade, which continued to be a dominant theme, and then advanced from control of the household manufacturing of textiles (1699) to the manufacture of iron products (1750).

But a wholly new level of sophistication in the British economic regulation of the colonies took place in the eighteenth century when Britain stepped in to control colonial monetary policy, which focused especially on the issue of paper currency. In many respects, this concern on the part of the mother country was a tribute to the increasing complexity and advancement of the American economy. Colonials themselves differed in their views on the merits of paper currency. Benjamin Franklin praised the use of paper money and suggested that it was a prerequisite for colonial prosperity (Document 8). Dr. William Douglass of Boston opposed the use of paper currency (Document 9). The issue of colonial monetary policy was elevated from the provincial to the imperial setting when British merchants urged Parliament to prohibit the issuance of paper currency by the American colonies (Document 10). In 1751 Parliament passed such an act affecting New England; in 1764 the act was extended to all the colonies.

Interestingly enough, no colonial spokesman ever challenged the right of the British to enact regulatory legislation even though they opposed by argument, petition, and pamphlets, specific measures, such as the Enumeration Act, the Molasses Act, or the Iron Act. Nor did any colonials seriously suggest that the entire system of regulation failed, in fact, to promote the general welfare of England—much less the colonies. A sweeping indictment of governmental restrictions, regardless of whether its purpose was to manipulate the English or the colonial economy, was made, however, by a celebrated Scottish political economist, Adam Smith (Document 11). Adam Smith considered most of the English regulatory acts harmful to the country's economic growth and thus at cross-purposes with the goal of a strong nation. Such measures, he suggested, did not attain the ends for which they were designed. The debate initiated by Adam Smith has yet to run its course.

DOCUMENT 1

JOSIAH CHILD, *A NEW DISCOURSE OF TRADE,*
(UNDATED, FOURTH EDITION)

Josiah Child wrote about almost every aspect of English economic policy, including the Navigation Acts and their effect. Certain of his contemporaries, such as Roger Coke, supported unsparingly every detail of the Navigation Acts, but Josiah Child was among those who tried to weigh carefully the advantages and

*disadvantages. Even so, Child in his analysis declared
the Enumeration Act of 1660 to be "one of the
choicest and most prudent" ever made in England.
In this account, he responds to the objections made
against it.*

Concerning the Act of Navigation

Though this Act of Navigation concluded a very beneficial Act for this Kingdom, especially by the Masters and Owners of Shipping, and by all Seamen; yet some they are, both wise and honest Gentlemen and Merchants, that doubt whether the Inconveniences it has brought with it, be not greater than the Conveniences.

For my own part, I am of opinion that in relation to Trade, Shipping, Profit, and Power, it is one of the choicest and most prudent Acts that ever was made in England, and without which we had not now been Owners of one half of the Shipping, nor Trade, nor employed one half of the Seamen which we do at present; but seeing time has discovered some Inconveniencies in it, if not Defects, which in my poor opinion do admit of an easy amendment; and seeing that the whole Act is not approved by unanimous consent, I thought fit to discourse a little concerning it, wherein, after my plain method, I shall lay down such objections as I have met with, and subjoin my answers, with such reasons as occur to my memory, in confirmation of my own opinion.

The objections against the whole Act are such as these:

Objection 1. Some have told me, that I on all occasions magnify the Dutch policy in relation to their Trade; and the Dutch have no Act of Navigation, and therefore they are certainly not always in the right, as to the understanding of their true interest in Trade, or else we are in the wrong in this.

I answer, I am yet to be informed where the Dutch have missed their proper interest in Trade, but that which is fit for one Nation to do in relation to their Trade, is not fit for all, no more than the same policy is necessary to a prevailing Army that are masters of the Field, and to an

Army of less force than to be able to encounter their
enemy at all times and places. The Dutch, by reason of
their great Stocks, low Interest, multitude of Merchants
and Shipping, are masters of the Field in Trade, and therefore have no need to build Castles, Fortresses, and places
of Retreat: such I account laws of limitation, and securing of particular Trades to the Natives of any Kingdom, because they, viz., the Dutch, may be well assured,
that no Nation can enter in common with them in any
Trade, to gain bread by it, while their own use of money is
at 5 per cent and others at 6 per cent and upwards, etc.,
whereas if we should suffer their Shipping in common with
ours in those Trades, which are secured to the English by
the Act of Navigation, they must necessarily in a few
years, for the reasons abovesaid, eat us quite out of them.

Objection 2. The second objection to the whole Act is:
Some will confess that as to Merchants and owners of
Ships the Act of Navigation is eminently beneficial, but
say, that Merchants and Owners are but an inconsiderable
number of men, in respect of the whole Nation, and that
the interest of the greater number, that our Native Commodities and Manufactures should be taken from us at the
best rates, and foreign Commodities sold us at the cheapest, with admission of Dutch Merchants and Shipping in
common with the English, by my own implication would
effect.

My answer is, That I cannot deny but this may be
true, if the present profit of the generality be barely and
singly considered; but this Kingdom being an Island, the
defence of which has always been our Shipping and Seamen, it seems to me absolutely necessary that Profit and
Power ought jointly to be considered, and if so, I think
none can deny but the Act of Navigation has and does
occasion building and employing of three times the number of Ships and Seamen, that otherwise we should or
would do, and that consequently, if our force at sea were
so greatly impaired, it would expose us to the receiving
of all kinds of injuries and affronts from our neighbours,
and in the conclusion render us a despicable and miserable people.

Objection to Several Parts of the Act of Navigation

Objection 1. The Inhabitants and Planters of our plantations in America, say, this Act will in time ruin their plantations, if they be not permitted at least to carry their sugars to the best markets, and not be compelled to send all to, and receive all Commodities from England.

I answer, If they were not kept to the rules of the Act of Navigation, the consequence would be, that in a few years the benefit of them would be wholly lost to the Nation, it being agreeable to the policy of the Dutch, Danes, French, Spaniards, Portuguese, and all nations in the world, to keep their external Provinces and Colonies in a subjection unto and dependency upon their Mother-Kingdom; and if they should not do so, the Dutch, who, as I have said, are Masters of the Field in Trade, would carry away the greatest of advantage by the plantations, of all the Princes in Christendom, leaving us and others only the trouble of breeding men, and sending them abroad to cultivate the ground, and have bread for their industry.

Query 1. Here, by the way, with entire submission to the greater wisdom of those whom it much more concerns, give me leave to query, whether instead of the late prohibition of Irish cattle, it would not have been more for the benefit of this kingdom of England, to suffer the Irish to bring into England, not only their live cattle, but also all other commodities of the growth or manufacture of that Kingdom, Custom free, or on easy Customs, and to prohibit them from trading homeward or outward with the Dutch, or our own plantations, or any other places, except the Kingdom of England? Most certainly such a law would in a few years wonderfully increase the Trade, Shipping, and Riches of this nation.

Query 2. Would not this be a good addition to the Act of Navigation, and much increase the employment of English Shipping and Seamen, as well in bringing from thence all the Commodities of that Country, as supplying that Country with Deals, Salt, and all other foreign Commodities, which now they have from the Dutch?

Query 3. Would not this be a means effectually to prevent the exportation of Irish wool, which now goes frequently into France and Holland, to the manifest and great damage both of England and Ireland?

Query 4. Would not this be a fortress or law to secure to us the whole Trade of Ireland?

Query 5. Would not this render that which now diminishes, and seems dangerous to the value of lands in England, viz., the growth of Ireland, advantageous, by increase of Trade and Shipping, and consequently augment the power of this Kingdom?

Objection 2. The second Objection to part of the Act of Navigation, is usually made by the Eastland and Norway Merchants, who affirm, that in effect their Trade is much declined since the passing the Act of Navigation; and the Danes, Swedes, Holsteiners, and all Easterlings, who by the said Act may import Timber, and other Eastern Commodities, have increased in the number of their Shipping, employed in this Trade, since our Act of Navigation, at least two third parts; and the English have proportionably declined in the number of theirs employed in that Trade.

I answer, That I believe the matter of fact asserted is true, as well as the cause assigned, viz., the Act of Navigation; and yet this should not make us out of love with that excellent law; rather let it put us upon contriving the amendment of this seeming defect, or inconvenience, the cure of which, I hope, upon mature consideration, will not be found difficult; for which I humbly propose to the wisdom of Parliament, viz., that a law be made to impose a Custom of at least 50 *l.* per cent on all Eastland Commodities, Timber, Boards, Pipe-Staves, and Salt, imported into England and Ireland upon any Ships but English built Ships, or at least such only as are sailed with an English Master, and at least three fourths English Mariners.

And that for these reasons:

Reason 1. If this be not done, the Danes, Swedes, and Easterlings, will certainly in a few years carry the whole Trade, by reason of the difference of the charge of building a Ship fit for that Trade there or here, viz., a Flyboat of 300 tons new built, and set to sea for such a voyage, may cost there 13 or 1400 *l.* which here would cost from 22 to 2400 *l.* which is so vast a disproportion, that it is impossible for an Englishman to cope with a Dane in that Navigation under such a discouragement; to ballance which there is nothing but the Stranger's Duty, which the Dane now pays, and may come to 5 or 6 *l.* per Ship per Voyage at most, one with another, which is incompatible with the difference of price between the first cost of the Ships in either Nation; and this is so evident to those who are conversant in those Trades, that besides the decrease of our Shipping, and increase of theirs which has already happened, ours in probability had been wholly beaten out of the Trade, and only Danes and Easterlings freighted, had we been necessitated to build English Ships, and had not been recruited on moderate prices by Flyboats (being Ships proper for this Trade) taken in the late Dutch war, and by a further supply of Scotch Prizes likewise, through his Majesty's permission and indulgence.

Reason 2. Because the number of Strangers' Ships employed in the aforesaid Trade yearly, I estimate to be about two hundred sail; which if such a law was made, must unavoidably be all excluded, and the employment fall wholly into English hands; which would be an excellent nursery, and give constant maintenance to a brave number of English Seamen, more than we can or do employ at present.

Reason 3. The Act of Navigation is now of seventeen or eighteen years standing in England, and yet in all these years not one English Ship has been built fit for this Trade, the reason of which is that before mentioned, viz., that it is cheaper freighting of Danes and Easterlands; and it being so, and all men naturally led by their profit, it seems to me in vain to expect that ever this Law will procure the building of one English Ship fit for that employment, till those Strangers are excluded this Trade for England; and much more improbable it is, that any should now be built than it was formerly, when the Act was first made, because Timber is now at almost double the price in England it was then; the consequence of which is, that if timely provision be not made by some additional law, when our old stock of Flemish prizes is worn out as many of them are already, we shall have very few or no Ships in this Trade.

The Objections which I have heard made to this Proposition, are, namely:

Objection 1. If such an imposition be laid on those gross Commodities imported by Strangers from this Trade, we shall want Ships in England to carry on the Trade, and so the Commodity will not be had, or else will come very dear to us.

I answer, If the Commodity should be somewhat dearer for the present, it would be no less to the Nation in general, because all freight would be paid to Englishmen; whereas the freight paid to Strangers (which upon those Commodities is commonly as much or more than the value of goods) is all clear loss to the Nation.

Secondly, If there should be a present want of Shipping, and the Parliament shall please to enjoin us to build English Ships for this Trade, this extraordinary good effect will follow.

It will engage us to do what we never yet did, viz., to fall to building of Flyboats (great Ships of burthen, of no force, and small charge in sailing) which would be the most profitable undertaking that ever Englishmen were engaged in, and that which is absolutely necessary to be done, if ever we intend to board the Dutch in their Trade and Navigation; these Flyboats being the Milch-Cows of Holland, from which they have sucked manifoldly greater profit than from all their Ships of force, though both I know are necessary; but if at first the Parliament shall think fit to enjoin us only to Ships sailed with an English Master, and three fourths English Mariners, the Danes and Easterlings being by this means put out of so great an employment for their Shipping, we shall buy Ships proper for this Trade on easy terms of them, perhaps for half their cost, which Undervalue in purchase will be a present clear profit to England.

Objection 2. If this be done in England, may not other Princes account it hard and unreasonable, and consequently retaliate the like upon us?

To answer this Objection, it is necessary to enquire what Kingdom and Country will be concerned in this Law.

1st, Then. Italy, Spain, and Portugal, will be wholly unconcerned.

2dly, So will France, who if they were concerned, can

take no offence, while they lay an imposition of 50 or 60 per cent upon our Drapery.

3dly, The Dutch and Hamburghers would not by such additional law be more excluded than now they are, and the latter would have an advantage by it, in case the Danes should (as it may be supposed they will) lay a tax upon our Shipping there; for the consequence of it would be, that much of those kinds of Commodities we should fetch from Hamburgh, where they are plentifully to be had, though at a little dearer rate, and yet none so dear, but that the Dutch fetch yearly thence 350 or 400 Ships loading of Timber, and other wooden Commodities.

4thly, The Swedes would have an apparent benefit by it, by turning a great part of the stream of our Trade for those Commodities to Gottenburgh, and divers other parts of Sweden, that are lately opened, and now opening, where very large quantities of Timber, Masts, and boards, likewise may be had, though some small matter dearer than in Norway. Besides, if the Swedes should expect no advantage, but rather loss by such amendment of our own laws, they have no reason to be angry, because they have lately made so many laws for encouragement of their own Shipping and Navigation, and consequently discouragement of ours, that do in effect amount to a prohibition of the English from sending their own Manufactures to Sweden in English Shipping, insomuch that the English Merchants when Swedish Shipping does not present, are forced many times to send their goods to Elsinore, to lie there till a Swedish Ship comes by to put them aboard of, and pay their factorage, and other charges, because if they should send them in English Ships, the Duties are so high in Sweden, that it is impossible for them to make their first cost of them.

5thly, The Easterlings, or Hans-Towns, though they were excluded this Trade for England with their shipping, of which they have little (the greatest share being carried away by the Danes) would be gainers by the increase of our Trade with them, for boards, timber, spruce deals, etc., at Dantzick, Quinsborough, and other places, which would be very considerable in case the King of Denmark should impose any considerable extraordinary tribute on our shipping, which brings me to the third objection.

Objection 3. If this be done, will not the King of Denmark lay a great imposition upon all our Shipping that trade into his Dominions, and also upon our Drapery, and other native English Commodities?

I answer, That whatever that King may do at first, I am presuaded [sic] after he has considered of it, he will be moderate in his Impositions, because he can hurt none but himself by making them great; for as to Drapery, and other English goods, his Country consumes none worth speaking of, and that charged with about 30 or 40 per cent. Custom already, nine tenths of all the Timber and boards we fetch from thence, being, in my opinion, purchased with ready Dollars sent from England and Holland; and if he should by a great Imposition totally discourage us from trading with his people, we should lay out that money with the Swedes, Hamburghers, Dantzickers, and others, where we have a sufficient supply, while the Danes would be exceedingly burthened with the lying of their goods upon their hands, there being in Norway great quantities of goods, viz., the coarse Hemlock Timber, commonly brought from Larwick, Tunsberry, Sandyford, Oskestrand, Hollumstrand, and many other parts, which no Nation in the World trades with them for, or will buy or use but the English only.

DOCUMENT 2

JOHN BLAND, *REMONSTRANCE AGAINST THE ENUMERATION ACT,*
LONDON (?), 1661

The Enumeration Act seriously affected the economy of the Chesapeake colonies, whose principal export was tobacco, and whose best markets were Holland and France. Sending tobacco exclusively to England when the consumer was ultimately a Dutch burgher worked a severe hardship on the Chesapeake planters, because their product was diverted from its natural market. Even with a system of re-exportation in which a large part of the duty on tobacco collected in the English customs was refunded upon reshipping, the added cost to the planter was excessive. The tobacco was unloaded in England, passed through customs, stored, and then reloaded for Holland or some other market. These costs added greatly to the price paid by the consumer, thus reducing the number of buyers, all of which depressed the price paid to the planter. If England could have absorbed all the tobacco produced by the Chesapeake colonies, no hardship would have resulted. But the amount of tobacco consumed by the English represented only a fraction of the total amount produced.

No wonder, then, that the Chesapeake planters complained as the economy of Virginia and Maryland fell upon distressing days. In this document, John Bland, a London merchant representing the planters, argues for suspension of the Enumeration Act, but both his effort and that of others trying to change English policy failed.

Most Humbly representing unto your Majesty the inevitable destruction of those Colonies, if so be that the late Act for encrese of Trade and shipping be not as to them dispenced with: for it wil not onely ruinate the inhabitants and Planters, but make desolate the largest fertilest, and most glorious Plantations under Your Majesties Dominion; the which, if otherwise suspended, will produce the greatest advantage to this Nations Commerce and considerablest Income to Your Majesties Revenue, that any part of the world doth to which wee trade.

And that the prejudice which this act bringeth to those Colonies may appear to your Majesty, I shall presume to desire that the following particulars in order to the discovery thereof may be taken into consideration, as it hath reference to the Territories of Virginia and Mariland, and then to those persons that first were the promoters of the same, for debarring the Hollanders trading to those Plantations, in the long Parliament, with their specious pretences alleged for the obtaining thereof, which are as followeth. . . .

First, I will say something concerning the Persons that did solicit and procure the prohibition of the Hollanders from trading into those Plantations.

Secondly, Wherefore the said Act against the Dutch was procured by them, and is still sought to be continued.

Thirdly, I shall take into consideration those three Motives, or Pretences, urged by the Ingrossers of the Virginia and Mariland trade, for the debarring the Hollanders from trading thither; and so speaking to each of them, demonstrate plainly, that what is alleged thereby to be an advantage to those Colonies, is quite contrary, and will in time utterly ruinate them, the commerce, our customes, and shipping here in England.

To the First, concerning the Persons that Procured the prohibition of the Hollanders from trading into Virginia and Mariland, I give account of them.

They are no Merchants bred, nor versed in foreign ports, or any Trade, but to those Plantations, and that from either Planters there or whole-sale Tobacconists and shopkeepers retailing Tobacco here in England, who know no more what belongs to the commerce of the World, or Managing new discovered Countries, such as Virginia and Mariland are, than children new put out Prentice; can it then be Rational, that such persons judgments should be taken or relyed upon for passing so important an Act?

To the second Particular, Why these men procured this Act, prohibiting the Hollanders trade into those Colonies at first, and its continuance now, was, and is, because they would keep still in their own hands that Trade which they had ingrossed, and have no body come there to hinder them, and that for the following reasons.

First, That for whatever goods they carried out of England to those Plantations, the Inhabitants should pay them what prices and rates they please to require, else they should have nothing at all of them to supply their necessities.

Secondly, To force the Planters to deliver them such Tobaccos, which by the labour and sweat of their browes they had made, at the rates they themselves trading thither would have it, whereby they got that oftentimes of the poor Planters for a halfpenny, which they made us pay for here in England by Retaile three or four shillings.

Thirdly, That if they could not yet get the Planters Tobaccoes at their own rates, but that the Planters would ship it themselves for England, then would not the Traders thither let the Planters have any Tunnage in their ships to England, except it were at such high freight, as the Tobacco comming for England could never yield what would satisfie the same; so that if they could not get the Planters Tobacco for nothing in the country, They would have it for nothing when it arrived in England.

Fourthly, That seeing the Hollanders could not go to Virginia and Mariland, the Traders thither might carry it to Holland from those colonies themselves, and so get (besides having the Tobacco for little or nothing of the Planters) the Duties the Hollander used to pay in the Country for what he expected thence; and also the custom, which ought by their own rule to have been paid in England.

By which I hope its apparent, that it was nor is not theire love to the Plantations, the commerce or to encrease the Duties in England, that caused them to seek the Hollanders prohibition from Virginia and Mariland, but their own private interests, not regarding if the colonies and all in them perished, so they might keep the said Trade still; surely then such men are not meet Judges for debarring of the Hollanders from trading to those Plantations.

To the third Particular wherein, it is to be considered, how destructive those three motives and pretences for the obtaining this Act of prohibition to the Hollanders from trading to Virginia and Mariland are to those Colonies, the commerce, and your Majesties customs here in England, I declare as followeth. To the First, in which it is alleged, That being the Hollander permits not us Trade in their Indian Dominion, why should we admit him Trade in ours?

A good reason it were, and justly retaliated, if Virginia and Mariland were stoared with and did produce such rich commodities as those Territories do, out of which the Hollanders doe debar us Trade, or that those our Plantations were inhabited with such ingenious men as theirs be, into which they wil not suffer us to trade.

But seeing Virginia and Mariland have no such rich commodities, nor ingenious people to produce them, nor plenty of anything but what may be had everywhere, is it not then a madness to hinder the Hollanders or any else from trading thither? Shall we, to put out one of their eyes, lose both our own? I do hope it will be more seriously considered, and not by following the humor of a few covetous, ignorant, self-seeking men destroy so many thousands of Your Majesties subjects planted in those parts, and thereby lose the best and hopefullest Plantation that belongs to this Nation; but permit the Hollanders, or any other Nations that will to trade thither, until Virginia and Mariland be capable to maintain it self by it self; then, and not till then, will it be convenient to debar Foreiners from trading thither.

The second Motive alledged for the obtaining this Act against the Hollanders trading to Virginia and Mariland, is, that it hinders our Trade, not onely there, but in England, whereby the general commerce is, and our Shipping are decreased.

To explain this, and to shew, that the promoters of the Hollanders prohibition from trading to Virginia and Mariland, by reason of their ignorance and unexperiencedness in the negotiations of the world, are very unfit for States-men, and to make Laws for whole Nations, when most of them have never been farther than in their own shops and Ware houses wherein they were bred; so that certainly it's hard for such, especially that mind onely their own profit and interest, to set Rules for others in those things which they understand not; but with grief in may be spoken, that though the sluggishness and sloathful neglect of our most experienced men in this Nation, and their unwillingness to take pains, or to appear in publick business, which chiefly may be attributed for their not being encouraged and countenanced, do thereby give too much leav to hairbrained Ignorance to obtain that which doth not onely overthrow themselves, but the most ingeniousest men, and our whole Nation, whereby, and that deservedly, all perish together.

Therefore before I proceed to the next particular, I pray that the State of Virginia and Mariland, as they now are in may be considered.

Virginia and Mariland are colonies, which though capable of better commodities, yet for the present affoard onely these, Tobacco chiefly, then in the next place Corn and Cattel, commodities almost in every country whatever to be had; withall they are such commodities, that except purchased in those Plantations so cheap as not elsewhere so to be had, none would ever go thither to fetch them, no not we our selves. Which being so, then certainly it cannot stand with wisdom to hinder the Hollanders from going thither, for unlesse what is there produced be fetched from thence, the Planters will have little encouragement to manure the ground, or trouble themselves to take so much pains as they do, for what, when obtained, they know not what to do therewith. Doth it not then hence appear, that unless as some plant, others go to buy what is planted, there can be no trade or commerce in such a place? Seeing what the commodities of Virginia and Mariland are is it not a great advantage to those Colonies to have them by every body fetched thence? And on the contrary, must it not needs be a disadvantage to the commerce there, not to do it? If therefore then we debar the Hollanders from going thither, see the inconveniences that will arise thereby.

The Hollander began to plant Tobacco in his own Territories, as soon as the Act for their prohibition from Virginia and Mariland in the long Parliment was obtained. Will he not proceed to plant greater quantities, and so totally supply himself by his own labour? Do we not force him to this ourselves, and so thereby cut off our own trade? Will he, after accustomed to the Tobacco of his own growth, ever regard that which is in Virginia? Will he ever afterwards be induced to fetch it thence, when he finds his profit higher at home? And will he ever buy that of us, when by passing so many hands, and so much charge contracted thereon, is made so dear, that he can have it cheaper in his own Territories? (Surely no.) Therefore it clearly appears, that being so, of necessity we must lose that Trade and Commerce.

And if it be alleged, the Tobacco planted in Holland is not so good as what comes from Virginia, none will buy Gold too dear, and being used once to bad, the best is not regarded; what grows in Holland for present spending is as good as any. Have we not in this Nation by reason of the dearness and Sophistication of Virginia's Tobacco, accustomed our selves so to Virginia, that little Spanish, though much better, is spent amongst us at this day? And certainly, experienced men will say, it is, and will be the overthrow of our Trade and commerce, to put any people upon necessities to seek that out in their own Territories, which we will not let them have from us, but with excessive cost and charge; which if it were otehwise to be had of us at easie rates they would not so much as think thereof to plant it themselves, of which, many experimental examples may be shown in order thereunto.

Again, If the Hollanders must not trade to Virginia how shall the Planters dispose of their Tobacco? The English will not buy it, for what the Hollander carried thence was a sort of Tobacco, not desired by any other people, nor used by us in England but merely to transport for Holland. Will it not then perish on the Planters hands? Which undoubtedly is not onely an apparent loss of so much stock and commoditie to the Plantations, who suffer thereby, but for want of its employment, an infinite prejudice to the commerce in general.

Then again, If you keep thence the Hollanders, can it be believed, that from England more ships will be sent than are able to bring thence what Tobacco England will spend? If they do bring more, must they not lose thereby both stock and Block, principal and charges? The Tobacco will not vend in England, the Hollanders will not fetch it from England; what must become thereof? Even flung to the Dunghil. Is not then this a destruction to the commerce? For if men lose their Estates, certainly trade cannot be encreased.

A farther prejudice doth evidently attend the commerce by this Act, not onely in debarring Hollanders from trading to those colonies, but thereby we do likewise debar ourselves; for by the Act, no English Ships can load any goods in Virginia and Mariland to transport to any country but our own Territories. Is not this absolutely against the very essence and being of Trade and commerce, and cuts off all industry or ingenious designes, and is in a manner quite against, and contrary to the intent of the Act it self, which I conceive is to find out a means, that the Hollanders cheap sailing should not overthrow our markets, our shipping going dearer set to sea than theirs?

Which I explain thus, a ship having loaden herself in Virginia and Mariland, with Tobacco, Beef, Pork, and Corn, must bring these commodities to England, or into other our Territories; being landed in England, is not the Hollander, arriving in that place, where those Goods are so landed, as free to buy them of the Importer as any other Merchant of England, that would transport them in our own ships? They then both going to one Market, hath not the Hollander the same advantage he ever had? and do what we can in such a case, will under-sell us. Is not this then a prejudice to the commerce and gives the Hollander that very benefit which we strive to keep from him?

Now as this is a prejudice to the commerce of Virginia and Mariland, so in the like it will hold in all our American Plantations; but I am, and it is my business at present onely, to plead for Virginia and Mariland, and to show its disadvantages to those colonies. Will not this contract a great deal of needless charges and hazardous voyages, and that upon such goods and commodities as Virginia and Mariland affoard, which will not keep in long and tedious voyages? Doth it not hereby then appear to be an absolute hindrance of trade and commerce, not onely to those places, but to ourselves here in England?

I demand then, If it would not be better to let our English ships, loading in those colonies, when laden, to go whither they please, and pay in the places where they do lade (if it will not be dispenced with otherwise), the same customs to your Majesty as they should have done in England, or give Bills from thence to pay it in England? Certainly this would be more beneficial to the commerce, and security both for the ships and goods and advantageous to your Majesty; for whilst they are comming to England they might be at the end of their intended voyages, and obtain a Market, which haply in England could not be had; and with the proceeds of those very goods return for England, and there produce more advantage to your Majesties customes, when as otherwise by making a double voyage run a hazard to lose all, so that by what herein hath been said, I hope it will appear, our commerce is rather hindred than furthered. . . .

DOCUMENT 3

A SHORT ANSWER TO AN ELABORATE PAMPHLET ENTITLED "THE IMPORTANCE OF SUGAR PLANTATIONS,"
1731

This document, one of a number of anonymous pamphlets written in the heat of the dispute over the prospective Molasses Act of 1733, reveals the pungency of the exchange and the precision of the arguments. Some of the surprises in the pamphlet are its omissions; no mention is made, for example, of the slave trade. The focus of the pamphlet is foreshadowed in its lengthy subtitle: "That the Bill now depending for Prohibiting the Commerce carried on between our Northern Colonies, and the Foreign Sugar Plantations, tends to the impoverishing and ruin of those Colonies; the weakening of the Power of the English Empire in those Parts; and the Damage and Loss of Great Britain; and would put it in the power of our Sugar Plantations to make us pay them what Price they please for their Sugars."

My Lord,

As there is a Bill now depending in your Lordship's House, and very sedulously sollicited by the Agents of Barbadoes, for the Prohibiting a profitable Trade which has been of late years carried on between the English Colonies on the Continent of America, and the French and Dutch Sugar Plantations, for supplying them with Lumber and Horses; and a Pamphlet is published to support so injurious an Attempt upon their Fellow-Subjects, with many Words, a very little Argument, and a great deal of false Reasoning and Misrepresentation: I will presume upon your Lordship's goodness to pardon me, in giving you the trouble of a few Remarks upon that Piece, in order to remove the wrong Impression which such artificial Compositions are apt to make upon Persons who have not been conversant in Affairs of that nature.

This Author sets out with telling us (*p. 4, and 5*) that *the Sugar Colonies are of the greatest Consequence to Great Britain, etc.*, and I am so ready to admit their being of great Consequence, that I wish we had double the number: But then I must tell him, that of all those Colonies, Barbadoes is become the least profitable to us; for it must be confest that those are the most profitable that can afford us their Commodities cheapest; but the Barbadians themselves make it an Argument for their Relief, that their Lands are worn out, and require a very great Charge in their Cultivation, so that they cannot afford their Sugars as cheap as others. And tho' I have heard of this Complaint for above Forty Years past, yet we see they go on and thrive still; and they themselves acknowledge, that the Profits of their Molosses and Rum (Commodities which their Predecessors made no advantage of, and yet sold their Sugars for less than half the Price they have been at of late years) are become so considerable, as to support the Charge of the whole Plantation. . . .

He tells us next, that the *Sugar Colonies bring a Profit and Advantage to Great Britain of a good* 1,200,000 l. *per Annum;* and thus he makes up the Account for us: *The Planters clear usually* 850,000 l. *which Sum, or much the greatest part of it,* he says, *is spent here by the Proprietors, who live in England, or else in Manufactures sent to the West-Indies, or to Guinea to purchase Negroes.* A notable stretch this! . . . Lastly he says, *we get little less than* 200,000 l. *more by the Duty, Commission, etc.*

As to the Commission, I will admit that the whole of that Sum would amount to above 20,000 *l.* but then would he have us believe that all the Sugars we import are consigned to Factors here for the proper Account of the Planters, and that our Merchants bring home none in return for the Cargoes they send out upon their own Accounts? For which methinks he might fairly have allowed us one half at least; and then for the Duty, 'tis a Tax paid really by the Consumer, and no National Gain, nor are the Planters any way concerned in it. And now what's become of this good 1,200,100 *l.* gain? I am sure it cannot be properly said that we gain any thing by what we spend at home, our real Gain arising only from what we export; and I am afraid that is now so dwindled away, as to reduce this mighty Sum to less than 100,000 *l.* per Annum; and surely 'tis a sign of a very bad Cause when Men are forced to strain their Invention to impose upon the World by such a way of Accounting, and such a sort of Arguing.

He says (*p.* 6, and 7) *Virginia, Maryland, Carolina, Pensilvania, New York, New Hampshire, and New Jersey, have but little Trade with the Foreign Sugar Colonies, and are no Parties in opposing this Bill.* No wonder if they did not oppose it, when they had not the least Notice of so malicious a Design being carried on against them: But if the Gentlemen who sollicit this Bill will be content to drop it for this Sessions of Parliament, I will submit to forfeit all my Credit in the World, if in the next, all these Colonies do not shew, by opposing it with all the Interest they are able to make, that they believe themselves to be very sensibly affected by this Bill, and that every one of them would be greatly injured thereby, if ever it should pass into a Law.

But he would have it, that *New England and Rhode Island are the only Colonies that oppose the Bill;* and he is pleased to represent them to be so inconsiderable, *as that the least Sugar Island was of ten times more Consequence to Great Britain, than both these put together:* he says, *their Imports scarce deserve that Name, and that their Exports consist in Hemp and Naval Stores unmanufactured,* etc. . . .

Now to answer all this Slander and Misrepresentation, I shall first observe, that the Accounts transmitted from the Custom-House shew, that the Value of the Manufactures we sent from hence to New England only in one Year, amounts to more than the one half of what was sent to all the Sugar Islands in the same Year; and as our Exports thither consist chiefly in British Manufactures, our Commerce with them will appear to be of much more consequence to this Kingdom, than that which for some years past we have held with the Sugar Colonies. For if, as he has granted, the New Englanders send us little of their own Product for our home Expence, they must pay us the Ballance in Money; whereas, on the other hand, if we spend the greatest part of the Sugar our selves which we bring from the Islands, and re-export little of it (as is really the case at present) 'tis apparent that we squander away our Estates in a Commodity which serves only to indulge our Luxury, and must lose proportionally in the Ballance of our Trade in general. What heed then is to be given to a Writer who has the Confidence to advance so extravagant an Assertion, as that the least Sugar Island was of more consequence to us than both those Colonies? He shews also the little regard he bears to Truth, when he affirms that the New England People have little occasion for our Manufactures, but can supply themselves with their own; whereas 'tis notorious that they buy of us to a very great value, and, excepting their making some sorts of Iron Ware, they have no Manufactures of their own worthy our Notice. Nor is the insinuation of their being supplied with Silk from the French less disingenuous, for I am well assured that 'tis utterly false in fact; and therefore his charging them positively with it again in *p*. 32 is a great abuse. The wipe also he gives them for building Ships for themselves and for Foreigners, is methinks very weak: Have they not built many a good Ship for ourselves cheaper than we can build them here? . . .

But I should tire your Lordship if I were to trace this Gentleman thro' all the Steps of his loose way of arguing; the Specimen I have already shewn you of what arises out of four Pages only, may suffice to give you an Idea of the whole Performance: I shall therefore for the future pass by many things which I think deserve little notice, and make my Remarks as short as possible on some places which may seem more material; and so I come on to *p. 9* where he pretends to *propose a Method to enable our Planters to supply foreign Markets as cheap as the French;* and that is, by *prohibiting the exportation of Horses, and Lumber, from our Colonies to theirs; and also the importation of all foreign Sugars, Rum, and Molasses into any of our Colonies; and this,* he says, *will effectually cramp and check the French in the Sugar Trade:* and he would persuade us that *this is as absolutely necessary as the prohibiting the carrying our Wooll to France.* . . .

I cannot but take notice how this Gentleman treats the Subjects settled in the Northern Colonies, as if they were separated from the Body, and as if we had little or no interest in them; whereas I think we ought to consider them all (as he would have us esteem the Sugar Colonies to be *p. 23*) as flesh of our flesh, and bone of our bone, and to have the same regard to their thriving and prosperity as a good Mother has to all her Children; for we may justly look upon them as contributing abundantly more to the strength and support of our Empire in those parts (and to our Riches too, 'till we can be enabled to export more Sugar) than all our Islands: but he is pleased to note to us (*p. 34*, and *35*) that *the profit they make by their Freights is gained only by themselves, and not by Great Britain;* and that *the multitude of Seamen they employ may prove of fatal consequence to us, as being kept there, and not returning home.* But a person less prejudiced would have considered that we are really benefited by the profits they make, because they lay out their Money with us; and that they are so far from hurting us, by detaining our Seamen, that they do indeed breed up abundance of as able Seamen of their own as perhaps any in the World, from which they afford very seasonable Recruits to our Men of War when they want them in those Parts.

Lastly, for a Corollary to his delusive Arguments he tells us, that *the Sugar Colonies are at present in a very bad and languishing condition: that their Duties are high, their Planters poor, their Soil worn out, and their Fortifications destroyed.* Which may be answered in a very few, but much truer words; that, in comparison with the Northern Colonies (and I may say with Great Britain itself), they are in a very good and flourishing condition; that they pay no Duties at all, for their Product, because how high soever the Duties are laid, they are all paid in the price of the Commodity by the last Consumer; their Planters are rich, or at least they appear to be so by the figure they affect to make; their Soil is not so worn out but that it yields them a Product far more profitable than any other Lands in the British Dominions; and if their Fortifications are destroyed, they may be ashamed of their own neglect and improvidence, since a trifling abatement in their exorbitant Luxury would always enable them to provide largely for all publick Services.

And now, my Lord, I have done with my Remarks, tho' I could have taken notice of many things more which a Man of knowledge and integrity would have been ashamed to advance; and shall hasten to a Conclusion, by giving you a short Idea of the true State of this controversy. The Sugar Planters began their improvements chiefly upon the Credit given them by the English Merchants, and paid their Creditors in Muscovado Sugar valued in Barbadoes at no more than 10 shillings per cent for Money it might be bought for less, and at this price it continued for many years. When they had overcome the difficulty of clearing their Lands, and erecting their Sugar Works, their profits encreased vastly, and even exceeded some Silver Mines, and they fell into an excess of Luxury beyond compare. After this our other Islands came to be settled, which afforded us such quantities of Sugar, that we re-exported a great part to our Neighbours, and in great measure beat the Portugueze out of that trade; and thus indeed our Sugar Plantations became very profitable to us. But as of late years we have vastly encreased the home expence of this Commodity, so that we have little to spare for re-exportation, the Planters have taken the advantage to raise their price upon us by degrees even to more than double, and if they carry this Bill, will have it in their power to impose almost what price they please upon us. But we have yet two ways to remedy this evil; one is, by settling more Sugar Colonies, which the Government ought to have at heart, and to set about it with vigour: The other is, to give a liberty to import Muscovado Sugars (paying the same Duty with our own), even from whencesoever we can get them cheapest; which is not thought an ill policy by other Nations, and which we our selves have sometimes done on other occasions, and never refuse it in the want of Corn. And this would immediately reduce our Planters to the necessity of lowering their prices and using us better, which we know they are well able to do without denying themselves in any thing, but what would be for their real good, a moderate abatement of their profusion: For we know that they are furnished with necessaries much cheaper than the French; and if their Predecessors were able to work themselves into Estates when they sold their Sugars for under 10 shillings per cent. I can see no reason why the present Gentlemen should not content themselves with 15.

On the other hand, the Northern Colonies are an industrious People, who may well be said to earn their bread with the sweat of their brows, and will continue to be more profitable to us (as I think I have demonstrated before) than our Sugar Islands, 'till these last shall furnish us with commodities that we can re-export with profit: and as the former have fallen into a profitable way of Trade (and no way detrimental to Old England) with the French and Dutch Settlements in America; and also have established a considerable Manufactury for Rum, and which is of great importance to the carrying on their Fisheries, they must needs look upon it as one of the greatest oppressions that ever was put upon an innocent and free People, if so many thousands should be turned out of their livelyhood, only to gratify the avaricious spirit of a few encroaching People, and therefore I hope this Bill will be better considered in your Lordship's House, and never suffered to pass; unless it be with a Proviso, That whenever the common Muscovado Sugar shall be sold in Barbadoes for above 15 shillings per cent, it shall and may be lawful for all and any of his Majesty's Subjects, to trade freely with any other Nation for the said Commodity, and to import it into any of His Majesty's Dominions. I most humbly beg your Lordship's Pardon for troubling you with so long an Epistle, and pray I may always have the honour to be

Your Lordship's Obedient Humble Servant.

DOCUMENT 4

JOSHUA GEE, *THE TRADE AND NAVIGATION OF GREAT BRITAIN CONSIDERED*, LONDON, 1729

Little is known about Joshua Gee, an Englishman who wrote several tracts on trade, except that his analytical essay found an extraordinarily receptive audience. Six editions of the essay were published over a period of more than three decades, and its influence long outlived the author. The full title of Gee's work, although typically eighteenth century, is a fair measure of its range and scope: "Shewing that the surest way for a nation to increase in riches is to prevent the importation of such foreign commodities as may be raised at home; that this kingdom is capable of raising within itself and its colonies materials for employing all our poor in those manufactures which we now import from such of our neighbors who refuse the admission of ours; some account of the commodities each country we trade with takes from us and what we take from them, with observations on the balance."

Gee concluded his lengthy appraisal with an observation that he could have readily used in his introduction: "The trade of a nation is of mighty consequence, and a thing that ought to be seriously weighed, because the happiness or misfortunes of so many millions depend upon it."

Now as it is plain, keeping the planters to the raising materials in the plantations is the certain way to enrich them, it is proper, for creating a right understanding and true friendship between the planters in the colonies, and for making the government, as well as the manufacturers here, easy, to come into the same measures that other nations have done, who have plantations abroad; for since the discovery of the American world, the several kingdoms that have colonies abroad, have thought convenient to spare some of their people for cultivating several commodities produced there, as well as to carry on a trade with the natives, and send their manufactures among them; but great care has been taken to prevent their natural-born subjects from going upon such manufactures as did interfere with theirs at home; for as people are the riches of a kingdom, if properly employed, it would be sad policy indeed for governments to spare them, be at the charge of protecting them abroad, and yet allow them to set up the manufactures of their mother kingdoms, whereby they would supply themselves, and in respect to trade and commerce, throw them into a state of independency, and the commodities for home-consumption, that were expected to be raised by their industry, entirely neglected. The Spaniards have very few of their own, yet it is said, they take care to discourage any of the manufactures of Europe being carried on in their plantations: they will not suffer the making of wines, oils, and many other things, because Old Spain should have the benefit of supplying them, and also that they may not be interrupted in raising the produce of their plantations, the Portuguese have done the like in the Brazils; and tho' they have none of their own, rather chuse to buy the manufactures of other European countries, because their planters should not be diverted from carrying on those of sugar and tobacco, and applying themselves to their mines. And we see what a mighty profit they produce to themselves, and what riches France, Holland, Italy, etc., gain by serving them with their manufactures: this, I think, ought to put us upon considerations, what we should gain if our colonies were duly regulated and encouraged, being capable to supply them with all such manufactures as they shall want, by the industry of our own inhabitants. The regulations France has made for turning every undertaking in their plantations to the good of their mother country, is so extraordinary, that it deserves imitation; of which I have elsewhere taken notice in this discourse.

We have not made inspection into affairs of this nature, as our neighbours have done, but when necessity forces us, we begin to stir.

Ireland is a particular instance of this. . . . For as this kingdom is the head and seat of the English empire, and is supported by its manufactures, trade, and navigation, and thereby enabled to give protection to all her dominions: it could not be expected they would suffer their subjects to transport themselves into Ireland, there to turn their rivals in the woollen manufacture. . . .

I should therefore think it worthy the care of the government, to endeavour by all possible means to encourage them [the colonies] in the raising of silk, hemp, flax, iron, pot-ash, etc., by giving them competent bounties in the beginning, and sending over judicious and skilful persons at the publick charge, to assist and instruct them in the most proper methods of management; which, in my apprehension, would lay a foundation for establishing the most profitable trade of any we have. And considering the commodious situation of our colonies along the sea-coast, the great convenience of navigable rivers in all of them, the cheapness of land, and the easiness of raising provisions, great numbers of people who are uneasy in several parts of Europe, would be glad to transport themselves thither to settle upon such improvements, which, when once set on foot, would easily be carried on without much farther assistance. Now as people have been filled with fears, that the colonies, if encouraged to raise rough materials, would set up for themselves; a little regulation would remove all those jealousies out of the way. . . . It is proposed, that no weaver there shall have liberty to set up any looms, without first registring at an office kept for that purpose under the governor of each province, his name and place of abode, and the name and place of abode of every journeyman that shall work with him: but if any particular inhabitant shall be inclined to have any linnen or woollen, etc., made of their own spinning, they should not be abridged of the same liberty that they now make use of, viz., to carry it to a weaver (who shall be licensed by the governor) and have it wrought up for the use of the family, but not to be sold to any person in a private manner, nor exposed at any market or fair, on forfeiture of——.

And in as much as they have been supplied with all their iron manufactures from hence, except what is used in the building of ships, and other country work, a great deal above one half of our own exports being supposed to be in nails; a manufacture which they allow has never hitherto been carried on among them; it is proposed, they shall for time to come never erect the manufacturing of any under the size of a two shilling nail, horseshoe nails excepted; that all slitting mills, and engines for drawing wire, or weaving stockings, be put down; and that every smith, who keeps a common forge or shop, shall register his name and place of abode, and the name of every servant which he shall employ; which licence shall be renewed once every year, and pay for the liberty of working at such trade.

That all negroes shall be prohibited from weaving either linnen or woollen, or spinning or combing of wool, or working at any manufacture of iron, further than making it into pig or bar iron: that they be also prohibited from manufacturing of hats, stockings or leather of any kind. This limitation will not abridge the planters of any privilege they now enjoy; on the contrary, it will turn their industry to promoting and raising those rough materials.

If the governor of each province was obliged to transmit an account of the number of master-smiths, master-weavers, master-combers, number of looms and number of journeymen employed in each manufactury, to the lords of Trade and Plantations, with an exact account of all new comers, and their last place of abode, they would always have opportunity of seeing the increase or diminution of the manufactures of the colonies, which may be encouraged or depressed, according to their wants, or the danger of their too much interfering with us.

It is to be hoped this method would allay the heat that some people have shewn (without reason) for destroying the iron works in the Plantations, and pulling down all their forges; taking away, in a violent manner, their estates and properties; preventing the husbandmen from getting their plough-shares, carts, or other utensils, mended; destroying the manufacture of ship-building, by depriving them of the liberty of making bolts, spikes, or other things proper for carrying on that work; by which article, returns are made for purchasing our woollen manufactures, which is of more than ten times the profit that is brought into this kingdom by the exports of iron manufactures.

Indeed, if they shall set up manufactures, and the government afterwards shall be under a necessity of stopping their progress, we must not expect that it will be done with the same ease that now it may.

If it should be objected, that it would be difficult to find out those manufacturers who keep looms or smiths forges, etc., to such I answer, that it cannot be more difficult than it is to find out ale-houses, and oblige them to take out licenses, or to collect the window-lights with us; for weavers and smiths, etc., are public employments, and known by every body in the parish; and consequently any assessment or rate may be levied upon them with as much ease as the window tax.

DOCUMENT 5

REASONS OFFERED AGAINST ENCOURAGING MAKING IRON IN AMERICA,
ca. 1750

When the Iron Act was under discussion in Parliament, Englishmen who were engaged in making pig iron opposed it. They stated that the act would drive some English producers out of business and that the Americans would export an inferior grade of pig iron. The overall English policy of opposing all manufactures was also employed to support their position. Using the national interest as a guideline, the regulation of the colonial economy by Britain hurt certain segments of the British trading and manufacturing community as much as it did the colonials. The following document is one of numerous petitions submitted to Parliament whose signers are unknown.

It was never thought the Interest of England to encourage the Colonies to Manufacture any Thing that was Manufactured in England; and the Iron Manufacture is the second in the Kingdom, which maintains at least 200,000 People; and, if lost, those People must be an heavy Burthen to their Parishes, particularly in the counties of Worcester, Stafford, Warwick, Salop, Lancaster, York, great Part of Wales, and other Places, and considerably lessen the Value of the Land and Rents in those counties.

Should Encouragement be given to the Colonies, especially to Virginia, 'twould not encourage our Navigation; for there's no Ship that comes from thence, but will bring a considerable Quantity of Iron, and her full Quantity of Tobacco also; and therefore not employ many more Ships in the Virginia Trade. And the Making of Iron in any other Parts of America, will occasion a larger Fleet to convoy the Ships from thence than from Sweden, should we have a War with any Nation whatever.

There is no Iron yet known proper for Steel made here, but the best Swedish; and the Steel Manufacture is very advantageous to England, at least Fifty per cent in Manufacturing.

There are Collieries in New-England, and the Smiths there buy Coals as cheap as a Smith in London; and by that and other Advantages, the People of New-England did Manufacture considerably; which being laid before the Honourable the House of Commons, they took off the Drawback from unmanufactured Iron and Steel Exported to America in the year 1711, being the Ninth of Queen Anne.

The Encouraging the Making of Iron in America, will put them upon Manufacturing, and they will supply themselves first, and all the Colonies; so that the Manufacturers here must starve. America cannot supply England with any Iron for many Years; and the Want of Iron is already sufficiently known to all Traders, Handicrafts, Husband-men, Shipwrights, Merchants, and others.

The Americans have the Advantage of 5*l.* per Tun and upwards, in Making of Iron in their Wood, and Oar, more than the English have; which will over and above pay the great Wages in America, and the Freight to England.

When there was an open Trade with Sweden, the Swedish Iron Imported into England paid annually 40,000*l.* Custom, which will be so much Loss to the Revenue if the Americans Import Iron free, and much more if a Bounty be given them, could they supply us.

DOCUMENT 6

REASONS FOR MAKING BAR, AS WELL AS PIG OR SOW-IRON IN HIS MAJESTY'S PLANTATIONS,
ca. 1750

Englishmen engaged in producing finished iron prod-ucts were eager to increase the supply of pig and bar iron, and, as expected, this group supported the Iron Act of 1750. Since at least 1736, these English enter-prisers encouraged colonial producers of bar and pig iron in the same spirit that certain groups in England encouraged the colonial production of pitch, tar, and turpentine. A correspondent to The Gentleman's Mag-azine *supported the idea of encouraging American pig iron and excluding the Swedes. "For Whereas the Swedish markets receive none of our British manu-factures in exchange of theirs, but drain us of our ready specie, and thereby consume the very vitals of the nation; our brethren of America on the contrary will, for their pig and bar iron, take the very same commodity back again manufactured into locks, nails, utensils, and other various implements necessary for their accommodation; so that the mother country has*

the benefit of employing her own hands for the col-
onies in the very same commodity they send her for
the common use of both."

Later in 1770, Arthur Young, in Travels to
Northern England, *observed of iron works near New-*
castle: "They use a great deal of American iron,
which is as good as Swedish, and for some purposes
better. They would use more of it, if larger quantities
were to be had, but they cannot get it." The follow-
ing document is one of a number of petitions submit-
ted to Parliament whose signers are unknown.

1. Except Bar as well as Sow-Iron be admitted, the
Quantity in the Plantations will fall much short of what
may be expected, it being hoped we may make more Sow-
Iron than our Market at Home can take off.

2. The Iron Works in England not being able to supply near one Third Part of the Bar-Iron demanded, must
occasion the same Importation as hath hitherto been from
Sweden, and consequently carry out our Bullion to purchase it, unless more Works be erected, which would still
create a further want of Wood.

3. This will prevent the Exportation of our Manufactures of Woollen, etc., which would be sent to purchase
it in our own Plantations; besides the Discouragement to
our Navigation, and the imploying of our Poor in the
Plantations and at Home.

4. To have a Supply of Iron, in his Majesty's Plantations, in case of a Rupture with Sweden or Spain, would
prevent the distressing our Manufactures; as hath so lately
happened to the Discouragement of Trade, and raising the
Price of Manufactured Iron Wares amongst us.

5. To extend this Law only to Sow or Pig Iron, would
in a great measure frustrate the good Design of the present
Bill now before this Honourable House.

6. The Manufacturing Iron into small Wares in the
Plantations can never be effected, till their Labour comes
to one Fourth Part of the Price that it now is: Iron being
made into Bars there for Forty Years past, and Nine or
Ten Iron-Works of many Years standing, and no Hin-

drance to our sending Iron-Wares from hence; which is a clear Demonstration that we are in no Danger.

7. Making Bar, as well as Sow-Iron, in the Plantations, will greatly increase the Quantity, and consequently the Riches of the Nation.

8. The want of Iron for this Two Years past, has created great Uneasiness in our Workmen, and put them under great Difficulties to subsist, and given Opportunity to our Neighbouring Countries to tempt them away.

Upon Examining the Imports for the Years 1714 and 1715, when a Free Trade was settled, we find imported in those Two Years above Forty Thousand Ton of Foreign Iron; which with the Swedish New Duties, and Tonnage on our Shipping, could not stand in so little as 12*l*. per ton.

That our usual Exports of wrought Iron is from 1900 to 2000 Ton yearly.

That about Six Hundred Ton thereof is exported to our Neighbouring Kingdoms of Europe.

That from 13 to 1400 Ton is annually exported to our Plantations; much about one Half thereof is sent to the Sugar-Islands, the rest to New England, Virginia, etc.

Those that are afraid of injuring our Manufactures, by making Bar-Iron in America, will not pretend any Danger of our Trade to the Sugar-Islands, for they can make no Iron; therefore allowing that full 700 Ton is now exported to the Continent, and that this Nation should lose all the Manufacturing thereof, and allowing full 12*s*. per Hundred for the Workmanship, it comes but to 8400*l*. For the first cost of the Iron must be deducted.

But 20,000 Ton of Iron at 12*l*. per Ton comes to 240,000*l*. and 'tis well known, Sweden takes nothing from us for their Iron, but our Bullion. And therefore on a Supposition, that 8400*l*. worth of Labour in the Iron Manufactories may be injured, we must be necessitated to send out our Gold and Silver Annually to supply us with Iron, which might be purchased with our Woollen and other Manufactures, and the Labour of our own People from our own Plantations, and keep us dependant on the Courtesy of Sweden, etc., for Iron and other Naval Stores, as we have been for many Years.

DOCUMENT 7

REASON AGAINST A GENERAL PROHIBITION OF THE IRON MANUFACTURE IN HIS MAJESTY'S PLANTATIONS,
ca. 1750

All restrictive acts contain some subtly hidden effect. In this statement of the colonial position, the author indicates that the terms of the Iron Act prohibited the colonials from manufacturing finished iron products for their fellow colonials. The Iron Act as passed did include such a clause, but it is doubtful whether the colonials honored it. It is significant that the terms of the act were considered "to bear hard on the common Rights and Liberties of Mankind."

The following document is one of a number of petitions submitted to Parliament whose signers are unknown.

I. If the Clause be taken in a strict Sense, all Iron Work for building Ships, Houses, Mills, and even what is necessary for Instruments to Till the Ground, will be forbid to be made there; whereby it will become impracticable to live in the Plantations, because this Sort of Iron Manufacture must be made on the Spot, that it may be framed and fitted to the Size of the Work.

II. To forbid his Majesty's Subjects the making any Sort of Iron Wares, when its for their own Necessary Use, and not for Exportation, seems to bear hard on the common Rights and Liberties of Mankind; especially, when the Ore is what their own Soil yields, and what is found but in small Quantities comparatively in the Mother Kingdom.

III. If such a Prohibition be thought just to prevent the Plantations from interfering with the Iron-Workers in this Kingdom, all other Tradesman may expect, in their Turns, to be forbid Working at their respective Callings.

For, by the same Reason, the People may be forbid making Cheese or Cyder, for fear of prejudicing the Manufactures in Cheshire and Herefordshire.

IV. It is humbly conceived, there is no Occasion for this Clause. All Labour is so excessively dear in the Plantations, that no Manufacture of the lesser Iron Wares can vend, or ever does there, but when it happens by Accident that there is a great Scarcity of the same Commodity made in Great Britain.

V. The Encouragement given in the Bill for the Importation of Bar Iron from the Plantations, by taking off the Duty, which is Three Pounds per Tun, is not sufficient to bring it in; of which there needs no other Proof, than that a Tun of Iron is worth Sixty Pounds in New-England, their money, and but Twenty Pounds here, to say nothing of the chargeable Freight thence; so that if the Clause pass, the Iron Ore in the Plantations will be of Use neither there nor here.

VI. It seems a farther Hardship, that the Subjects Abroad should be permitted to forge their Ore into Bars, but not to run or cast it into Pots and other Implements, because the same Fire, and even the same Heat, will suffice for both.

It is therefore humbly prayed, That the Clause prohibiting any Kind of Iron Wares to be made in the Plantations, tho' for their own Use, and not for Exportation, be left out of the Bill.

DOCUMENT 8

BENJAMIN FRANKLIN, *A MODEST ENQUIRY INTO THE NATURE AND NECESSITY OF PAPER CURRENCY,*
1729

The decision to increase or decrease the amount of money available or determine exchange rates cuts to the marrow of a market-oriented capitalistic society;

this fact is as true today as it was in the eighteenth century. Once again, British policy represented an unintentional tribute to the vigor and maturity of the colonial economy. The issue of paper currency was the focus of intra-colonial (see Part IV) as well as colonial-mother-country debate. In the following document, Benjamin Franklin declares that appropriate issues of paper currency by the colonials are needed to achieve prosperity.

There is no Science, the Study of which is more useful and commendable than the Knowledge of the true Interest of one's Country; and perhaps there is no Kind of Learning more abstruse and intricate, more difficult to acquire in any Degree of Perfection than This, and therefore none more generally neglected. Hence it is, that we every Day find Men in Conversation contending warmly on some Point in Politicks, which, altho' it may nearly concern them both, neither of them understand any more than they do each other.

Thus much by way of Apology for this present *Enquiry into the Nature and Necessity of a Paper Currency*. And if any Thing I shall say, may be a Means of fixing a Subject that is now the chief Concern of my Countrymen, in a clearer Light, I shall have the Satisfaction of thinking my Time and Pains well employed.

To proceed, then,

There is a certain proportionate Quantity of Money requisite to carry on the Trade of a Country freely and currently; More than which would be of no Advantage in Trade, and Less, if much less, exceedingly detrimental to it.

This leads us to the following general Considerations.

First, A great Want of Money in any Trading Country, occasions Interest to be at a very high Rate. And here it may be observed, that it is impossible by any Laws to restrain Men from giving and receiving exhorbitant Interest, where Money is suitably scarce: For he that wants Money will find out Ways to give 10 per cent when he cannot have it for less, altho' the Law forbids to take more than 6 per cent. Now the Interest of Money being high is prejudicial to a Country several Ways: It makes Land bear a low Price, because few Men will lay out their Money in Land, when they can make a much greater Profit by lending it out upon Interest: And much less will Men be inclined to venture their Money at Sea, when they can, without Risque or Hazard, have a great and certain Profit by keeping it at home; thus Trade is discouraged. And if in two Neighbouring Countries the Traders of one, by Reason of a greater Plenty of Money, can borrow it to trade with at a lower Rate than the Traders of the other, they will infallibly have the Advantage, and get the greatest Part of that Trade into their own Hands; For he that trades with Money he hath borrowed at 8 or 10 per cent cannot hold Market with him that borrows his Money at 6 or 4. On the contrary, A plentiful Currency will occasion Interest to be low: And this will be an Inducement to many to lay out their Money in Lands, rather than put it out to Use, by which means Land will begin to rise in Value and bear a better Price: And at the same Time it will tend to enliven Trade exceedingly, because People will find more Profit in employing their Money that Way than in Usury; and many that understand Business very well, but have not a Stock sufficient of their own, will be encouraged to borrow Money; to trade with, when they can have it at a moderate Interest.

Secondly, Want of Money in a Country reduces the Price of that Part of its Produce which is used in Trade: Because Trade being discouraged by it as above, there is a much less Demand for that Produce. And this is another Reason why Land in such a Case will be low, especially where the Staple Commodity of the Country is the immediate Produce of the Land, because that Produce being low, fewer People find an Advantage in Husbandry, or the Improvement of Land. On the contrary, A Plentiful Currency will occasion the Trading Produce to bear a good Price. . . .

As we have already experienced how much the Increase of our Currency by what Paper Money has been made, has encouraged our Trade; particularly to instance only in one Article, Ship-Building; it may not be amiss to observe under this Head, what a great Advantage it must be to us as a Trading Country, that has Workmen and all the Materials proper for that Business within itself, to have Ship-Building as much as possible advanced: For every Ship that is built here for the English Merchants, gains the Province her clear Value in Gold and Silver, which must otherwise have been sent Home for Returns in her Stead; and likewise, every Ship built in and belonging to the Province, not only saves the Province her first Cost, but all the Freight, Wages and Provisions she ever makes or requires as long as she lasts. . . . Now as Trade in general will decline where there is not a plentiful Currency, so Ship-Building must certainly of Consequence decline where Trade is declining.

Thirdly, Want of Money in a Country discourages Labouring and Handicrafts Men (which are the chief Strength and Support of a People) from coming to settle in it, and induces many that were settled to leave the Country, and seek Entertainment and Employment in other Places, where they can be better paid. For what can be more disheartning to an industrious labouring Man, than this, that after he hath earned his Bread with the Sweat of his Brows, he must spend as much Time, and have near as much Fatigue in getting it, as he had to earn it. And nothing makes more bad Paymasters than a general Scarcity of Money. And here again is a Third Reason for Land's bearing a low Price in such a Country, because Land always increases in Value in Proportion with the Increase of the People settling on it, there being so many more Buyers; and its Value will infallibly be diminished, if the Number of its Inhabitants diminish. On the contrary, A Plentiful Currency will encourage great Numbers of Labouring and Handicrafts Men to come and Settle in the Country, by the same Reason that a Want of it will discourage and drive them out. Now the more Inhabitants, the greater Demand for Land (as is said above) upon which it must necessarily rise in Value, and bear a better Price. . . . Now the Value of House-Rent rising, and Interest becoming low, many that in a Scarcity of Money practised Usury, will probably be more inclined to Building; which will likewise sensibly enliven Business in any Place; it being an Advantage not only to Brickmakers,

Bricklayers, Masons, Carpenters, Joiners, Glaziers, and several other Trades immediately employed by Building, but likewise to Farmers, Brewers, Bakers, Taylors, Shoemakers, Shop-keepers, and in short to every one that they lay their Money out with.

Fourthly, Want of Money in such a Country as ours, occasions a greater Consumption of English and European Goods, in Proportion to the Number of the People, than there would otherwise be. Because Merchants and Traders, by whom abundance of Artificers and labouring Men are employed, finding their other Affairs require what Money they can get into their hands, oblige those who work for them to take one half, or perhaps two thirds Goods in Pay. By this Means a greater Quantity of Goods are disposed of, and to a greater Value. . . . As A plentiful Currency will occasion a less Consumption of European Goods, in Proportion to the Number of the People, so it will be a means of making the Balance of our Trade more equal than it now is, if it does not give it in our Favour; because our own Produce will be encouraged at the same Time. And it is to be observed, that tho' less Foreign Commodities are consumed in Proportion to the Number of People, yet this will be no Disadvantage to the Merchant, because the Number of People increasing, will occasion an increasing Demand of more Foreign Goods in the Whole.

Thus we have seen some of the many heavy Disadvantages a Country (especially such a Country as ours) must labour under, when it has not a sufficient Stock of running Cash to manage its Trade currently. And we have likewise seen some of the Advantages which accrue from having Money sufficient, or a Plentiful Currency.

The foregoing Paragraphs being well considered, we shall naturally be led to draw the following Conclusions with Regard to what Persons will probably be for or against Emitting a large Additional Sum of Paper Bills in this Province.

1. Since Men will always be powerfully influenced in their Opinions and Actions by what appears to be their particular Interest: Therefore all those, who wanting Courage to venture in Trade, now practise Lending Money on

Security for exhorbitant Interest, which in a Scarcity of Money will be done notwithstanding the Law, I say all such will probably be against a large Addition to our present Stock of Paper-Money; because a plentiful Currency will lower Interest, and make it common to lend on less Security.

2. All those who are Possessors of large Sums of Money, and are disposed to purchase Land, which is attended with a great and sure Advantage in a growing Country as this is; I say, the Interest of all such Men will encline them to oppose a large Addition to our Money. Because their Wealth is now continually increasing by the large Interest they receive, which will enable them (if they can keep Land from rising) to purchase More some time hence than they can at present; and in the mean time all Trade being discouraged, not only those who borrow of them, but the Common People in general will be impoverished, and consequently obliged to sell More Land for less Money than they will do at present. And yet, after such Men are possessed of as much Land as they can purchase, it will then be their Interest to have Money made Plentiful, because that will immediately make Land rise in Value in their Hands. Now it ought not to be wondered at, if People from the Knowledge of a Man's Interest do sometimes make a true Guess at his Designs; for, *Interest,* they say, *will not Lie.*

3. Lawyers, and others concerned in Court Business, will probably many of them be against a plentiful Currency; because People in that Case will have less Occasion to run in Debt, and consequently less Occasion to go to Law and Sue one another for their Debts. Tho' I know some even among these Gentlemen, that regard the Publick Good before their own apparent private Interest.

4. All those who are any way Dependants on such Persons as are above mentioned, whether as holding Offices, as Tenants, or as Debtors, must at least *appear* to be against a large Addition; because if they do not, they must sensibly feel their present Interest hurt. And besides these, there are, doubtless, many well-meaning Gentlemen and Others, who, without any immediate private Interest of their own in View, are against making such an Addition, thro' an Opin-

ion they may have of the Honesty and sound Judgment of some of their Friends that oppose it (perhaps for the Ends aforesaid), without having given it any thorough Consideration themselves. And thus it is no Wonder if there is a *powerful* Party on that Side.

On the other Hand, Those who are Lovers of Trade, and delight to see Manufactures encouraged, will be for having a large Addition to our Currency: For they very well know, that People will have little Heart to advance Money in Trade, when what they can get is scarce sufficient to purchase Necessaries, and supply their Families with Provision. Much less will they lay it out in advancing new Manufactures; nor is it possible new Manufactures Should turn to any Account, where there is not Money to pay the Workmen, who are discouraged by being paid in Goods, because it is a great Disadvantage to them. . . .

And since a Plentiful Currency will be so great a Cause of advancing this Province in Trade and Riches, and increasing the Number of its People; which, tho' it will not sensibly lessen the Inhabitants of Great Britain, will occasion a much greater Vent and Demand for their Commodities here; and allowing that the Crown is the more powerful for its Subjects increasing in Wealth and Number, I cannot think it the Interest of England to oppose us in making as great a Sum of Paper Money here, as we, who are the best Judges of our own Necessities, find convenient. And if I were not sensible that the Gentlemen of Trade in England, to whom we have already parted with our Silver and Gold, are misinformed of our Circumstances, and therefore endeavour to have our Currency stinted to what it now is, I should think the Government at Home had some Reasons for discouraging and impoverishing this Province, which we are not acquainted with. . . .

DOCUMENT 9

DR. WILLIAM DOUGLASS, *A DISCOURSE CONCERNING THE CURRENCIES OF THE BRITISH PLANTATIONS IN AMERICA,* 1740

William Douglass, a practicing physician in Boston who later wrote a history of the British settlements in America, denounced the use of paper currency in the colonies. His view as a "sound money" man was less typical than Franklin's non-ideological approach, but it was effective in persuading Massachusetts Bay to reduce its paper currency issues. An English admirer, upon reading Douglass' Discourse, exclaimed: "Had I the power, the author should be invited to this country against the next meeting of Parliament."

The many Schemes at present upon the Anvil in Boston, for emitting enormous Quantities of Paper Currencies; are the Occasion of this Discourse. The Writer does not vainly pretend to dictate to Government, or prescribe to Trade; but with a sincere Regard to the publick Good, hath taken some Pains, to collect, digest, and set in a proper Light, several Facts and Political Experiences especially relating to Paper Currencies; which tho' plain in themselves, are not obvious to every Body. If any Expressions should sound harsh, they are not to be understood as a Reflection upon this Province in general: It was always my Opinion, That the Province of the Massachusetts-Bay, is by far the most vigorous and promising Plant (with proper Cultivation) of all the British Plantations; in the best of Countries at Times, bad Administrations, and private evil Men of Influence have prevailed. The Author is not a transient Person, who from Humour or Caprice, or other Views may expose the Province; but is by Inclination induced, and by Interest obliged to study the Good of the Country. . . .

In all Sovereignties in Europe where Paper-Money was introduced, great Inconveniencies happened; upon cancelling this Paper Medium all those Inconveniencies did vanish.

1. In Sweden, Baron Gortz, by imposing Government Notes (and Munt tokyns) reduced the People to extreme Misery (this was one of the principal Crimes alledged against him when he suffered capital Punishment) but these being called in, and the Coin settled upon the same Foundation as it was before Charles XIIth Accession, Sweden flourished as formerly.

2. The late Regent of France, by the Advice of Mr. Law, did form a Project *A*. 1720, and by his arbitrary Power, endeavoured to put it on Execution; to defraud State Creditors and others, by banishing of Silver Currency, and by substituting a Paper Credit: the Effect was, the greatest Confusion, and almost utter Subversion of their Trade and Business: The Remedy was (Mr. Law having sneaked off, became a Profugus, and at last died obscurely) after a few Months the Court of France were obliged to ordain, that there should be no other legal Tender but Silver-Coin; and Commerce has flourished in France more than ever. At present, under the wise Administration of Cardinal Fleury (who allows of no Paper Currencies, nor Re-coinages, which had the same Effect in depreciating nummary Denominations in France, that frequent and large Emissions of Paper-Money have in our Colonies) their Trade bids fair to outdo the Maritime Powers (as Great Britain and Holland are called) and has a much better Effect in advancing the Wealth and Glory of France, than the Romantick butcherly Schemes of Conquest over their Neighbours, under the Administrations of Richelieu, Mazarine and others, in the Reigns of Lewis XIII and XIV.

3. In Great Britain *A*. 1716, were current four and a half Millions of Pounds Sterling in Exchequer Notes, being the largest Quantity current at one Time: although they bore about half of legal Interest, and not equal to one third of the concomitant national Silver Currency; they laboured much in Circulation, and the Government to prevent their being depreciated, was obliged to give considerable Pre-

miums to the Bank for cancelling some of them, and circulating the remainder.

It is not easily to be accounted for, how England, France and Holland, have tacitly allowed their several American Colonies; by Laws of their several Provinces, by Chancerings in their Courts of Judicature, and by Custom; to depreciate from Time to Time, the Value of their original Denominations, to defraud their Principals and Creditors in Europe. The British Plantations have not only varied from Sterling, but have also very much varied from one another; to the great Confusion of Business, and Damage of the Merchant. This will appear plain by inserting at one View the State of the Currencies in the several British Plantations; whereof some are per Exchange, some in Spanish Silver Coin, and some in Paper Money called Colony or Province Bills of publick Credit.

Originally and for some Years following in all the English American Colonies, 5s Denomination was equal to an English Crown Sterl. after some Time Pieces of Eight, being the general Currency of all foreign American Colonies, became also their Currency; and they remitted or gave Credit to the Merchants at Home (by Home is meant Great Britain) a Piece of Eight (value 4s 6d Sterl.) for a Crown or 5s Sterl. this was a Fraud of 11 per cent. In sundry of our Colonies were enacted Laws against passing of light Pieces of Eight; these Laws not being put in Execution, heavy and light Pieces of Eight passed promiscuously; and as it always happens, a bad Currency drove away the good Currency; heavy Pieces of Eight were shipped off. This current Money growing daily lighter, a Difference was made between heavy Money which became Merchandize, and light Money in which they paid their Debts gradually from 10, 15, 20, to 25 per cent as at present in Jamaica: this was another and continued Course of cheating their Creditors and Employers at Home. From a Complaint of Merchants and others dealing to the Plantations; Queen Anne by Proclamation, and the Parliament of Great Britain afterwards by the Proclamation Act, ordered, that after *A*. 1709, *A heavy Piece of Eight and other Pieces in Proportion to their Weight, in all our Colonies should pass not* *exceeding 6*s *Denomination.* This Act continues to be observed in none of our Colonies, excepting in Barbadoes, and Bermudas. Virginia Currency was formerly, and continues still better than what the Act directs. . . .

Thus we see, that particularly in our Paper Money Colonies, the Currencies have incredibly depreciated from Sterling, and from one another. Exchange with Great Britain being at this Time (February 1739) in New England 450 per cent in New-York, Jerseys, and Pensylvania 70 to 75 per cent in Maryland 100 per cent in North Carolina 900 per cent in South Carolina 700 per cent worse than Sterling.

To make a Bill or Note bearing no Interest, and not payable till after a dozen or score of Years, a legal Tender (under the highest Penalties as in New-York and Jerseys) in Payment of Debts, is the highest of despotick and arbitrary Government: France never made their State Bills a common Tender. Our Paper Money Colonies have carried the Iniquity still further; the Popular or Democratick Part of the Constitution are generally in Debt, and by their too great Weight or Influence in Elections, have made a depreciating Currency, a Tender for Contracts done many Years before; that is, they impose upon the Creditor side in private Contracts, which the most despotick Powers never assumed. An Instance of a still further arbitrary Proceeding in relation to Paper Money was an Act of Assembly in New Jerseys *A.* 1723, whereby Executions for Debt were stayed until Paper Money should be issued.

The Mystery of the infatuation of our Colonies running Headlong into a depreciating Paper Currency may be this: In many of our Plantations of late Years, by bad Management and Extravagancies, the Majority of the People are become Debtors, hence their Elected Representation in the Legislature have a great Chance to be generally of the Debtors Side: or in other Words, the Representatives being generally Freeholders, and many of them much in Debt; by large Emissions their Lands rise in Denomination Value while their Debts become really less, and the Creditor is defrauded in Part of his Debt. Thus our Colonies have defrauded more in a few Years than bad Administrations in Europe have formerly done in some Centuries. The great Damage done to the generous Merchants at Home, and to the industrious fair Dealers amongst our selves, call aloud, for some speedy and effectual Relief from the supreme Legislature the Parliament of Great Britain. . . .

The Mischiefs arising from a large Paper Currency are,

I. With regard to the particular and immediate Sufferers thereby.

1. The Labourers and Trades-men, who in all Countries, are the Heads which feed the Belly of the Common Wealth, and therefore deserve our chief Regard. How much they have suffered and continue to suffer is obvious: For Instance, a Carpenter when Silver was at 8s per Oz. his Wages were 5s a Day all Cash. The Town House *A.* 1712 was built at this Rate; whereas at present *A.* 1739 from the bad Influence of Paper Money Silver being 29s per Oz. he has only 12s a Day, equal only to 3s 4d of former Times; and even this is further reduced, by obliging him to take one half in Shop Goods at 25 per cent or more Advance above the Money Price: this Iniquity still grows, by reducing the Goods Part to the least vendable; the Shopkeeper refusing to let them have Provisions, West India Goods, or Goods of Great Britain that are in Demand.

To make the Case more familiar, Suppose a Tradesman laying in his Winter Store, when Wages were at 5s with one Day's Labour he purchases 15 Pound of Butter being 4d per Pound (I use Butter because it rises the most uniformly of all Provisions); at present his 12s a Day purchases only 7 Pound of Butter at 20d a Pound. The Clergy or settled Preachers to Congregations in Boston, no Offence in classing them with Labourers, when Silver was at 5s had 3 *l.* per Week; at present Silver at 29s per Oz. they have only 6 *l.* to 8 *l.* equal to 40s of former Times.

The Shopkeepers are become as it were Bankers between the Merchants and Tradesmen, and do impose upon both egregiously. Shop Notes that great and insufferable Grievance of Tradesmen, were not in Use until much Paper Money took Place: this Pay in Goods which generally are of no necessary Use (Provisions and West India Goods at this Time are removed from that Denomination) encourage Extravagance in Apparel and Furniture much above our Condition.

2. The Merchants of Great Britain Adventurers to New England, because of their largest Dealings have suffered most. Their Goods are here generally sold at a long Credit, while the Denominations of the Money in which they are to be paid, continues depreciating; so that they are paid in a less Value than was contracted for: thus our Bills have successively depreciated from 8s per Oz. Silver *A*. 1713, to 29s in this Year 1739; that is, if we could suppose the same Person to have constantly followed this Trade (without extraordinary Hits) for that space of Time, he must have reduced his Estate after the rate of 8s only for 29s. For every Shilling in the Pound that Silver rises in Price, or, which is the same, for every Shilling in the Pound that the Denomination of our Paper Money depreciates, the Creditor actually looses 5 per cent of his Debt.

There have been from Time to Time seeking Factors, who to procure Business from Home, have entred into Engagements which could not possibly be complied with: these having little or nothing of their own to loose, soon make desperate Work of it; become Bankrupts, and from a general insensibility of discredit, do notwithstanding keep their Countenance as before.

Many Factors to dazzle their Employers for a Time, and in the mean while to procure more Consignments, send Home a high Account of Sales, by the Shopkeepers giving a great Advance in Consideration of a very long Credit, and to be drawn out in Shop Notes. This Practice has so much prevailed, that it is now become a fixed tho' pernicious and ruinous Custom.

As Paper Money pays no Debts abroad, the Factor is obliged to give an extra Quantity of it, to purchase Silver, and other Returns; which can be exported, to satisfy Debts; in this Shape also the Merchant becomes a Sufferer.

3. Widows, Orphans, Funds for Charity at Interest, and all other Creditors, by Bonds, Notes and Book Debts, acquired by Industry, good Management, and Frugality, are great Sufferers from Time to Time: For Instance, from Autumn *A*. 1733 to Autumn *A*. 1734 Silver rose from 22s to

27s per Oz. this was a Loss of 23 per cent of the Principal.

II. The repeated large Emissions of Paper Money are the Cause of the frequent rise of the Price of Silver and Exchange; that is, of the publick Bills of Currency depreciating in all the Paper Money Colonies; which do as regularly follow the same, as the Tides do the Phases or course of the Moon. When no larger Sums are emitted for some Time, than what are cancelled of former Emissions, Silver and Exchange are at a Stand; when less is emitted than cancelled (which seldom happens) Silver and Exchange do fall. This is plain to a kind of Demonstration, from the Instance in the History of our Paper Money Emissions in New England. . . .

III. Large repeated Emissions of publick Bills of Credit, called Paper Money, is no addition to the Medium of Trade. No Country can have an indefinite or unlimitted Credit; the further a Country endeavours to stretch its Credit beyond a certain Pitch, the more it depreciates. . . . Here it is plain that the more Paper Money we emit our real Value of Currency or Medium becomes less, and what we emit beyond the trading Credit of the Country does not add to the real Medium, but rather diminishes from it, by creating an Opinion against us, of bad Oeconomy and sinking Credit.

IV. This infatuation in favour of Paper Money has had a mutinous bad Effect upon the Civil Government, in several of our Colonies. The Representatives of the People, have frequently refused to provide for the necessary Charges of Government, and other wholesome Laws, because the Governours and Councils, would not (in breach of their Instructions from the Crown) concur in emitting large Sums of Paper Money to defraud the industrious Creditor and fair Dealer. I shall mention only a few Instances. In S. Carolina *A.* 1719, the People deposed the Proprietors Governour on this Account: it is true, the King did not much resent this Mutiny; perhaps, that the Proprietors might be weary of their Property and Government; and accordingly seven of the eight Proprietors, for a small Consideration, did *A.* 1729 resign and sell to the Crown: Upon Governour Johnson's arrival in S. Carolina *A.* 1731, there had been no Supply granted in the four preceeding

Years. The Government of the Massachusetts-Bay, has from Time to Time been distressed, by our Representatives refusing Supplies for the necessary Charges of Government, and other publick Affairs neglected on this Account: Our present Governour's Fortitude and steady Adherence to the King's Instructions, and his having shortned the long Periods of Emissions for Charges of Government (I am under no Obligation to flatter) are highly laudable. New Hampshire Representatives for five Years preceeding *A.* 1736 granted no Supply. As the French humour of building Forts, to protect their Settlements against an Enemy, and as the Spanish humour of Devotion, in building Churches and Convents, is perverted, by their becoming Nurseries of Idleness and other Vices, so the English Liberty and Property of the Subject, in many of our Plantations are somewhat abused, to levelling and licentiousness; it is true, all Men are naturally equal, but Society requires subordination.

V. Long Credit, is not one of the least of the bad Effects of Paper Money. People run in Debt, endeavour after a long Credit, and refuse paying their Debts when due; because while Bills are continually depreciating, the longer the Debt is outstanding, they pay their Creditors with a less and less Value, than was contracted for. . . .

A general Clamour for a depreciating Paper Currency, is a certain Sign of the Country being generally in bad Circumstances, that is, in Debt; because all Creditors who by their Industry and Frugality have acquired Rents, Bonds, Notes and Book Debts, loose by its depreciating; and the Debtors (the Idle and Extravagant Part of the People) come off easy by the Creditors loss. Seeing they who are desperately in Debt, and want to pay a smaller Value than contracted for, or they who have nothing to loose, are generally of the Party for Paper Money; this ought to be a strong Prejudice against it, with sober thinking Men.

DOCUMENT 10

PETITION OF THE MERCHANTS OF LONDON TO PARLIAMENT, 1751

Within the colonies the people were divided in their views as to appropriateness of the issuance of paper money, whereas the English merchants abhorred its use in any form. In 1751 the influential English merchants trading with New England took steps to encourage Parliament to prohibit further issues of paper money by the colonies. The petition which follows, and others like it, led to the Currency Act of 1751, which prohibited the New England colonies from making new issues of paper money and required the gradual reduction of the issues in existence. In 1764, this prohibition was extended to all the colonies, thus expanding the range of imperial regulation of colonial economic life as represented by its most sophisticated economic tool—monetary policy.

A petition of the merchants of London, trading to his Majesty's colony of Rhode Island, whose names are thereunto subscribed, in behalf of themselves, and of many of the most considerable of the inhabitants of the said colony, was presented to the House, and read; alleging, that the currency, or medium of commerce of a country, being the standard and measure by which the worth of all things bought and sold is estimated and determined, it ought to be fixed invariably; otherwise property can neither be ascertained nor secured, by any plan or method whatsoever; and setting forth, that the currency of the government of the colony of Rhode Island is so far from being fixed, that it has sunk in its value above one half within these last seven years; whereby the petitioners, and all the other creditors of the colony, have been greatly defrauded; and all those who reside in the said colony, whose effects or estates have consisted in money, or bills of publick credit, so called, amongst whom are numbers of widows and orphans, have been grievously injured, oppressed, and almost ruined; and that the said colony of Rhode Island hath now outstanding the sum of 525,335 *l.* in bills of publick credit, emitted at several times, partly upon loan, and partly to supply the colony treasury; and that the sum upon loan is 390,000 *l.* the value of which, at the times of issuing, was 78,111 *l.* sterling, and the present sterling value is but 35,445 *l.* as appears by a particular state thereof, to the said petition annexed; and further alleging, that the bills emitted to supply the treasury, by acts of assembly, ought to be sunk, or drawn in by a tax; but that the government of the said colony hath hitherto delayed the execution of these acts, no tax having yet been levied for that purpose: and further setting forth, that several petitions for a new bank, or another emission of paper bills of publick credit, have been lately preferred to the present general assembly of the said colony, and the house of deputies there, though a number of petitions, from the most considerable inhabitants of the said colony, were presented against it; and the same were strongly opposed by some of the deputies in the said house, as being totally unnecessary, and in no respect wanted, as tending to depreciate greatly the large quantity of old bills, then outstanding; and as the same might be destructive to the privileges and interest of the colony, and subject them to the royal displeasure; notwithstanding all which, and notwithstanding the address of this House to his Majesty, in the year 1740, in relation to the large and frequent emissions of paper currency in the British plantations in America, and the royal pleasure signified thereon to the governor of Rhode Island, by the then Lords Commissioners of Trade and Plantations; whereby they were acquainted, that his Majesty, in pursuance of the said address of this House, had sent circular instructions to the several colonies, more immediately under his government, not to pass any more bills for the issuing of paper money, without a clause inserted therein (as proposed by the said address) to suspend the execution till his Majesty's pleasure should be signified thereupon; and were at the same time admonished and advised to pay all due regard to his Majesty's intentions, and to the sense of this House, in this matter; and notwithstanding this House, on the 30th of May 1749, presented another address to his Majesty, to have a particular account laid before this House, at their then next session, of the tenor and amount of all the bills of credit which had been created and issued in the several British colonies and plantations in America, as well those under proprietors and charters, as under his Majesty's immediate commission and government; and which address had been likewise signified to the governor of the said colony of Rhode Island; yet notwithstanding these, and all other remonstrances to the contrary, and in defiance and contempt of the royal pleasure, and of the authority of this House, the said deputies did, at their session in August last, pass a vote for emitting 50,000 *l.* in bills of a new tenor, to be let out on loan, which are equal in value to 400,000 *l.* in bills of their present currency of the old tenor, and exceed in value the whole of their present currency, upon loan, by 10,000 *l.;* and that the said house of deputies appointed a committee of four of their members to prepare and bring forward, a bill for that purpose, which the petitioners have no doubt was soon after passed; and further alleging, that the value of bills of the old tenor has been reduced much more than one-half since its emission, and by this new emission will be still further reduced, so as not to be worth one-fourth of the value it was originally issued for; and yet these bills are made a legal tender in all payments whatsoever, let the stipulation of the contract be what it will; and that the landholders of this colony, having generally mortgaged their farms or plantations, as a security for the bills of credit they have taken upon loan, have found it their interest to multiply such bills, that they may depreciate and lessen in value, and which they have recourse to, as a legal expedient of wiping away their debts without labour; whereby the laudable spirit of industry is greatly extinguished, and his Majesty's trading subjects, inhabiting in the said colony, greatly discouraged for want of produce and remittances, and the petitioners, the merchants of London, defrauded of at least three parts in four of the sums really and bona fide due to them: and therefore praying the House to take the premises into their serious consideration, and to provide such means as shall be effectual to prevent and restrain the legislature or authority of the government of the said colony of Rhode Island, from making or emitting any more bills of publick credit, without his Majesty's royal permission; and to cause the said intended emission to be stopped or recalled; and to prevent them from circulating or being offered, or taken in payment of debts; and to prevent and restrain them from passing any acts, whereby any extant bills of publick credit may be either debased in value, or postponed in their period of being drawn in; and that the House will be pleased to interpose in this matter, in such manner as shall seem meet, to relieve the petitioners frem the injury and oppression of such a flood of fluctuating sinking paper bills of publick credit.

Ordered, that the said petition be referred to the consideration of a committee: and that they do examine the matter thereof; and report the same, with their opinion thereupon, to the House.

DOCUMENT 11

ADAM SMITH, "CONCLUSION OF THE MERCANTILE SYSTEM" FROM *THE WEALTH OF NATIONS,* 1776

It remained for a talented Scottish political economist, Adam Smith, to challenge the entire rationale of the British regulatory system. The colonials argued against the enactment of specific measures, but even during the pre-revolutionary crisis they did not question the right of Britain to invoke such regulation, nor did any colonial write as sweeping and penetrating an indictment as that of Adam Smith. The colonials presumed that the mother country was obligated to protect its self-interest, which entailed enacting measures restricting the colonial economy as long

*as these measures were clearly within the sphere of
power to be exercised by the mother country.*

*What Adam Smith suggests (ironically, in the
same year that the* Declaration of Independence *was
signed) is that British economic regulation of its colonies was not only unsound in theory but also that
these same regulations actually curtailed the prosperity of the mother country. The regulations did not
achieve, he concludes, the objective for which they
were designed.*

Though the encouragement of exportation, and the
discouragement of importation, are the two great engines
by which the mercantile system proposes to enrich every
country, yet with regard to some particular commodities,
it seems to follow an opposite plan: to discourage exportation and to encourage importation. Its ultimate object, however, it pretends, is always the same, to enrich the country
by an advantageous balance of trade. It discourages the exportation of the materials of manufacture, and of the instruments of trade, in order to give our own workmen an
advantage, and to enable them to undersell those of other
nations in all foreign markets: and by restraining, in this
manner, the exportation of a few commodities, of no great
price, it proposes to occasion a much greater and more
valuable exportation of others. It encourages the importation of the materials of manufacture, in order that our own
people may be enabled to work them up more cheaply, and
thereby prevent a greater and more valuable importation of
the manufactured commodities. I do not observe, at least
in our statute book, any encouragement given to the importation of the instruments of trade. When manufactures have
advanced to a certain pitch of greatness, the fabrication of
the instruments of trade becomes itself the object of a
great number of very important manufactures. To give any
particular encouragement to the importation of such instruments, would interfere too much with the interest of
those manufactures. Such importation, therefore, instead of
being encouraged, has frequently been prohibited. Thus the
importation of wool cards, except from Ireland, or when
brought in as wreck or prize goods, was prohibited by the

3d [law] of Edward IV; which prohibition was renewed by the 39th of Elizabeth, and has been continued and rendered perpetual by subsequent laws. . . .

The exportation, however, of the instruments of trade, properly so called, is commonly restrained, not by high duties, but by absolute prohibitions. Thus by the 7th and 8th of William III, chapter 20, section 8, the exportation of frames or engines for knitting gloves or stockings is prohibited under the penalty, not only of the forfeiture of such frames or engines, so exported, or attempted to be exported, but of forty pounds, one half to the king, the other to the person who shall inform or sue for the same. In the same manner, by the 14th of George III, chapter 71, the exportation to foreign parts, of any utensils made use of in the cotton, linen, woollen and silk manufactures, is prohibited under the penalty, not only of the forfeiture of such utensils, but of two hundred pounds, to be paid by the person who shall offend in this manner, and likewise of two hundred pounds to be paid by the master of the ship who shall knowingly suffer such utensils to be loaded on board his ship.

When such heavy penalties were imposed upon the exportation of the dead instruments of trade, it could not well be expected that the living instrument, the artificer, should be allowed to go free. Accordingly, by the 5th of George I, chapter 27, the person who shall be convicted of enticing any artificer of, or in any of the manufactures of Great Britain, to go into any foreign parts, in order to practise or teach his trade, is liable for the first offence to be fined in any sum not exceeding one hundred pounds, and to three months imprisonment, and until the fine shall be paid; and for the second offence, to be fined in any sum at the discretion of the court, and to imprisonment for twelve months, and until the fine shall be paid. By the 23d of George II, chapter 13, this penalty is increased for the first offence to five hundred pounds for every artificer so enticed, and to twelve months imprisonment, and until the fine shall be paid; and for the second offence, to one thousand pounds, and to two years imprisonment, and until the fine shall be paid.

By the former of those two statutes, upon proof that

any person has been enticing any artificer, or that any artificer has promised or contracted to go into foreign parts for the purposes aforesaid, such artificer may be obliged to give security at the discretion of the court, that he shall not go beyond the seas, and may be committed to prison until he give such security.

If any artificer has gone beyond the seas, and is exercising or teaching his trade in any foreign country, upon warning being given to him by any of his majesty's ministers or consuls abroad, or by one of his majesty's secretaries of state for the time being, if he does not, within six months after such warning, return into this realm, and from thenceforth abide and inhabit continually within the same, he is from thenceforth declared incapable of taking any legacy devised to him within this kingdom, or of being executor or administrator to any person, or of taking any lands within this kingdom by descent, devise, or purchase. He likewise forfeits to the king all his lands, goods, and chattels, is declared an alien in every respect, and is put out of the king's protection.

It is unnecessary, I imagine, to observe how contrary such regulations are to the boasted liberty of the subject, of which we affect to be so very jealous; but which, in this case, is so plainly sacrificed to the futile interests of our merchants and manufacturers.

The laudable motive of all these regulations, is to extend our own manufactures, not by their own improvement, but by the depression of those of all our neighbours, and by putting an end, as much as possible, to the troublesome competition of such odious and disagreeable rivals. Our master manufacturers think it reasonable that they themselves should have the monopoly of the ingenuity of all their countrymen. Though by restraining, in some trades, the number of apprentices which can be employed at one time, and by imposing the necessity of a long apprenticeship in all trades, they endeavour, all of them, to confine the knowledge of their respective employments to as small a number as possible; they are unwilling, however, that any part of this small number should go abroad to instruct foreigners.

Consumption is the sole end and purpose of all production; and the interest of the producer ought to be attended to, only so far as it may be necessary for promoting that of the consumer. The maxim is so perfectly self-evident, that it would be absurd to attempt to prove it. But in the mercantile system, the interest of the consumer is almost constantly sacrificed to that of the producer; and it seems to consider production, and not consumption, as the ultimate end and object of all industry and commerce.

In the restraints upon the importation of all foreign commodities which can come into competition with those of our own growth or manufacture, the interest of the home consumer is evidently sacrificed to that of the producer. It is altogether for the benefit of the latter, that the former is obliged to pay that enhancement of price which this monopoly almost always occasions.

It is altogether for the benefit of the producer that bounties are granted upon the exportation of some of his productions. The home consumer is obliged to pay, first, the tax which is necessary for paying the bounty, and secondly, the still greater tax which necessarily arises from the enhancement of the price of the commodity in the home market.

By the famous treaty of commerce with Portugal, the consumer is prevented by high duties from purchasing of a neighbouring country a commodity which our own climate does not produce, but is obliged to purchase it of a distant country, though it is acknowledged that the commodity of the distant country is of a worse quality than that of the near one. The home consumer is obliged to submit to this inconveniency, in order that the producer may import into the distant country some of his productions upon more advantageous terms than he would otherwise have been allowed to do. The consumer, too, is obliged to pay whatever enhancement in the price of those very productions this forced exportation may occasion in the home market.

But in the system of laws which has been established for the management of our American and West Indian colonies, the interest of the home consumer has been sacrificed to that of the producer with a more extravagant profusion than in all our other commercial regulations. A great empire has been established for the sole purpose of raising up a nation of customers, who should be obliged to buy from the shops of our different producers all the goods with which these could supply them. For the sake of that little enhancement of price which this monopoly might afford our producers, the home consumers have been burdened with the whole expense of maintaining and defending that empire. For this purpose, and for this purpose only, in the two last wars, more than two hundred millions have been spent, and a new debt of more than a hundred and seventy millions has been contracted over and above all that had been expended for the same purpose in former wars. The interest of this debt alone is not only greater than the whole extraordinary profit, which, it ever could be pretended, was made by the monopoly of the colony trade, but than the whole value of that trade, or than the whole value of the goods, which at an average have been annually exported to the colonies.

It cannot be very difficult to determine who have been the contrivers of this whole mercantile system; not the consumers, we may believe, whose interest has been entirely neglected; but the producers, whose interest has been so carefully attended to; and among this latter class our merchants and manufacturers have been by far the principal architects. In the mercantile regulations, which have been taken notice of in this chapter, the interest of our manufacturers has been most peculiarly attended to; and the interest, not so much of the consumers as that of some other sets of producers, has been sacrificed to it.

PART IV

The Politics of Internal Controversy

ALTHOUGH the American colonies developed similar political institutions modeled upon English experience and practice (see Part II), political issues within each colony were usually of a dual nature. Geographic and demographic factors produced special issues, but more often questions or problems faced in one colony were repeated in others. The list of internal political issues is long: the conflict between constituents within a colony for a stake in the Indian trade; the struggle among geographic sectors for governmental subsidies to build roads or improve waterways; the relationship between church and state; the resentment of the older settlers toward the new, often non-English, migrants; the emergence of political alignments along the "old country" lines—the German vote or the Scots-Irish vote; the procurement, control, and distribution of uncultivated land; and taxes and monetary policy, to select the most obvious.

Most of these issues lay directly in the mainstream of political development; but certain ones were far more important in one colony than in another. Monetary policy was a more significant issue in South Carolina and Massachusetts Bay than in North Carolina. The issue of church and state was more urgent in New England where each colony except Rhode Island had an established church than in Pennsylvania which had no established church, whereas the reverse was true on the issue of the new non-English migration. In Part IV, the arguments surrounding five sets of internal political issues are explored: the relationship of church and state, which also involved the question of religious toleration; reapportionment to correct grave injustices in representation; the role of the Negro in American society; the stance of the colonial government in relationship to the colonial economy; and finally, the clash of economic interests within a colony.

The issue of the relationship between church and state and the relative degree of religious toleration of dissenting religious sects—an issue that affected the majority of the colonies—arose immediately in Massachusetts Bay, whose goal was to establish a Bible Commonwealth. John Cotton, the most distinguished of the Puritan divines (Document 1), responded to inquiries from England by stating that civil authority would be exercised solely by church members, which meant, of course, an intimate relationship between church and state. Nor is this arrangement shocking, because similar close relationships existed in every other country of the Western world. When Roger Williams, after banishment from Massachusetts Bay in 1636, founded Rhode Island and stipulated that its settlers might exercise freedom of religion, his policy marked a dramatic departure from customary practice.

The issue of toleration in its political, religious, and social context was debated in an exchange between John Cotton and Roger Williams. The latter led off with *The Bloody Tenet of Persecution* (Document 2). Nathaniel Ward, minister at Ipswich in Massachusetts, called for strict religious conformity in a celebrated essay entitled *The Simple Cobler of Aggawam in America* (Document 3).

In the Chesapeake colonies, the same kind of struggle took place, although with reduced intensity. From the outset, the Church of England was the established church in Virginia. In Maryland, with its Catholic proprietor and substantial Catholic population, no one church of the seventeenth century was the legally established one. But when the Protestant population greatly exceeded that of the Catholics, the Baltimore proprietor feared that the

Catholic minority would be persecuted—which is what eventually happened. In an effort to protect the Catholics, however, Maryland, urged by Lord Baltimore, passed the Toleration Act of 1649 (Document 4).

The issue of church and state, although somewhat deflated, continued to reassert itself as a political as well as a social and intellectual issue. In 1689, England passed a Toleration Act to which American colonials often referred as the constitutional and legal precedent against religious persecution. The problem persisted, however, as is evident in the middle of the eighteenth century when Samuel Davies, a Presbyterian minister in Anglican Virginia, protested that the English Toleration Act was not being honored (Document 5), and Connecticut, to protect its Congregational Church establishment against itinerant preachers of the Great Awakening, enacted legislation to "correct abuses in ecclesiastical affairs" (Document 6).

A second internal political issue that aroused a strong response in colonial America was the question of reapportionment of representation to the colonial assembly. As population grew much more rapidly in one section of the colony in relation to others, constituents in swiftly expanding areas were usually seriously underrepresented. A protest from the newer and rapidly growing counties in New York indicates the dimension of this issue (Document 7), and a pointed petition from the constituents of Philadelphia reveals that urban underrepresentation was a similar development (Document 8). Internal political issues in the colonies had a history of being escalated into a broader political framework, namely, the policy-making authority of Britain. In this case, the Crown, in 1767, specifically forbade any colony to reapportion or establish new counties without royal consent, a serious encroachment upon colonial self-government (Document 9).

The most lasting internal political issues often arose from sharp conflicts in economic interest. One such category is labor. In 1744, several ship's carpenters in Charleston petitioned the South Carolina legislature, accusing one of their competitors of using black slave labor in repairing ships with the obvious result that they, Anglo-Saxon carpenters, were being thrown out of work (Document 10).

The political aspects of slavery were not confined to the competitive position of the blacks as a labor force. Negro slavery in the society, including the subject of emancipation, became a political issue, sometimes subtly screened but at other times forthrightly stated as in the case of the Quakers in America (Document 11). What the white man conceived of as the role of the slave is unmistakably revealed in a sermon by Thomas Bacon of Maryland, preached to a congregation of slaves (Document 12).

Vital economic interests were inevitably reflected in the political arena, and the intervention of governmental authority in the productive process provoked political debate. Colonial governments frequently regulated the price of commodities or labor. In the case of Virginia, the colonial authorities, reacting to a pronounced and sweeping demand from their constituency, intervened to control tobacco production, notably by specifying the procedure to be followed in preparing tobacco for shipment to any overseas market. Overproduction in certain years aroused such violent feeling that planters took the law into their own hands by forcibly limiting the number of tobacco plants (Document 13), but the government stepped in to stop them. In 1713 Governor Spotswood of Virginia introduced inspection of tobacco (Document 14), but because he tried to use the jobs created by the legislation to form a Crown party, this effort also failed. The issue remained unresolved until the colonial legislature itself, searching for some solution to its dilemma, passed legislation to control the quality of the tobacco exported from Virginia (Document 15).

A clash of political-economic interests occurred when the colonials began to develop banks to fulfill the needs of a maturing economy. Banking and monetary policy are interdependent, and the conflict over monetary policy (see Part III, where the merits of paper money are debated) is related to colonial disputes over banks. Dr. William Douglass of Boston wrote a biting condemnation of the Massachusetts Land Bank of 1740 (Document 16). His pamphlet, in turn, was analyzed point by point by an anonymous supporter of the bank (Document 17). The internal debate on the issue of the bank, like the issues of church and state and of representation, was eventually elevated to a higher authority when the British merchants appealed to Parliament to intervene in negating the Massachusetts Land Bank on the theory that merchants would be forced to accept paper money based on the land bank resources (Document 18). Parliament thereupon enacted legislation prohibiting the chartering of banks in the colonies.

The implication is obvious: As the colonies matured, internal political issues became increasingly interwoven with a more fundamental issue, the extent or limitation of British authority over its colonies.

DOCUMENT 1

JOHN COTTON, *CERTAIN PROPOSALS MADE BY LORD SAY, LORD BROOKE, AND OTHER PERSONS OF QUALITY, AS CONDITIONS OF THEIR REMOVING TO NEW ENGLAND, WITH ANSWERS THERETO,* 1636

The establishment of the Puritan Church in Massachusetts Bay was fundamental to the character of that colony. This close relationship between church and state was a source of strength, but it was also a source of friction and, consequently, weakness. John Cotton, the most distinguished of the New England Puritan divines, prepared the following document after consulting with "the mindes of such leading men amongst us." Cotton answered the queries of English Puritans who were considering a migration from the homeland to either Massachusetts Bay or Connecticut, but who settled ultimately in Connecticut.

The point John Cotton makes is unmistakable: The civil authority will be exercised exclusively by church members. However, this position should not be misinterpreted. Despite the intimate relationship between church and state, the civil authority was always to exercise supremacy over the church, while

*the magistrates, and not the ministers, managed Massa-
chusetts Bay.*

Demand. That, for the present, the Right Honorable
the Lord Viscount Say and Seale, the Lord Brooke, who
have already been at great disbursements for the public
works in New-England, and such other gentlemen of approved sincerity and worth, as they, before their personal
remove, shall take into their number, should be admitted
for them and their heirs, gentlemen of the country. But,
for the future, none shall be admitted into this rank but
by the consent of both houses.

Answer. The great disbursements of these noble person-
ages and worthy gentlemen we thankfully acknowledge,
because the safety and presence of our brethren at Connecticut is no small blessing and comfort to us. But, though
that charge had never been disbursed, the worth of the
honorable persons named is so well known to all, and our
need of such supports and guides is so sensible to ourselves, that we do not doubt the country would thankfully
accept it, as a singular favor from God and from them, if
he should bow their hearts to come into this wilderness and
help us. As for accepting them and their heirs into the
number of gentlemen of the country, the custom of this
country is, and readily would be, to receive and acknowledge, not only all such eminent persons as themselves and
the gentlemen they speak of, but others of meaner estate,
so be it is of some eminency, to be for them and their heirs,
gentlemen of the country. Only, thus standeth our case.
Though we receive them with honor and allow them pre-
eminence and accommodations according to their condition, yet we do not, ordinarily, call them forth to the
power of election, or administration of magistracy, until
they be received as members into some of our churches,
a privilege, which we doubt not religious gentlemen will
willingly desire (as David did in Psal. xxvii:4) and christian churches will as readily impart to such desirable persons. Hereditary honors both nature and scripture doth
acknowledge (Eccles. xix:17) but hereditary authority
and power standeth only by the civil laws of some com-

monwealths, and yet, even amongst them, the authority
and power of the father is no where communicated, together with his honors, unto all his posterity. Where God
blesseth any branch of any noble or generous family, with
a spirit and gifts fit for government, it would be a taking
of God's name in vain to put such a talent under a bushel,
and a sin against the honor of magistracy to neglect such
in our public elections. But if God should not delight
to furnish some of their posterity with gifts fit for magistracy, we should expose them rather to reproach and
prejudice, and the commonwealth with them, than exalt
them to honor, if we should call them forth, when God
doth not, to public authority.

Demand. That the rank of freeholders shall be made
up of such, as shall have so much personal estate there, as
shall be thought fit for men of that condition, and have
contributed, some fit proportion, to the public charge of
the country, either by their disbursements or labors.

Answer. We must confess our ordinary practice to be
otherwise. For, excepting the old planters, i.e. Mr. Hum-
phry, who himself was admitted an assistant at London,
and all of them freemen, before the churches here were
established, none are admitted freemen of this commonwealth but such as are first admitted members of some
church or other in this country, and, of such, none are excluded from the liberty of freemen. And out of such
only, I mean the more eminent sort of such, it is that
our magistrates are chosen. Both which points we should
willingly persuade our people to change, if we could make
it appear to them, that such a change might be made according to God; for, to give you a true account of the
grounds of our proceedings herein, it seemeth to them,
and also to us, to be a divine ordinance (and moral) that
none should be appointed and chosen by the people of
God, magistrates over them, but men fearing God (Ex.
xviii:21) chosen out of their brethren (Deut. xvii:15)
saints (1 Cor. vi:1). Yea, the apostle maketh it a shame
to the church, if it be not able to afford wise men from
out of themselves, which shall be able to judge all civil
matters between their brethren (ver.5). And Solomon

maketh it the joy of a commonwealth, when the righteous are in authority, and the calamity thereof, when the wicked bear rule (Prov. xxix:2).

Objection. If it be said, there may be many carnal men whom God hath invested with sundry eminent gifts of wisdom, courage, justice, fit for government.

Answer. Such may be fit to be consulted with and employed by governors, according to the quality and use of their gifts and parts, but yet are men not fit to be trusted with place of standing power or settled authority. Ahitophel's wisdom may be fit to be heard (as an oracle of God) but not fit to be trusted with power of settled magistracy, lest he at last call for 12,000 men to lead them forth against David (2 Sam. xvii:1,2,3). The best gifts and parts, under a covenant of works (under which all carnal men and hypocrites be) will at length turn aside by crooked ways, to depart from God, and, finally, to fight against God, and are therefore, herein, opposed to good men and upright in heart (Psal. cxxv:4,5).

Objection. If it be said again, that then the church estate could not be compatible with any commonwealth under heaven.

Answer. It is one thing for the church or members of the church, loyally to submit unto any form of government, when it is above their calling to reform it, another thing to chuse a form of government and governors discrepant from the rule. Now, if it be a divine truth, that none are to be trusted with public permanent authority but godly men, who are fit materials for church fellowship, then from the same grounds it will appear, that none are so fit to be trusted with the liberties of the commonwealth as church members. For, the liberties of the freemen of this commonwealth are such, as require men of faithful integrity to God and the state, to preserve the same. Their liberties, among others, are chiefly these. 1. To chuse all magistrates, and to call them to account at their general courts. 2. To chuse such burgesses, every general court, as with the magistrates shall make or repeal all laws. Now both these liberties are such, as carry along much

power with them, either to establish or subvert the commonwealth, and therewith the church, which power, if it
be committed to men not according to their godliness,
which maketh them fit for church fellowship, but according to their wealth, which, as such, makes them no better
than worldly men, then, in case worldly men should prove
the major part, as soon they might do, they would as
readily set over us magistrates like themselves, such as
might hate us according to the curse (Levit. xxvi:17) and
turn the edge of all authority and laws against the church
and the members thereof, the maintenance of whose peace
is the chief end which God aimed at in the institution of
Magistracy (1 Tim. ii:1,2).

DOCUMENT 2

ROGER WILLIAMS, *THE BLOODY TENET*, 1644

*Roger Williams came to New England in 1631 and
later accepted a position as teacher in the Salem
Church of Massachusetts Bay. A man of great talent
with a marvelous indifference to his own interests,
Williams said and wrote what he believed—which
often offended others. He was banished from Massachusetts Bay in 1636 and founded the colony of
Rhode Island.*

   The quaint title of Williams' discourse, The
Bloody Tenet, *masks a critical subject, the bloody
tenet of persecution for the sake of conscience, an
issue as relevant in the contemporary world as in the
seventeenth century. In the 1640s the Puritans in
England and America were engaged in a complex
and intense debate about the relationship of the
church and state and, in particular, the question of
religious toleration. In this document, Williams lays
down the framework of the debate which was addressed to his English countrymen, who were engaged
in bitter civil strife, as well as to his fellow church-*

men in New England. The Bloody Tenet *initiated a
series of counter-responses between John Cotton and
Williams: Cotton's* The Bloody Tenet Washed and
Made White *and Williams'* The Bloody Tenet Yet
More Bloody.

First, That the blood of so many hundred thousand
soules of Protestants and Papists, spilt in the Wars of
present and former Ages, for their respective Consciences,
is not required nor accepted by Jesus Christ the Prince
of Peace.

Secondly, Pregnant Scripturs and Arguments are
throughout the Worke proposed against the Doctrine of
persecution for cause of Conscience.

Thirdly, Satisfactorie Answers are given to Scriptures,
and objections produced by Mr. Calvin, Beza, Mr. Cotton,
and the Ministers of the New English Churches and others
former and later, tending to prove the Doctrine of persecution for cause of Conscience.

Fourthly, The Doctrine of persecution for cause of
Conscience, is proved guilty of all the blood of the Soules
crying for vengeance under the Altar.

Fifthly, All Civill States with their Officers of justice
in their respective constitutions and administrations are
proved essentially Civill, and therefore not Judges, Governours or Defendours of the Spirituall or Christian state and
Worship.

Sixthly, It is the will and command of God, that (since
the comming of his Sonne the Lord Jesus) a permission
of the most Paganish, Jewish, Turkish, or Antichristian
consciences and worships, bee granted to all men in all
Nations and Countries: and they are onely to bee fought
against with that Sword which is only (in Soule matters)
able to conquer, to wit, the Sword of Gods Spirit, the
Word of God.

Seventhly, The state of the Land of Israel, the Kings
and people thereof in Peace and War, is proved figurative
and ceremoniall, and no patterne nor president for any
Kingdome or civill state in the world to follow.

Eightly, God requireth not an uniformity of Religion
to be inacted and inforced in any civill state; which in-

forced uniformity (sooner or later) is the greatest occasion
of civill Warre, ravishing of conscience, persecution of
Christ Jesus in his servants, and of the hypocrisie and destruction of millions of souls.

Ninthly, In holding an inforced uniformity of Religion
in a civill state, wee must necessarily disclaime our desires
and hopes of the Jewes conversion to Christ.

Tenthly, An inforced uniformity of Religion throughout a Nation or civill state, confounds the Civill and Religious, denies the principles of Christianity and civility,
and that Jesus Christ is come in the Flesh.

Eleventhly, The Permission of other consciences and
worships then a state professeth, only can (according to
God) procure a firme and lasting peace (good assurance
being taken according to the wisedome of the civill state
for uniformity of civill obedience from all sorts).

Twelfthly, lastly, true civility and Christianity may
both flourish in a state or Kingdome, notwithstanding the
permission of divers and contrary consciences, either of
Jew or Gentile. . . .

While I plead the Cause of Truth and Innocencie
against the bloody Doctrine of Persecution for cause of
conscience, I judge it not unfit to give alarme to my selfe,
and all men to prepare to be persecuted or hunted for
cause of conscience.

Whether thou standest charged with 10 or but 2 Tal-
ents, if thou huntest any for cause of conscience, how
canst thou say thou followest the Lambe of God who so
abhorr'd that practice?

If Paul, if Jesus Christ were present here at London,
and the question were proposed what Religion would they
approve of: The Papists, Prelatists, Presbyterians, Inde-
pendents, etc., would each say, Of mine, of mine.

But put the second question, if one of the severall sorts
should by major vote attaine the Sword of steele: what
weapons doth Christ Jesus authorize them to fight with in
His cause? Doe not all men hate the persecutor, and every
conscience true or false complaine of cruelty, tyranny?

Two mountaines of crying guilt lye heavie upon the

backes of All that name the name of Christ in the eyes of Jewes, Turkes and Pagans.

First, The blasphemies of their Idolatrous inventions, superstitions, and most unchristian conversations.

Secondly, The bloody irreligious and inhumane oppressions and destructions under the maske or vaile of the Name of Christ, etc.

O how like is the jealous Jehovah, the consuming fire to end these present slaughters in a greater slaughter of the holy Witnesses? Rev. 11.

Six yeares preaching of so much Truth of Christ (as that time afforded in K. Edwards dayes) kindles the flames of Q. Maries [Queen Mary's] bloody persecutions.

Who can now but expect that after so many scores of yeares preaching and professing of more Truth, and amongst so many great contentions amongst the very best of Protestants, a fierie furnace should be heat, and who sees not now the fires kindling?

I confesse I have little hopes till those flames are over, that this Discourse against the doctrine of persecution for cause of conscience should passe currant (I say not amongst the Wolves and Lions, but even amongst the Sheep of Christ themselves) yet *liberavi animam meam,* I have not hid within my breast my souls belief: And although sleeping on the bed either of the pleasures or profits of sinne thou thinkest thy conscience bound to smite at him that dares to waken thee? Yet in the middest of all these civill and spirituall Wars (I hope we shall agree in these particulars).

First, how ever the proud (upon the advantage of an higher earth or ground) or'elooke the poore and cry out Schismatickes, Hereticks, etc., shall blasphemers and seducers scape unpunished? Yet there is a sorer punishment in the Gospel for despising of Christ then Moses, even when the despiser of Moses was put to death without mercie, Heb. 10: 28, 29. He that beleeveth not shall bee damned, Marke 16: 16.

Secondly, what ever Worship, Ministry, Ministration, the best and purest are practised without faith and true perswasion that they are the true institutions of God, they are sin, sinfull worships, Ministries, etc. And however in

Civill things we may be servants unto men, yet in Divine and Spirituall things the poorest pesant must disdaine the service of the highest Prince: Be ye not the servants of men, 1 Cor. 14 [vii: 23].

Thirdly, without search and triall no man attaines this faith and right perswasion, 1 Thessal. 5. Try all things.

In vaine have English Parliaments permitted English Bibles in the poorest English houses, and the simplest man or woman to search the Scriptures, if yet against their soules perswasion from the Scripture, they should be forced (as if they lived in Spaine or Rome it selfe without the sight of a Bible) to beleeve as the Church beleeves.

Fourthly, having tried, we must hold fast, 1 Thessal. 5, upon the losse of a Crowne, Revel. 13 [iii: 11], we must not let goe for all the flea bitings of the present afflictions, etc., having bought Truth deare, we must not sell it cheape, not the least graine of it for the whole World, no not for the saving of Soules, though our owne most precious; least of all for the bitter sweetning of a little vanishing pleasure.

For a little puffe of credit and reputation from the changeable breath of uncertaine sons of men.[:]

For the broken bagges of Riches on Eagles wings: For a dreame of these, any or all of these which on our death-bed vanish and leave tormenting stings behinde them: Oh how much better is it from the love of Truth, from the love of the Father of lights, from whence it comes, from the love of the Sonne of God, who is the way and the Truth, to say as he, John 18: 37, For this end was I borne, and for this end came I into the World that I might beare witnesse to the Truth.

DOCUMENT 3

NATHANIEL WARD, *THE SIMPLE COBLER OF AGGAWAM IN AMERICA,* 1647

Nathaniel Ward, minister at Ipswich, was among those who replied to the arguments of Roger Wil-

liams, arguing against toleration and separation of church and state. Ward and John Cotton made the issue of toleration a peculiarly internal one, upholding the current practice of Massachusetts Bay, for example, to demand religious conformity and ignore the forces pressing for change.

First, such as have given or taken any unfriendly reports of us New-English, should doe well to recollect themselves. We have been reputed a Colluvies of wild Opinionists, swarmed into a remote wilderness to find elbowroom for our Phanatic Doctrines and practises; I trust our diligence past, and constant sedulity against such persons and courses, will plead better things for us. I dare take upon me, to be the Herauld of New-England so far, as to proclaim to the World, in the name of our Colony, that all Familists, Antinomians, Anabaptists, and other Enthusiasts shall have free Liberty to keep away from us, and such as will come to be gone as fast as they can, the sooner the better.

Secondly, I dare aver, that God doth no where in his word tolerate Christian States, to give Tolerations to such adversaries of his Truth, if they have power in their hands to suppress them.

Here is lately brought us an Extract of a Magna Charta, so called, compiled between the Sub-planters of a West-Indian Island; whereof the first Article of constipulation, firmly provides free stable-room and litter for all kind of Consciences, be they never so dirty or jadish; making it actionable, yea, treasonable, to disturb any man in his Religion, or to discommend it, whatever it be. We are very sorry to see such professed Prophaneness in English Professors, as industriously to lay their Religious foundations on the ruine of true Religion; which strictly binds every Conscience *to contend earnestly for the Truth: to preserve unity of Spirit, Faith and Ordinances, to be all like minded, of one accord; every man to take his Brother into his Christian care, to stand fast with one spirit, with one mind, striving together for the faith of the Gospel;* and by no means to permit Heresies or Erronious Opinions: But God abhorring such loathsome beverages, hath in his righteous judgment blasted that enterprize, which might otherwise have prospered well, for ought I know; I presume their case is generally known ere this.

If the Devil might have his free option, I believe he would ask nothing else, but liberty to enfranchize all false Religions, and to embondage the true; nor should he need: It is much to be feared that lax Tolerations upon State-pretences and planting necessities, will be the next subtle Stratagem he will spread to distate the Truth of God, and supplant the Peace of the Churches. Tolerations in things tolerable, exquisitely drawn out by the lines of the Scripture, and pensil of the Spirit, are the sacred favours of Truth, the due latitudes of Love, the fair Compartments of Christian fraternity: but irregular dispensations, dealt forth by the facilities of men, are the frontiers of error, the redoubts of Schisme, the perillous irritaments of carnal and spiritual enmity.

My heart hath naturally detested four things: The standing of the Apocrypha in the Bible; Foreigners dwelling in my Country, to crowd out Native Subjects into the corners of the Earth; Alchymized Coines; Tolerations of divers Religions, or of one Religion in segregant shapes: He that willingly assents to the last, if he examines his heart by day-light, his Conscience will tell him, he is either an Atheist, or an Heretick, or an Hypocrite, or at best a captive to some Lust: Poly-piety is the greatest impiety in the World. . . .

Not to tolerate things meerly indifferent to weak Consciences, argues a Conscience too strong: pressed uniformity in these, causes much disunity: To tolerate more than indifferents, is not to deal indifferently with God: He that doth it, takes his Scepter out of his hand, and bids him stand by. Who hath to do to institute Religion but God. The power of all Religion and Ordinances, lies in their Purity: their Purity in their Simplicity: then are mixtures pernicious. I lived in a City, where a Papist Preached in one Church, a Lutheran in another, a Calvinist in a third; a Lutheran one part of the day, a Calvinist the other, in the same Pulpit: the Religion of that Place was but motley and meagre, their affections Leopard-like.

If the whole Creature should conspire to do the Creator a mischief, or offer him an insolency, it would be in nothing more, than in erecting untruths against his Truth, or by sophisticating his Truths with humane medleyes: the removing of some one iota in Scripture, may draw out all the life, and traverse all the Truth of the whole Bible: but to authorise an untruth, by a Toleration of State, is to build a sconce against the walls of Heaven, to batter God out of his Chair: To tell a practical lye, is a great Sin, but yet transient; but to set up a Theorical untruth, is to warrant every lye that lyes from its root to the top of every branch it hath, which are not a few. . . .

Concerning Tolerations, I may further assert. . . .

He that is willing to tolerate any Religion, or discrepant way of Religion, besides his own, unless it be in matters meerly indifferent, either doubts of his own, or is not sincere in it.

He that is willing to tolerate any unsound Opinion, that his own may also be tolerated, though never so sound, will for a need hang God's Bible at the Devils girdle.

Every toleration of false Religions, or Opinions hath as many Errors and Sins in it, as all the false Religions and Opinions it tolerates, and one sound one more.

That State that will give Liberty of Conscience in matters of Religion, must give Liberty of Conscience and Conversation in their Moral Laws, or else the Fiddle will be out of Tune, and some of the strings crack.

He that will rather make an irreligious quarel with other Religions than try the Truth of his own by valuable Arguments, an peaceable Sufferings; either his Religion, or himself is irreligious. . . .

It is said, Though a man have light enough himself to see the Truth, yet if he hath not enough to enlighten others, he is bound to tolerate them, I will engage my self, that all the Devils in Britanie shall sell themselves to their shirts, to purchase a Lease of this Position for three of their Lives, under the Seal of the Parliament.

It is said, That Men ought to have Liberty of their Conscience, and that it is Persecution to debar them of it: I can rather stand amazed than reply to this: it is an astonishment to think that the braines of men should be parboyl'd in such impious ignorance; Let all the wits un-

If there be room in England for

Familists		Manes
Libertines		Lemures
Erastians		Dryades
Antitrinitarians		Homodryades
Anabaptists		Potamides
Antiscripturists		Naiades
Arminians		Hinnides
Manifestarians		Pierides
Millinarians	the room	Nereides
Antinomians	for	Pales
Socinians		Anonides
Arrians		Parcades
Perfectists		Castalides
Brownists		Monides
Mortalians		Charites
Seekers		Heliconides
Enthusiasts,	Good Spirits,	Pegasides,
etc.	but very Devils.	etc.

In a word room for Hell above ground.

der the Heavens lay their heads together and find an Assertion worse than this (one excepted) I will Petition to be chosen the universal Ideot of the World.

It is said, That Civil Magistrates ought not to meddle with Ecclesiastical matters.

I would answer to this so well as I could, did I not know that some Papers lately brought out of New-England, are going to the Press, wherein the Opinions of the Elders there in a late Synod, concerning this point are manifested, which I suppose will give clearer satisfaction than I can.

The true English of all this their false Latin, is nothing but a general Toleration of all Opinions; which motion if it be like to take, it were very requisite, that the City would repair Pauls with all the speed they can, for an English Pantheon, and bestow it upon the Sectaries, freely to assemble in, then there may be some hope that London will be quiet in time.

But why dwell I so intolerable long about Tolerations, I hope my fears are but Panick, against which I have a double cordial. First, that the Parliament will not though they could: Secondly, that they cannot though they would grant such Tolerations. God who hath so honoured them with eminent Wisdom in all other things, will not suffer them to cast both his, and their Honour in the dust of perpetual Infamy, do what they can; nor shall those who have spent so great a part of their substance in redeeming their Civil Liberties from Usurpation, lose all that remains in enthralling their spiritual Liberty by Toleration.

DOCUMENT 4

THE MARYLAND TOLERATION ACT, 1649

The Maryland Toleration Act did not bring complete religious freedom, as is so often assumed, and as a reading of this document will quickly prove. Nor did it come about because of a profound humanistic conviction on the part of Lord Baltimore, the Maryland proprietor. The act was a pragmatic solution to a serious problem. The Catholics in originally Catholic Maryland had become a minority of the population although still powerful politically. They were in great danger of being ill-treated by the Protestant majority. The Toleration Act, it was believed, was a way of providing protection for Catholics while at the same time representing a nod in the direction of the English government, which in 1649 and for a dozen years thereafter was firmly under the control of the English Puritans.

Nonetheless, the document is important because it did provide modest although impermanent protection for Catholic Marylanders and set a precedent to which others could refer. Despite Baltimore's Catholic background and his desire to use Maryland as a refuge for Catholics persecuted elsewhere, the Catholic Church never became the established church. In the eighteenth century this distinction was given to the Church of England.

An Act Concerning Religion.

Forasmuch as in a well governed and Christian Common Weath matters concerning Religion and the honor of God ought in the first place to bee taken, into serious consideracion and endeavoured to bee settled, Be it therefore ordered and enacted by the Right Honourable Cecilius Lord Baron of Baltemore absolute Lord and Proprietary of this Province with the advise and consent of this Generall Assembly:

That whatsoever person or persons within this Province and the Islands thereunto belonging shall from henceforth blaspheme God, that is Curse him, or deny our Saviour Jesus Christ to bee the sonne of God, or shall deny the holy Trinity the father sonne and holy Ghost, or the Godhead of any of the said Three persons of the Trinity or the Unity of the Godhead, or shall use or utter any reproachfull Speeches, words or language concerning the said Holy Trinity, or any of the said three persons thereof, shalbe punished with death and confiscation or forfeiture of all his or her lands and goods to the Lord Proprietary and his heires.

And bee it also Enacted by the Authority and with the advise and assent aforesaid, That whatsoever person or persons shall from henceforth use or utter any reproachfull words or Speeches concerning the blessed Virgin Mary the Mother of our Saviour or the holy Apostles or Evangelists or any of them shall in such case for the first offence forfeit to the said Lord Proprietary and his heirs Lords and Proprietaries of this Province the summe of five pound Sterling or the value thereof to be Levyed on the goods and chattells of every such person soe offending, but in case such Offender or Offenders, shall not then have goods and chattells sufficient for the satisfyeing of such forfeiture, or that the same bee not otherwise speedily satisfyed that then such Offender or Offenders shalbe publiquely whipt and bee imprisoned during the pleasure of the Lord Proprietary or the Lieutenant or cheife Governor of this Province for the time being. And that every such Offender or Offenders for every second offence shall forfeit tenne pound sterling or the value thereof to bee levyed as aforesaid, or in case such offender or Offenders shall not then have goods and chattells within this Province sufficient for that purpose then to bee publiquely and severely whipt and imprisoned as before is expressed. And that every person or persons before mentioned offending herein the third time, shall for such third Offence forfeit all his lands and Goods and bee for ever banished and expelled out of this Province.

And be it also further Enacted by the same authority advise and assent that whatsoever person or persons shall from henceforth uppon any occasion of Offence or otherwise in a reproachful manner or Way declare call or denominate any person or persons whatsoever inhabiting, residing, traffiqueing, trading or comerceing within this Province or within any the Ports, Harbors, Creeks or Havens to the same belonging an heritick, Scismatick, Idolator, puritan, Independant, Prespiterian popish prest, Jesuite, Jesuited papist, Lutheran, Calvenist, Anabaptist, Brownist, Antinomian, Barrowist, Roundhead, Separatist, or any other name or terme in a reproachfull manner relating to matter of Religion shall for every such Offence forfeit and loose the somme of tenne shillings sterling or the value thereof to bee levyed on the goods and chattells of every such Offender and Offenders, the one half thereof to be forfeited and paid unto the person and persons of whom such reproachfull words are or shalbe spoken or uttered, and the other half thereof to the Lord Proprietary and his heires Lords and Proprietaries of this Province. But if such person or persons who shall at any time utter or speake any such reproachfull words or Language shall not have Goods or Chattells sufficient and overt within this Province to bee taken to satisfie the penalty aforesaid or that the same bee not otherwise speedily satisfyed, that then the person or persons soe offending shalbe publickly whipt, and shall suffer imprisonment without baile or maineprise [bail] untill hee, shee or they respectively shall satisfy the party soe offended or greived by such reproachfull Language by asking him or her respectively forgivenes publiquely for such his Offence before the Magistrate or cheife Officer or Officers of the Towne or place where such Offence shalbe given.

And be it further likewise Enacted by the Authority and consent aforesaid That every person and persons within this Province that shall at any time hereafter prophane the Sabbath or Lords day called Sunday by frequent swearing, drunkennes or by any uncivill or disorderly recreacion, or by working on that day when absolute necessity doth not require it shall for every such first offence forfeit 2s 6d sterling or the value thereof, and for the second offence 5s sterling or the value thereof, and for the third offence and soe for every time he shall offend in like manner afterwards 10s sterling or the value thereof. And in case such offender and offenders shall not have sufficient goods or chattells within this Province to satisfy any of the said Penalties respectively hereby imposed for prophaning the Sabbath or Lords day called Sunday as aforesaid, That in Every such case the partie soe offending shall for the first and second offence in that kinde be imprisoned till hee or shee shall publickly in open Court before the cheife Commander Judge or Magistrate, of that County Towne or precinct where such offence shalbe committed acknowledg the Scandall and offence he hath in that respect given against God and the good and civill Governement of this Province, And for the third offence and for every time after shall also bee publickly whipt.

And whereas the inforceing of the conscience in matters of Religion hath frequently fallen out to be of dangerous Consequence in those commonwealthes where it hath been practised, And for the more quiett and peaceable governement of this Province, and the better to preserve mutuall Love and amity amongst the Inhabitants thereof, Be it Therefore also by the Lord Proprietary with the advise and consent of this Assembly Ordeyned and enacted (except as in this present Act is before Declared and sett forth) that noe person or persons whatsoever within this Province, or the Islands, Ports, Harbors, Creekes, or havens thereunto belonging professing to beleive in Jesus Christ, shall from henceforth bee any waies troubled, Molested or discountenanced for or in respect of his or her religion nor in the free exercise thereof within this Province or the Islands thereunto belonging nor any way compelled to the beleife or exercise of any other Re-

ligion against his or her consent, soe as they be not un-
faithfull to the Lord Proprietary, or molest or conspire
against the civill Governement established or to bee established in this Province under him or his heires. And that
all and every person and persons that shall presume Contrary to this Act and the true intent and meaning thereof
directly or indirectly either in person or estate willfully to
wrong disturbe trouble or molest any person whatsoever
within this Province professing to beleive in Jesus Christ
for or in respect of his or her religion or the free exercise
thereof within this Province other than is provided for in
this Act that such person or persons soe offending, shalbe
compelled to pay trebble damages to the party soe wronged
or molested, and for every such offence shall also forfeit
20s sterling in money or the value thereof, half thereof
for the use of the Lord Proprietary, and his heires Lords
and Proprietaries of this Province, and the other half for
the use of the party soe wronged or molested as aforesaid, Or if the partie soe offending as aforesaid shall refuse
or bee unable to recompense the party soe wronged, or to
satisfy such fyne or forfeiture, then such Offender shalbe
severely punished by publick whipping and imprisonment
during the pleasure of the Lord Proprietary, or his Lieutenant or cheife Governor of this Province for the tyme
being without baile or maineprise.

And bee it further alsoe Enacted by the authority
and consent aforesaid That the Sheriff or other Officer or
Officers from time to time to bee appointed and authorized
for that purpose, of the County Towne or precinct where
every particular offence in this present Act conteyned shall
happen at any time to bee committed and whereupon there
is hereby a forfeiture fyne or penalty imposed shall from
time to time distraine and seise the goods and estate of
every such person soe offending as aforesaid against this
present Act or any part thereof, and sell the same or any
part thereof for the full satisfaccion of such forfeiture,
fine, or penalty as aforesaid, Restoring unto the partie soe
offending the Remainder or overplus of the said goods or
estate after such satisfaccion soe made as aforesaid.

The freemen have assented.

DOCUMENT 5

SAMUEL DAVIES, LETTER TO REVEREND DOCTOR DODDRIDGE,
2 OCTOBER 1750

Samuel Davies was a notable Presbyterian minister, trained at the College of New Jersey, who gained a large and devoted following in upcountry Virginia. In Virginia, where the Anglican Church was the established church, dissenting sects required a special license from the Burgesses. As his letter indicates, Davies who had a license to serve several congregations was chafing to enlarge the dissenter church in Virginia. In his argument, he appeals to the English Toleration Act of 1689. Anglican clergymen in the colony submitted petitions to the Bishop of London opposing Davies. The Bishop, interestingly enough, when asked by partisans to intervene, responded: "But give me leave to set you right in one thing, and to tell you that my name neither is or can be used to any such purpose. The Bishop of London and his Commissarys have no such power in the plantations; and I believe they never desired to have it, so that if there be any ground for such complaint, the civil Government only is concerned."

The Church of England has been established in this Colony since its first plantation and there were not above four or five Dissenters that I know of within a hundred miles of this till about six years ago. Religion, alas! was just expiring and a strict form of Godliness was very rare. The Clergy were generally degenerated from the Calvinistical articles of their own Church and careless about strengthening the things which remained and were ready to die (and many of the Laiety were extremely corrupted in their principles and manner). I am sorry Sir that I have occasion to give an account that may so much as seem to be invidious; but I do it to exalt the rich Grace of God which pitied us in our low condition and not to asperse another denomination.

About six years ago it pleased the Lord to open the Eyes of one Sam Morice a Lay Man by reading some Old Authors particularly Luther on the Galatians, Flavel, Bunyan, etc., who thereupon endeavored to awaken his neighbours whom he saw like to perish in security round about him, by serious conversation with them and reading profitable Books (and these private means were effectual for conviction of Sundry), thus they spent their Sabbaths for some time not knowing that there was any Minister upon Earth now a days whose doctrine would agree with their sentiments (which I may observe by the way were generally Calvinistical tho' unhappyly corrupted in a few instances by an Antinomian tincture which has since been thoroughly cured), at length they had opportunity of inviting Mr. Robinson, a Member of our Synod and a painful, unwearied Minister of the Gospel who now rests from his labours, to preach amongst them and the Providence which gave them this opportunity was really remarkable, but I have not time to relate the circumstances of it; he preached but four week days successively among them and the number of his hearers was daily increased, some being excited to attend from a curiosity and an affectation of novelty and others by nobler motives. The word ran and was glorified. A General Concern about religion was spread through the neighbourhood, and some hundreds, I believe, were brought anxiously to enquire what shall we do to be saved? Sundry of whom have since given good evidences that their concern has issued in a believing resignation of themselves to God through the Glorious Redeemer. After this they applied to our Synod for a Minister, though about 300 miles distant, but the number of our Ministers being not at all proportioned to our vacancies in many parts we would only send some of them to officiate amongst them for a few Sabbaths about once a year; till about two years ago when, as I observed, I was sent to take the pastoral charge of them. These transient labours of my Brethren were extensively blessed and when in their absence the people associated to read and pray, the Lord was in the midst of them, so that now there are seven Meeting Houses in and about this country where about six years ago there were not 7 Dissenters. The nearest of these Meeting houses are 12 or 15 Miles apart and at each of them large Congregations are wont to assemble who generally hear with eager attention, and tho' the Religious commotion is not so apparent now as formerly, yet the Son is still quickening whom He will and the prospect of success is encouraging. This supports me under the fatigue of my Ministration which seems unavoidable at present for the Number of our Ministers is so small and our vacancies in various parts so many that I have thought it my duty to take the seven Meeting houses under my Ministerial care.

I have also comfortable hope that Ethiopia will soon stretch out her hands unto God for a considerable number of Negroes have not only been proselyted to Christianity and baptized but seem to be the genuine seed of Abraham by Faith. There are as many as 1,000 of them in this colony, and some 100 of them are the property of my people. I have baptized about 40 of them in a year and a half, 7 or 8 of whom are admitted into full communion and partake of the Lord's Supper. I have also sundry catechumens who, I hope, will be added to the Church after farther instruction.

Sir, favour us with your prayers that we may see greater things than these for tho' the Lord has done great things for us, for which we are glad, and which I would mention with the warmest gratitude, yet I have cause to complain that my success at present is not equal to what the posture of affairs would seem to promise according to common observation, which I oftimes impute to my own unfitness to move in so large a sphere. If I am acquainted with the temper of my own mind I do not rejoice in the increase of our numbers as captures from the Established Church, and if I do, I am sure your generous spirit would abhor it. The Kingdom of God is not meat and drink, but righteousness and peace and joy in the Holy Ghost, and if Men are walking the Heavenly Road, it affords me but little uneasiness that they are not of my mind about every circumstance, and notions of things will not be wholly the same till we view them in light of celestial day, but if their journey with us be attended with a disposition to receive the truth as it is in Jesus, if the cause of it be a weariness of the Ministry of such as did not direct them what they should do to be saved and speak a word in season to their weary Souls, and if their general conduct be so happily changed as to argue a change of heart as well as of sentiment in lesser points, I think, Sir, it is matter of solid joy to the most Catholic spirit.

But it has been an unhappiness to lie under the odium of the Government and Clergy as incendiaries and promoters of Schism, and sundry measures have been and still are pursued to restrain and suppress us. Sundry of the people have been indicted and fined and tho' our side are willing to comply with the act of Toleration (as I have actually done), yet the Government, under a variety of Umbrages has endeavored to infringe upon my Liberties and to exclude my Brethren from settling here. It has been alleged that the act of tolleration does not extend to this Colony (tho' by the by our Legislature has expressly adopted it so far at least as to exempt Protestant Dissenters from penalty for absenting themselves from Church), and the Counsel have lately determined that a dissenting Minister has no right to more meeting houses than one, in consequence of which they have superseded a Licence granted by a County Court for an Eighth Meeting house amongst a number of people that live 20 or 30 Miles distant from the nearest of the seven Meeting houses formerly Licensed by the General Court, and I fear will confine me entirely to one; which will be an intolerable hardship to the people, as they are so dispersed that they can not convene at one place. I should be glad, Sir, to have your sentiments on this point, and particularly that you would inform me whether a dissenting Minister is tollerated with you to have more Meeting houses than one in case the bounds of his congregation require it.

The President of the Counsel lately informed me that he had written to the Bishop of London to lay the affair before the King and Council for advice. I can't charge his Honor with designed partiality but I have the utmost reason to conclude his representation is defective. I hope therefore, Dear Sir, you will use your interest in our behalf as far as your imperfect acquaintance with our affairs will permit.

To qualify you to interceed for us I would further observe, that we claim no other liberties than those granted by the act of toleration and those only upon our compliance with all its requirements that all our Ministers attest their Orthodoxy by subscribing the West-Minster Confession of Faith and Catechism at their Licensure and Ordination and such of the articles of the Church of England as that act imposes on us when we settle in this Colony; that we attest our Loyalty by taking the usual Oaths to His Majesty's person and Government, and by all other public and private methods that belong to our province; and that our very enemy don't pretend to impeach us of any practical immorality.

DOCUMENT 6

CONNECTICUT'S ACT TO REGULATE ABUSES AND TO CORRECT DISORDERS IN ECCLESIASTICAL AFFAIRS,
1742

In the eighteenth century, the Great Awakening, a sweeping and powerful religious revivalist movement which gained a popular and enthusiastic following among laymen and a few clergymen, challenged the established churches, calling them dead congregations preached to by dead men. The established churches responded by invoking the civil authority to curb the enthusiasm, particularly by placing a ban on itinerant clergy. This act declares, in effect, that the state itself is threatened if these piercing dissenting voices are permitted to be heard.

Whereas, this Assembly did by their act, made in the seventh year of the reign of her late Majesty Queen Anne, establish and confirm a confession of faith, and an agreement for ecclesiastical discipline, made at Saybrook, Anno

Domini 1708, by the Reverend Elders and [the] Messengers delegated by the churches in this Colony for that purpose; under which establishment his Majesty's subjects, inhabiting in this Colony, have enjoyed, great peace and quietness, until [till] of late sundry persons have been guilty of disorderly and irregular practices; whereupon this Assembly, in October last, did direct to the calling of a General Consociation, to sit at Guilford in November last, which said Consociation was convened accordingly; at which Convention it was endeavored to prevent the growing disorders amongst ministers that have been ordained or licensed by the Associations in this government to preach; and likewise to prevent divisions and disorders among the churches and ecclesiastical societies, settled by order of this Assembly; notwithstanding which, divers of the ministers, ordained as aforesaid, and others licensed to preach by some of the Associations allowed by law, have taken upon them, without any lawful call, to go into parishes immediately under the care of other ministers, and there to preach to and teach the people; and also sundry persons, some of whom are very illiterate, and have no ecclesiastical character or any authority whatsoever to preach or teach, have taken upon them publicly to teach and exhort the people in matters of religion, both as to doctrine and practice; which practices have a tendency to make divisions and contentions among the people in this Colony, and to destroy the ecclesiastical constitution established by the laws of this government, and likewise to hinder the growth and increase of vital piety and godliness in these churches, and also to introduce unqualified persons into the ministry; and more especially where one Association doth intermeddle with [the] affairs that by the platform and agreement abovesaid, made at Saybrook aforesaid, are properly within the province and jurisdiction of another Association; as by licensing persons to preach and ordaining ministers: Therefore,

Be it enacted by the Governor, Council, and Representatives in General Court assembled, and by the authority of the same, that if any ordained minister, or other person licensed as aforesaid to preach, shall enter into any parish not immediately under his charge, and shall there preach or exhort the people, shall be denied and secluded the benefit of any law of this Colony, made for the support and encouragement of the gospel ministry, except such ordained minister or licensed person shall be expressly invited and desired so to enter into such other parish, and there to preach and exhort the people, either by the settled minister and major part of the church in [of] said parish, or, in case there be no settled minister, then by the church or society within such parish.

And it is further enacted by the authority aforesaid, that if any Association of ministers shall undertake to examine or license any candidate for the gospel ministry, or assume to themselves the decision of any controversy, or as an Association to counsel or [and] advise in any affair that by the platform or agreement above mentioned [made at Saybrook aforesaid,] is properly within the province and jurisdiction of any other Association, then and in such case every member that shall be present in such Association, so licensing, deciding or counselling, shall be each and every of them denied and secluded the benefit of any law in this Colony, made for the support and encouragement of the gospel ministry.

And it is further enacted [by the authority aforesaid], that if any minister or ministers, contrary to the force, intent and meaning of this act, shall presume to preach in any parish not under his immediate care and charge, the minister of the parish where he shall so offend, or the civil authority, or any two of the committee of such parish, shall give information thereof in writing, under their hands, to the clerk of the parish, or society where such offending minister doth belong, which clerk shall receive such information, and lodge and keep the same on file in his office; and no Assistant or Justice of the Peace in this Colony shall sign any warrant for the collecting any minister's rate, without first receiving a certificate from the clerk of the society or parish where such rate is to be collected, that no such information as is above mentioned hath been received by him, or lodged in his office.

And it is further enacted [by the authority aforesaid], that if any person whatsoever, that is not a settled and ordained minister, shall go into any parish, and without the express desire and invitation of the settled minister of such parish, if any there be, and the major part of the church, or if there be no such settled minister, without the express desire of the church or congregation within such parish, publicly preach and exhort the people, shall for every such offence, upon complaint made thereof to any Assistant or Justice of the Peace, be bound to his peaceable and good behavior until the next County Court, in that county where the offence shall be committed, by said Assistant or Justice of the Peace, in the penal sum of one hundred pounds lawful money, that he or they will not again offend in like kind; and the said County Court may, if they see meet, further bind the person or persons offending as aforesaid to their peaceable and good behavior, during the pleasure of said Court.

And it is further enacted [by the authority aforesaid], that if any foreigner or stranger, that is not an inhabitant within this Colony, including as well such persons that have no ecclesiastical character or license to preach, as such as have received ordination or license to preach by any Association or Presbytery, shall presume to preach, teach or publicly [to] exhort, in any town or society within this Colony, without the desire and license of the settled minister and the major part of the church of said town or society, or at the call and desire of the church and inhabitants of such town or society, provided that it so happen that there is no settled minister there, that every such preacher, teacher or exhorter, shall be sent as a vagrant person, by warrant from any one Assistant or Justice of the Peace, from constable to constable, out of the bounds of this Colony.

A MEMORIAL OF SEVERAL AGGRIEVANCES AND OPPRESSIONS OF HIS MAJESTY'S SUBJECTS IN THE COLONY OF NEW YORK IN AMERICA,

UNDATED, *ca.* 1750

Where population increases rapidly while the number of political representatives remains fixed, the proportionate relationship between representatives and people is quickly lost. The American colonies grew from a population of 250,000 in 1700 to 2 million in the 1760s. The middle colonies, which were settled late, grew most rapidly. The political issue of underrepresentation for many parts of these colonies was especially keen, although the issue arose sporadically at one time or another within each colony during the eighteenth century. In this document an underrepresented county of New York pleads for reapportionment.

When the Enemies of the Nation had, by their wicked Councils and trayterous Intreagues, brought our Nation to the very Brink of being swallowed up by Popish Superstition and Arbitrary Government, it pleased the Almighty God by his wonderful Omnipotence to bring in Peace and settle his Most Sacred Majesty, King George, upon the British Throne; and it is to be hoped, that his Subjects in distant Countries, and in particular those of the Colony of New-York, may in some Measure feel the Influence of his Happy Government, and be in due time relieved from all Oppressions. . . .

The Governor, Commissioners and Council took upon them the Legislative Power, and the people were governed by their Ordinances, until Governor Dungan came to be over them, then an Assembly were called, which Privilege was then declared to be the Peoples Right; and some

time after an Act of Assembly passed, That the Persons
to be Elected to sit as Representatives in the General Assembly from time to time, for the several Cities, Towns,
Counties, Shires, Divisions or Mannors of this Province,
and all Places within the same, shall be according to the
Proportion and Number hereafter expressed; that is to
say, For the City and County of New-York four, for the
County of Suffolk two, for Queens-County two, for
Kings-County two, for the County of Richmond two, for the
County of Westchester two, for the County of Ulster two,
for the County of Albany two, for the Mannor of Ransler-
wick one, and for Dukes County two, and as many more as
their Majesties, their Heirs and Successors shall think fit
to establish; That all Persons chosen as aforesaid, or the
major Part of them, shall be deemed and accounted the
Representatives of this Province in General Assembly, and
such Acts made by them, consented to by the Governor
and Counsel, shall be the Laws of the Province, until they
are disallowed by their Majesties, their Heirs and Successors, or expire by their own Limitation. And though by
this Act, their Majesties, their Heirs and Successors may
establish as many more, as they shall think fit: It is not
to be thought that our Most Gracious Sovereign King
George, will establish so many in such Places, that they
may live upon other Parts of the Government, and great
Injustice be done thereby, neither give Power to his Governor so to do; But that His Most Sacred Majesty would
have Justice done: Notwithstanding of late there hath
been Precepts issued out for choice of Representatives in
what Part and Places of the Government as he pleaseth.
So that notwithstanding the Law, they are raised to the
Number of Twenty-Five; and now the Minor Part of
the People in the Government have the Major Part of the
Assembly, and for their Interest Oppress a great Part of
the People, and they lie under great Disadvantages; as may
appear by the following Proportion of a 4000 *l.* Tax, and
several other Particulars upon the several Counties in the
Colony, here is an Account of the Men, Inhabitants in
each County, and their Representatives in the Assembly;
also the Quota of Tax in the same.

	Number of Men	Assembly Men	Quota of Tax		
			l.	*s.*	*d.*
In the City and County of New-York	1200	4	885	00	0
County of Albany, with Ranslerwick	540	4	175	10	0
Kings County	420	2	730	00	0
Queens County	1000	2	644	10	0
County of Suffolk	800	2	680	10	0
County of Ulster	620	2	311	10	0
County of Westchester	630	3	240	00	0
County of Richmond	350	2	226	13	4
Orange County	65	2	60	00	0
Dutchess County	60	2	46	06	8
	5685	25	4000	00	0

By this Plan it is evident, that the several Counties are
very unequally Represented, as well with Regard to the
Number of Inhabitants in each, as to the Taxes they pay;
And to this Disproportion of Assembly-Men is to be ascribed the unequal Taxing of the several Counties, without
respect to their Number of People, their Riches and Commerce. To evince this it will appear, that Kings-County,
Queens-County, and County of Suffolk, which contain 2220
Men, have only Six Representatives in Assembly, and are
taxed at 2055 *l.* whereas all the other Counties, having in
them 3465 Men, and so many Representatives that they
are taxed only at 1945 *l.* So that at this time there is up
Hudsons-River Ten Assembly-Men, in Albany, Ransler-
wick, Ulster, Orange and Dutchess Counties, and all those
Ten represent, do not pay in one Tax so much as one
County on the Island of Nassau, where they have but
two in each County. And for what Disbursements and
Services done on the same Island, for publick Service
there is very little if any thing paid them: When for
publick Disbursements and Services done up Hudsons-
River (do but give it the Name for their Majesties Service)
altho' it be to draw Trade to them, or to go to purchase
Land for themselves, it is brought to the Assembly to put
the Charge upon the Country; and for the most part they
get twice so much as others in part of the Government
would demand for the same Service, if it were for the
Publick. It is a Privilege to have an Assembly, if it were
as near as may be according to the Number of the People
in each County, that Justice and Right might be done:

But to have the Name and nothing of the Nature, is but a Snare to the greatest Part of the People in the Colony, and would be easier for them that there was not any Assembly, than to have such an One as endeavour to live upon their Neighbours, and not by them, and shall be called True and Loyal Subjects, complying to all Proposals for some Mens Advantage; when others, endeavoring to have Justice and Right done, and speak anything for Property and Liberty of the Subjects, shall be looked upon as Criminals. . . .

A great Part of the Aggrievances and Injustice done in the Colony may be ascribed to an unequal Proportion of Representatives; and if not redressed, may ruin the Colony. If there were an equal Proportion of them, as near as may be according to the Number of the People in each County, then they might in the strongest Manner unite Hearts of all the Subjects, and put an effectual End to all the Feuds and Animosities that have obstructed Prosperity in the Colony for a course of many Years. . . .

DOCUMENT 8

A PETITION FROM INHABITANTS OF PHILADELPHIA,
14 FEBRUARY 1752

Underrepresentation for the expanding frontier in the American colonies had its urban counterpart. Philadelphia was the fastest growing city in the British colonies. Yet its two representatives to the legislature in 1700, when it was little more than a rural village, remained two in 1750 when the city was estimated to have a population of 25,000. This inequality of representation provoked protests and petitions, of which this document is one.

A Petition from divers Inhabitants of the City of Philadelphia was presented to the House and read, setting forth, that at the first Settlement of this Province, the worthy Founder wisely intended to give every Part of the Inhabitants a Share in the legislative Government thereof, agreeable to natural Equity; that in the Infancy of the said City, when the Number and Wealth of its Inhabitants were small, compared with the Counties, and its foreign Trade very inconsiderable, two Representatives might then be deemed near a Proportion; but since by the great Increase of the Inhabitants, and Settlement of Merchants and Artificers, the Trade of the Province has chiefly centered in the said City, and the Advantage of its Commerce and Navigation being more extensive and important, they humbly conceive a considerable Addition to the Number of its Representatives both equitable and necessary; that it is evident since the late Division of Counties, and in Consequence an additional Number of County Members, how unequally the said City, being the Metropolis of the Province, is represented by two Members only, and how much its equitable Share in Government is diminished; and therefore praying this House would grant them Relief in the Premises, by making such an Addition to the Number of Representatives for the said City, as they in their Wisdom shall judge reasonable.

Ordered to lie on the Table.

DOCUMENT 9

ROYAL INSTRUCTIONS TO THE GOVERNORS OF THE COLONIES FORBIDDING ALTERATION IN REPRESENTATION, 24 JULY 1767

Almost all internal political issues ultimately became the object of imperial attention. Whereas representation, broadly conceived, was considered by the colonials as within their authority, the Crown, by injecting itself into this crucial issue, magnified it into imperial proportions with intercolonial and intracolonial undertones.

Additional Instruction to Our trusty and Wellbeloved

Lord William Campbell	Governor of Nova Scotia
John Wentworth Esquire	Governor of New Hampshire
Sir Henry Moore	Governor of New York
William Franklin Esquire	Governor of New Jersey
Sir Jeffery Amherst	Governor of Virginia
John Eliot Esquire	Governor of West Florida
Sir William Trelawney	Governor of Jamaica
William Woodley Esquire	Governor of Leeward Islands
William Spry Esquire	Governor of Barbados
George S. Bruere Esquire	Governor of Bermuda
William Shirley Esquire	Governor of Bahama
Robert Melville Esquire	Governor of Granada

Whereas Laws have at several times been passed in many of Our Colonies and Plantation in America, by which certain Parishes and Districts have been empowered and Authorized to send Representatives to the General Assemblies of the respective Colonies in which the said Parishes and Districts lie, and sundry other Regulations have been introduced by those Laws relative to the said Assemblies; It is Our Will and Pleasure, and We do hereby require and command that you do not upon any pretence whatever give your assent to any Law or Laws to be passed in Our [Colony, Province, Island] under your Government, by which the number of the Assembly shall be enlarged or diminished the duration of it ascertained, the qualifications of the Electors, or the Elected, fixed or altered or by which any Regulations shall be established with respect thereto, inconsistent with Our Instructions to you Our Governor, as prejudicial to that Right or Authority which you derive from us in virtue of Our Royal Commission and Instructions.

DOCUMENT 10

REMONSTRANCE OF JOHN DANIELL, JOHN YERWORTH, GEORGE HESKETT, JOHN SCOTT, AND DAVID BROWN . . . SHIP CARPENTERS,
25 JANUARY 1744

On January 21, 1744, a petition was submitted to the South Carolina Commons House of Assembly by Andrew Ruck and other shipwrights, complaining that blacks in great numbers were being employed in the repair of ships. This petition and the response to it reveal one aspect of the internal political-economic issue of slavery. Specifically, the Ruck petition stated: "That there were such a Number of Negro Men chiefly employed in mending, repairing and caulking of Ships, other Vessels and Boats, and working at the Shipwright's Trade and Business in this Town, Harbor and other Places near the same, that the Petitioners, who were white Persons, and had served their Times to the Trade of a Shipwright, could meet with little or no Work to do, and that themselves and their Families were reduced to Poverty, and should be obliged to leave the Province or run the Risque of starving if they were not relieved, and met with some Encouragement for the future. And that no white Man of the same Trade could upon his Arrival here expect to meet with any Encouragement to settle, or go get any Work at his Business. And therefore humbly praying that his Excellency and their Honours would be pleased to take the Premises into Consideration, and to grant them such Relief therein, as to their Excellency and Honours in their Great Wisdom and Goodness should seem meet."

Then the Remonstrance of John Daniell, John Yerworth, George Heskett, John Scott and David Brown was read, setting forth that the Remonstrants were by Trade

Ship Carpenters, Inhabitants of Charles Town, who, by a long industrious Prosecution of their Trade, had from Time to Time been enabled to make Purchases of several Negro Slaves. That, with great Care and Pains, they had trained up those Slaves to be useful to them in the Exercise of their Trade, and to be necessary for the Support of them and their Families, when by Age or Infirmity they became incapable of Labor. That Complaint had been lately made to his Excellency and to their Honours, by Andrew Ruck in behalf of himself and sundry other Shipwrights in Charles Town, "that by Reason of the frequent Employment of such Slaves they could meet with no Work nor Encouragement, and that they and their Families were thereby reduced to Poverty, and must leave the Province or run a Risque of starving." That they, the said Remonstrants (without anywise remarking how far their private Properties were concerned in this Matter, or how far they were secured in the Use of their Slaves by the Laws of the Land, leaving that to the Consideration of his Excellency and their Honours) begged Leave, only by the Evidence of a few Facts, to discover unto them that the above Complaint was in itself altogether without Foundation; that the Use of their Slaves apparently had been, and in all Probability would be, for the Interest of his Majesty and of this Province; and that those Complainants were wanting in Nothing to maintain themselves and their Families with as much Credit as the Remonstrants had done, but Industry and a more frugal Way of Life.

And that the Facts are as follows, on the seventh Day of March 1741/2, Captain Thomas Frankland, before his Entry on his Station at New Providence, had Occasion to refit and new mast his Majesty's Ship the Rose; and for that Purpose applied to all the Ship Carpenters of this Place, but that notwithstanding his earnest Sollicitations, and large Offers of Reward, he could procure but one Man. And that if any others went on board they were compelled thereto by his Honour the Lieutenant Governour. That, in the Month of September last, a Survey was ordered on the Bottom of his Majesty's Sloop the Spy, and it was found necessary by the Surveyors to shift

many of her Planks. Captain Newnham applied himself
to John Daniell to procure as many white Men Carpenters
as possible (Spanish Privateers being then upon the Coast)
but not more than one white Man could be got. In October
last Captain Charles Hardy was under the same Necessity
with Captain Newnham, and met with the like Difficulty
in obtaining white Men, for not one of all those who now
complain for Want of Work could, by any Means, be
then procured to work, except one John Thompson. That
on the first Day of December, one thousand seven hundred and thirty-nine, Mr. Benjamin Godin had immediate
Occasion to bring his Crop to Market, and, for that Purpose, wanted his Boat new bottomed; these Ship Carpenters, finding his urgent Necessity, refused to work at less
than fifty Shillings per Diem, which he was obliged to
give them. And, in July, one thousand seven hundred and
forty-one, the Honourable Edmond Atkin Esquire had his
Boat detained in Town upwards of ten Days, and also his
Sloop was detained three Weeks after she was cleared at
the Custom House for Want of the Work of a Carpenter,
although he offered any Rate and to pay the Money beforehand, and particularly to one Clase, one of the Complainants.

From all which it was evident that those Men had
no real Ground of Complaint for Want of Work. That
many Times they had refused to work at all, or, if obliged
to it by Necessity, only on extravagant Wages. That his
Majesty's Ships had been refitted and repaired only by the
Assistance of the Remonstrants' Slaves, and that without
those Slaves the worst Consequences might ensue. His
Majesty's Ships might remain by the Walls at the Discretion of the Complainants. Merchants who were bound
by Charter-party to load Vessels, within a limited Time,
might be drawn into heavy Demurrage. And no Planter
could be certain of performing his Agreement with the
Merchant, for the Delivery of his Rice, while such Men
had it in their Power to take or refuse Work upon their
own Terms. That the Remonstrants were fully convinced
that there was Business in this Place sufficient for three
Times the Number of Ship Carpenters. And that the Complaints that had been made to his Excellency and their

Honours, as aforesaid, was with no other View than to ingross the whole Trade into their own Hands, and thereby to have it in their Power to make their own Prices. All which the Remonstrants most humbly submit to the Consideration of his Excellency and their Honours.

DOCUMENT 11

[ANTHONY BENEZET], *INSTRUCTIONS REGARDING NEGRO-SLAVES ISSUED BY THE SOCIETY OF FRIENDS IN ITS MONTHLY MEETING,* 1754

Agitation against slavery was expressed as early as the late seventeenth century. The Society of Friends frequently led such protests. In 1671, George Fox counseled his fellow Friends to "train [the slaves] up in the fear of God." On another occasion, he declared: "Let me tell you it will doubtless be very acceptable to the Lord, if . . . masters of families here, would deal so with their servants, the negroes and blacks whom they have bought with their money, [as] to let them go free after they served faithfully a considerable term of years, be it thirty years after, more or less, and when they go and are made free, let them not go away empty handed."

Few men thought in terms of immediate and forthright emancipation. Nonetheless the seed was planted. Every Quaker group in America, including those living in the southern colonies, was asked to consider the manumission of its slaves. The following document, emanating from the Quaker seat, Philadelphia, reflects the conflict between moral condemnation and an established social institution, as well as the subdued language of the appeal for abolition.

"Dear Friends. It hath frequently been the concern of our Yearly Meeting, to testify their uneasiness and disunity with the importation and purchasing of negroes and other slaves, and to direct the overseers of the several meetings, to advise and deal with such as engage therein; and it hath likewise been the continued care of many weighty Friends, to press those that bear our name, to guard as much as possible, against being in any respect concerned in promoting the bondage of such unhappy people; yet as we have with sorrow to observe, that their number is of late increased amongst us, we have thought proper to make our advice and judgment more public, that none may plead ignorance of our principles therein; and also again earnestly exhort all, to avoid in any manner encouraging that practice, of making slaves of our fellow creatures.

"Now, dear Friends, if we continually bear in mind the royal law of 'doing to others as we would be done by,' we should never think of bereaving our fellow creatures of that valuable blessing, liberty, nor endure to grow rich by their bondage. To live in ease and plenty, by the toil of those, whom violence and cruelty have put in our power, is neither consistent with Christianity nor common justice; and we have good reason to believe, draws down the displeasure of heaven; it being a melancholy, but true reflection, that where slave keeping prevails, pure religion and sobriety decline; as it evidently tends to harden the heart, and render the soul less susceptible of that holy spirit of love, meekness and charity, which is the peculiar character of a true Christian. How then can we, who have been concerned to publish the gospel of universal love and peace among mankind, be so inconsistent with ourselves, as to purchase such who are prisoners of war, and thereby encourage this anti-Christian practice: and more especially as many of those poor creatures are stolen away, parents from children and children from parents; and others, who were in good circumstances in their native country, inhumanly torn from what they esteemed a happy situation, and compelled to toil in a state of slavery, too often extremely cruel. What dreadful scenes of murder and cruelty those barbarous ravages must occasion, in the country of those unhappy people, are too obvious to mention. Let us make their case our own, and consider

what we should think, and how we should feel, were we
in their circumstances. Remember our blessed Redeemer's
positive command, 'to do unto others as we would have
them to do unto us;' and that with what measure we meet,
it shall be measured to us again. 'And we intreat all to
examine, whether the purchasing of a negro, either born
here, or imported, doth not contribute to a further importation, and consequently to the upholding all the evils
above mentioned, and promoting man-stealing, the only
theft which by the Mosaic law was punished with death.
'He that stealeth a man and selleth him, or if he be found
in his hands, he shall surely be put to death.'—Exod.
xxi: 16.

"The characteristic and badge of a true Christian, is
love and good works. Our Saviour's whole life on earth,
was one continued exercise of them. 'Love one another,'
says he, 'as I have loved you.' How can we be said to
love our brethren, who bring, or for selfish ends, keep
them in bondage? Do we act consistent with this noble
principle, who lay such heavy burthens on our fellow
creatures? Do we consider that they are called, and sincerely desire that they may become heirs with us in glory;
and rejoice in the liberty of the sons of God, whilst we
are withholding from them the common liberties of mankind? Or can the Spirit of God, by which we have always
professed to be led, be the author of those oppressive and
unrighteous measures? Do we not thereby manifest, that
temporal interest hath more influence on our conduct
herein, than the dictates of that merciful, holy, and unerring Guide?

"And we likewise earnestly recommend to all who
have slaves, to be careful to come up in the performance
of their duty towards them; and to be particularly watchful over their own hearts; it being by sorrowful experience
remarkable, that custom, and a familiarity with evil of
any kind, have a tendency to bias the judgment, and
deprave the mind; and it is obvious, that the future welfare of these poor slaves who are now in bondage, is
generally too much disregarded by those who keep them.
If their daily task of labour be but fulfilled, little else perhaps is thought of; nay, even that which in others would

be looked upon with horror and detestation, is little regarded in them by their masters, such as the frequent
separation of husbands from wives, and wives from husbands, whereby they are tempted to break their marriage
covenants and live in adultery, in direct opposition to the
laws both of God and man. As we believe that Christ
died for all men, without respect of persons; how fearful
then ought we to be of engaging in what hath so natural
a tendency to lessen our humanity, and of suffering ourselves to be inured to the exercise of hard and cruel
measures, lest we thereby in any degree, lose our tender
and feeling sense of the miseries of our fellow creatures,
and become worse than those who have not believed.

"And dear Friends, you, who by inheritance, have
slaves born in your families, we beseech you to consider
them as souls committed to your trust, whom the Lord
will require at your hands; and who, as well as you, are
made partakers of the Spirit of Grace, and called to be
heirs of salvation. Let it be your constant care to watch
over them for good, instructing them in the fear of God,
and the knowledge of the gospel of Christ, that they may
answer the end of their creation, and God be glorified and
honoured by them, as well as by us; and so train them
up, that if you should come to behold their unhappy situation in the same light that many worthy men who are at
rest have done, and many of your brethren now do, and
should think it your duty to set them free, they may be
the more capable to make a proper use of their liberty.
Finally, brethren, we intreat you in the bowels of gospel
love, seriously to weigh the cause of detaining them in
bondage. If it be for your own private gain, or any other
motive than their good, it is much to be feared, that the
love of God and the influence of the Holy Spirit is not the
prevailing principle in you, and that your hearts are not
sufficiently redeemed from the world; which that you,
with ourselves, may more and more come to witness,
through the cleansing virtue of the holy spirit of Jesus
Christ, is our earnest desire."

DOCUMENT 12

THOMAS BACON'S SERMON TO NEGRO SLAVES,
1743

The impact of black slavery on American colonial life was pervasive, but as a factor in politics the slave was usually outside of specific political discussion. The role of the slave was assumed but unstated. The slaves, who, of course, had no political spokesman, were barred from the traditional American expectations of a better life, of progress, of working to improve one's status, with the result that the slave was alienated from the mainstream of American life. In the following document, a sermon preached by a Maryland minister, Thomas Bacon, to a group of slaves, reveals the white man's view of the slaves' political and social role and argues for a docile, obedient servant who willingly accepts all earthly burdens.

Knowing, that whatsoever good thing any man doeth, the same shall he receive of the Lord, whether he be bond or free.

My well-beloved Black Brethren and Sisters,

When you were last here, I endeavoured to shew you, That God made you and all the world, and that he made you and all mankind to serve him; That it is he who places every man in the station or rank which he holds in the world, making some kings, some masters and mistresses, some tradesmen and working people, and others servants and slaves. That every one of us is obliged to do the business he hath set us about, in that state or condition of life to which he hath been pleased to call us: And that whoever is doing his business quietly and honestly in the world, and living as a christian ought to do, is serving of God, though his condition be ever so low and mean; and will be as much taken notice of, and as highly favoured by God at the last day, as the greatest prince upon earth, for God is no respecter of persons. I also laid before you, that you ought to serve God for your own sakes, because you have souls to be saved, and if you should lose them, you are undone for ever: That every one who dies, and goes into another world, must go either to heaven or hell; and that there is no other way of escaping everlasting punishment in hell, or being eternally happy in heaven, but by serving God while he spares our life upon earth.

I then went on to shew you, what duty you owe to God in particular, that you ought to look upon him as your great and chief master, to whom you must one day answer for every thing you have done in this life: That he is always looking upon you, and taking notice of your behaviour, so that if you could deceive all the world, you cannot deceive God: That you ought to love God above all things, or else he will not love you, which would be the most dreadful thing that could happen to you: That if you love God sincerely, you will be afraid of doing any thing that is bad, because his holy spirit is grieved to see men destroy their souls by their wickedness: That if the love of God is not strong enough to keep you from doing what is bad, and vexing and offending him thereby, you ought, at least, to dread his terrible judgments; for that he is able, not only to destroy your bodies, and strike you dead in a moment, but also to cast both body and soul into hell, which will certainly be the portion of all such, as provoke him to anger by leading wicked lives: That you ought to worship God both in publick and in private: in publick, by coming to church as often as you have leave and opportunity; and in private, by praying to him for every thing you want, and giving him thanks for all his goodness to you, which you may easily do, when you are walking, or working, in the house, or in the field: That you ought to reverence and honour Almighty God, and keep from all cursing and swearing, or making any light, foolish, vain use of his great and holy name: And that you must keep from all lying, because God hates all such as tell lies, and will give them over to the devil, who is the father of all lies and liars.

In the next place I endeavoured to shew you, how

you ought to behave towards your masters and mistresses; and to make it plain to you, that as God himself hath set them over you here in the nature of his stewards or overseers, he expects you will do every thing for them, as you do for himself: That you must be obedient and subject to them in all things, and do whatever they order you to do, unless it should be some wicked thing which you know that God hath forbidden, in which case you are to refuse, but in no other: That you must not be eye-servants, that is, such as will be very busy in their masters presence, but very idle when their backs are turned: For your head master, Almighty God, is looking on you, and though you may escape being found out, or punished by your owners for it, yet you cannot deceive God, who will punish you severely in the next world for your deceitful dealing in this: That you must be faithful and honest to your masters and mistresses, not wasting their substance, or letting any thing, belonging to them, perish for want of your care; because that is next to stealing—for the master's loss is the same as if he had been robbed of it: And that you are to serve your owners with cheerfulness, respect, and humility, not grumbling, or giving any saucy answers, but doing your work with readiness, mildness, and good nature; because your sauciness and grumbling is not so much against your owners, as it is against God himself, who hath placed you in that service, and expects you will do the business of it as he hath commanded you. . . .

Now, to suit this rule to your particular circumstances; Suppose you were masters and mistresses, and had servants under you, would you not desire that your servants should do their business faithfully and honestly, as well when your back was turned, as while you were looking over them? Would you not expect that they should take notice of what you said to them? That they should behave themselves with respect towards you and yours, and be as careful of every thing belonging to you as you would be yourselves? You are servants, do therefore as you would wish to be done by, and you will both be good servants to your masters, and good servants to God, who requires this of you, and will reward you well for it, if you do it for the sake of conscience in obedience to his command.

Again, suppose that you were people of some substance, and had something of your own in the world, would you not desire to keep what you had? And that no body should take it from you, without your own consent, or hurt any thing belonging to you? If, then, you love your neighbor as yourself, or would do by others as you could wish they would do by you, you will learn to be honest and just towards all mankind, as well as to your masters and mistresses, and not steal, or take away any thing from any one, without his knowledge or consent: You will be as careful not to hurt any thing belonging to a neighbour, or to do any harm to his goods, his cattle, or his plantation, or to see it done by others, as you would be to hurt yourself, or any thing you had of your own: And will behave yourselves towards all mankind with the same honesty and good will, as you could wish they would do to you in the like case.

Your fellow servants are more particularly to be looked upon as your brethren: Your common station, as slaves, your complexion, and your marriages one among another in different families, make you nearer to each other than all the rest of the world, except your owners. And, poor and ignorant as you are, you may do much good, and prevent much harm, by behaving one towards another as brothers and sisters ought to do, and as God requires of you. And, considering all things, you must be miserable creatures indeed, if you will not be loving and affectionate, kind and honest among yourselves. But for fear you should mistake my meaning, I will first describe to you, what true love and affection is, and then endeavour to shew you in particular, how you ought to behave one towards another. . . .

Suppose any of you to have been wicked creatures, idle, drunken, swearing, thievish, lewd people; and being at length overtaken by the hand of God, and laid down on a painful, sick bed, without any hopes of recovery, with all the terrors of conscience about you, and nothing before you but death, and the fearful apprehensions of being miserable for ever—what a dreadful state of mind must you then be in! And what would you then give, that you had been blessed with a true friend in your former days, one that had so much real love for you, as to have warned you of your danger, and have hindered you, by his kind advice, from running such lengths of wickedness as you had done? And would you not then think, that such a friend would have been of more value to you, than the whole world? You have it in your power to be such true friends and lovers one to another: And though you can give but little bodily help, you can do what is far better, you can help each other on in the way towards heaven. You can, nay, you ought to check one another, when you see any thing doing amiss: You can encourage each other in doing what is right and good: You can pray together, and you can pray for one another: You can, on a Sunday evening, talk about the good advice you have heard in Church, and by telling it to such as could not be there, may do them much good, and, at the same time, by thus repeating these things, they will be the stronger fixed in your own memory, so as to be of lasting service to yourselves: You can, by a good example, prevent a great deal of wickedness and indecency, in your meetings and conversations one among another: And where you find that your sober, friendly advice, will do no good with them, you may terrify your companions from doing bad things, by threatening to complain of them; and by such means as these you may help to save their souls, and get a blessing upon yourselves and families. But, Oh, my brethren! I am grieved to say it, you are so far from doing this that I fear many of you rather encourage and help one another on in wickedness, and go hand in hand towards destruction, rather than strive to assist one another in the way to heaven! . . .

DOCUMENT 13

THE SECRETARY OF VIRGINIA REPORTS ON SELF-REGULATION WITHOUT BENEFIT OF LEGISLATION, 8 MAY 1682

Colonial regulation of economic activity was exercised by each colonial government. Wages and prices, for example, were regulated in seventeenth-century Massachusetts Bay by the General Court. Internal economic regulation did not often develop into a political issue over an extended period of time. Land laws in each colony were usually formulated by the ruling group which displayed just enough generosity in land distribution to avoid an open contest between the landed and the landless, the latter being relatively few in number.

Tobacco regulation, however, was a persistent political issue in Virginia because first, tobacco remained the principal money crop for a hundred years; second, the problems that arose in marketing tobacco were such that there was seldom universal agreement on the most effective legislation to establish proper marketing practices and to raise prices; and third, the regulation of tobacco affected the small and large planters alike.

In the following document, the secretary of the colony of Virginia reports to the Lords of Trade. Tobacco prices were so low that some planters favored using force to reduce production to obtain what they considered justice for their cause, higher prices for tobacco.

I have bad news to write. Not only is the peace of the Colony endangered by unruly and tumultuous persons, but at present it is suffering much from a combination of many inhabitants of Gloucester county. They have entered into a resolution to force a law of their own wills that no tobacco should be planted this year. To effect this the more readily they began operations on the 1st of this month by cutting up their own plants, and thence proceeded from plantation to plantation, telling the planters that if they were unwilling to have their plants cut up they would create willingness in them by force. In an hour's time they destroy as many plants as would have employed twenty men for a whole summer to bring to perfection. These outrages were in progress near three days before the Lieutenant-Governor had any intelligence thereof. The Council, which was sitting in General Court at Jamestown, at once issued proclamations to restrain such proceedings, and, to make them the more effectual, sent Colonel Kemp, of the Gloucester Militia, a Councillor and a worthy gentleman, with orders to march with such a force of horse and foot as might be necessary to suppress the mutineers. The 5th instant he marched with a party of horse, came upon a party of two and twenty of the mutineers, surrounded them with his troops, and took every one of them in the very act of destroying plants. Two of the principals, incorrigible rogues, are committed, the rest submitting and giving assurance of good behaviour, were remitted. I hope that by this time other parties of the mutineers may have been reduced, though it is to be feared that the contagion will spread. We received news to-day that the county next adjoining, New Kent, had broken out into the like spoiling of plants, and have taken the same measure of sending the militia to suppress it. Lest the infection should spread further, orders have been issued to the commanders of the militia in each county to provide a party of horse to be in continual motion, by which vigilance we have some hope that the growth of the insurrection may be prevented. I should have no doubt of it, did I not know that the necessities of the inhabitants, owing to the low price of tobacco, have made them desperate, and caused them to resolve on a law of cessation of their own making. But it is to be feared that the mere destruction of tobacco plants will not satiate their rebellious appetites; if they increase, and find out the strength of their own arms, they will not keep themselves within bounds. . . .

DOCUMENT 14

LIEUTENANT-GOVERNOR SPOTSWOOD AND THE INTERNAL REGULATION OF TOBACCO, 29 DECEMBER 1713

Governor Spotswood, an able administrator and a loyal partisan of the Crown, attempted to use the genuine grievances of the planters to effect an end that he considered desirable: the establishment of a governor's political party, a court party. Many planters continued to find the marketing practices for tobacco chaotic and undesirable and the low prices an abomination. Raise the level of quality by inspection, urged Spotswood, send a better commodity, and thus receive a better price. Spotswood finally obtained the adoption of a law establishing tobacco inspection points throughout the waterways of Virginia. The Governor expected to appoint his favorites in the assembly to positions as tobacco inspectors, which would give him leverage, so he thought, to obtain from the Burgesses the laws he desired. But Spotswood miscalculated, because the electorate of Virginia voted out those who supported the Governor's plan, and in 1717 the tobacco inspection law was repealed.

I gave your Lordships an account in my last of some preparatory steps towards the Act herewith sent, for preventing frauds in the tobacco payments. After the many discouragements which that Trade laboured under, both here and in Great Britain, It was necessary to enquire from what Root so many Evils did proceed. This has been judged to be owing to the ill-management of Tobacco here, many people making it for no other end than to pay off Debts and levies, for which purpose they think it good enough how mean soever it be, and others making such a sort as several of the Out Port Traders in Great Britain most eagerly seek after (especially of late), and seeing

House Sweepings and the worst of Trash is a sort, too, which they come hither to purchase and that they have been known to pour Salt Water upon such Tobacco so soon as they have gotten it on board, it may be reasonably suspected if what they carry home rather diminishes than increases the dutys at the Custom House and serves for no other Use than Vile practices, whereby the Staple Commodity of this Country has been brought into Disesteem and the markets thereof entirely ruined in Europe.

This Law, therefore, by obliging all Planters to have their Tobacco viewed by a Sworn Officer in the manner your Lordships may see more fully from the several parts of the Act, has made provision against the exportation of all such Trash as is said to be allowed by the Customs House Officers in the Out Ports as damaged Tobacco and thereafter frequently re-exported without the benefit of the Draw-back, and thus it is hoped the reputation of Virginia Tobacco may be retrieved when none but such as is found to be worth paying the duty at home shall be sent to forreign markets. It has likewise very justly provided against the passing bad Tobacco in any manner of payments within this Colony, so that her Majesty's Quit Rents, several Officers' Salarys and all the Public credit will hereafter be raised by so much as is the difference between Trash and good Tobacco; for, as I have before remarked, it is the general notion of the Country that the worst sort is good enough for these purposes. Besides the convenient method that this Act establishes for the making all Payments by the Agent's notes, which are to pass like Bank-Bills, will give an opportunity to collect the quit rents at a cheaper Rate than hitherto they have been. The main design of the Port-Act, which was recommended to my Predecessor, Governor Nott, to endeavour to get passed, is, I presume, compassed by this Act, since that Ships will by means thereof be hereafter loaded in half the time they are now, and that the Collectors and Naval Officers may certainly know to a hogshead the Tobacco that is Shipt home to Great Britain, and to a Pound that which is exported for the Plantations.

What I have had at heart, and what I have had in a former Session in vain attempted, vizt., to make the Bene-fices of the Clergymen valuable and the collecting their Income more just and easy to them, to the end good and able Divines might reckon it worth their while to come over to Supply the Churches here, and that they might not be diverted from their Studys, as several now are, by running up and down their Parishes to gather in their Salary Tobacco—This, I say, is by this Act effectually Obtained.

Thereby, I have, in a great measure, I think, cleared the way for a Governor towards carrying any reasonable point in the House of Burgesses, for he will have in his disposal about forty Agencys, which one with another are likely to yield nigh 250 Pounds Per annum each; these, my intentions are to dispose of among the most considerable men of the Colony, and principally to gratify with a Place all the members of the Assembly who were for the bill. By this means the staple of Tobacco will have a better Security for its perpetual Establishment and constant Encouragement than any other Manufacture, and the Propositions of several Countys which frequently used to be presented to the House of Burgesses for the setting up other Manufactures, will not be so favourably heard in that House when the majority of its Members shall be engaged by their Interest to advance the making of Tobacco chiefly. Besides in aiming at this Law I had in view (for I must own my Self to be not only principally concerned in framing the Bill, but even from the beginning the Sole Author of the Scheme) to put a check to some dishonest courses in Tobacco payments which by use were grown so habitual and general that it was to be feared at long run there would scarce be found Men in Virginia who durst make a Law to prevent those Fraudulent dealings; and I was apprehensive of ill consequences if the Vulgar's Standard of Right and Wrong prevailed any longer, for there are a set of People whom all the meaner sort of Planters cry up for honest, for Lovers and Patriots of their Country, and for Friends to the Poor, and this general Character often sets them up for candidates in the Election Field (where the Votes and humours of the lowest Mob do at present decide who shall be the Representatives in Assembly), and also recommends them for Tobacco receivers to Merchants and Masters of Ships, who come hither to purchase that commodity. But

a few Years' Observation has made me perceive that the
Vulgar in these parts reckon him only the Honest Man who
inclines to favour their Interest. He is the lover of this
Country who in all Controversies justifies the Virginian,
and [in] all Dealings is ready to help him to overreach the
Forreigner; He is the Patriot who will not yield to whatever
the Government proposes, and can remain deaf to all
Arguments that are used for the raising of Money, and
lastly, him they call a poor man's Friend who always carrys
Stilliards to weigh to the needy Planter's advantage, and
who never judges his Tobacco to be Trash. Of this set of
People there was such a number in the lower House that it
was with some Address and great struggle the Bill was got
to pass there, for tho' their Understandings be not above
the level of their Electors, and that they could not advance
one solid Argument against it, yet they readily discovered
that this Bill was to cut them out of their Popular interest
and profitable way of living, and thereupon they opposed
it most violently with their Nays. Except this last sort of
Men with their Defendants, there are scarce any within this
Government but who rejoyce at this new Law, and your
Lordships may be assured that a very fair Score of benefits is opened to the People here when the whole Council
and all the Sencible Members of the lower House unanimously laboured to carry this Extraordinary point. I cannot foresee that any Objection can be made at home to this
Law, unless that some may possibly say that the navigation
will be lessened by not Shipping all the Tobacco which is
made, and that it seems to take of[f] some hands from
planting, who may perhaps fall upon the British manufactures. To this I answer, that it plainly appears by the Naval
Officers' Books, that of late years, ever since Trash has been
so abundantly exported to the ruine of the Markets in Europe, the number of Hogsheads shipt off has been less by
some Thousands, for it is well known here that the considerable Crop Masters who are able to Cloath their Familys
by what substance they happen to have beforehand in Great
Britain, will not drudge on with all their hands at Tobacco
when it does not yield a living price, but employ them in
other services and wait till the Market rises again; besides,
too, the natural consequences of this Act will be that Hogs-

heads will not exceed the lawful standard, that they will be less pressed, and that the Tobacco will be less stemmed, whereby the number of Tonns must increase. And as to the rest of the Objection, if it should prove true that any hands fall of [off] from Planting, 'tis evident enough they must be those of the Careless, idle planter, from whom the British Manufactures are in less danger than from the Careful, Industrious Planter, if he should be necessitated to take some other course to Cloath his Family than by making Tobacco. I have, My Lords, been the more perticular in my Observations upon this Act, because it is looked upon to be the most Extraordinary one that ever passed a Virginia Assembly, and such an one as those persons to whom I first communicated my thoughts, and to whom the Temper of these Assemblys are well known, believed I could never have compassed. I hope your Lordships will be so well satisfyed with the honest Design of it and the advantages which in all probability will arise thereby, that it will meet with your Lordships' approbation, so that it may be put in Execution according to the time it is to commence. . . .

DOCUMENT 15

RESPONSE TO THE TOBACCO ACT, 1729

The vigorous reaction against Spotswood's Tobacco Inspection Act, measured by the number in the assembly who failed reelection, did not end the problem. For the next dozen years regulation of tobacco production and marketing was under constant discussion. By 1729 a regulatory act was adopted to restrict the number of plants grown and to inspect the tobacco to be shipped out of Virginia. It stated that every tithable person—white males over 16 and male and female black slaves over 16—could, with minor exceptions, tend no more than 6,000 plants. Vestrymen in the parishes were to enforce the act in the months of June and July, the appropriate time in the tobacco growing season. Because, as the act stated, "many frauds are committed by false and promiscuous packing and by putting trash and bad Tobacco into bundles to the great prejudice of the trade of this colony," regulations were introduced specifying the proper procedure for packing the tobacco into hogsheads. Tobacco was also to be inspected before shipping.

The colony watched the experiment with hope but also with suspicion. Some rioting broke out in the Northern Neck of Virginia in defiance of the law. But many planters who originally opposed the law came around to support it as did Robert "King" Carter, who at first thought good tobacco was being destroyed. When prices rose, however, and the inspection was carried out without serious political overtones, he wrote in 1732: "The Country are wonderfully fond of the tobacco law. May God grant we find the good effects of it from the Tryal to relieve us out of the dismal circumstances we are under."

In this address by the Burgesses to Governor William Gooch, a popular leader, the assembly argues for continuance of the law despite the riots and tumults in isolated sections of the colony.

We His Majesty's most Loyal and Dutiful Subjects, the Representatives of the People of this Colony, now met in Assembly, do sincerely return You our Thanks, for Your kind Speech to the Council and this House; but more especially for the great Care and Pains You have taken, in Supporting the Act passed at our last Session, for Improving the Staple of Tobacco, against all the Opposition it has met with in Great Britain: Wherein we are surprised to find any There seeming to be affected with a greater Tenderness for the poor Planters, than the whole Legislature of this Colony, and accusing Our Body of a Design to oppress them; when no Hardship or Inconvenience can possibly be laid upon them, which will not be felt by Us, in a greater Degree: But it is Matter of great Consolation to us, that this Imputation has made no Impression upon His Sacred Majesty, whose Wisdom and Justice is very conspicuous, in leaving us to be justified by Experience: And we persuade ourselves, that, as the wretched and deplorable State of the Tobacco Trade, made it necessary for us to put it under some Regulation, no better Expedients can be proposed, than Destroying that which is not fit to be sold in any Market in the World, and Preventing by a careful Inspection, the many Frauds that have manifestly contributed to reduce that Commodity to so low a Price, as cannot defray the Expence of Making it: And we flatter ourselves, that all reasonable Men will be convinced, from the short Experience they have had of the Honesty and Impartiality of Those who are intrusted with the Execution of this Law, that these Ends will in great Measure be attained, and the Trade restored to such a Condition, as may at least enable us to live by it.

The late Tumults, which have been raised by an inconsiderable Number of ignorant, deluded People, who have dared to threaten the Government with open Violence, is to us a Subject of Contempt, as well as Abhorrence, and cannot turn us from our just Purposes, nor discourage us to hope for the Continuance of His Majesty's good Opinion of our Proceedings. Yet we cannot but acknowledge and approve Your Prudence in suffering the Offenders to attone for their Boldness by a peaceable and submissive Deportment, without undergoing any other Punishment than the Shame and Reproach of their own Misdoings.

And we do assure You, That we are so well disposed to give Satisfaction to every Body, in this important Business, that nothing shall be wanting, on our Parts, to amend whatever may appear the least Inconvenience, either to the People Here, or the Merchants in Great-Britain, and to remove all just Occasions of Complaint against any Part of the Law, which we desire so sincerely to cherish and support.

And, feeling we have hitherto succeeded very well in all our Consultations, by Your Assistance, and the Influence and Credit You have in England, we beg the Continuance of Your Affection, Zeal and Vigilance for the Good of this People, so happily conducted by Your wife and unexceptionable Administration.

Ordered, That the said Address be fairly transcribed,

and presented by the whole House: And that the Committee who prepared the same, so wait on the Governor, to know when he will be attended with it.

DOCUMENT 16

[DR. WILLIAM DOUGLASS], *A LETTER TO MERCHANT IN LONDON CONCERNING A LATE COMBINATION IN THE PROVINCE OF MASSACHUSETTS BAY . . . TO IMPOSE OR FORCE A PRIVATE-CURRENCY CALLED LAND-BANK MONEY,*
21 FEBRUARY 1740

In 1740, a group of Massachusetts men from a broad range of economic backgrounds—merchants, enterprisers, and farmers—incorporated a land bank. It became important in fact and as a symbol, because it implied that the colonials were empowered to control their own internal financial system.

Dr. William Douglass of Boston, an anti-paper money man, sternly opposed the Massachusetts Land Bank, although he did not disapprove of all banks. He based his position on the land bank on a critical appraisal of its possible inflationary consequences. Douglass' sharp criticism awakened English mercantile and imperial interests, and eventually the establishment of any colonial bank was forbidden. In this document, Douglass argues for the elimination of the land bank.

I have the favour of yours of 1st December per the *Bladen,* with Copies of the Reports of the Board of Trade and Plantations, and of the Committee of Council for Plantation Affairs; concerning our Land-Bank so called: I observe that having examined into the Nature of the Scheme, and of the refusal of the House of Representatives to pay any regard to the Governour's Message concerning the same; they approve of the Governour and Councils

Proceedings, and do declare that the said Scheme appears to them to be not only Illegal, but of dangerous Tendency; and must create great Confusion, and Interruption in Business, as well to the Traders in New-England, as in Great Britain; and in Order that the said Land-Bank may be as speedily and effectually suppressed as possible, they are pursuing Methods to put a Stop to the same, until such Time as the Legislature of Great Britain shall take the State of the Paper Currencies of all the Plantations into Consideration.

You desire a particular Account of this *monstrous* (as you call it) *Combination*, lately made, to evade Resolves of Parliament, and King's Instructions. . . .

The Land-Bank, or Manufactory Scheme (the designed Subject of this Letter), being a late Combination of a vast Multitude of necessitous, idle, and extravagant Persons; with all the Signs of a genuine Bubble; contrived to have what they call Money, at an easy Rate; and to pay their Debts in a precarious fallacious Kind of Bills, very ill, or not at all, secured; of no determined Value; bearing no Interest; not payable (the Possessor cannot oblige to an Acceptance) until after twenty Years, and being a very large Sum (equal to all the then provincial Bills of New-England) of Six hundred thousand Pounds, will, if not remedied, depreciate all Paper Currencies, that are not determined by a Silver Value, consequently prove a great Prejudice to private Property in the Province, and great Loss and Damage to the Merchants of Great-Britain, trading to New-England.

Your Surmise is groundless, That perhaps some of our Merchants, who have suffered much by depreciating publick Bills, have, jesuitically, and as it were behind the Curtain, prompted the unthinking Multitude, to a Scheme, running into unheard of Extremities of Sum, and Period; and at this critical Time, when all Paper Money is under the Censure of the Boards and Parliament of Great-Britain, on purpose to bring the Parliament under the Necessity of speedily and effectually suppressing Paper Money of all Kinds.

The Rise of this Scheme, was from a few evil-minded Men, contrived only for their own Benefit, and have admitted a great Multitude of Subscribers, by their Numbers to give it a Circulation, and to contribute towards indemnifying them against all Acts of Government. Its being contrived only for the Benefit of the Directors, appears by their Constitution.

1st, They are to be Directors in Perpetuity.

2dly, They are to have a Negative in all Resolves of general Meetings.

3dly, Their Sallaries, other Charges of Management, and their living sumptously, at Free-Cost, will amount to Two per cent per annum, of the original Stock; (the original South Sea Stock of Ten Millions was allowed only Eight thousand Pounds for Management, which is scarce One 12th per cent per annum). They design to convert Sixty thousand Pounds of the principal Stock into Trade, that they may have a greater Latitude of imposing upon the Partnership. The Bank of England, and all other well constituted Banks, are restricted from trading, that their Stock may remain good at home, ready to answer all Demands. Their ludicrous Pretence is, That since the Merchants will not sell them Goods for this worthless Money, they will import all sorts of Merchandise, for the Benefit of the Partnership: Their Directors cannot seriously pretend to understand Trade, only one of their Number is called Merchant, or rather a Factor for some Marooners or Logwood-Cutters, in the Bay of Honduras.

4thly, They alter the Articles of Partnership at Pleasure, without Consent of a general Meeting, pretending, (contrary to all good Regulation) that private Consent of the Members, without Deliberation or Debate, is sufficient; this is the Reason of their Scheme being so often botched: Their Scheme now sent to you, is their last, as it stands in the County Register; it was refused a Record in the Secretary's Office: How soon it may be altered, we know not.

5thly, The County Registers being lately searched by Order of the Governour and Council, to find out the civil and military Officers, guilty in this Combination; It was discovered, That the principal Projectors, or Bubblers, the Directors, etc., had given no Security to the Partnership for their good Management, and for their Quota of this Money, taken up some Months since: The sham Reason

they give, of being very busy; is not only weak, but fully
discovers the Cheat and Imposition; because in all well
ordered honest Schemes, the Directors, or Managers, are
the first who give Security.

You desire to know the Nature of our landed Interest,
which by these evil-designing Men, is set up in competition
with the trading Interest. In Great-Britain, the Landed-
Interest consists generally of Gentlemen very Rich, with
valuable Rent-Rolls; Our Freeholders generally are labouring Men, who earn less, and fare worse, than many in
Boston, and without any Rent-Rolls. Indulge me here, to
cast a Vail, over the Nakedness of our Country: This
Country seems designed by Nature for Trade, not for Produce: We Import Provisions at much easier Rates from the
Southern Provinces, than we can afford to raise them here.
I am concerned in Lands, and therefore can have no sinister End in disparaging of them. On the other side, Our
Trade is not Inferiour to that of any of his Majesty's Plan-
tations; and Our Navigation much exceeds any of them. The
Truth is shortly this; The Debtor part of the Country
(which is vastly the most numerous) are contriving to
baulk their Creditors by reducing the Denominations of
Money (by their huge and ill-secured Emissions) to a
small or no Value; that they who have laudably acquired
Fortunes by Industry and Frugality, may reap no Benefit
thereof, but be upon a level with the Idle and Extravagant:
We all have learnt by Experience that large Emissions with
distant Periods, have sunk a great Part of Debts, without
any Consideration.

The Projectors gave to this *Bubble* the specious Name
of, *A Bank*—It has not the least Affinity to Banking. Banking is issuing of Cash-Notes, payable upon Demand: or
Merchants having lodged their Cash, the Bank transfers
Cash from one Merchant's Folio, to that of another, when
required.

1st, This Sham-Bank has no Stock in their Treasury;
and the Face of their Bills promising to accept them for
Stock in the Treasury is an arrant Bubble: It is true,
that for some short Time the Directors decoyed some Gra-
ziers and Hog-Drivers, to part with their Provisions for
this their Land-Bank Money, but have shipped it off in

Trade for the Profit of the Directors, and perhaps to help to indemnify themselves when obliged to make good the Bills by them signed.

2dly, These Bills, tho' carrying no Interest, cannot make an effectual Demand of Acceptance till after Twenty Years, and then not payable in current Cash, but in Goods of an Arbitrary Assortment and Value.

3dly, As Produce and Manufacture are more valuable than depreciating Bills; all Payments of the Partnership of Interest, and Parts of Principal, will be in these Bills; and consequently no Produce, or Manufacture, will be found in their Treasury.

4thly, Being no Body-Corporate, they are under no Limitation: The Directors, who are for this very Purpose the Signers, may and will emit Bills in *indefinitum*, or until at length their Value become near equal to the Charge of manufacturing them.

5thly, If we can suppose their Board of Bill-Makers to be honest-Men, and that in Conscience (they having no other Check but Conscience) they emit no more than according to their first Articles, as they have no exclusive Patent, any other Number of desperate Men may follow the same Money-making Trade, and Bills may multiply as in the former Case.

6thly, In other Countries, the Opulent, the Honest, the Men of Credit, become Bankers; here the Indigent, the Debtors, the Fraudulent, set up for Bankers: A Bank of a Numerous, but poor People, who pretend to circulate 600,000 *l.* without any Stock.

7thly, To compleat the Farce, the Securities for circulating and paying off these Bills, are within themselves, and may be stifled at Pleasure. . . .

The Projectors and Managers of this Scheme have Debauched the Minds of the People, by Instilling unto them some pernicious Principles, destructive of all Society, and good Government:

1st, That common Consent, or the Humour of the Multitude, ought to be the *Ratio Ultima* in every Thing and particularly in Currencies; whereas not only according to the Constitution of Great-Britain, but of all polite Governments, Money or Currencies are the Prerogative of the

Sovereigns, and have followed the universal Custom of Merchants, whereby Silver from its own natural Qualifications, could not avoid becoming the universal Medium of Trade. If we may suppose a Country entirely separated from the trading Part of the World, common Consent may admit of any Thing for a Currency, according to the Humour, or Profit of the Projectors; but this will fluctuate from one thing to another, until at length the most proper Material obtain a permanent Consent: It is doubtless a high Misdemeanour to assert strenuously, the Priviledge of the People, to emit and pass any Thing as a Currency, in defiance, of the King's prerogative of Currencys. Middleton, a neighbouring Town, has lately unanimously voted, that This Bank-Money shall be received as Cash for Town-Rates.

2dly, That every Landed Man, even to the mortgaging of his last Acre, has a Right to make Money: This is a most destructive and wicked Principle, the Security and Bulwark of a Country, are these People who have valuable Possessions and Effects to loose; whereas they who are much in Debt, become desperate, and bad Subjects, and have nothing to hinder them from relinquishing their Country to the first Invader.

3dly, That the Industrious Merchants, and frugal monied Men, are the Bone of a Country; because they expect their Debts and Dues to be honestly paid: Whereas a Country without Trade is of little Value, and would soon return to its primitive Waste. People of Genius for Trade grow rich by the Labour of Peasants, and the Peasants or Labourers happy by being employed: This Province noted for Trade would soon become a Habitation of rude Rusticks.

4thly, To value themselves as being formidable by their Numbers, Two Thousand Principals, as they publish, and many Thousand Abettors: This is Ruffian like, by Superiority of Numbers, to endeavour to make honest People buy the Rabbit. Such dangerous bare-faced Combinations, are not to be connived at in Government; they openly threaten, that in the next Assembly, no Body shall be a Representative, or of the Council, but those who are Principals or Abettors in this Scheme; and thus have formed an *Imperium in imperio*. If this Wickedness of

Combinations, under the Name of Banking, should spread into our neighbouring Charter Governments (in Providence of Rhode-Island they have gone some Lengths in it) where all the Negatives, or Branches of the Legislature are elective by the People; they would become Masters in all Affairs of Legislature and Government; their Dependance upon and Subjection to Great-Britain, would soon vanish. At this Time, in Neglect or Contempt of the Resolves of Parliament, and subsequent King's Instructions, Connecticut have emitted One hundred and eight thousand Pounds, and Rhode Island, Eighty thousand Pounds, Province Bills.

5thly, By the inclosed News-Papers, printed in Boston, you may see, and we here upon the Spott do daily hear, how the Managers spirit the People to Mutiny, Sedition, and Riots: One gives it for Law, That no Orders from the Boards at Whitehall, nor Acts of Parliament, can put a Stop to their Proceedings; Others say, We shall humble the proud Merchants; That if the Merchants will not receive these Bills in Pay, they must blame themselves for any Outrages that may happen; That We had as good perish by the Sword as by Famine, that is, by being Dragooned, as by Want of Money; That upon a French Invasion, if we submit, We cannot be worse than at present; that is poor and in Debt; because the Government or private Combinations will not let us have Paper Money, to the Ruin of the good People of the Province.

Upon desire to know what has been done by the Government of the Province towards their Suppression: One of the Negatives, I mean the House of Representatives, stand out; so that the Legislature can do nothing. The Governour and Council have acted with much Prudence and Fortitude; and are dismissing all Officers, Civil and Military, of their Appointment, who are concerned in this Combination; only the Chairman of the Directors, and the Indorser, their Commissions or Warrants being from Great-Britain, cannot be dismissed; but their Dismission, by their Constituents at home, may be expected.

You take the Liberty to surmise, a Liberty which you would not allow to me:

1st, That for the present, the most summary Way of proceeding against this Combination, would be, To send for the Treasurer, Directors, and Indorser, to Great-Britain, by a Messenger, with a Secretary of State's Warrant, to bring them upon Examination, concerning this high Crime and Misdemeanour: But this would ruin them in their small Fortunes, and render them less capable to satisfy the Possessors of the Bills, when returned upon them.

2dly, That the Mortgages of Lands in the Partnership cannot be sued out by the Managers; because there was no valuable Consideration received. Thus the Possessors having only the Estates of the Signers liable, would not receive above Two Shillings in the Pound.

3dly, That the Possessors having had sufficient Warning from the Government, can claim none of their Compassion.

We hope that the Government, who are the Parents and Guardians of the People, will act, as natural Parents do with their Children, guilty of some Follies, after repeated Admonition.

In all Bubbles, Combinations, etc., the Guilt of the Projectors and Managers is from a corrupt Principle; but the Error in their Followers, the Multitude, is only from a Mistake in Judgment.

I have now given you my Thoughts of this singular Piece of Iniquity, in the most impartial Manner I am able, and hope it will be satisfactory to you, assuring you I am, with all possible Respect. . . .

DOCUMENT 17

(ANONYMOUS), *A LETTER TO THE MERCHANT IN LONDON TO WHOM IS DIRECTED A PRINTED LETTER RELATING TO THE MANUFACTORY UNDERTAKING,* 27 FEBRUARY 1740

This document responds point by point to Dr. William Douglass' censorious critique of the land bank. In addition to a specific response to the questions raised by Douglass, the author addresses a more profound issue, namely, the constitutional issue of the bank as it affected the Crown and the colonies.

I take the Freedom to send you and them the following Remarks on that Author's Performance, whereby it will appear . . . how industrious some among us . . . is to represent the said Manufactory Scheme, in odious Colours, and thereby excite to Resentment against it, which they could never do, if they treated it with Truth, and related the Facts as they really are. . . .

Next he comes to the Manufactory Scheme, the main Subject of his Letter, as he says. And here, I doubt not, Sir, but the hard Names, scurrilous Epithets, extravagant Glosses, and Ungentlemanly Language, with many plain and obvious Contradictions (Things never needed in a good Cause), which this Author in his unconnected Ramble over this Scheme, and its Undertakers, has used, will induce you to give little Credit to his Performance; yet give me Leave Sir, for the more full discovery of this Hard-Mouthed Author, and for clearing the Scheme, and its Promoters, from his scandalous Reflections (tho' I confess one can hardly come so near him without Defilement), to examine his Assertion in Point of Fact, and his Conclusions with respect the Event of this Affair.

And first he begins with the Subjects of this Undertaking; which he calls *a vast Multitude of Necessitous, Idle, and Extravagant People, combining to have Money at an easy Rate, of no determinate Value, which the possessor cannot oblige them to accept, until after twenty Years, and with this to pay their Debts, which will depreciate the other Currencies, prejudice private Property, and damage the Merchants of Great Britain trading to New England.*

To which I Answer, that as to the Numbers being Great that are actually concerned in it, it is true, but not the tenth Part of those that are in Heart in favour of the Scheme, and think it the best calculated Method for the Province's Good, that has yet been thought of, but that said Partners are a Combination of such as he represents, is as far from Truth as his Epithets are from the Rules of Decency and good Manners, or which is all one, as the

East from the West. Can it be supposed, Sir, that the great
Number of Officers Civil and Military selected out of the
People by a wise Governour and Council, and performing
so well, as that no Complaints were ever brought against
one of them for Male-Administration, besides numbers of
Gospel Ministers now concerned in this Scheme, could deserve such a Character? Would such Numbers of Officers
(not Partners) as of late have resigned their Commissions
(that they might be free to give those Bills a Credit) have
done so to take Part with a Combination of such despicable Mortals in a Design to cheat Mankind, and in which
they must share equally with others? But this (instead of
Reason), has been their Treatment all along.

As to the easy Rate by which the Partners have their
Money, there's no Argument in that, nor Truth in Assertion, that they are not obliged to receive it till twenty Years,
or that the Bill is of no determinate Value, that it bears no
Interest; all this is notoriously false. . . .

As to these Bills depreciating others, not on a Silver
Foundation, there will be none of them to suffer at the
End of one Year, for that compleats the Term of their
Redemption; his Consequence therefore that they will hurt
private Property and the British Merchants, fails and comes
to nothing.

And here I would propose to them, Which will hurt
them most, whether to have Money circulating to pay for
their Goods in Ships built, and Cargoes bought, in about
six Months, as has been the Case when the Manufactory
Bills are taken? Or whether to wait twice that Time, as
some Refusers, I am informed, have done, and the Keel not
yet laid, or Cargoes bought, for want of Money, and perhaps will not till their Debtor breaks, or by some other
Accident they are defeated of their Debt? But then, our
Author lays Stress on the length of the Period, and the
largeness of the Sum. As to that of the Period, the Partners
Obligation to take the Bills at any Time, as before related,
is an Answer. And as to the largeness of the Sum, had there
been the same Provision in the Province Bills, the Rise of
Silver had never affected them as it did. To clear this, pray
observe, that when A gave B an advance Price for Silver,
that sunk the Province Bills so much, as A advanced in his

Purchase. B, who thought he had got by the Bargain, soon found his Mistake; for none alive was obliged to receive the Bills of him in Trade, at a higher Value than he received them of A, and so the Bills sunk in Value in Trade, just as they did in their Purchase of Silver. . . .

But our cavilling Author will say, What's all this without sufficient Security for the Performance, and accordingly tells you, that the Bills are very Ill, or not at all secured. For Answer to which, I shall inform you, Sir, what the Security is, and leave you to judge for your self, what Reason there is for this Objection. Every Partner Mortgages a Real Estate (saving a very few who gave Personal Security in Boston) exclusive of Buildings, Timber, Wood, and wooden Fences, which are prized at nothing, to the Value of one and a half of the Money he takes out, done by five Men on Oath: The Deeds Conditioned for the yearly Payment of a twentieth Part of the Principal, and three per cent Interest. To inforce these Payments, each Partner gives a Covenant, obliging himself to make them, according to the Tenor of his Mortgage; as also to pay his Rateable Proportion of all manner of Losses that may any Ways happen; besides many other Things contained therein for the better Security of the Possessor; to which Purpose all the Instruments are made. Now Sir, if he pays not, Action of Covenant broken may be brought, and on Judgment obtained, Execution may be Levied on his other Estate from Year to Year, and Payment to Payment, and his whole Mortgage lies to secure the last Payment only: Hence if all they are worth will make good their Engagements, it is liable. The Directors Security as such, besides Instruments executed to each other, obliging to the faithful Discharge of their Trusts, is a Covenant they give to each of the Partners, expressing the Particulars of their Duty; on failure of which each Partner has his Action against each Director, by Vertue of said Covenant, which secures against all Suggestions of Corruption in the Directors.

With respect to the Surmise he pretends you make of the Merchants jesuitically promoting the Scheme in order to get all Paper Currencies suppressed, whether this is Genuine or not, I can't tell. But this is certain, that the Term is well adapted; for at that Game, it's notorious, he is never exceeded, and but seldom equalled. Then again (as tho' hurried by some Evil Spirit) he repeats his Abuses of the Contrivers, says the Scheme was contrived for their Use, and in the same Breath says, it is only contrived for the Directors Use, who to be sure were mostly other Persons; for the first Projector of the Scheme is no Officer. . . .

Then he wrangles and finds Fault with their Trade, and calls them Ludicrous, because they Import that which others won't sell us, and that which we can't do without; whereas the Bank of England, and all other Banks well constituted (he must mean established by Law) are prohibited Trade. And these desire the same Thing, when alike circumstanced (their Trade not being a chosen Circumstance) but are loath to starve in the mean Time. But then they don't understand Trade. This ought to move his Compassion, rather than his Anger. That he and his Brethren force them to Business of which they are not capable. His diminitive Appellation of the Gentlemen of the Bay, is very ungenerous and ungrateful, they having contributed vastly to the Assistance of our Trade, and to the Wealth of this very Author in particular.

His next Freak is about *the Alteration of the Scheme,* which he thinks none have a Right to do but himself, he having altered as before mentioned; and what then, if it be for the better (which he don't deny) and compleated before any Obligation was made, why should he be angry? . . .

In his Answer to your Desire *to know the Nature of our landed Interest,* he ought to have told you, "that it is almost ruined by our Trade; as our Merchants manage it. It's true, Sir, Our Fore-Fathers spent their Blood and Treasure, many of them, in subduing this Wilderness, and its savage Inhabitants; and the Land being cultivated is generally exceeding Good, for so cold a Climate; the People orderly, vertuous, and industrious, but the want of Money and Hands to labour (too great a Proportion going to Sea) has brought them to the Pass our Author speaks of. Tho' he has his own Ends in casting his Veil over their Nakedness; otherwise he might have discovered the Means which made them so, which would be little to his Credit.

The Truth is this, that the Import too much encouraged, or Export too much neglected and discouraged, has built up a few on the ruins of many; the natural Effect of such a State. . . .

That of the Assortment and Value of the Goods in which the Bills are to be paid, I answer thus; All the Goods in the Treasury are the Property of the Possessor (so far as his Bills will reach) and consequently he will take which he pleases. And the Case vastly differs from a Bond, where two Species are mentioned, as discharging Conditions; there the Creditor is intitled to but one, but here to all, therefore has his Choice. As to the Value, it being at the Market Price, the Debtor has no more Right to decide that than the Creditor; but of this also before.

His third, that the Bills will supply the Treasury, and no Manufactures paid: I Answer, that's impossible, because the Sum to be paid in is bigger than what is emitted, and consequently Manufactures must supply the Deficiency. And as to what Bills are paid in, they must be procured of the Possessor, and by them who must receive the Bills at the declared Value, and then who is hurt? Tho' all possible Means will be used, that Manufactures be produced for a Reason herein mentioned.

His fourth, viz., That the Directors (the Company not being a Body Politick) may emit what Bills they please, so none must be had, least too much be emitted. However, a Law easily prevents this. But if the Argument proves any Thing, it proves too much, as by the Consequence aforesaid, and so must be rejected.

The same answers his fifth.

His sixth describing who may set up a Bank, as well suits the Land Bank Partners, after all his Scurrility and foul Language, as it does the Silver Schemers. And I dare (were it convenient) put the Issue of the Case upon it. As to others following the Example, it is vertually answered in his fourth.

His seventh, that the Security being among themselves, may be shifted at Pleasure. I Answer, Can they blot out the Face of the Bill in the Possessor's Hand? If so, there may be Danger, otherwise it's irrational to suppose the Directors will suffer, much less agree to cancel or stifle the Securitys, while the Bill stands out against them, and must prove their Ruine. What can be more invidious?

No wonder the Government rejected the Scheme in 1714, as he next relates, when the Signers of the Bills, the only Persons the Possessors could come at, were to have no Security given to them, as appears, to enable them to redeem the Bills. But no doubt this Author when it suits his Design, will conclude that whatever once were the Sentiments of the Government, must always be right (let Circumstances alter as they will) and 'tis a wonder we are not charged with Rebellion, for our proceeding contrary to what was their Mind twenty six Years ago. But tho' we escape here, he now draws up a heavy Charge indeed, viz., of debauching People's Minds, instilling Principles into them destructive of the Government, and so he goes on with a long Detail of Particulars, equally ridiculous, and equally false, calculated purely to influence the Power at Home against this People, to procure a Dissolution of our Constitution, doubting of his half Vote for the future. When in Fact (saving some Opposition made to the Merchants [by Abuse extorted] and that in a very small Degree, to what they have given) there is not the least Foundation in Truth for all these Assertions. But this Instrument of Cruelty, with just the same Reason, takes the same Methods which his Predecessors the old Pharisees did, when they wanted Argument to hunt down the Christian Religion and its Promoters, they thought to Effect it by representing them as Seditious and Disturbers of Government; and what was the Effect of their own Opposition, as now, was unjustly charged on them that peaceably suffered under it.

I shall select and Answer his most material Points, as that in his first, That *for the People strenuously to assert the emitting and passing any Thing as a Currency, in defiance of the King's Prerogative is a high Crime,* is answered before. *Middletown* he says, *have Voted to receive those Bills as Cash for Town Rates;* intimating that by the Words (*as Cash*) they invaded the King's Prerogative: But this is a false Recital of their Words, and (I fear) wilful, and discovers a consciousness in this Author that a bare offering or receiving of the said Bills in lieu of

Money or any thing else, which was their Case, was no
Invasion on the Prerogative; therefore he perverts the
Words on Purpose to serve his Design, at which he has
an excellent Faculty. The Words are, "that they would
receive the Bills in Town Rates," which no more infringes
the Prerogative, than to have said, they would pay in Corn,
or any other Commodity, which some Towns have done
before them, and were never taxed with invading the
Prerogative.

As to his second, *why Landed Men have not a Right
to make Money as well as they that have none,* or why
they will relinquish their Country, sooner to an Invader,
or why *they must necessarily be supposed to be in Debt,*
or why *their making Money* (he means Bills) *is from a
destructive and wicked Principle,* as he asserts, being beyond me to discover, I pass it by.

His Glosses in his third, are intirely groundless. No
Sir, we value our Selves on a just and honest Trade, equal
to our Ability. 'Tis the Excess only we are against: should
be glad to enlarge our Ability, and hope by this Scheme
to effect it (our Produce being thereby improved) in an
honest and thrifty way, and not by a Bankrupt Trade as
at present, make our selves a Bankrupt People, the necessary and natural Effects of such a Trade.

The Substance of his fourth is this, *that the People
in the Charter Governments, being greatly in Favour of
this Undertaking, will,* it's like, *exercise their Charter Liberty in chusing such to Rule them, as they think will promote it;* and so, says he, our *Dependance on Great Britain
would vanish, Neglects of Resolves of Parliament, and
King's Instructions will ensue* (he seems to have changed
his Mind since Governour Burnet's Day); he had better
have spoken plain, and said, it is best to take away the
Charters, least the People by Vertue of them, should make
Choice of such as would promote, what they judged for
the publick Good, instead of others who may deserve the
contrary Character, which is the grand Reason of a Charter: or in other Words, least the People by their Charter
Priviledge, should give check to any arbitrary Proceedings
that have or may happen, and so he is for absolute Mon-

archy, and destroying the Constitution, not only here but of the Nation also.

As to his fifth, *that the People are by the Managers of the Scheme excited to Mutiny, etc., that they tell them, that the Lords at Whitehall, nor Acts of Parliament can stop their Proceedings; that if the Merchants won't take the Bills they must blame themselves for any Outrages that may happen; that we had as good perish by the Sword as by Famine; that on a French Invasion, if we submit, it can't be worse, as appears,* he says, *by the printed Papers sent home,* I Answer: It is hard to determine what Property of the Devil discovers itself most in this Relation, Malice or Falshood both being carried to the Height. But I leave it to the Papers he refers to (abating some Strokes on the Merchant by their hard and cruel Usage extorted) and let them be searched for the Test of this Author's Veracity in this Affair; and will be answerable for it, that scarce one in five Thousand of the Landed Men of these Provinces would quit their Allegiance to his present Majesty, and His Royal House, while the Blood in their Veins would keep them in Life; and none later than the Managers he refers to, and so monstrously abuses. . . .

Thus Sir, have I given you some Remarks on his Work, passing over much of his Fallacy, which Pity to him would not allow me to expose. I have also given you a summary Account of the Manufactory Undertaking, with the Manner of Proceeding, and the Necessity thereof. I should have been more particular had Leisure admitted. I hope, Sir, by what is said, you will be convinced that it is another Thing, than it has been represented to be, by those that are it's Enemies.

DOCUMENT 18

THE PETITION OF LONDON MERCHANTS TO PARLIAMENT,
11 FEBRUARY 1741

The issues involved in the colonial confrontation on the merit of the Massachusetts Land Bank were forwarded to Britain. At this stage, the British merchants intervened, fearing that British goods sent to New England would be paid for by depreciating land bank currency issues. Parliament then passed an act that declared the Massachusetts Land Bank to be illegal and thus void.

A petition of the several merchants of London, and others, whose names are thereunto subscribed, in behalf of themselves, and great numbers of merchants, traders, and other inhabitants, in the province of the Massachusets Bay, in America, was presented to the House, and read; setting forth, that while his Majesty and this House have exerted their authority and utmost care, not only to prevent the increase of paper money in America, but even to sink and discharge what has already issued under the publick authority, by virtue of acts of assembly there, John Coleman Esquire, and a very great number of private persons, in the Massachusets Bay, his associates, have, without any authority, assumed a power to erect themselves into a company or society there, by the name of the land bank, and have chosen and appointed directors, treasurers, and officers, to carry on the same under large yearly salaries, avowedly for the purpose of issuing paper bills or notes, to a very large amount, to be redeemable twenty years hence, or at some other remote distance of time; and have actually issued out their notes, and, by their numbers and influence, endeavour to force a currency for the same; and this, notwithstanding that the most considerable inhabitants in the Massachusets Bay in due time opposed such scheme, and petitioned the general assembly there to discountenance and suppress that pernicious project; and notwithstanding that his Majesty's governor, with the advice of the council there, by publick proclamations, did discourage the same; so that, by means of the said land bank, the quantity of paper money there is greatly increased, and many frauds, losses, and prejudices, are likely to ensue to the petitioners, and others, if not timely prevented; and that several of the petitioners have humbly petitioned his Majesty in Council, for relief against the said Coleman's scheme, and the Lords of the committee of his Majesty's most honourable Privy-Council, and the Lords Commissioners for Trade and Plantations, to whom the petition has been referred, have concurred in opinion, that that scheme was of dangerous tendency, and fit to be suppressed as speedily and effectually as possible, and have given all the orders that were possible for them to give, that the governors should continue in the meantime to discourage the said scheme; and that, although the said Coleman's scheme would here in Great Britain be an high offence, and attended with heavy punishments, and might easily be suppressed, as being within the act of the sixth year of his late Majesty King George the First, chapter the 18th, sections 18, 19, 20, yet his Majesty's Attorney and Sollicitor-General, to whom the method for prosecuting the persons concerned in the said scheme was in the course of the said petition referred, have reported their opinion, that that act does not extend to America; and that nothing can effectually be done to put a stop thereto, but by the interposition of a positive law; so that, notwithstanding all the endeavours used by the petitioners, without the aid of Parliament, no remedy can be had against those persons who have already presumed to set on foot this fraudulent project; but all the care taken by his Majesty, from time to time, and his repeated royal orders and instructions on the head of paper money, as well as the care and inquiry of this House, will be totally evaded and eluded, and many other persons may take upon themselves also to set on foot other like projects in America: and therefore praying the House to take the premises into their consideration, and to hear the petitioners, by their counsel; and that the said act of Parliament, of the sixth year of his late Majesty King George the First, may be extended to the British plantations in America, by express words, with proper clauses and powers, and with such penalties, forfeitures, and disabilities, on all persons offending against the same, or with such other relief in the premises as to the House shall seem proper.

The House was moved, that the 18th and 19th sections of an act, made in the sixth year of the reign of his late Majesty King George, intituled, An act for better securing certain powers and privileges intended to be granted by his Majesty, by two charters, for assurance of ships and merchandizes at sea, and for lending money upon bottomry, and for restraining several extravagant and unwarrantable practices therein mentioned, might be read:

And the same being read accordingly;

Ordered, that leave be given to bring in a bill to explain and amend so much of the said act as relates to the extravagant and unwarrantable practices therein mentioned: and that Sir John Barnard, Colonel Bladen, Mr. Walpole, Mr. Sandys, and Sir George Caswall, do prepare, and bring in, the same.

✳ PART V ✳

Constitutional Contest
Between Colony and Crown

THE contest between England and its colonies in which the political authority of the mother country and the political rights of the colonials were constantly re-defined is a principal theme of early American history. The framework in which this contest was staged generally found the governor, who represented the Crown, pitted against the assemblies, who represented the colonials. Five prominent and representative issues, each affecting the constitutional relationship between the colonies and mother country, are included in this unit: the issue of the governor's salary; biennial and triennial acts defining the right of the assembly to meet without a summons from the governor; the right of an assembly rather than the governor to choose its speaker; the complicated issue of defense; and the right of colonials to prohibit the importation of slaves. Issues discussed in previous units, such as the right of a legislature to reapportion itself or control monetary policy, can also be viewed as part of the controversy between the mother country and its colonies in defining the authority of each.

Every colonial assembly at one time or another confronted the issue of whether or not it would provide a permanent revenue to pay the salary of the governor. The Massachusetts House of Representatives argued that if such action were taken, the colonists' fundamental rights under the colonial charter would be infringed and their rights as Englishmen and as colonials compromised (Document 1). Governor Burnet responded by saying that the position of the House was a "mere invention" to avoid providing the funds (Document 2). Burnet contended that the king's instructions were part of the constitution of England and thus were the supreme law for the colonies. The assembly considered the instructions of the Crown a guideline to action, but not as constitutionally binding.

Whether or not an assembly should determine the frequency of its own meeting was another sensitive issue, and the terms of the North Carolina Biennial Act, which called for a scheduled session at least once every two years, illustrate one side of this argument (Document 3). The fear prompting the act was the danger that the governor would fail to summon an assembly and instead rule unchallenged for an indeterminate number of years, thus bringing about arbitrary and unrepresentative government. North Carolina, together with other colonies, relied on the English Triennial Act of 1694, calling for sessions of a Parliament at least once every three years, as a precedent for its own action. In most colonies, a biennial act was not signed by the governor, or, if it was, the home government immediately declared it void. In North Carolina, because of early indifference on the part of the Crown, its Biennial Act was still in force twenty years later, until Governor Gabriel Johnston (Document 4) requested its repeal, which was eventually granted after a legal opinion ruled it invalid (Document 5).

The right to elect a speaker was an issue that struck a responsive note in colonial minds and hearts. Self-government for the colonists implied the selection of their own legislative leaders. In New Hampshire, as in most other colonies, debate on the question was passionate with frequent appeals to the constitutional rights of Englishmen. The assembly projected arguments in favor of its right to select a speaker (Document 6), while the governor declared the choice a critical part of royal prerogative (Document 7).

Insofar as British policy was concerned, each colony

was expected to defend its own frontier, but this sometimes proved ineffective, particularly in the eighteenth century when the French or the Spanish, each with Indian
allies, confronted the expanding English colonies on a
broad intercolonial front. The wars in Europe spilled over
into America, where the growing economic and political
power of the New World influenced, increasingly, diplomatic relationships in Europe (see Part VI).

In Pennsylvania, the problem of defense was complicated by two special factors: the Quakers who controlled
the colony opposed war and thus the government failed to
take either defensive or offensive measures; furthermore,
the manpower of Pennsylvania was comprised in part of
indentured servants, so when the British looked for recruits in wartime, these servants became a tempting target.
These problems provoked a broader question: What authority and responsibility did England possess for the defense of its empire, and what authority and responsibility
remained with the colonials? In Pennsylvania, the assembly
opposed defense measures (Document 8), while the governor supported them (Document 9). In each case practical as well as theoretical questions were debated.

An issue profoundly affecting the Southern colonies
and, later, the United States, was that of the prohibition
of slave importation. During the eighteenth century, each
Southern colony—except Georgia—tried repeatedly to discourage if not end directly the importation of slaves by
enacting an exceedingly high import duty, akin in some
respects to a protective tariff. In every case, Britain declared such duties invalid, because of the conviction that
British economic welfare depended upon a flourishing slave
trade. In a South Carolina act to impose a heavy duty on
slaves, the colonials stated their motives quite clearly
(Document 10). The English position is clarified by Malachy Postlethwayt, an English political economist (Document 11).

That the colonials, after more than a century of practical experience, were prepared to claim that they had inviolate rights, is revealed in resolutions adopted by the
Virginia House of Burgesses in 1764 (Document 12), a
year before the enactment and subsequent struggle over the

Stamp Act which led ultimately to the American Revolution. By the 1760s, the colonials held to the position that they enjoyed certain rights of self-government by reason of their being Englishmen; these rights, they believed, could not be rescinded. In contrast, the British held to the view that any practice of self-government exercised by the colonials was a privilege extended to them by the royal grace and favor, privileges that could be withdrawn without colonial consultation. The confrontation between the colonies and the mother country from 1765 to 1776 was, then, an extension of a collision over the interpretation of the constitutional relationship existing between the colonies and the mother country, which recurred consistently during the entire eighteenth century.

DOCUMENT 1

MASSACHUSETTS HOUSE OF REPRESENTATIVES ON THE GOVERNOR'S SALARY, 11 SEPTEMBER 1728

The colonial assemblies found that control of the governor's salary was an effective weapon in encouraging him to sign bills that they wished to adopt. Occasionally, as was the case with Governor Glen of South Carolina, the assembly offered "large sums of money, to . . . be raised under collour of Reimbursing me my Expenses amongst the Indians" if he, in this particular instance, would approve a controversial money bill.

To counter this weapon, the Crown issued instructions to the governors asking for the establishment of a permanent revenue by the respective colonial legislatures to pay the governor's salary. Virginia, for example, enacted an export tax on tobacco for this purpose, but more often than not the colonial assemblies refused to honor the royal request. The response of the Massachusetts House of Representatives to the royal instructions is indicative of

*other colonial responses because it employs the pro-
visions of the colonial charter, the validity of colonial
experience, and the precedence of British theory and
practice to support its case.*

Whereas His Excellency the Governour at the opening
of this present Session laid before this Court His Majesties
23d Instruction which relates to a stated Salary instead
of the ordinary Allowances which by the former Method
and Practice of this Court has been from time to time made
for the Support of the Governour (which Instruction is
entered at large in the Journal of this House, *p.* 2).

The House after Consideration had thereon proceeded
in their usual way of an Allowance, and granted the Sum
of Seventeen Hundred Pounds to His Excellency the Governour to enable Him to manage the publick Affairs of the
Government, and defrey his Charge in coming here, assuring His Excellency that although the House had not fixed
a stated Salary for His Excellency, yet that an ample and
honourable Allowance would from time to time be made
to enable Him to manage the publick Affairs, and that the
said Grant was made as an earnest thereof. His Excellency
in His Message to the House informed them that He was
utterly disabled from consenting to the Resolve for that
Grant, it being contrary to His Majesties Instruction:
Whereupon the House chose a Committee to join with a
Committee of the Honourable Board to prepare a proper
Answer to the said Message; and pursuant to a Message
from the Board, as entered (*p.* 18) purporting that they
had not yet passed upon the Report of the Committee in
answer to His Excellency's Message, apprehending it necessary even from the tenour of the said Report for this
Court to make a new Grant, the former Grant not having
been accepted, The House proceeded to resolve, That the
Sum of Fourteen Hundred Pounds be paid to His Excellency the Governour to enable him to manage the Affairs
of the Government, and the Sum of Three Hundred Pounds
to defrey his Charges in coming, and chose a Committee
to consider the Report of the Committee on His Excellency's Message to both Houses, with the Vote of the Honourable Board who reported thereon, as entered (*p.* 23)

assuring His Excellency of the readiness of this Court to improve the Powers vested in them by the Royal CHARTER of imposing and levying proportionable and reasonable Rates and Taxes, and disposing of the same in providing for His ample and honourable Support, and praying His Excellency's Acceptance of the Grant then made and therewith presented, which Report was accepted by the House, and together with the two Votes, viz., Fourteen Hundred and Three Hundred Pounds was sent up for Concurrence; His Excellency returned an Answer declaring that a Support given in such a precarious manner as has been usual here could not possibly be Honourable because it implied no sort of Confidence in the Government, and made the Support of it visibly depend on an entire Compliance with every thing demanded by the other Branches of the Legislature etc., and that he could never accept of a Grant of this kind.

Upon which a Committee of both Houses was appointed to consider and report on His Excellency's Message, who reported thereon (as entered *p.* 31, 32, 33) therein alledging that the CHARTER impowers the General Assembly to raise Money for the Support of the Government according to such wholesome and reasonable Laws as they should judge to be for the good and welfare of the Province, and that it was against the Design of the Power so vested in them for the Court to pass any Acts pursuant to that Instruction, apprehending that the passing of such Acts had a direct tendency to weaken if not destroy our happy Constitution, by our giving away the great and almost only Priviledge that gives Weight to the House of Representatives, which is the making Grants of Money as the exigence of Affairs requires; which Report was accepted by the House but not by the Board, The Vote of the Board for Non-Acceptance of the said Report was accompanied with a Draft of an Answer to His Excellency's Message, sent down for Concurrence, which Draft altho' it recites the Opinion of the Board that the great End proposed in the Power granted by the Royal CHARTER would be best answered without establishing a fixed Salary, yet the House apprehending that the said Draft was in many respects deficient did non-concur the same, and then proceeded to put the Question with a Preamble, *Whether passing an Act for fixing a Salary on the Governour or Commander in Chief for the time being would not be hurtful to the Inhabitants of this Province, and therefore contrary to the plain End and Design of the Power vested in them by the Royal CHARTER which is to make wholesome and reasonable Orders and Laws as they shall judge to be for the good and welfare of the Province?* Which was Resolved in the Affirmative, and sent up for Concurrence, and was sent down again with a Message from the Board that they thought it improper and unsafe to pass on the Question, for that it was not only expressed in doubtful terms, but the method of Resolving matters of such a Nature by answering Questions is inconvenient and altogether new and without precedent.

The House then passed it into a Vote viz., That passing such an Act will be dangerous to the Inhabitants of this Province etc., which they sent up for Concurrence; The Board Non-Concurred the Vote, adding that they apprehended that a Salary might be granted for a certain time to His Excellency our present Governour without danger to the Province. The House ordered that a Conference should be had with the Honourable Board on the subject matter of the said Vote which was attended, and the House observing that it was alledged by the Board that they could not concur in said Vote, in as much as it was said in the Preamble thereof that the Council and Representatives had granted an ample and honourable Support for the Governour, which the Board could not say because it was not expressed for what time the Sum was granted; thereupon being returned to their own Chamber, the House sent up the Vote for Concurrence leaving out the Preamble. The Board sent down the Vote concurred with the Amendment which with the said Amendment stands thus, Voted, *That the passing an Act for fixing a Salary on the Governour or Commander in Chief without Limitation of time may prove of ill Consequence to this Province:* Which was read and non-concurred, and the House adhered to their own Vote, and sent it up for Concurrence. The Board Non-Concurred the Vote of the House and insisted on their own Vote. The House having passed a Resolve for the Supply of the Treasury sent a Message to His Excellency desiring that they might rise. His Excellency signified in Answer thereto, that He could not agree to a Recess 'till His Majesties 23d Instruction was complied with. The House made Reply renewing their desire to Rise; His Excellency sent a Message urging a Compliance. The House sent a Message to His Excellency expressing the Reasons why they could not in Faithfulness to their Country come into a fixed Salary, ardently moving that they might be permitted to return to their several homes.

His Excellency sent a Message in Reply in the Conclusion whereof he put the House upon considering what advances they could make towards a Compliance; His Excellency's Message being read and debated on, The Question was put, *Whether the House would take under Consideration the setling a temporary Salary?* and it passed in the Negative. And then the Question was put, *Whether the House with Safety to the People they represent could come into any other Method for Supporting the Governour than what had been heretofore practiced?* It passed in the Negative. The House renewed their Desire to Rise, and received His Excellency's Answer, assuring them that unless His Majesties Pleasure had its due Weight with them, their Desires would have very little with Him. On Saturday the Honourable Board sent down for Concurrence a Vote of Council that it was expedient for this Court now to ascertain a Sum as a Salary for His Excellency's Support, as also the term of Time for the Continuance of the same which was Non-Concurred.

Now although we have after the best manner we are capable of thinking or acting for the publick Good come into the many Votes and Resolutions before-mentioned, and with a pure and sincere desire aimed at the Weal and Prosperity of this Province, and are still fully of the same mind, yet whereas several Members have desired to know the Minds of their Principals, therefore this House to prevent any Misrepresentations that may be made to the several Towns in this Province have concluded upon this Account of the Proceedings in this Affair and the Reasons and Grounds thereof to be transmitted to the several Towns by their Representatives, if they see cause, from whence it may plainly appear that we dare neither come into an Act for fixing a Salary on the Governour for ever, nor for a limited time, viz.

1. Because it is an untrodden path which neither we nor our Predecessors have gone in, and we cannot certainly foresee the many Dangers there may be in it, and we must depart from that way which has been found safe and comfortable.

2. Because it is the undoubted Right of all Englishmen by *Magna Charta* to raise and dispose of Moneys for the publick Service of their own free accord without any Compulsion.

3. Because this must necessarily lessen the Dignity and Freedom of the House of Representatives in making Acts and raising and applying Taxes etc., and consequently cannot be thought a proper method to preserve that Ballance in the three Branches of the Legislature, which seems necessary to form maintain and uphold our Constitution.

4. Because the CHARTER fully impowers the General Assembly to make such Laws and Orders as they judge for the good and welfare of the Inhabitants; and if they or any part of them judge this not to be for their good, they neither ought nor can come into it, for, as to act beyond, or without the Powers granted in the CHARTER, might justly incur the Kings Displeasure; so not to act up and agreable to those Powers might justly be deemed a betraying the Rights and Priviledges therein granted: Moreover if we should now give up this Right, we shall open a Door to many other Inconveniencies.

DOCUMENT 2

GOVERNOR BURNET OF MASSACHUSETTS ON THE GOVERNOR'S SALARY
17 SEPTEMBER 1728

William Burnet was the son of a distinguished English clergyman, Bishop Gilbert Burnet, who participated in and wrote about the Glorious Revolution

*of 1688. As governor of New York from 1720 to
1728, William Burnet served with distinction, especially in formulating a long-range policy of diplo-
macy with the Indians and checking the expansion of
the French. Moreover, he prepared a firm written
defense of the colonial position on the issuance of
paper money, a novel stand for any English governor.*

*Burnet was appointed governor of Massachusetts
in 1728 just in time to confront the constitutional
issue of the governor's salary. He spoke for the imperial interest and against what he regarded as an encroachment by the colonial assembly upon royal authority. In this document, he replies specifically to
the arguments presented by the Massachusetts legislature, recorded in the preceding document.*

Gentlemen of the House of Representatives,

I Thought it proper to delay answering your Message
of the 12th Instant, in which you desired to Rise that you
might advise with your Towns, till I had seen the Draught
which you had accepted as what might be necessary to
advise the Towns how far the Court had proceeded in the
matter of a Salary to the Governour; for by your Vote of
the 7th appointing a Committee to draw it up, you seemed
to allow that your own going home would be needless,
since you resolved to transmit to them what might be necessary, and since upon that they might if they pleased send
you Directions how to act for them.

But you have now carried the thing much further, for
you conclude, *that you dare neither come into an Act for
fixing a Salary on the Governour for ever, nor for a limited
time,* what then can it signify *to know the minds of your
Principals and advise with your Towns* since you *dare not*
take their Advice, if it should differ from your own Opinion, all your meaning therefore can only be that you would
go home to give Advice to your Towns, but that you are
fully resolved to take none from them, which is not a very
respectful Treatment of those who have Chosen you to
represent them: You say, *That the House to prevent any
Misrepresentations that may be made to the several Towns
in this Province have concluded upon this Account of the*

*Proceedings in this Affair, and of the Grounds and Reasons
thereof;* It were to be wished you had pursued this Design
impartially, instead of which you have set forth the
Strength of the Argument on one side and concealed it on
the other, so that your Account can only serve to mis-
inform those who rely upon it, and this the generality of
People in the Country will naturally do, if they are not
warned of their Danger of being misled, for it cannot be
supposed that they will have the time or take the pains
to compare it with the pages of the Votes as they are cited,
but will of course expect that you have taken all that is
material out of them. Now as this has not been done, I
thought my self obliged in Justice to the publick, to point
out the defects and mistakes of this Account, and to set the
matter once more in a true Light, that as you have found
your selves at a loss to give any Reply to my long Message
of the 3d Instant, you may have as little success in your
design of filling the minds of the People with the same
wrong Notions, which have already been and are so easy
to be confuted. In the very beginning you omit taking any
notice at all of my Speech in which I observed, *That
Parliaments had made it a Custom to grant the Civil List
to the King for Life, and that the same Maxims that made
Great Britain shine would make you flourish.*

You begin with His Majesties 23d Instruction (*p.* 2)
where you omit mentioning, That His Majesty had declared your Compliance necessary to preserve his favour
and your not shewing an immediate regard to his Pleasure
therein an undutiful Behaviour, which would oblige Him
to lay the Affair before the Legislature at home, but when
you come to your own first Resolve (*p.* 6) to grant 1700 *l.*,
you insert it at length and almost word for word; then
again when you come to my Message (*p.* 11) you only
say that I informed you that I *was utterly disabled from
consenting to the Resolve of that Grant, it being contrary
to His Majesties Instruction,* but you should have mentioned my Reason, *because it was the very thing against
which this Instruction was levelled as done in order to
keep the Governour the more dependent on the Council
and Representatives;* just after you give a very particular
Account of your Proceedings with the Council and your

second Grant, and your Message with it (*p.* 18, 22, 23) and then you give a short account of the Allegations of my Message (*p.* 28) omitting what I insisted on to support and prove them, viz., *That Gentlemen knew in their Consciences that the Allowances for the Governour's Salary had been kept back till other Bills of moment had been consented to;* you had once put off this Charge with a turn as if Salarys always looked forward, but as I have since shewn this to be plainly contrary to the proceedings of last Winter, you now very prudently say nothing at all about it, nor what gave occasion to it.

The next thing you mention is a draught of your own (*p.* 31, 32, 33) which was never offered to me, and consequently not answered, and therefore you find it convenient to give some account of it in this place; whereas you say but a word or two of a like Paper delivered to me afterwards (*p.* 52, 53) which contains much the same matter with this draught, and not one word of the Contents of my Reply to it (*p.* 55, 56, 57) except something of the Conclusion, which Reply was so full that you have thought fit to drop the Dispute upon it; and so that you might mention your own Arguments without being discovered to conceal my Answers, you bring them in only on this former Occasion, but I will restore them to their proper place, and go on in order to observe, that you give all the particulars of a Dispute you had with the Council at full length (*p.* 35, 38, 39, 41, 42, 43) and then at once grow very short again when you come to mention any thing that came from me; you just say of my Answer to your Message (*p.* 47) that I signified I *could not agree to a Recess 'till His Majesties 23d Instruction was complied with,* without mentioning a very short and strong reason which I had given for it, *because I should thereby make your immediate Regard to His Majesties Pleasure impossible;* then you run over your Reply (*p.* 49) and my Message (*p.* 50) and your Message with Reasons (*p.* 52, 53) and my Reply (*p.* 55, 56, 57) with such precipitation (tho' the last were the two longest Papers that had passed between us) that one would think you were unwilling to have them read and considered, which, as it has a quite different effect with me I am willing to stop a little where you are so much in a hurry, and shew in this place that all that you mentioned before out of your draught (*p.* 31, 32, 33) is sufficiently answered in a few words of my Reply (*p.* 55, 56, 57) as follows, *I cannot see why you apprehend that passing Acts pursuant to the Instruction has a direct tendency to weaken your happy Constitution especially since you now acknowledge what I had formerly observed, that each Branch of the Legislature* (*and consequently the Governour*) *ought to be enabled to support his own Dignity and Freedom, which is all that is intended by the Instruction.*

After that you are got beyond this long Reply of mine, which you make so much haste to pass by, then you are at leisure to give an ample Account of your own proceedings (*p.* 58) and afterwards of the latter part of my Answer (*p.* 59) which you insert at length, but think proper to say nothing of the beginning of it, where I informed you *that I thought my Duty would not permit me to agree to a Recess,* and where I make a kind of Appeal to you by saying that *I had given you my Reasons and answered all your Objections;* to which you never replied, and yet you seem not to desire that the Country should know that the Dispute remains in such a state as will incline every impartial person to believe that I have Truth and Justice on my side. You finish your Narrative with mentioning your last difference with the Council (*p.* 62) and then although you had already brought together every Circumstance that you thought made for you, and omitted what seemed to make most strongly against you: You seem still apprehensive that People may not be enough prejudiced in your Favour, and therefore you conclude all with four Reasons at length, which contain the substance of your former Allegations, as if they were unanswerable, or at least had never been answered, whereas in Fact I have given a sufficient Reply to every thing contained in them, and therefore it would have been no more than a piece of Justice to me to have set down the substance of my Answers as fully as the Reasons themselves, but since that is not done as I might have expected, I think it necessary to do it my self in the fairest manner, by first repeating your Grounds and Reasons word for word, from whence you say *it may plainly appear, that you dare neither come into an Act for*

*fixing a Salary on the Governour for ever, nor for a limited
time.*

*1st. Because it is an untrodden path which neither you
nor your Predecessors have gone in, and you cannot certainly foresee the many dangers there may be in it, and
you must depart from that way which has been found safe
and comfortable.*

In answer to this I have already shewn (*p. 50*) *that the
same methods which are found no ways to prejudice the
Rights and Liberties of the People of Great Britain nor of
other Colonys cannot prejudice those of this Province;* and
again upon your replying, *That the British Constitution differed from yours in many respects,* I said (*p. 56*) *That I
took the chief difference to have been in the use made of
the Constitution, which has been no ways to your advantage, for by Great Britain's keeping up to the Constitution
publick Credit still continues at the height, notwithstanding
the vast Charges and Debts of the Nation; but with you
Credit has fallen lower and lower in an amazing manner,
and this has proceeded plainly from the want of a sufficient Check in the other Branches of the Legislature to the
sudden and unadvised Measures of former Assemblies.* By
this you might have seen how safe and comfortable your
way of Granting Allowances so as to keep the Governour
dependent has been, since it produced nothing less than the
Fall of publick Credit. But since you seem not to be satisfied with what has been already observed against your first
Reason, I must remind you that your lessening Governour
Shute's Salary in pursuance of this Way of making Allowances as you please from time to time, was no slender motive of his going home, and complaining of the divers Incroachments on the King's Prerogative committed by the
House of Representatives, and that upon a Hearing of
Seven Articles of his Charge, the Council for the House of
Representatives expressly declared, *that they did not insist
upon, or claim on the behalf of the House of Representatives any Right or Authority in the Matters charged upon
them by the 1st, 3d, 5th, 6th, and 7th.* And that His late
Majesty in Council ordered *an Explanatory Charter to be
granted upon the 2d and 4th Articles,* with this Conclusion,
That if such Explanatory Charter shall not be accepted,

and a just regard shewed to His Majesties Royal Preroga-
tive by the House of Representatives for the future in all
the particulars aforesaid, it may be proper for the Con-
sideration of the Legislature what further Provision may
be necessary to support and preserve His Majesties just
Authority in this Province, and prevent such presumptuous
Invasions for the future: So safe was your Way that it
helped in a great measure to bring this Complaint upon
the House, which ended in obliging those who appeared
for you to a Confession to many of your illegal Proceedings, and in putting you under a necessity of accepting an
Explanatory Charter, that your former One might not be
brought into Parliament, where Mr. Agent Dummer's
Letter, which I sent to you on the 12th Instant shews
plainly enough, what Fate it was like to have undergone.
What Comfort this Way may have given to those then
employed by the Country I shall not determine, but all
the Comfort the People had from it was an immense
Charge without succeeding in any one particular. I hope
by this time I have sufficiently shewn, how safe and comfortable your usual Way has been.

I come now to your 2d Reason,

2dly. Because it is the undoubted Right of all English-
men by Magna Charta to raise and dispose of Moneys for
the publick Service of their own free accord without Com-
pulsion.

To this it has been answered (*p.* 28) *that the Right of*
Englishmen can never entitle them to act in a wrong man-
ner, and therefore the Priviledge in your CHARTER to
raise Money for the Support of the Government is therein
expressed to be by wholesome and reasonable Laws and
Directions, and consequently not by such as are hurtful to
the British Constitution, and that by your *usual Way the*
Governour must either be deprived of the undoubted Right
of an Englishman, which is to act according to his Judg-
ment, or the Government must remain without Support;
and again (*p.* 56) I produced to you an undeniable Instance of the House's making use of this Way last Winter
in order to compel the Lieut. Governour to a Compliance,
so that I have proved that you have done the very thing
you here complain of. But I may again call upon you to

shew where the Compulsion lies: Is waiting with patience
'till you shew a due Regard to His Majesties Pleasure any
Compulsion? Is not His Majesties Favour free to be continued or withdrawn as well as you are free to raise or
not to raise Money? And is not the Governour as free to
keep the Court setting or not as he judges proper? But I
must repeat to you what I observed to you before (*p.* 57)
*That you seem to allow the Governour's Powers only so
far as he uses them according to your Pleasure, but in
using your own Powers you take it very ill to be directed
by any Body.*

Your 3d Reason is,

*3dly. Because this must necessarily lessen the Dignity
and Freedom of the House of Representatives in making
Acts and raising and applying Taxes etc., and consequently
cannot be thought a proper Method to preserve that Ballance in the three Branches of the Legislature which seems
necessary to form maintain and uphold your Constitution.*

In answer to this I have already observed (*p.* 56)
*That the fall of Credit here has proceeded from the want
of a sufficient Check in the other Branches of the Legislature to the sudden and unadvised Measures of former
Assemblies, so that if ever you hope to come near the
Happiness of Great Britain it must be by supporting those
parts of the Legislature which of late have been too much
depressed, but are in themselves necessary to guard the
Liberties and Properties of the Inhabitants as well as the
House of Representatives.* I have shewn (*p.* 57) that you
cannot be in earnest when you say, *that other things which
depend on a Governour are vastly more than a Counter-
ballance to his Support or Subsistence, and just after you
cast an odious Aspersion on an undoubted Branch of the
Power lodged with the Governour, which is to keep the
Court together as long as he thinks the publick Affairs require it.* I will only add now that all the World will think
it very odd in you to talk of the Danger of not preserving
the Ballance in the three Branches of the Legislature while
you have a majority of three to one in the Choice of the
Council, and while you leave but Five Hundred Pounds
to be disposed of by the Governour and Council during a
Recess.

Your 4th Reason is,

4thly. *Because the CHARTER fully impowers the General Assembly to make such Laws and Orders as they shall judge for the good and welfare of the Inhabitants, and if they or any part of them judge this not to be for their good they neither ought nor can come into it, for as to act beyond or without the Powers granted in the CHARTER might justly incur the Kings Displeasure, so not to act up and agreable to those Powers might justly be deemed a betraying the Rights and Priviledges therein granted: Moreover, if you should now give up this Right you should open a Door to many other Inconveniences.*

In answer to this I must remind you, that I observed (*p. 57*) That *as I was still of Opinion that as you have acted upon mistaken Notions, I could not give over hopes of your coming to see things in that true Light in which I flattered my self I had stated the Point in Question.* I may again renew my Appeal, whether I have not answered all your Objections, and if so, then how can I think that you have reason to judge the fixing a Salary not to be for your good; a bare assertion of that kind without proof can go for nothing with the publick, and it must always be supposed that any stiffness that has no real foundation will go off in time. But to cut off all pretence as if the Granting what is now proposed were against the Powers of your CHARTER, I will set down the words of the Statute of the 25th of Edward the first, King of England, Chap. 6, Entitled a Confirmation of the Great Charter, *That for no Business from henceforth we shall take such manner of Aids, Tasks nor Prices, but by the common assent of the Realm, and for the common Profit thereof, saving the ancient Aids and Prices due and accustomed.* I will likewise set down the words of the Statute of the 34th of the same King Chap. 1, which was Enacted to make the former more full and certain—*No Talliage or Aids shall be taken or levied by Us or Our Heirs in Our Realm without the good will and assent of Arch-Bishops, Bishops, Earles, Barons, Knights, Burgesses, and other Freemen of the Land.* These Clauses of Acts of Parliament are as strong at least as any words in your Charter, which gives no power of raising and disposing of Money greater than those of all Englishmen, and yet I defy you to shew that these Acts of Parliament or any other were ever pretended to be an Objection against granting to the King a Revenue for Life, which appears to have been done, and much more time out of mind by the Preamble of the first of James the first, Chap. 33, which is too long to be inserted in this place, but where you will find that the same Dutys of Tunnage and Poundage that had been granted to Henry the 7th, Henry 8th, Edward the 6th, Queen Mary, Queen Elizabeth, and other the Kings Progenitors, Kings of England, were given to King James the first, *To have, take, enjoy and perceive the Subsidies aforesaid and every of them, and every part and percel of them to the Kings Majesty during his Life natural.* So that it is a mere Invention without any ground to say, that a Charter to grant Moneys is any reason against granting them either for a limited or an unlimited time. And since this is now so fully proved I hope you will no longer be amused with so wrong a notion.

Your last Observation of *the many other Inconveniencies to which a Door will be opened,* cannot be answered 'till it is explained what those Inconveniencies are, and it looks as if at the very end of your Paper you felt the Imperfections of it, since you are reduced to call for Help from what you have not mentioned, and which I may justly believe to be of no more force than what you have.

DOCUMENT 3

THE NORTH CAROLINA BIENNIAL ACT, 1715

The colonial assemblies not only attempted to control the number of representatives and the extent of each constituency (see Part IV), but they also favored triennial and biennial acts whereby they might insure a meeting of the colonial assembly every three or two years regardless of whether or not the governor summoned one. The reason behind such acts

*was a desire to continue unbroken colonial self-gov-
ernment. The colonials referred to English precedent,
particularly the Triennial Act of 1694, adopted by
Parliament to guard against the possibility of arbitrary government by a king who might try to rule
without reference to or consultation with Parliament.*

*The North Carolina assembly, while still under
proprietary rule, passed the Biennial Act of 1715.
The act states forthrightly the expectations of assembly rule and the assembly's role in the colonial
government. Note that no reference is made to being
summoned by the governor, and in many respects,
the governor and his powers are ignored. But the act
incorporates the colonial arguments for legislative action as a fundamental ingredient in the operation of
the political system of the colonies and the empire.*

Act Relating to the Biennial and Other Assemblys and Regulating Elections and Members.

I. Whereas His Excellency the Palatine and the rest
of the true and Absolute Lord's Proprietors of Carolina,
having duely considered the priviledges and immunities
wherewith the Kingdom of Great Brittain is endued and
being desirous that this their province may have such as
may thereby enlarge the Settlement and that the frequent
sitting of Assembly is a principal, safeguard of 'their People's priviledges, have thought fit to enact. And Be It
Therefore Enacted by the said Pallatine and Lords Proprietors by and with the advice and consent of this present
Grand Assembly now met at Little River for the North
East part of the said province:

II. And it is Hereby Enacted that for the due election
and Constituting of Members of the Biennial and other
Assemblys it shall be lawfull for the Freemen of the respective precincts of the County of Albemarle to meet the
first Tuesday in September every two years in the places
hereafter mentioned. . . .

III. And Be It Further Enacted that it is and may be
lawfull for the inhabitants and freemen in each Precinct in
every other County or Counties that now is or shall be
hereafter erected in this Government aforesaid to meet as

aforesaid at such place as shall be judged most convenient by the Marshall of such county, unless he be otherwise ordered by the special commands of the Governor or Commander in Chief to choose two freeholders out of every precinct in the county aforesaid to sit and vote in the said Assembly.

IV. And Be It Further Enacted that the Burgesses so chosen in each precinct for the Biennial Assembly shall meet and sitt the first Monday in November then next following, every two years, at the same place the Assembly last satt except the Pallatines Court shall by their proclamation published Twenty days before the said meeting appoint some other place and there with the consent and concurrence of the Pallatine Court shall make and ordain such Laws as shall be thought most necessary for the Good of this Government. Provided allways and nevertheless that the Powers granted to the Lord's Proprietors from the Crown of Calling, proroguing and dissolving Assemblys are not hereby meant or intended to be invaded, limited or restrained.

V. And It Is Hereby Further Enacted by the Authority aforesaid that no person whatsoever Inhabitant of this Government born out of the allegiance of His Majesty and not made free; no Negroes, Mulattoes, Mustees or Indians shall be capable of voting for Members of Assembly; and that no other person shall be allowed or admitted to vote for Members of Assembly in this Government unless he be of the Age of one and twenty years and has been one full year in the Government and has paid one year's levy preceding the Election.

VI. And Be It Further Enacted that all persons offering to vote for Members of Assembly shall bring a list to the Marshall or Deputy taking the Pole containing the names of the persons he votes for and shall subscribe his own name or cause the same to be done: And if any such person or persons shall be suspected either by the Marshall or any of the candidates not to be qualified according to the true intent and meaning of this Act, then the Marshall, Deputy Marshall, or other Officer that shall be appointed to take and receive such votes and list—shall have power to administer an oath or attestation to every such suspected person of his qualification and ability to choose Members of Assembly and whether he has not before given in his list at that Election.

VII. And Be It Further Enacted that Every Officer or Marshall which shall admit of or take the vote of any person not truly qualified according to the purport and meaning of this Act (provided the objection be made by any candidate or Inspector) or shall make undue return of any person for Member of Assembly shall forfeit for such vote taken, so admitted and for such Return Twenty pounds to be employed for and towards the building of any Court House, Church or Chapel as the Governor for the time being shall think fitt; but if no such building require it then to the Lord's Proprietors and Twenty Pounds to each person which of right and majority of votes ought to have been returned: to be recovered by Action of Debt, Bill, Plaint or Information in any Court of Record in this Government wherein no Essoign Wager of Law or Protection shall be allowed or admitted.

VIII. And Be It Further Enacted that every Marshall or Officer whose business and duty it is to make returns of Elections of Members of Assembly, shall attend the Assembly the first Three days of their sitting (unless he have leave of Assembly to depart) to inform the Assembly of all matters and disputes as shall arise about Elections and shall show to the Assembly the List of the Votes for every person returned and have made complaints of false returns to the Assembly; every Marshall or other Officer as aforesaid which shall deny or refuse to attend as aforesaid shall forfeit the sum of Twenty pounds to be recovered and disposed of in such manner and form as the Forfeitures before by this Act appointed.

IX. And Be It Further Enacted that whatsoever Member or Representative so elected as aforesaid shall faile in making his personal appearance and giving his attendance at the Assembly precisely on the day limited by the Writt (or on the day appointed for the meeting of the Biennial Assembly, when the election is for the Biennial Assembly) shall be fined for every day's absence during the sitting of the Assembly (unless by disability or other impediment to be allowed by the Assembly) Twenty Shillings to be levied by a Warrant from the Speaker and to be applied to such uses as the Lower House of Assembly shall think fitt.

X. And Be It Further Enacted that every member of Assembly that shall be elected as aforesaid after the Ratifying of this Act shall not be qualified to sitt as a Member in the House of Burgesses before he shall willingly take the Oath of Allegiance and Supremacy the Adjuration Oath and all such other Oathes as shall be ordered and directed to be taken by the Members of Parliament in Great Britain.

XI. And Be It Further Enacted that the quorum of the House of Burgesses for voting and passing of Bills shall not be less than one full half of the House and that no Bills shall be signed and Ratified except there be present Eight of the Members whereof the Speaker to be one. And in case that eight Members shall meet at any Assembly those eight shall have full power to adjourn from day to day till a sufficient number can assemble to transact the Business of the Government.

DOCUMENT 4

GOVERNOR GABRIEL JOHNSTON'S REQUEST TO REPEAL THE BIENNIAL ACT, 18 OCTOBER 1736

Gabriel Johnston served as governor of North Carolina from 1733 to 1752. Compared with the usual tenure, his term was a long one. Soon after assuming office, Johnston found the Biennial Act of 1715 a particular annoyance, in part because it obviously reduced the power of the governor and in part because of practical considerations. The Governor addressed his request for its repeal to the Board of Trade.

I sent your Lordships the only Copies of our Laws I could procure last December with such remarks as my bad state of health would then permit me to make. I did venture at that time to desire you to advise His Majesty to repeal as soon as possible the Biennial Law and to order that no Precinct should on any Pretence whatsoever be Represented by more than two members and to discharge me from consenting to Erect any new Precinct without His Majestys permission. I am still confirmed in my Opinion of this matter, and I am satisfied we never shall have a Reason[able] Assembly while this Act subsists. I have by this Conveyance sent an attested Copy of the said Biennial Law and shall only observe (1) That it is highly unreasonable that any Assembly should presume to meet without His Majestys Writt, and therefore I dissolved them when they mett last. (2) The six Precincts in the County of Albemarle have in each five Members making thirty, and the number of People in it is I am sure not fifteen thousand, which is by much too large a Representation. (3) The whole lower House by this means consists of forty six and it is impossible to pick out in the whole Province so many fitt to do business. (4) The greatest objection is that there must be a new election every two years which is too short a time to settle a Country which has been so long in confusion, and men of sense who sincerely mean the Publick good are so much afraid of the next Elections that they are obliged to go in with the majority whose Ignorance and want of education makes them obstruct everything for the good of the Country even so much as the Building of Churches or erecting of schools or endeavouring to maintain a direct Trade to Great Britain. If your Lordships approve of this I beg no time may be lost but I may have this Repealed by the way of Virginia and South Carolina by June next at farthest and the Governors of these Provinces may have orders to forward it. This one thing would contribute to the quiet and settlement of this Country more than I am able to Express. . . .

DOCUMENT 5

DISPOSITION OF THE BIENNIAL ACT, 1737

When Governor Johnston's request to repeal the Biennial Act of 1715 reached the Board of Trade in England, the question was referred specifically to Francis Fane, its legal counsel. In the document that follows, Fane advises that the act be declared null and void, a recommendation that was eventually accepted. The fate of the North Carolina Biennial Act was also typical of the history of colonial triennial acts. In each case, with rare exceptions such as in South Carolina, these acts were nullified by the Crown.

Francis Fane to Council of Trade and Plantations. By an Act passed in Carolina in the time of the Lords Proprietors relating to biennial and other assemblies and regulating elections and members, I observe that there is a power given to the assembly of this colony to meet without the consent of the Crown. The charter to the Lords Proprietors does not warrant this proceeding. The power of calling of parliaments is admitted to be an inherent privilege in the Crown, and I believe this is the first instance that such an attempt has been made to deprive the Crown of it. I think you should show your disapprobation of a law which in so high a degree encroaches upon the prerogative of the Crown. But I must observe to you, if the facts are true which are stated in the memorial of Mr. Smyth the Chief Justice, I think it cannot be considered as an Act in force, not having received a due confirmation agreeable to the rules settled by the Lords Proprietors themselves.

DOCUMENT 6

THE PREROGATIVES OF THE ASSEMBLY IN CHOOSING A SPEAKER,
10 JANUARY 1748

In almost every colony a struggle arose between the colonial assemblies and the Crown, represented by the governor, over the issue of choosing a speaker. The assemblies believed that this power should be reserved exclusively to them, because the speaker was their legislative leader. If the governor's choice prevailed, the person selected could block assembly legislation, control committee assignments, and serve the governor by informing him of the proposed legislative strategy of the assembly. For these reasons, the assembly, in this case the assembly of New Hampshire, sought control over the appointment of the speaker, basing its action on British precedent and colonial experience.

May it please your Excellency

With your Excellency's permission we will make a short recapitulation of the Several Messages passed between your Excellency and this House touching your Excellency's Power to Negative a Speaker and Introduce Members amongst us not Warranted by Law Usage or Custom or any other Authority that we Can find. Then we'll make a Short Remark or two on what is past and Suggest a few Authoritys which we think full in Point Against what your Excellency Requires and then give our final Resolution on the Premises.

Your Excellency first sent to this House your Direction to Choose a Speaker; we immediately Did it And informed your Excellency what we had done. Your Excellency's next message was to inquire whether the Members as you were pleased to Call them Returned from Chester and South Hampton Voted in the Choice of a Speaker.

To which we Replyd the Gentlemen which Appeared from Chester and South Hampton Did not vote in the Choice of a Speaker.

Then your Excellency was pleased to Send us your Disapprobation of our Choice of a Speaker and to Direct us to proceed to the Choice of Another And to Declare that no Choice would be Approved of Unless the persons who had been Excluded before were admitted to Vote in the new Choice

To which we Humbly Replyd that as Soon as your Excellency would be pleased to show us your power to Negative a Speaker we would immediately Submit to it and proceed to Another Choice And as Soon as your Excellency would evince to us that the pretended members had a Right to Sit And Vote in this House we would immediately admit them. But till Such Evidence should be produced both in the one Case and the other we Could not See the way Clear to Comply with what your Excellency had Required.

Then your Excellency was pleased to Reply that when your message should be fully obeyed in the Choice of a New Speaker And the two persons from Chester and South Hampton Admitted to Vote in the Second Choice that then you should be Ready to Give us a Satisfactory Answer to things we had a Right to inquire into and not till then

Thus Stands the Case Between your Excellency and this House And this is the Seventh day Since the Session Commenced without our being permitted to enter upon the Common and ordinary business of the Province Unless we would yield to your Excellency two important points of Priviledge which we were and are full in the opinion your Excellency had no Right to Demand.

After your Excellency was pleased to begin a dispute with us did we not indeavor to shorten it in a Becoming manner.

When your Excellency inquired whether the persons Returned from South Hampton and Chester were admitted to Vote did we not immediately Answer that they were not Tho perhaps upon a Critical Examination into the Rights of Governours it would be found that your Excellency had no Right to make Such an inquisition yet how Readily did we yield it And here we would humbly ask why your Excellency Chose Rather to inquire whether the persons Returned from Chester and South Hampton Voted than whether the members Sent from Portsmouth and Dover Did—Does not the Question imply that your Excellency apprehended the Chester and South Hampton persons would not be Admitted And what could such Apprehensions be Grounded on But a Consciousness that your Excellency had no power to impose them upon us.

Then Sir with Respect to the message we Sent to your Excellency Requesting to see your Power for Negativing a Speaker And Admitting the two persons from Chester and South Hampton, Can your Excellency imagine that such a Reply should be Satisfactory to a Senatorian Assembly. Your Excellency Required of us what we thought Unlawfull and therefore we prayed you would show us your Right to Command and promise; As Soon as your Excellency should do so we would immediately Obey—But Lo, what was your Reply—That when your Message is fully obeyed you would give us a Satisfactory Answer to what we had a Right to inquire into. What is this but insisting that we should first take a Leap in the Dark and then your Excellency would Order a Light to be held to us that we might Discern whether we had leaped Right or wrong.

And now Sir with Respect to the authoritys we promised to Suggest and first in Regard to the Power of Negativing a Speaker we find in Bishop Burnets history of his own times that in the year 1679 It was said the House had the Choice of their Speaker in them and that their presenting the Speaker was only a Solemn Shewing him to the King Such as was presenting the Lord Mayor and Sheriffs of London in the Exchequer but that the King was bound to Confirm their Choice—Again The point was Setled that the Right of Electing was in the House and that Confirmation was a thing of Course. Thus far the Bishop. And thus we presume the Case Stands between the King and the House of Commons at this day. If your Excellency Knows it to be otherwise we Beseech you to Communicate it to us that we may Act According to knowledge for We Abjure all implicit faith in Politicks As well as Religion

And are resolved to See with our Own Eyes And Act According to our own Understanding.

Again we find a Grant Made to a Governour of a Neighbouring Province by Letters patent from King William and Queen Mary in the third year of their Reign That he with the Council And Assembly should make Orders, Laws, Statutes and Ordinances, Directions and Instructions for the Welfare of the Province and that he the Governour should have a Negative Voice upon all Such Orders, Laws, Statutes and Ordinances and in all Elections and Acts of Government whatsoever to be passed by the General Court or Assembly or in Council And Tho' this power is Greater than what we think is Contained in your Excellency's Commission yet his Majesty King George the first in the twelfth year of his Reign Explicitly Says that no Provision is made in the Said Letters Patent meaning those above mentioned touching the Nomination and Election of A Speaker nor any reservation made for his being Approved or Disapproved by a Governour.

Upon your Excellency's Considering what we have offered on this Point We humbly hope your Excellency will be pleased to retract your Disapprobation of Our Choice of a Speaker or Shew us that you have a Right to maintain it. As to calling members of Assembly from Unpriviledged places if your Excellency will be Referred to President Cutt's Commission which was the first for this Province it will we apprehend Easily End the Dispute for by it you may See that in the Very first formation And founding this Government the People were Ordered by the King to have a hand in it. And while there was no Assembly yet in the Province and the first was to be called for a first there must be the King Says to the President and Councill that within a Limitted time they shall issue a Summons for Convening a General Assembly Observing such Rules and Methods and Appointing such time and Place of Meeting As the Electors shall think fit. And Agreeable to this in forming the Government of a Neighbouring Province it was Appointed by the Crown that they should have two members from every Town in their first Assembly And that they with the other Branches of the Legislature should

Determine what members should be afterwards Sent to Represent the Country Towns and Places.

What we would further add is the Custom and Usage of the Province According to which by your Excellency's Commission General Assemblys are to be Called which as we Apprehend has always been that the Admission of Any new member was by Vote or Act of General Assembly And for this we would Refer your Excellency to a Message Sent to your Excellency by a former Assembly when this Same thing was in Dispute About four years ago.

Upon the whole we Say once more if your Excellency will shew us that you have a Power to Negative a Speaker we will proceed to Another Choice And if your Excellency will shew us that you have a Right to introduce Chester and South Hampton Persons into this House Against the Common Custom and Usage of the Province We will admit them But in Case no Such Evidences are produced:

Voted and Resolved That we do and will Adhere to our Right and Privilege in both those Cases As well as in all other According to the Laws, Usage and Custom of the Province and are fully Determined not to proceed to the Choice of Another Speaker nor to Admit the two persons from Chester and South Hampton aforesaid but upon the Conditions before mentioned And this we Humbly offer as the final Result of this House Upon these two Points.

DOCUMENT 7

THE GOVERNOR'S PREROGATIVES IN CHOOSING A SPEAKER,
15 FEBRUARY 1748

Governor Benning Wentworth of New Hampshire, a native son, spoke in behalf of the royal prerogative, basing his position on the instructions drawn up by the Board of Trade. In most cases, the colonial assemblies won the right to appoint the speaker, but in

*New Hampshire, a rare case, Governor Wentworth's
clever maneuvering prevented the assembly from gaining this advantage.*

To the members of the Assembly returned on his
Majestys Writ to serve in General Assembly—

If in any manner you have had his Majestys Instruction Given at White Hall June 30th 1748 signified to the
members of the General Assembly Determining the Right
to be in the Crown of Lawfully Extending the Priviledge
of sending Representatives, to such new Towns as his
Majesty shall Judge worthy thereof, it was all his Majesty
intended, when I am commanded by said Instructions to
signifie his Majestys Pleasure therein to the members of
the said General Assembly.

As to the method of Doing it, and time when I hope
I may be permitted to be the sole Judge and therefore
you may not Expect any other part of the Royal Instruction than what has been laid before you. The Kings Instructions being to govern me and for you to obey.

You seem to cavell at the Language of the Royal Instruction, but when you will give yourselves time to cool
a little I am perswaded you will find the English to be
Sterling, and that it needs no further Explanation.

It will be needless to put the people you Represent to
any further expence in disputing about the names of the
towns the members are called from, which you have hitherto refused a seat with the other members; Because I
have by vertue of my Commission called them from such
Towns as I thought worthy thereof—and if I had thought
ten other Towns worthy of sending Representatives I
should in obedience to the Royal Instruction have supported their Election as zealously as I shall the Election
of Colonel Blanchard and Mr. Packer and the other new
members; In the Execution whereof I am sure of his Majesty's approbation, and as sure that your conduct will be
Esteemed the Highest Act of Disobedience, and if you could
but lay aside the strong Prejudice some of you brought
with you, you must honestly confess, that you have as far
as in your power been striping a sett of honest industrious

People of a Priviledge which his Majesty has Determined have an equal Right with yourselves.

I shall pass by the Irregularities and Indecencies of the other parts of what you call your message of the 14th Instant, and shall only take Notice of what relates to the choice of a new Speaker. The King's Commission and Instructions are and shall be the measure of my conduct in the administration of my government, and by them I have a negative on every act of Government, and consequently full power to Negative one or more Speakers and if my authority will not convince you clearer Evidence may be had at White Hall where some Gentlemen seem very fond of going and where any misconduct of mine will be impartially considered. But I would advise you to be certain of the justness of your cause before you presume so far: For if you should have the misfortune to miscarry it would illustrate my conduct which would neither answer your purposes nor intentions. Be pleased Gentlemen once more to take under your consideration how long you have disobeyed his Majesty's Commands in not proceeding to the choice of a Speaker after the Speaker presented to the Chair was Disapproved by me, whereby you have put a stop to the administration of my Government so far as was in your Power.

Be pleased likewise to consider the Error you have made proceeding to debar Gentlemen called to serve their King and Country by the same Authority with your selves from a seat in the House of Representatives before you had the least shadow of power to justify you. If you had proceeded against these Gentlemen after you were Qualified to act as a seperate Branch of the Legislature, it might have been less Expensive to the Publick and for which I believe the people you represent would have thank't you. But as you have thought fit to act otherwise I am Indispensably bound in obedience to the Royal Commands to support the King's Authority in every branch of it and to use my utmost Endeavors in support of his Instructions.

DOCUMENT 8

THE PENNSYLVANIA ASSEMBLY OPPOSES THE GOVERNOR ON DEFENSE MEASURES, JULY 1740

The defense of the English colonies in America was considered a shared responsibility between the Crown and the colonies. The Crown frequently sent instructions to a governor requesting that his colony provide troops for a military expedition or for deployment to defend a group of colonies against a common danger.

In 1739–1740, England was engaged in a war with Spain known as the War of Jenkins' Ear. In general, the war was popular with the colonies, especially the Southern colonies, who regarded Spanish Florida as a threat. The British carried out an expedition, with miserable results, to scourge the Spanish possessions in the West Indies, using volunteers from the English continental colonies as one of the principal military forces. The call for troops from the colonies included Pennsylvania, the colony of the Quaker pacifists. For the Quakers, however, the issue with which they were faced was primarily economic and political, not moral, and they argued strenuously against the extent of British power in military policy.

May it please the Governor,

We have often had Occasion to acquaint the Governor, that the greater Number of the present Assembly are of the People called Quakers, principled against bearing of Arms, or applying Money to any such Purposes: Desirous however to demonstrate our Obedience to our present Sovereign King George, by yielding a ready and chearful Compliance in the Matters recommended to us, so far as our religious Perswasions would permit; and willing to give ample Testimony of the Loyalty and sincere Affec-

tions of his loving Subjects within this Province; we determined at our last Meeting, that a Sum of Money should
be raised for the Use of the Crown, exceeding, in Proportion, as we think, what is given in some neighbouring
Colonies. Several Difficulties occured to us whilst that Matter was under our Consideration. The publick Accounts
were then unsettled, and it was unknown what Money remained in the Treasury. We observed also great Numbers
of bought Servants, belonging to the Inhabitants of this
Province, encouraged to that Purpose, had enlisted in the
King's Service, and were detained from their Masters, to
their great Loss, and to the Injury of the Publick, which
we thought called loudly upon us to endeavour to redress.
These, and other Considerations, took up so much of our
Time, that our Harvest was full ripe; the Officers were
enlisting our Servants in great Numbers in the Country,
and Labour in this young Colony, excepting what is performed by these Servants, difficult to be obtained. The
Necessity of attending the Harvest, and our Speaker's Engagements to be absent at that Time in the Proprietary
Affairs, determined us to adjourn to the Eighteenth Day
of next Month, by which Time we expected the Publick
Accounts would be settled, and the Circumstances of the
Treasury better known. We were the rather induced to
this, because the Governor seemed to represent our Treasury full, and our Abilities of giving great: Whereas we
had, and still have, different Sentiments. For if it be considered, that great Charges have arisen on the Paper
Money, by the annual Payments given to the Proprietor
for obtaining the said Act; and for printing, signing, and
providing Materials to that End; and that considerable
Sums are drawn out for finishing and enclosing the State-
house; and the yearly Expenses of Government; the Ex-
changing of old Money for New, and other Debts due from
the Province; it will take up so much of the Publick
Money, as we apprehend will leave the Treasury in a much
worse State than the Governor has represented it.

Our affairs being thus circumstanced, we think ourselves very hardly used, in having a Small Recess, which
we thought, and yet think, could not be attended with
any great Inconvenience, so severely censured by the Gov-

ernor in the Writs by which we are now called together, as having adjourned ourselves, "To the great Prejudice of his Majesty's Service, notwithstanding the Governor's pressing Instances to the contrary."

To shew a becoming Zeal in executing the Commands of the Crown, is laudable, and will, no doubt, meet with a proper Acceptance from thence: But whilst the Governor is pleased to assume so much to himself, it seems hard not to allow us any; when in Matters, wherein our Consciences are not concerned, we could as chearfully give Demonstration of it as any of our Fellow Subjects.

The Obstacles we formerly met with are not as yet lessened, but increase, so as to render it a Duty, we think indispensibly necessary, to apply for Relief. The Governor is pleased to let us know, that the Troops enlisted in the King's Service are not so numerous as might be expected from a Province so populous, altho' Seven Companies are already compleated: But by what Rules this Estimate is made, we are very much at a loss to determine. Were we to form any Judgment from the whole Number expected, and the Abilities of the Inhabitants of this Province, compared with others on the Continent, we should think Three of the Seven Companies a full Proportion: And if we are rightly informed, are as many, if not more, than was expected from this Government, exclusive of the Territories. Besides, from the best Account we have hitherto gained of the Seven Companies which have been raised within this Government, there are Several Hundreds of bought Servants, whose Masters, if they are detained from them, must totally lose their Service, and the Publick the Benefit of their Labour. A Calamity, we persuade ourselves, the Crown never intended should befal any of its Dominions.

The Governor indeed has been pleased to tell us, "Had our Zeal been seasonably exerted, he doubted not a Number of Freemen might have been found here, etc., and that it was not then probable a Number of Men should be raised in Time, etc., without receiving Servants, unless a sufficient Bounty were immediately given, etc."

But had the Governor been pleased to recollect what had happened in this Province, it must be known to him, that Servants were encouraged to enlist, and that the Names of those who enlisted were directed to be concealed; which Concealment, and the severe Treatment those Masters who applied for their Servants received from the Persons appointed to take the Names of such as should apply to enlist themselves, gave the Servants an Opportunity of escaping from their Masters, and the King's Service, which many of them did, to the entire Loss of their Masters, before the Assembly had any Opportunity of giving a Bounty to Freemen, had they been so disposed.

The King and Parliament of Great-Britain seem desirous to encourage the Importation of White Servants into the Colonies of America, rather than Negroes; and have from time to time made Acts which seem to be directed to this End; but if the Property of the Master is so precarious, as to depend on the Will of his Servant, and the Pleasure of an Officer, it cannot but be expected there will be fewer Purchasers for the future, and that Trade consequently much discouraged. Besides, the Masters of these Servants have Reason to think their Properties unjustly invaded; and it will not be easy to shew, that any Goods, in which they have the most absolute Property, may not with equal Reason be taken from them as their Servants.

The Applications we have had by Petitions from the Masters, and our own Observation of the Difficulties many of them undergo, render them Objects worthy of Relief; and we therefore earnestly request the Governor, on their Behalf, that he would give Directions to discharge and deliver those Servants already enlisted within this Province, to their Masters, and that none may be enlisted for the future.

It must afford but a very melancholly Prospect, to discover the Farmer and Tradesman, whose Subsistance, and the Subsistance of their Families, very much depend on the Labour of their Servants, purchased, perhaps, at the Expence of the most they were worth, deprived of that Assistance, and put under the greatest Difficulties; the former, to secure what he has already sown, and to cultivate and to sow what is absolutely necessary to subsist on another Year; and the latter to carry on his Trade and Business; all owing to the Caprice of the Servant, and Will of an Officer, under pretence of serving the Crown, when hardly any greater Disservice could be done it. The Regard our

King has ever shewn to the Liberties and Properties of his Subjects, in every Part of his Dominions, sufficiently demonstrate to us, that no Thought so injurious ever entered his Royal Breast; and the Grievance is now become so great, and so general, that we conceive it would be inconsistent with that Duty we owe to the Crown, and the Trust reposed in us by our Country, should we give any Money without first seeking for Redress.

DOCUMENT 9

GOVERNOR THOMAS OF PENNSYLVANIA REPLIES TO THE ASSEMBLY,
2 AUGUST 1740

Even though he was the head of a proprietary colony, Pennsylvania, Governor George Thomas supported the position that the British were entitled to recruit according to the king's instructions. He states that the Crown's prerogatives included questions of defense and war, and he responds to the problem of the recruitment of indentured servants who enlisted at the expense of their masters.

Gentlemen,

In Answer to your Message of the Thirty-first of last Month, I recommend to you a Review of your Proceedings at your last Meeting. But lest his Majesty's Service should suffer by any Neglect of mine, and as Interest and Prejudices may blind some amongst you, who have otherwise good Intentions; it may be necessary for me to make some Observations upon them, as well as upon your last Message.

In my Speech of the Second of July last, I recommended to you, "To give a Bounty, as was done in some other Governments, to encourage Freemen to enlist," and expressed my Apprehensions, "That unless such Bounty were given, a Number of Men, sufficient to answer his Majesty's Expectations from a Province so populous, would not be raised, without receiving Servants."

In your Address to me of the Seventh of July, you tell me, That you cannot chearfully accede to the Measures recommended from thence; that is (from what goes before) from the Crown, and Government of your Mother Country. And then you say, That you cannot preserve good Consciences, and come into the Levying of Money, and appropriating it to the Uses recommended to you in my Speech; because it is repugnant to the religious Principles professed by the greater Number of the present Assembly, who are of the People called Quakers. But you made no Answer to what I said concerning Servants.

This I looked upon as a positive Refusal to comply with his Majesty's Eighth Instruction: But as the latter Part carried an Insinuation, that I had recommended something different from that Instruction; to cut off all Pretence for differing with me, I recommended to you "a Compliance with that Instruction," in his Majesty's own Words.

On the Ninth I informed you, "That a considerable Number of Men were enlisted, and that the Levies would be compleated in a reasonable Time, unless you discouraged them by delaying the necessary Supplies;" and I then recommended "a speedy Provision for them." To this Message you never vouchsafed to give me any Answer, so far were you from complaining of the Enlisting of Servants at that Time.

On the Eleventh you sent me the Resolution of your House, to be delivered verbally by two of your Members; but as it related to a Matter so strongly recommended by his Majesty, I desired that the Members would return to the House, and bring it in Writing, for fear of Mistakes, either through Defect of their Memories or my own. And upon their Return, they did deliver it in Writing, acquainting me, That the House had made a considerable Progress in a Bill for raising of Money for the Use of the Crown; but it being Harvest Time, it would be injurious to the Country Members to stay the Completion of it: That there was a Rumour about the Town of the Probability of a Peace between Great-Britain and Spain: And for these Reasons you adjourned to the Eighteenth of August, notwithstanding my Instances to the contrary.

In this Resolution you were so far from making Complaints of the King's Officers having received Servants, who had voluntarily enlisted themselves, that you say, you had made a considerable Progress in a Bill for raising Money for the Use of the Crown. But to shew how little you were in earnest in that Bill, you adjourned to the Eighteenth of August, upon the Rumour of a Probability of a Peace (which no Man heard any Thing of but yourselves) to go Home to your Harvest, notwithstanding his Grace the Duke of Newcastle, in his Letter of the Fifth of April, which was laid before your House, and read there, says, "That Colonel Spotswood will receive his Majesty's Directions to sail with such a Number of the Troops as he can get together, so as to be at the Place appointed for the general Rendezvous by the latter End of August."

Colonel Gooch having, since that Adjournment, "pressed me earnestly to provide Transports and Provisions for the Troops, so as that they may be at the Capes of Virginia by the Middle of September," I called you by writ to meet me the Twenty-eighth of July. As you now find that the Time presses, and that you are obliged to come to the Point, to avoid complying with his Majesty's Instructions, the Bill for raising of Money for the Use of the Crown is vanished; and instead of it a Message is sent to me, demanding a Discharge of all such Servants as have voluntarily enlisted themselves, before you will raise any Money for his Majesty's Service.

In Answer to this new Demand, I say, That my Warrants to the Officers to enlist Men were general, and pursuant to the King's Orders; and the Officers inform me, that they did not receive any Servants till they met them travelling upon the Road to New-York to enlist there, and were well informed that many had gone thither before.

That to all that have applied to me for a Discharge for their Servants, I have given Notes, directed to the Officers, desiring them to discharge such Servants, if they can be persuaded to return to their Masters, and it can be done consistent with the Service. And as many have from thence been discharged here, so the Discharge of some has been procured by me from other Governments.

That I shall continue this Method, that the King's Service, and the Interest of the Masters of Servants, may go

Hand in Hand; and I doubt not, before the Troops embark, most People will be better satisfied than if the Officers had denied to receive them; as they would have run away, and enlisted themselves in other Governments, on account of the Bounty given, or better Provision made there for them. But as to discharging them all at once, it will be injurious to the King's Service; and if I may judge from what has happened already, breed such a Mutiny, as will not be very easy for me to quell; since upon Captain Thinn's returning some Servants back to their Masters, Freemen, as well as Servants, laid down their Arms, and declared, that they would go into other Governments, where the King's Soldiers were better used; and were about immediately to disband, had not the Captain's Temper and Presence of Mind found a Way to satisfy them.

That I shall not take upon me to determine, whether a Person indented for a Term of Years may enlist himself in the King's Service; tho' I have the Opinions of many able Lawyers upon it; and most of them give it for the Affirmative, with greater Strength of Reason and Law, in my Judgment, than those that hold the Negative. . . .

It must appear very extraordinary, that the King's Affairs should be postponed till you can find Leisure from your private Affairs to settle the Publick Accounts; or that the Officers receiving some Servants into the King's Service, should be thought a sufficient Reason for refusing what his Majesty so justly expects from a People who have, as yet, borne no Part of the Burden of a War, undertaken for the Preservation of their Property, when the Subjects in Britain chearfully pay very heavy Taxes. . . .

If you can shew me that you have contributed in the minutest Particular to the Execution of his Majesty's Orders, tho' so pressingly and affectionately recommended to you by his Majesty; or how one Man could have been raised in Time for this Expedition by any Encouragement given by you; I will readily acknowledge, and publish to the World, the Share of Merit due to you.

If his Majesty's Instructions, declaring, that he does not fix any Quota of Men; and his Grace the Duke of New-Castle's Letter, signifying his Majesty's Pleasure, that I am to raise as many Men as I possibly can, notwithstanding the Proportion of Arms carried by Colonel Blakeney; are not of equal Authority with any Information you pretend to have received, I confess myself incapable of satisfying you: But from your whole Conduct there appears good Reason to conclude, that to save your Money, you would have been pleased, that not even one Company had been raised here.

Altho' your Principles will not allow you to raise Men, or even, it seems, to support them when they are raised, you are ready enough to censure the Conduct of others who have been more zealous in the Execution of his Majesty's Commands. When you want an Addition of Paper Money, your Province is represented as very populous, and your Trade very great; but when you are called upon for Men or Money, your Numbers and your Abilities are very much diminished. I have seen, and informed myself of much of this Continent, and I can venture from thence to affirm, that, next to New-England, this Province is the most populous, and the best able to spare a Sum of Money for carrying on this glorious Undertaking; New-York, and other Governments, having been at a very great Expence in building Forts, and maintaining their Frontiers.

As it makes for your Purpose, you have greatly aggravated the Number of Servants enlisted, by calling them several Hundreds. . . .

I should be glad you would shew your Duty to his Majesty, and your Gratitude for the Powers and Privileges the People of your Society enjoy here, more than in any other Part of his Majesty's Dominions, by Actions as well as Words. If your Principles are inconsistent with the End of Government, at a Time when his Majesty is put under a Necessity of procuring Reparation for his injured Subjects by Arms, why did not your Consciences restrain you from solliciting for a Station, which your Consciences will not allow you to discharge, for the Honour of his Majesty, and the Interest of those you represent? For it is a Piece of Injustice to involve a People, of which you are not above one Third in Number, in the ill Consequences that must attend a Government under such a Direction.

Before you applied yourselves with great Industry to obtain an uncommon Majority in this Assembly, for op-

posing my endeavours to put the Province into a Posture
of Defence, the Government enjoyed such a Tranquility,
as gave every honest Man great Pleasure of Mind; but
since, the Defence of the Province has not only been
opposed, but the Rights of the Corporation of this City
(generously granted by your first great Proprietor) have
been attacked; Emissaries have been frequently employed
to promote Petitions for various Ends; and the Publick
Money has been spent in Contests with me, without doing
one single Act for the Service of your King, or the People you represent. This is a Behaviour very different from
that Spirit of Christianity you profess, and I think as different from that of your Friends in England.

DOCUMENT 10

AN ACT TO IMPOSE DUTIES ON THE IMPORTATION OF SLAVES, 1740

*In the Southern colonies, slavery emerged as a dis-
puted issue between the colonies and the mother
country. The issue of slavery, as it formed in the
eighteenth century, was based on fear, defense, and
profit—not on morality. As they came to recognize
the problems of a large slave population, most Southern colonies tried to impose a highly restrictive import duty to discourage if not prohibit the importation of slaves. The British, over a period of fifty
years, struck down these attempts, which encouraged
Jefferson in the first draft of the Declaration to include in his indictment of the king the statement,
"He [the king] has prostituted his negative for suppressing every legislative attempt to prohibit or restrain this execrable commerce," an assertion that
was eliminated in the final version because it offended New England merchants and certain Southern planters. After the Stono Rebellion of 1739 in
South Carolina, this particular act was adopted by its*

colonial legislature, the Commons House of Assembly.

An Act for the better strengthening of this Province, by granting to His Majesty certain taxes and impositions on the purchasers of Negroes imported, and for appropriating the same to the uses therein mentioned, and for granting to His Majesty a duty and imposition on Liquors and other Goods and Merchandizes, for the use of the Publick of this Province.

Whereas, the great importation of negroes from the coast of Africa, who are generally of a barbarous and savage disposition, may hereafter prove of very dangerous consequence to the peace and safety of this Province, and which we have now more reason to be apprehensive of from the late rising in rebellion of a great number of the negroes lately imported into this Province from the coast of Africa, in the thickest settlements of this Province, and barbarously murdering upwards of twenty persons of his Majesty's faithful subjects of this Province, within about twenty miles from the capital of this Province; and whereas, the best way to prevent those fatal mischiefs for the future, will be to establish a method by which the importation of negroes into this Province should be made a necessary means of introducing a proportionable number of white inhabitants into the same; and whereas, in order to effect this good purpose, it is fit and necessary that a sufficient fund should be appropriated by the laws of this Province for the better settling the frontiers, and also the several townships laid out in this Province, pursuant to his Majesty's royal instructions, and which, unless it be speedily effected, the settlement of the said townships and other frontier parts of this Province will be very greatly hindered, if not entirely obstructed; and whereas, his most sacred Majesty, by the one hundred and fourteenth article of his royal instructions to his Excellency Robert Johnson, Esq., late Governour of this Province, reciting that whereas several merchants of Great Britain, trading to South Carolina, have complained that by certain Acts of Assembly now in force in the said Province, duties are imposed on negroes imported there, and made payable by the importer, and have desired that the said duties may for the future be made payable by the purchasers, and not by the importer, submitting nevertheless, that the importer or his factor shall be security to the publick for the payment of the said duty, in case of the purchaser's failure, it was, by the said instruction, declared to be his Majesty's will and pleasure that his said Excellency should endeavour to get a law passed for explaining and altering the laws for collecting the said duties on negroes, agreeable to the desire of the said merchants: For the complying therefore with his Majesty's royal will and pleasure, and for the effectual raising and appropriating a sufficient fund for the better settling his Majesty's townships and the other frontier parts of this Province with white inhabitants, by which we may be the better enabled to suppress any future insurrection of negroes and slaves, and to repel any attempts of his Majesty's enemies against the peace of this Province, and may also have a fund for discharging such other demands as may be made for the necessary security thereof; We, his Majesty's faithful and loyal subjects, the Commons House of Assembly, now met in General Assembly, do cheerfully and unanimously give and grant unto his most sacred Majesty, his heirs and successors, the several taxes, aids and impositions, hereinafter mentioned, for the uses, and to be raised, appropriated, paid and applied, as is hereinafter directed, and do humbly pray that it may be enacted,

I. *And be it enacted,* by the Honourable William Bull, Esquire, Lieutenant Governour and Commander-in-chief, in and over his Majesty's Province of South Carolina, by and with the advice and consent of his Majesty's honourable Council and the Commons House of Assembly of this Province, and by the authority of the same, That from and immediately after the passing of this Act until the end and term of fifteen months then next ensuing, and from and immediately after the expiration of the term of four years and three months next ensuing the passing of this Act, there shall be imposed and paid by all and every the inhabitants of this Province and other person and persons whomsoever, first purchasing any negro or other slave within the same which hath not been the space of six months within this Province, a certain tax or sum of ten pounds current money for every such negro and other slave of the height of four feet and two inches and upwards; and for every one under that height, and above three feet two inches, the sum of five pounds like money; and for all under three feet two inches (sucking children excepted), two pounds ten shillings like money, which every such inhabitant of this Province and other person and persons whomsoever shall so buy or purchase as aforesaid: And that immediately from and after the expiration of the said term of fifteen months next after the passing of this Act, for and during the term of three years thence next ensuing, and no longer, there shall be imposed on and paid by all and every the inhabitants of this Province and other person and persons whosoever first purchasing any negro or other slave within the same, which hath not been the space of six months in this Province, a certain tax or sum of one hundred pounds current money for every such negro and other slave of the height of four feet and two inches and upwards; and for every one under that height, and above three feet two inches, the sum of fifty pounds like money; and for all under three feet two inches (sucking children excepted), the sum of twenty-five pounds like money; which said sums of ten pounds, five pounds, two pounds ten shillings, and one hundred pounds, fifty pounds, and twenty-five pounds, current money, respectively, shall be paid by such purchaser for every such slave, at the time of his, her or their purchasing the same, to the publick treasurer of this Province for the time being, for the uses hereinafter mentioned, set down and appointed, under the pain of forfeiting all and every such negroes and slaves for which the said taxes or impositions shall not be paid, pursuant to the directions of this Act; the one half to his Majesty, his heirs and succesors, for the uses hereinafter mentioned, and the other half to him or them that will seize, sue and inform for the same, by any action, bill, plaint or information, in any court of record in this Province, wherein no essoign, protection or wager of law shall be admitted or allowed; any law, usage or custom to the contrary thereof in any wise notwithstanding.

II. *And be it further enacted* by the authority aforesaid, That the better to secure, collect and gather in the

said taxes from the said persons so first purchasing any
such negroes or other slaves as aforesaid, all and every
person and persons whatsoever in this Province, who from
and immediately after the passing of this Act, shall import
into this Province, or shall have any negroes or other
slaves to sell or dispose of, either in their own right or in
the right of any other person or persons, which negroes or
slaves shall have not been the space of six months in this
Province, every such importer or other person and persons,
shall before he or they shall sell or dispose of such negroes
or slaves, or any part thereof, give notice in writing under
his hand, of such intended sale or disposal, to the country
waiter for the time being, that is to say, of the time when,
the place where, and the number and quantity of such negroes and slaves so intended to be sold or disposed of,
under the penalty of forfeiting the sum of one hundred
pounds current money for every slave such person or persons shall sell or otherwise dispose of, for any term or time
whatever before such notice given as aforesaid; the one
half to his Majesty for the uses hereinafter mentioned, and
the other to him or them who will sue or inform for the
same, to be recovered as aforesaid.

III. And whereas, by reason of the length of time that
by the Act for granting to his Majesty a duty and imposition on negroes, liquors and other goods and merchandizes,
for the use of the publick of this Province, was given to
the merchants and factors for paying unto the publick
treasurer the duty imposed by that Act on the importation
of negroes, it hath sometimes happened that divers poor
protestants who have arrived in this Province, as well before the importation of such negroes as between the days
of such importation and the days of payment of the said
dutys arising by reason of such importation, have been
disappointed, and not met with that speedy supply or been
so soon settled as the exigency of their case did require,
or as they otherwise would have been had such dutys been
payable instantly, on such importations, which hath proved
of great discouragement to the poor protestants coming to
this Province, and of manifest detriment to the speedy
settlement of the said townships: For prevention therefore
of the like mischiefs for the future, and that the treasury

may be supplied with present provision for the relief and subsistence of poor protestants, *Be it enacted* by the authority aforesaid, That all and every person and persons who shall first buy or purchase any negroes or other slaves as aforesaid, shall and they are hereby obliged to pay the said taxes of ten pounds, five pounds, two pounds ten shillings, and one hundred pounds, fifty pounds and twenty-five pounds, current money, as the case shall require, for every such negro and other slave they shall so buy or purchase as aforesaid, to the publick treasurer, before he or they remove the said slave or slaves, or cause the same to be removed from the place where he shall buy or purchase the same, and shall take a receipt or certificate for the same from the said treasurer (which he is hereby required to give without fee or reward), and the said receipt or certificate shall be directed to the country waiter or waiters for the time being, and shall particularly mention the sum paid and the number of slaves for which the same was paid, and shall be a permit to the said waiter or waiters to suffer such person so obtaining the same, to remove and carry away the slaves therein mentioned; and such waiter and waiters is and are hereby directed and required to make a regular entry of every such receipt or certificate in a book to be fairly kept by him or them for that purpose, and duly to file the original.

IV. *And be it further enacted* by the authority aforesaid, That the said country waiter or waiters, and the waiter or waiters for the time being, is and are hereby authorized, impowered and required, upon having notice or information of any such sale or intended sale of any negroes or other slaves as aforesaid, to give diligent and constant attendance at the place and places of such sale, and in case he or they shall find that any person or persons shall have purchased or bought any negro or other slave as aforesaid, or shall attempt to remove or carry away any such negroe or slave without first having paid the said respective tax and obtained a receipt or certificate as aforesaid, and producing the same to the said waiter or waiters, that then it shall and may be lawful to and for such waiter or waiters, and he and they is and are hereby impowered to seize and take all and every such negroes and other slaves as aforesaid, and the said negroes and slaves so seized as aforesaid, are hereby declared forfeited to all intents and purposes whatsoever; and if the said negroes or slaves cannot be found, then the purchaser shall forfeit the value of them, the one moiety to his Majesty for the uses hereinafter mentioned, the other moiety to the said waiter or waiters, to be recovered as aforesaid: Provided always, that if any person or persons who shall hereafter import any negroes or slaves into this Province, shall before the landing thereof give sufficient security by bond, made payable to his Majesty for the uses mentioned in this Act, to the satisfaction of the publick treasurer, to pay on behalf of the several purchasers the tax or imposition hereby laid and imposed on such negroes or slaves, within three months after the entry of the same, it shall and may be lawful for the said publick treasurer to give a permit for the landing such negroes or slaves, and in such case the waiter or waiters before mentioned, shall be freed and discharged from attending on the sale of such negroes or slaves.

V. *And be it further enacted* by the authority aforesaid, That every person and persons whatsoever, who from and immediately after the passing of this Act, shall import into this Province any negroes or other slaves, or their factors or agents to whom the same shall be consigned, shall be and they are hereby obliged and required, within forty-eight hours after such importation, to make an entry of all and every such negroes and slaves upon oath, in the office of the publick treasurer of this Province for the time being, upon pain of forfeiting the sum of one hundred pounds current money, for every such negro and other slave that shall be so imported, and of which no such entry shall be made as aforesaid within the time aforesaid, to be recovered as aforesaid; and all such negroes and other slaves imported as aforesaid, and which shall be landed or attempted to be landed as aforesaid, in any part of this Province before such entry made as aforesaid, shall and are hereby declared to be forfeited, the one half to his Majesty for the uses hereinafter mentioned, and the other half to him or them who will seize and sue, or inform for the same, to be recovered as aforesaid. . . .

DOCUMENT 11

MALACHY POSTLETHWAYT, *THE ADVANTAGES OF THE AFRICAN TRADE,* 1772

Fundamentally, the British took the position that any interference with the slave trade touched the economic well-being of the empire. The British merchants were most persistent in this view, because they were deeply engaged in the trade, particularly from 1713 onward, when, by the Treaty of Utrecht, the British received the Assiento, the exclusive right to supply the Spanish colonies in America with slaves.

British political economists gave their blessing to the slave trade, regarding it as a cornerstone of British commercial prosperity. No respectable writer on commerce took a contrary position, and Malachy Postlethwayt, whose writings influenced the young Alexander Hamilton, was no exception.

The most approved Judges of the commercial Interests of these Kingdoms have ever been of Opinion, that our West-India and African Trades are the most nationally beneficial of any we carry on. It is also allowed on all Hands, that the Trade to Africa is the Branch which renders our American Colonies and Plantations so advantagious to Great-Britain; that Traffic only affording our Planters a constant Supply of Negroe-Servants for the Culture of their Lands in the Produce of Sugars, Tobacco, Rice, Rum . . . Fustick, Pimento, and all other our Plantation-Produce: So that the extensive Employment of our Shipping in, to, and from America, the great Brood of Seamen consequent thereupon, and the daily Bread of the most considerable Part of our British Manufacturers, are owing primarily to the Labour of Negroes; who, as they were the first happy Instruments of raising our Plantations; so their Labour only can support and preserve them, and render them still more and more profitable to their Mother-Kingdom.

The Negroe-Trade therefore, and the natural Consequences resulting from it, may be justly esteemed an inexhaustible Fund of Wealth and Naval Power to this Nation. And by the Overplus of Negroes above what have served our own Plantations, we have drawn likewise no inconsiderable Quantities of Treasure from the Spaniards, who are settled on the Continent of America; not only for Negroes furnished them from Jamaica, but by the late Assiento Contract with the Crown of Spain; which may probably again be revived, upon a Peace being concluded with that Kingdom.

What renders the Negroe-Trade still more estimable and important, is, that near Nine-tenths of those Negroes are paid for in Africa with British Produce and Manufactures only; and the Remainder with East-India Commodities. We send no Specie or Bullion to pay for the Products of Africa, but, 'tis certain, we bring from thence very large Quantities of Gold; and not only that but Wax and Ivory; the one serves for a foreign Export without the least Detriment to our own Product; the other is manufactured at Home, and afterwards carried to foreign Markets, to no little Advantage both to the Nation and the Traders. From which Facts, the Trade to Africa may very truly be said to be, as it were, all Profit to the Nation; the direct Trade thither affords a considerable national Ballance in our Favour, and is apparently attended with such a Series of advantagious Consequences, that no other Branch whatever of our foreign Traffic admits of.

And it may be worth Consideration, that while our Plantations depend only on Planting by Negroe-Servants, they will neither depopulate our own Country, become independent of her Dominion, or any way interfere with the Interests of the British Manufacturer, Merchant, or Landed Gentleman: Whereas were we under the Necessity of supplying our Colonies with White-Men instead of Blacks, they could not fail being in a Capacity to interfere with the Manufactures of this Nation, in Time to shake off their Dependency thereon, and prove as injurious to the Landed, and Trading-Interests as ever they have hitherto been beneficial.

Many are prepossessed against this Trade, thinking it a barbarous, inhuman, and unlawful Traffic for a Christian Country to Trade in Blacks; to which I would beg leave to observe; that though the odious Appellation of Slaves is annexed to this Trade, it being called by some the Slave-Trade, yet it does not appear from the best Enquiry I have been able to make, that the State of those People is changed for the worse, by being Servants to our British Planters in America; they are certainly treated with great Lenity and Humanity: And as the Improvement of the Planter's Estates depends upon due Care being taken of their Healths and Lives, I cannot but think their Condition is much bettered to what it was in their own Country.

Besides, the Negroe-Princes in Africa, 'tis well known, are in perpetual War with each other; and since before they had this Method of disposing of their Prisoners of War to Christian Merchants, they were wont not only to be applied to inhuman Sacrifices, but to extream Torture and Barbarity, their Transplantation must certainly be a Melioration of their Condition; provided living in a civilized Christian Country, is better than living among Savages: Nay, if Life be preferable to Torment and cruel Death, their State cannot, with any Colour of Reason, be presumed to be worsted.

But I never heard it said that the Lives of Negroes in the Servitude of our Planters were less tolerable than those of Colliers and Miners in all Christian Countries. However, while our Rivals in Trade receive great national Emolument by the Labour of these People, this Objection will be of little Weight with those who have the Interest of their Country at Heart; or indeed the Welfare of the Negroes.

But to resume the Subject. As the present Prosperity and Splendor of the British Colonies have been owing to Negroe-Labour; so not only their future Advancement, but even their very Being depends upon our pursuing the same Measures in this Respect as our Competitors do.

That our Colonies are capable of very great Improvements, by the proper Application of the Labour of Blacks, has been urged by the most experienced Judges of Commerce. And if it be good Policy to purchase as little from, and sell as much to foreign Nations of our own Produce and Manufactures, 'tis certainly very unwise and impolitic in us not to encourage our Plantations to the extent they are capable of; in order to supply ourselves at least from thence with what we can't do without; and take from other Nations such Essentials only, as neither our own Country, or our Plantations will afford us.

From these Considerations it has been wisely proposed to extend the Planting of Coffee, Cocoa, Indigo, Cochneal, Logwood, Hemp, Flax, Naval Stores, and making of Pot-ash, and variety of other Products, which those Lands admit of. Whereby, instead of being under the disadvantagious Necessity of purchasing such valuable and useful Merchandize of other Nations, we might easily become capable, not only of supplying ourselves, but exporting to others considerable Quantities of our Plantation-Produce. This would turn the ballance of Trade in our Favour, with Countries where 'tis now against us; and enable our Colonies to encrease their demand for British Manufactures, in Proportion to our Demand for their Produce.

But all Improvements proposed to be made in our Plantations, have always presupposed the Well-Being and Prosperity of our African-Trade; to the End that they might not be destitute of a constant Supply of Negroes for those Purposes: Without which, instead of Improvement, nothing but Distress and Poverty could ensue in all the British Colonies, while France, by wiser Measures, would render their Colonies still more opulent, and consequently a more formidable Nursery of Naval Power.

And however mean an Idea some may entertain of the Advantages arising from the direct Trade to Africa, it can proceed from nothing but want of being duly acquainted therewith. Was all the Gold that has, or easily might have been brought from thence, coined at the Tower, with some Impression to distinguish it from all other Gold, as was formerly done, we should soon be sensible, that we need be little beholding to any other Nation for that valuable Metal; for were we to extend our Commerce into Africa, to the Pitch it will admit of, we must certainly export thither, of the British Produce and Manufacture, considerably more than we do to any one Country in the whole World.

The Continent of Africa is of great Magnitude, the Country extremely populous, and the Trade and Navigation now well known, easy, and not hazardous. As the Natives in general stand in great Need of European Commodities, so they have valuable Returns to make us; and such too, that do in no respect interfere either with the Produce and Manufactures of these Kingdoms, or her American Plantations; which ought never to be forgot, it being the State of no other Branch of Trade carried on by the whole British Empire. . . .

DOCUMENT 12

RESOLUTION OF THE VIRGINIA HOUSE OF BURGESSES ON COLONIAL AUTHORITY, 14 NOVEMBER 1764

Each issue that arose between the mother country and the colonies can be incorporated into an important and more general heading, the contest for authority. What authority did the colonials possess? What were the limits of power for the colonial assembly? Were those limits to be defined by agreement between the mother country and the colonies, or were they to be defined exclusively by Britain? If the latter position were valid, the colonials could exercise only that authority England wished to give them. Under these circumstances, England could restrict or enlarge the colonial authority at will, or, for that matter, eliminate colonial authority altogether. Colonial rights, under these conditions, were entirely subject to the ups-and-downs of royal grace and favor.

Whatever the validity of the theory held by the Crown and Parliament—and the British clung to it until the American Revolution—the colonials had developed a precise position regarding their own constitutional authority. In this document, the proceedings of the Virginia House of Burgesses in 1764

are an articulation of the views of the assembly in
particular and the colonials in general. They an-
ticipated the Stamp Act crisis of 1765 and fore-
shadowed what might happen if Parliament decided
to levy taxes in America.

Resolved, That a most humble and dutiful Address be presented to his Majesty, imploring his Royal Protection of his faithful Subjects, the People of this Colony, in the Enjoyment of all their natural and civil Rights, as Men, and as Descendents of Britons; which Rights must be violated, if Laws respecting the internal Government, and Taxation of themselves, are imposed upon them by any other Power than that derived from their own Consent, by and with the Approbation of their Sovereign, or his Substitute: And professing, that as these People have at all Times been forward and zealous to demonstrate their Loyalty and Affection to his Majesty, and especially by a ready Compliance with the Requisitions of the Crown to bear their Part in the late War, which they engaged to do with the more Alacrity, from a Confidence that the Royal Benignity would never suffer them to be deprived of their Freedom (that sacred Birthright and inestimable Blessing) so they would be willing to contribute their Proportion of any Expenses necessary for the Defence and Security of America, as far as Circumstances of the People, already distressed with Taxes, would admit of, provided it were left to themselves to raise it, by Modes least grievous.

Resolved, That a Memorial be prepared to be laid before the Right Honourable the Lords Spiritual and Temporal in Parliament assembled, intreating their Lordships, by a proper and reasonable Interposition and Exertion of their Power, not to suffer the People of this Colony to be enslaved or oppressed by Laws respecting their internal Polity, and Taxes imposed on them in a Manner that is unconstitutional; and declaring our Hopes that the Preservation of the Rights of any of his Majesty's faithful Subjects will be thought by their Lordships as an Object worthy the Attention of those hereditary Guardians and Protectors of British Liberty and Property, and especially as the Subversion of those Rights, in the Instance of taxing the People of Virginia, at this Time, when they are most grievously burthened by the Expenses of the late War, must diminish that Consumption of Manufactures furnished to them by their Mother Country, by which her wealth is very greatly augmented, and her Prosperity continued.

Resolved, That a Memorial be prepared to be laid before the Honourable the House of Commons, to assert, with decent Freedom, the Rights and Liberties of the People of this Colony as British Subjects, to remonstrate that Laws for their internal Government, or Taxation, ought not to be imposed by any Power but what is delegated to their Representatives, chosen by themselves, and to represent that the People are already taxed, for several Years to come, so heavily, for Expenses incurred in the late War, amounting to near Half a Million, that an Increase of that Burthen by the Parliament, at this Time, would be not only a Violation of the most sacred and valuable Principle of the Constitution, but such an Oppression as would probably draw after it a Desolation in many Parts of the Country, and must divert those of the Inhabitants, who could not remove from it, to manufacture what Articles they have hitherto been supplied with from the Mother Country, and consequently one grand Source of Wealth and Prosperity will be stopped up.

Resolved, That the Committee appointed to correspond with the Agent of this Colony in Great Britain pursuant to an Act of Assembly For appointing an agent, be directed to answer the Letter of the 25th of June last from the Committee of the House of Representatives of the Province of Massachusetts Bay to the Honourable the Speaker of the House of Representatives for the Province of Virginia, and to assure that Committee that the Assembly of Virginia are highly sensible of the very great Importance it is, as well to the Colony of Virginia, as to America in general, that the Subjects of Great Britain in this Part of its Dominions should continue in Possession of their ancient and most valuable Right of being taxed only by Consent of their Representatives, and that the Assembly here will omit no Measures in their Power to prevent such essential Injury from being done to the Rights and Liberties of the People.

✳ PART VI ✳

The Politics of
International Rivalry

EIGHTEENTH-CENTURY America was very much like
the twentieth century in the close interrelation of foreign
and domestic affairs. Almost every colonial in English
America, whether he lived on the seaboard or the frontier,
recognized that an episode in some other part of the world
could directly affect his personal welfare. An incident in
France might cut off the West Indian market for colonial
staples; war could disrupt trade channels and prevent
frontiersmen from finding buyers for their furs and skins.
By the same token, a confrontation between the English
or French or Spanish colonies in the New World affected
Europe.

The diplomats of the Western world in the eighteenth
century held as their goal a world balance of power. According to their theory, if world equilibrium were achieved,
peace would ensue automatically because an aggressor nation disturbing such an equilibrium would be met with a
countervailing force and thus gain nothing. The problem
of such a formula is that no nation remains constant. Some
grow stronger while others become weaker. As a result international groupings also become unstable. In the early
eighteenth century, for example, France, having grown
powerful on the continent during the reign of Louis XIV,
disturbed the delicate equilibrium by advancing forcibly its

northern boundary at the expense of the Low Countries. Other nations of Europe, including England, formed a coalition to counter the French threat.

As the American colonies of England, France, and Spain matured and developed vigorous economic and political resources in the eighteenth century, they became an increasingly important component in the balance-of-power concept. The exclusive right of the British, acquired by treaty, to furnish the Spanish colonies with slaves, for example, not only strengthened the British interests in the New World but also its international commercial position. When the colonial proportion of the total British trade increased from one-sixth to one-third, the importance of its possessions in America was greatly enhanced. Indeed, because of the rising importance of the English possessions, the relative strengths of Spain, France, and England in America required reappraisal—and readjustment—if the balance of power was to be maintained. But English economic growth and the acquisition of French territory in the New World at the end of the Great War for Empire (1755–1763) tipped the balance of power dramatically in favor of Britain.

These mainstreams represent the politics of international rivalry in which the American colonies of all nations played a starring role. Written at the end of the seventeenth century, the Memoir for the Marquis de Seignelay (Document 1) outlines the position of France with regard to the North American continent. The end of the seventeenth and the beginning of the eighteenth century corresponds with a policy of French expansion in Europe, which alarmed England and most other nations of Europe. A barometer of English concern is found in the speech of King William to the English Parliament (Document 2).

King William's speech marked the beginning of an intensive struggle between England and France, each supported by respective European allies in a conflict known as the War of Spanish Succession (1701–1713). The French monarchy, in attempting to unite the throne of France with that of Spain, not only disrupted the balance of power in Europe but also affected the American colonies, because Spanish and French possessions there bordered on those of England, so that any French-Spanish alliance constituted a serious threat to the existence of the English colonies.

The war ended with the Treaty of Utrecht in 1713. The terms of the treaty provided that the French and Spanish thrones be separated forever. Obviously, this provision had repercussions for the New World as well as the Old. Moreover, Spain granted Britain the Assiento, the exclusive right to provide the Spanish colonies in America with slaves for thirty years; the British government and commercial interests regarded this right as the cornerstone of English trade. Britain also received strategic territory in Europe, namely, Gibraltar, the gateway to the Mediterranean, and the island of Minorca. Further gains were Hudson's Bay, Newfoundland, Acadia (in North America), and St. Christopher (in the West Indies). From 1713 onward, the diplomats of Western Europe made every effort to preserve among the great powers the equilibrium established by the Treaty of Utrecht.

The objective of the treaty and its achievement, however, did not completely coincide. Within a few years, Alexander Spotswood, Lieutenant-Governor of Virginia, spoke out unhesitantly about the French threat to the English colonies in America (Document 3); the French responded that the English colonies were plotting war. In an informal exchange the governors of New York and Canada explored their differences (Document 4).

The confrontation between the Spanish and English colonies in America also created tension and conflict. England forced the issue in 1733 by founding the colony of Georgia in territory that Spain regarded as its legitimate possession. Although the founding of Georgia is often attributed to humanistic impulses within England, that is, for providing a colony for imprisoned English debtors, two equally vital motives prompted the British to take this step: one, mercantilist in character, to employ English labor to advantage by transferring debtors from prison in England, where they were a charge upon the public, to Georgia, where, hopefully, they would produce goods needed by Britain; and two, imperial in character, in which England deliberately extended its territory in the New World to curb the possible expansion of Spain.

Spain protested against the English action, even taking the trouble to assemble proof for its claim to the territory of Georgia (Document 5). Determined steps were taken by both sides: Spain made a *pacte de famille* (a family pact) with France in which the latter agreed to defend Spanish territory in America, including Georgia; undeterred, the English attempted unsuccessfully to reduce St. Augustine, the Spanish fortress on the Atlantic coast, and continued to argue in behalf of their claim to Georgia territory (Document 6). The conflict between Spain and England evoked a penetrating discussion of the issues by the Duke of Newcastle, the British Secretary of State (Document 7). Powerful Indian nations located along the Appalachian Mountain ridge played a significant role in these diplomatic maneuvers, a fact fully recognized by the Indian leaders themselves and by most experienced colonials. Governor Glen of South Carolina stressed the vital position of the Indians in the balance of power in Europe and America (Document 8).

Beginning about 1750, the great confrontation between England and France reached a new level of intensity. At that time the French prepared an official policy statement condemning "the British agression" in the West Indies, in Florida, and in the Ohio River Valley (Document 9). The same year the Marquis de la Galissoniere prepared a complementary document entitled "The Importance and Necessity of Preserving Canada and Louisiana" (Document 10). The British denounced the French action of erecting a series of forts from the Great Lakes southward to the Ohio River, westward on the Ohio to the Mississippi River, and down the Mississippi to its mouth. The British government decided to warn the French in North America against encroachment upon what it considered British territory and sent the appropriate instructions to Governor Robert Dinwiddie of Virginia. Dinwiddie chose a relatively unknown young militia officer, George Washington, to deliver the warning to the French. In a sense, Washington's account of his journey into the disputed territory (Document 11) thoroughly Americanized the conflict between Britain and France. The response of the British monarch in 1756 to a letter of the King of France argued for the official British position on the Ohio lands and other territorial questions (Document 12), thus further intensifying the conflict between these two powers.

The war that ensued (1756–1763), known in Europe as the Seven Years' War, in America as the French and Indian War, and more recently rechristened "The Great War for Empire" by the historian Lawrence Gipson, swept across every continent of the world except Australia. India, Europe, Africa, the Caribbean, and North America were all involved in the military operations. In each arena of war the British gained the upper hand. As a result, in a brief memorandum, the French minister, Duc de Choiseul, laid down acceptable terms to end the war (Document 13).

The role of the American colonies in the European balance of power took a new turn with the Peace of Paris of 1763 which ended the Seven Years' War. France realized that one way to curtail British power was to encourage independent action on the part of Britain's American colonies. British loss of the American colonies would weaken England and restore the balance which had been tipped heavily in Britain's favor because of its overwhelming victory in the Great War for Empire.

Before 1763 the response of the English colonies in America to British imperial policies had been restrained because of the persistent French threat on its borders. With the elimination of this threat in 1763, the English colonies in America were freer to set their own course. Peter Kalm, a celebrated Swedish traveler, recognized this fact as early as the 1740s (Document 14). So did France. Beginning in the early 1760s, the French government sent agents to America to report on the degree of American dissatisfaction with English rule. This information (Document 15) served as a barometer of American dissension, foreshadowing precisely the position that the French would take in the American Revolution when, to serve their own interests, they helped the American cause. In this sense, the American Revolution comprises a chapter in the politics of international rivalry of the eighteenth century.

DOCUMENT 1

MEMOIR FOR THE MARQUIS DE SEIGNELAY REGARDING THE DANGERS THAT THREATEN CANADA AND THE MEANS TO REMEDY THEM,
JANUARY 1687

The direct confrontation between England and France on the North American continent was clearly fore-shadowed late in the seventeenth century by border clashes and by rivalry in obtaining Indian allies. Whereas in the European balance of power France under Louis XIV had been considered the disturbing element and the aggressor nation, in Canada (New France) the English plantations in America were regarded as the threat. On their part, the English colonials spoke of a Catholic conspiracy in the New World and of the growing French trade with the Indians. The international rivalry of the eighteenth century on the North American continent was not only to establish additional colonies but also to play for the higher stake of global supremacy.

Canada is encompassed by many powerful Colonies of English who labor incessantly to ruin it by exciting all our Indians, and drawing them away with their peltries for which said English give them a great deal more merchandise than the French, because the former pay no duty to the King of England. That profit attracts towards them, also, all our Coureurs de bois and French libertines who carry their peltries to them, deserting our Colony and establishing themselves among the English who take great pains to encourage them.

They employ these French deserters to advantage in bringing the Far Indians to them who formerly brought their peltries into our Colony, whereby our trade is wholly destroyed.

The English have begun by the most powerful and best disciplined Indians of all America, whom they have excited entirely against us by their avowed protection and manifest usurpation of the sovereignty they claim over the country of those Indians which appertains beyond contradiction to the King for nearly a century without the English having, up to this present time, had any pretence thereto.

They also employ the Iroquois to excite all our other Indians against us. They sent those last year to attack the Hurons and the Outawas, our most ancient subjects; from whom they swept by surprise more than 75 prisoners, including some of their principal Chiefs; killed several others, and finally offered peace and the restitution of their prisoners, if they would quit the French and acknowledge the English.

They sent those Iroquois to attack the Illinois and the Miamis, our allies, who are in the neighborhood of Fort Saint Louis, built by M. de La Salle on the Illinois River which empties into the River Colbert or Missisipi; those Iroquois massacred and burnt a great number of them, and carried off many prisoners with threats of entire extermination if they would not unite with them against the French.

Colonel Dongan, Governor of New-York, has pushed this usurpation to the point of sending Englishmen to take possession, in the King of England's name, of the post of Mislimakinac which is a Strait communicating between Lake Huron and the Lake of the Illinois [Lake Michigan], and has even declared that all those lakes, including the River Saint Lawrence which serves as an outlet to them, and on which our Colony is settled, belong to the English.

The Reverend Father Lamberville, a French Jesuit who, with one of his brothers, also a Jesuit, has been 18 years a Missionary among the Iroquois, wrote on the first of November to Chevalier de Callières, Governor of Montreal, who informed the Governor-General thereof, that Colonel Dongan has assembled the Five Iroquois Nations at Manatte where he resides, and declared to them as follows:

1st, That he forbids them to go to Cataracouy or Fort

Frontenac and to have any more intercourse with the French.

2d, That he orders them to restore the prisoners they took from the Hurons and Outawacs, in order to attract these to him.

3d, That he is sending thirty Englishmen to take possession of Missilimakinak and the lakes, rivers and adjoining lands and orders the Iroquois to escort them thither and to afford them physical assistance.

4th, That he has sent to recall the Iroquois Christians belonging to the Mohawks who reside since a long time at the Saut Saint Louis, in the vicinity of the Island of Montreal, where they have been established by us, and converted by the care of our Reverend Jesuit Fathers, and that he would give them other land and an English Jesuit, to govern them.

5th, That he wishes that there should not be any Missionaries except his throughout the whole of the Five Nations of Iroquois, and that the latter send away our French Jesuits who have been so long established there.

6th, That if they are attacked by Monsieur de Denonville the latter will have to do with him.

7th, That he orders them to plunder all the French who will visit them; to bind them and bring them to him, and what they'll take from them shall be good prize.

The Iroquois—He accompanied his orders with presents to the Five Iroquois Nations, and dispatched his thirty Englishmen, escorted by Iroquois, to make an establishment at Missilimakinak.

The Iroquois plunder our Frenchmen every where they meet them, and threaten to fire their settlements which are much exposed and without any fortifications.

These measures, and the discredit we are in among all the Indians for having abandoned our allies in M. de la Barre's time, for having suffered them to be exterminated by the Iroquois and borne the insults of the latter, render war again absolutely necessary to avert from us a general Indian Rebellion which would bring down ruin on our trade and cause eventually even the extirpation of our Colony.

War is likewise necessary for the establishment of the Religion, which will never spread itself there except by the destruction of the Iroquois: so that on the success of hostilities, which the Governor-General of Canada proposes to commence against the Iroquois on the 15th of May next, depends either the ruin of the Country and of the Religion if he be not assisted, or the Establishment of the Religion, of Commerce and the King's Power over all North America, if granted the required aid.

If men consider the Merit in the eyes of God, and the Glory and utility which the King will derive from that succor, it is easy to conclude that expense was never better employed since, independent of the salvation of the quantity of souls in that vast County to which His Majesty will contribute by establishing the faith there, he will secure to himself an Empire of more than a thousand leagues in extent, from the Mouth of the River Saint Lawrence to that of the River Mississippi in the Gulf of Mexico; a country discovered by the French alone, to which other Nations have no right, and from which great Commercial advantages, and a considerable augmentation of His Majesty's Revenues will eventually be derived.

The Marquis de Denonville, whose zeal, industry and capacity admit of no addition, requires a reinforcement of 1,500 men to succeed in his enterprise. If less be granted him, success is doubtful and a war is made to drag along, the continuation of which for many years will be a greater expense to His Majesty than that immediately necessary to guarantee its success and prompt termination.

The Iroquois must be attacked in two directions. The first and principal attack must be on the Seneca Nation on the borders of Lake Ontario, the second, by the River Richelieu and Lake Champlain in the direction of the Mohawks.

Three thousand French will be required for that purpose. Of these there are sixteen companies which make 800 men and 800 drafted from the militia, 100 of the best of whom the Governor-General destines to conduct 50 canoes which will come and go incessantly to convey provisions. Of the 3,000 French he has only one-half, though he boasts of more for reputation's sake, for the rest of the militia are necessary to protect and cultivate the farms of the Colony, and a part of the force must be employed in guarding the posts of Fort Frontenac, Niagara, Tarento, Missilimakinak so as to secure the aid he expects from the Illinois and from the other Indians, on whom, however, he cannot rely unless he will be able alone to defeat the Five Iroquois Nations.

The Iroquois force consists of two thousand picked Warriors (*d'élite*) brave, active, more skilful in the use of the gun than our Europeans and all well armed; besides twelve hundred Mohegans (*Loups*), another tribe in alliance with them as brave as they, not including the English who will supply them with officers to lead them, and to intrench them in their villages.

If they be not attacked all at once at the two points indicated, it is impossible to destroy them or to drive them from their retreat, but if encompassed on both sides, all their plantations of Indian corn will be destroyed, their villages burnt, their women, children and old men captured and their warriors driven into the woods where they will be pursued and annihilated by the other Indians.

After having defeated and dispersed them, the winter must be spent in fortifying the post of Niagara, the most important in America, by means of which all the other Nations will be excluded from the lakes whence all the peltries are obtained; it will be necessary to winter troops at that and some other posts, to prevent the Iroquois returning and reestablishing themselves there, and to people those beautiful countries with other Indians who will have served under us during this war.

As operations commence on the 15th of May, it is necessary to hasten the reinforcement and to send it off in the month of March next in order that it may arrive in season to be employed, and that it be accompanied by munitions of war and provisions, arms and other articles required in the estimates of the Governor-General and Intendant of Canada.

The vast extent of this country and the inconveniences respecting the command which may occur during the war suggest the great necessity of appointing a Lieutenant-Governor over it, as well to command the troops there in the absence, and under the orders, of the Governor-General as to enforce these throughout all parts of the Colony beyond the Island of Montreal towards the great lakes which are at a considerable distance from Quebec.

The Marquis de Denonville who sees the necessity of establishing that office is of opinion that Chevalier de Callières, Governor of the Island of Montreal, is eminently qualified for it by his application and industry in the King's service, and his experience in war, said Chevalier de Callières having served twenty years with reputation in his Majesty's armies throughout the whole of his glorious campaigns.

DOCUMENT 2

KING WILLIAM OF ENGLAND ADDRESSES PARLIAMENT ON THE FRENCH QUESTION,
31 DECEMBER 1701

King William of Holland and his wife Mary, daughter of King James II of England, mounted the English throne at the invitation of Parliament after James II fled to France in 1688. William III was a firm opponent of French expansion in Europe, either by the acquisition of territory or the development of overpowering political coalitions. He viewed with alarm a move by Louis XIV to install a Catholic pretender to the English throne; moreover, William saw the maneuver of Louis to gain control of the Spanish throne as a giant step toward French domination of Europe and America and thus the world —which was, in fact, the objective of the French sovereign.

My Lords and Gentlemen; I promise myself you are met together full of that just sense of the common danger of Europe, and the resentment of the late proceedings of the French king, which has been so fully and universally expressed in the loyal and seasonable Addresses of my people. The owning and setting up the pretended Prince of Wales for king of England, is not only the highest indignity offered to me and the nation, but does so nearly concern every man, who has a regard for the Protestant Religion, or the present and future quiet and happiness of his country, that I need not press you to lay it seriously to heart, and to consider what further effectual means may be used, for securing the Succession of the Crown in the Protestant line, and extinguishing the hopes of all Pre-. tenders, and their open and secret abettors. By the French king's placing his Grandson on the throne of Spain, he is in a condition to oppress the rest of Europe, unless speedy and effectual measures be taken. Under this pretence, he is become the real Master of the whole Spanish Monarchy; he has made it to be intirely depending on France, and disposes of it, as of his own dominions, and by that means he has surrounded his neighbours in such a manner, that, though the name of peace may be said to continue, yet they are put to the expence and inconveniencies of war. This must affect England in the nearest and most sensible manner, in respect to our trade, which will soon become precarious in all the variable branches of it; in respect to our peace and safety at home, which we cannot hope should long continue; and in respect to that part, which England ought to take in the preservation of the liberty of Europe.

In order to obviate the general calamity, with which the rest of Christendom is threatened by this exorbitant power of France, I have concluded several Alliances, according to the encouragement given me by both houses of Parliament, which I will direct shall be laid before you, and which, I doubt not, you will enable me to make good. There are some other Treaties still depending, that shall be likewise communicated to you as soon as they are perfected. It is fit I should tell you, the eyes of all Europe are upon this Parliament; all matters are at a stand, till your resolutions are known; and therefore no time ought to be lost. You have yet an opportunity, by God's blessing, to secure to you and your posterity the quiet enjoyment of your Religion and Liberties, if you are not wanting to yourselves, but will exert the ancient vigour of the English nation; but I tell you plainly, my opinion is, if you do not lay hold on this occasion, you have no reason to hope for another. In order to do your part, it will be necessary to have a great strength at sea, and to provide for the security of our ships in harbour; and also that there be such a force at land, as is expected in proportion to the forces of our Allies.

Gentlemen of the House of Commons; I do recommend these matters to you with that concern and earnestness, which their importance requires. At the same time I cannot but press you to take care of the public credit, which cannot be preserved but by keeping sacred that maxim, that they shall never be losers, who trust to a Parliamentary security. It is always with regret, when I do ask aids of my people; but you will observe, that I desire nothing, which relates to any personal expence of mine; I am only pressing you to do all you can for your own safety and honour, at so critical and dangerous a time; and am willing, that what is given, should be wholly appropriated to the purposes for which it is intended. . . .

I should think it as great a blessing as could befall England, if I could observe you as much inclined to lay aside those unhappy fatal animosities, which divide and weaken you, as I am disposed to make all my subjects safe and easy as to any, even the highest offences, committed against me. Let me conjure you to disappoint the only hopes of our enemies by your unanimity. I have shewn, and will always shew, how desirous I am to be the common father of all my people. Do you, in like manner, lay aside parties and divisions. Let there be no other distinction heard of amongst us for the future, but of those, who are for the Protestant Religion, and the present establishment, and of those, who mean a Popish Prince, and a French government. I will only add this; if you do in good earnest desire to see England hold the balance of Europe, and to be indeed at the head of the Protestant interest, it will appear by your right improving the present opportunity.

DOCUMENT 3

GOVERNOR ALEXANDER SPOTSWOOD TO THE BOARD OF TRADE,
14 AUGUST 1718

Alexander Spotswood became Lieutenant-Governor of Virginia in 1710. He was an able leader who worked unceasingly in the king's interest, often to the dismay and disaffection of the Virginians. On one question, however, the governor and his constituents did see eye to eye—the threat of the French in America. In asserting that the French were enveloping the British settlements in America by their expansion northward from Louisiana and southward from Quebec, Spotswood spoke for Virginians and for all English settlers. He further advocated a countermove, settlement of Englishmen into the hinterland of the North American continent. His plea is made to the Board of Trade, the principal policy-making group within the British government from 1696 to the Revolution.

The Memorial mentioned in Your Lordships' Letter concerning the French Settlements at Louisiana, and the consequences thereof, By some mistake was omitted to be sent, but tho' I'm ignorant of the facts set forth in that Memorial, Yet having of a long time endeavoured to informe myself of the situation of the French to the Westward of Us, and the Advantages they Reap by an uninterrupted Communication along the Lake, I shall here take the Liberty of communicating my thoughts to Your Lordships, both of the dangers to which his Majesty's Plantations may be exposed by this new Acquisition of our Neighbours, and how the same may be best prevented. I have often regretted that after so many Years as these Countrys have been Seated, no Attempts have been made to discover the Sources of Our Rivers, nor to Establishing

Correspondence with those Nations of Indians to the Westward of Us, even after the certain Knowledge of the Progress made by French in Surrounding us with their Settlements.

The Chief Aim of my Expedition over the great Montains in 1716, was to satisfye my Self whether it was practicable to come at the Lakes. Having on that occasion found an easy passage over that great Ridge of Mountains which before were judged Unpassable, I also discovered, by the relation of Indians who frequent those parts, that from the pass where I was It is but three Days' March to a great Nation of Indians living on a River which discharges itself in the Lake Erie; That from the Western side of one of the small Mountains, which I saw, that Lake is very Visible, and cannot, therefore, be above five days' March from the pass aforementioned, and that the way thither is also very practicable, the Mountains to the Westward of the Great Ridge being smaller than those I passed on the Eastern side, which shews how easy a Matter it is to gain possession of those Lakes.

Having also informed myself of that extensive Communication which the French maintain by means of their water Carriage from the River St. Lawrence to the mouth of Mississippi, I shall here set down the route from Montreal (a place well known and distinguished in the ordinary Mapps), to Maville, their Chief Town in their New Settlement of Louisiana, according to the account given me by three French Men, who had often Travelled that way, and were taken in a late Expedition under the Command of the Governor and Lieutenant-Governor's Sons, of Montreal, and is as follows:

French Leagues

From Montreal up St. Lawrence River, to Fort Frontenac, at the Entrance of Lake Ontario, is	60
The Length of Lake Ontario, which is Navigable,	60
Up the River to the Falls of Niagara, where there is a necessity of Land Carriage,	3
From Niagara to the Lake Erie,	100

Up the River Michigan, which falls into Lake Erie,	60
From the River Michigan to the River Occabacke, a Land Carriage of,	3
Down the River Occabacke till it falls into the River Mississippi,	200
Thence down Mississippi to Maville,	360

By this Communication and the forts they have already built, the Brittish Plantations are in a manner Surrounded by their Commerce with the numerous Nations of Indians seated on both sides of the Lakes; they may not only Engross the whole Skin Trade, but may, when they please, Send out such Bodys of Indians on the back of these Plantations as may greatly distress his Majesty's Subjects here, And should they multiply their Settlements along these Lakes, so as to joyn their Dominions of Canada to their new Colony of Louisiana, they might even possess themselves of any of these Plantations they pleased. Nature, 'tis true, has formed a Barrier for us by that long Chain of Mountains which run from the back of South Carolina as far as New York, and which are only passable in some few places, but even that Natural Defence may prove rather destructive to us, if they are not possessed by us before they are known to them. To prevent the dangers which Threaten his Majesty's Dominions here from the growing power of these Neighbors, nothing seems to me of more consequence than that now while the Nations are at peace, and while the French are yet uncapable of possessing all that vast Tract which lies on the back of these Plantations, we should attempt to make some Settlements on the Lakes, and at the same time possess our selves of those passes of the great Mountains, which are necessary to preserve a Communication with such Settlements.

As the Lake Erie lyes almost in the Center of the French Communication, and, as I observed before, not above 5 days' March from the late discovered passage of Our great Mountains, That seems the most proper for forming a Settlement on, by which we shall not only share with the French in the Commerce and friendship of those Indians inhabiting the banks of the Lakes, but may be able to cutt off or disturb the communication between Canada and Louisiana, if a War should happen to break out. If such a Settlement were once made, I can't see how the French could dispute our Right of Possession, the Law of Nations giving a Title to the first Occupant, and should they think fitt to dispossess us by force, We are nearer to Support than they to attack. As this Country is the nearest of any other to Supply such a Settlement, and as I flatter my Self I have attained a more exact knowledge than any other Englishman Yet has of the Situation of the Lakes, and the way through which they are most accessible over Land, I shall be ready to Undertake the Executing this project if his Majestie thinks fitt to approve of it. Your Lordships will easily imagine there can be no great pleasure in an Expedition of this Nature through an uninhabited Wilderness, and where the only Humane kind expected to be met with are such as must either be gained by much Industry or compelled by force to afford a passage to Strangers; Yet, having been from my Infancy employed in the Service of my Country, I shall not grudge any fatigue which may contribute to its benefits; And for the Charge, his Majesty has at present a Bank of Quitrents here sufficient to defray it, without issuing any Sums out of his Treasury at home, and I dare venture with such a Body of Men to reconnoitre the Country and find out a proper Post to be fortifyed on the Lakes as the produce of one year's Quitrents might suffice for their pay, Provisions and all other incident Charges, referring my Self to his Majesty's bounty for what my own particular Services shall deserve if ever I return. To make any greater Effort, 'till an Exact discovery be made of the fittest place to forme the proposed Settlement, would be running into Expences upon an uncertainty of Success; for having had the honor to serve nine years under my Lord Cadogan as Lt. Quarter Master General of her late Majesty's Army in Flanders, I have Learned by Experience how much the knowledge of a Country contributes to the facilitating the Execution of Military Projects, and that Without the one the other must prove abortive. And this inclines me to propose the Carrying on this design Gradatim, than attempting to make a Settlement at once without knowing whether it will prove of consequence to the End proposed.

DOCUMENT 4

THE GOVERNORS OF NEW YORK AND CANADA EXPLORE THEIR DIFFERENCES, 1721

The climax of the first phase in the contest between France and England in North America was the War of Spanish Succession, 1701–1713. France attempted to gain control of the Spanish throne, which would place the English and Spanish colonies in the New World under a single head and ally Spain and France in Europe against England and Holland. England organized a counterforce of allies from Western and Central Europe, which defeated France. According to the concluding peace, the Treaty of Utrecht (1713), the thrones of France and Spain were to be separate. England received strategic territorial possessions: Gibraltar, the gateway to the Mediterranean, the island of Minorca, Newfoundland, and Acadia in North America, as well as undisputed sovereignty over Hudson's Bay. Last, but not least, England received the Assiento, the right to supply slaves to the Spanish colonies for thirty years.

The Treaty of Utrecht became the point of reference for all future diplomatic discussions. Its terms were regarded as the model for a balance of power among contending nations. The following exchange between Governor Burnet of New York and Governor Vaudreuil of Canada reflects the enormous impact of this treaty and its persistence in North American discussions of war and peace.

[Governor Burnet to the Marquis de Vaudreuil, 11 July 1721]

Your letter of the 26th March to Colonel Peter Schuyler, which he has communicated to me, induces me to do myself the honor of writing to you by Mr. Cuyler, who requests my passport to go to Canada on his private affairs, and who is highly deserving of whatever favor I may have in my power to grant him. I reckon that I shall confer a very great pleasure on him when I afford him this opportunity of most respectfully kissing your hands.

I assure you, Sir, that I regret exceedingly having experienced, on arriving in this country in September last, so much to oppose the inclination I felt to salute you by a notification of my arrival. I heard such a high eulogium of your family and of your own excellent qualities, that I flattered myself with a most agreeable neighborhood, and was impatient to open a correspondence in which all the profit would be on my side. But I had not passed two weeks in the province when our own Indians of the Five Nations came to advise me, that the French were building a post in their country at Niagara; that Sieur de Joncaire was strongly urging them to abandon the English interest altogether and to join him, promising them that the Governor of Canada would furnish better land near Chambly, to those who would remove thither; and would uphold the rest against the new Governor of New-York, who was coming only with a design to exterminate them; that the French flag has been hoisted in one of the Seneca castles, and that this Nation appeared quite ready to revolt from their obedience to our Crown. This news did, indeed, surprise me, and caused me to doubt what course to pursue on occasion of the ill observance of the articles of the Peace of Utrecht, by which the Five Nations have been conceded to the English. The intelligence afterwards became still more interesting; I was informed that the Indians were about to receive Priests and a Blacksmith from the French; that an effort was making to persuade them to close the passage through their country to the English, in case the latter should disturb the post at Niagara, and that M. de Longueuil had gone thither for that purpose, and to complete the seduction of the Indians from their ancient dependence on Great Britain.

You will not consider it strange if this news obliged me to advise the Court of the condition in which I found affairs on the frontier, and to await orders so as to understand in what manner I should comport myself at this conjuncture. I was always in expectation of these additional orders, that I may write to you more fully on this subject, but as you were pleased to mention to Colonel Schuyler some rumors that were afloat, and which alarmed you, I considered it my duty to show you that if some misunderstanding is beginning to arise, it is due entirely to the French.

You will perceive, by the Treaty of Utrecht, that all the Indians are to be at liberty to go to trade with one party and the other; and if advantage be taken of the post at Niagara to shut up the road to Albany on the Far Indians, it is a violation of the Treaty which ought justly to alarm us, especially as that post is on territory belonging to our Indians, where we were better entitled to build than the French, should we deem it worth the trouble.

You say, Sir, that your orders, as well as mine, are, not to undertake any thing until the Treaty respecting the Limits, which will regulate every thing. Why, then, be so hasty, on your side, to seize disputed posts before the arrangement be made? I regret, exceedingly, that whilst the intelligence continues so good between the two Crowns in Europe, the proceedings of the French, in these Colonies, has been so different. I wish to believe that such is done, in part, without your knowledge; that the most of these disorders are due to this Joncaire, who has long since deserved hanging for the infamous murder of Montour, which he committed. I leave you to judge whether a man of such a character deserves to be employed in affairs so delicate, and in which every occasion of suspicion ought to be carefully avoided. You see, Sir, that I speak to you in all frankness, and that I see, with pain, every thing that can cause ill blood among numbers in this Country. The danger would not be ours.

I hope, Sir, you will follow the dictates of your natural disposition, and place things on a better footing, whereunto I shall be always ready to contribute whatever will depend on me, and to endeavor, by all means, to convince you that I am, with all the esteem in the world . . .

[Marquis de Vaudreuil to Governor Burnet, 24 August 1721]

It affords me pleasure to take advantage of the return of Mr. Cuyler, who handed me the letter you did me the honor to write me on the 11th of July last, to present you my humble thanks for the first intelligence, you were pleased to convey to me, of your safe arrival at New-York, and of the favorable opinion towards me with which you assumed your government. I beg of you to do me the kindness to be persuaded that to retain you in those sentiments, which afford me a very sensible pleasure, I shall exert myself as much as I have done with Mr. Huneter, who has always honored me with his friendship.

I am greatly obliged to you, Sir, for the frankness with which you have been pleased to explain to me the subjects you believe you have of complaint, and I flatter myself that you will permit me, when answering them article by article, to state to you, with the same frankness, that I do not consider them well founded.

You complain that the French have established a post at Niagara, which you have been informed is intended to stop your communication with the Indians who are to be at liberty to trade with one side and the other, according to the Treaty of Utrecht; and you pretend that, as the Five Nations of Indians have been ceded to the English, the French have no right to settle on the territory which, you say, is dependant on them; that this post being on the lands of the Five Nations, the English have a better title to establish themselves on it than the French, and that, inasmuch as my orders are not to undertake any thing until the conclusion of Treaty of Limits, which will arrange the disputes, I must not seize this disputed post before the arrangement be completed. I have the honor to observe to you hereupon, that you are the first English Governorgeneral who has questioned the right of the French, from time immemorial, to the post of Niagara, to which the English have, up to the present time, laid no claim; that it is upwards of fifty years since that post has been occupied by the late Sieur de la Salle, who had an establishment there, and had vessels built there to navigate Lake Erie; that his Majesty had a fort there thirty-four years ago with a garrison of 100 men, who returned thence in consequence of the sickness that prevailed there, without this post, however, having been abandoned by the French, who have ever since always carried on trade there until now, and without the English being permitted to remain there; also, that there has never been any dispute between the French and the Five Nations, respecting the erection of that post, and that the latter always came there to trade with the same freedom that they repair to other French territory, as well as to that which is reputed English.

I flatter myself, Sir, that this establishment will disabuse you of the idea you appear to entertain, that this post is an infraction of the Treaty of peace, and ought not to be erected until the limits had been settled, inasmuch as it is not of a more recent date, nor more objectionable to the English, than Fort Frontenac, from which I do not think you would propose that I should withdraw the garrison until the arrangement of the limits be concluded; such arrangement referring only to territory which the English dispute with the French, and not to what has always belonged to them. This is the reason for my requesting Mr. Schuyler, on hearing of the rumor last winter that the English of Albany intended to go to Niagara with a force of 200 men, to inform me of the truth of that intelligence, observing to him that this proceeding would be an infraction of the treaty of Peace, inasmuch as it would be troubling the peaceable possession of this post which the French enjoyed from all time; a circumstance that obliges me to request you not to permit any English people to go there to trade, as I could not help having them pillaged, which I should greatly regret.

Respecting the report you received, that the establishment of this post closes the path to our Far Indians who could no longer go to trade with the English, I have the honor to observe to you, that they will always enjoy the same privilege of going to the English that they have hitherto had, and that no Indian in my government has been compelled to trade with the French rather than with the English. The proof of this is evident, for a great number of their canoes went again this year to Albany, and those domiciled in the neighborhood of Montreal and Three Rivers trade there almost altogether.

Regarding your representation that it has been reported to you that Sieur Joncaire was strongly urging the Indians of the Five Nations to abandon the English entirely and to side with the French; that I would furnish better land

near Chambly to those who would come and settle there;
that I would uphold those who would remain in their
ancient villages against the Governor of New-York, who
was coming only with the design of exterminating them;
that the French flag had been hoisted in one of the Seneca
Castles, and that this Nation appeared disposed to withdraw from their allegiance to his Britannic Majesty; I can
assure you, Sir, that such false information can be communicated to you by none but evil-disposed persons who
are endeavoring to disturb the Peace, since it is certain
that I never entertained an idea of drawing any Indians of
the Five Iroquois Nations to the neighborhood of Chambly,
and that I even do not prevent the Iroquois of the two
Villages domiciled in the neighborhood of Montreal going
to live with those of the Five Nations whenever they desire to do so; that Sieur de Joncaire has not held any other
discourse, and that no French flag is hoisted among the
Senecas.

You observe to me that you have been also notified,
that the Indians of the Five Nations were about to receive
French Priests and a Blacksmith, and that M. de Longueuil
had gone to that country for such purpose, and to put a
finishing hand to persuading the Indians to withdraw from
their ancient dependence. In reply to this, I have the honor
to observe to you, that M. de Longueuil is adopted by the
Onontaguez, and that his family belongs to those of that
Nation; that the same is the case with Sieur de Joncaire,
whose family is, in like manner, adopted by the Senecas,
which has obliged them to go thither almost daily at their
solicitation.

The Senecas have twice sent me delegates from their
villages urgently to entreat of me to send them two Missionaries, having expressed to me their regret at the with-
drawal of those they formerly had. I told them by M. de
Longueuil that if they would come to get some, I would
have them supplied, not considering myself at liberty to
refuse this favor to Indians who believed themselves to be
independent, and with whom I am ordered to maintain
good intelligence. As for the rest, although the Treaty of
Utrecht looks upon the Indians as the subjects of France
or of England, we treat our Indians as Allies, and not as

subjects, and I question if the English did otherwise in regard to the Five Iroquois Nations, who are neither more humble nor more submissive than those attached to us.

In regard to their demand for a Blacksmith. This is nothing new, since the Senecas required that one should be furnished them by the last Treaty, which the French made with them twenty years ago.

I conclude from all you write me respecting Sieur de Joncaire, a Lieutenant of the King's troops kept in this Colony, that you have been misinformed as to his character and qualities, as he possesses none but what are very good and very meritorious, and has always since he has been in this country most faithfully served the King. It was by my orders that he killed the Frenchman named Montour, who would have been hanged had it been possible to take him alive and to bring him to this Colony.

I hope, Sir, these explanations will not be less satisfactory to you than were those to Mr. Hunter, which I furnished him about four years ago in answer to a letter he wrote me on the reports rendered him by the Merchants of Albany, somewhat similar to those which gave rise to your complaints; for, having discovered that they were false, he informed me that he should not hereafter attach credit so easily to any representations from those people on such subjects. I flatter myself, also, that you will be fully persuaded of my attention to prevent the occurrence of any thing on this side which may create ill-will between the Nations, without, however, my feeling any apprehension of danger, should a rupture unfortunately occur; for the great numbers you believe to be on your side did not prevent the people of New-York suffering considerably during the last war, whilst those of this country then enjoyed the same tranquillity that they now do, and if the people belonging to your government have not experienced the horrors of the war, it is because the Five Iroquois Nations presented me with some Belts, to beg of me not to commit any hostilities in the direction of New-York; a request I did not wish to refuse, in consideration of the fact that they had invariably resisted the urgent solicitations of the English to unite with them in hostilities against the French, and had always lived in friendship with us, which was sufficiently strong to enable me to prevail on them to unite with me in operations against the English, had I been disposed to excite them to such a course, instead of contenting myself with not requiring any thing from them except to take no part in that war, and to remain neuter.

DOCUMENT 5

ARREDONDO'S PROOF OF SPAIN'S TITLE TO GEORGIA,
1742

The decision by England to found the colony of Georgia in 1732 upset the delicate balance of power existing in Europe and America and promoted the rapprochement between Spain and France against England. The Spanish considered the founding of Georgia an encroachment upon their territory in the New World and a signal that England's growing power would be realized at the expense of Spain and France. The most immediate diplomatic reaction was an agreement between France and Spain, dated 1733, called the Family Pact. It pledged both countries to the defense of Spanish territory in America. English dominance in the New World, they agreed, would jeopardize the balance of power in Europe as well as in America in favor of England. In this document proof is offered by Spain of its legitimate and longstanding claims to the territory of Georgia.

For Great Britain to pretend to some show of right to the territory which she is now occupying under the name of Georgia, it would not be sufficient merely to demonstrate that it was deserted and unoccupied by any kind of inhabitants since before the year 1670. Besides this, two impossible things should be alleged and proved in order that the possession conceded by the agreement of Article 7 might fall with some legality to the British

Crown, as that of the other regions fell to it. One is that England held and possessed it before the treaty; the other is that the Spaniards were not the owners and inhabitants, as they really were, in the year of its ratification.

In addition to these attempts, so contradictory to each other, it would also be necessary to show that the dates of the patents issued to the Company of New Georgia were anterior to the year 1670, and not sixty-two years after its ratification. But since all the world knows that they were granted in 1732, how can the British Minister, without causing astonishment and amazement, draw the inference that "the predecessors of his British Majesty were in possession of the dominion called Georgia before the conclusion of the treaty?" The inconsistencies are manifest in themselves.

No one can fail to see that it would be necessary for the English subjects who were living in this territory to have the gift of invisibility, and the need to live incompatibly incorporated with the Spaniards who dwelt in it until the year 1702 without any one knowing of their presence; and that they must have removed to some other place after the formation of the Company of Georgia. For it is evident and notorious that this province has not had, and has not now, any other inhabitants than those that Oglethorpe brought with him to settle it, and those which the said Company has subsequently sent.

The British Minister tries to draw the inference from the treaty "that the predecessors of his British Majesty had granted to his subjects before it was ratified the country between 36° 30' and 29°, inclusive, etc." Laying aside all the proofs given to the contrary, but granting how improbable this would be if the subjects of Spain were actual owners of it, as they indeed were, it should be replied that in none of the articles agreed upon is there a word or expression to be found which gives any indication that the Court of Spain had had any notification whatever of the concessions he speaks of, or that his Catholic Majesty had recognized or consented to the fixing of the limits in accordance with the patents of Great Britain, much less that the province and country called Georgia had always been possessed as a part of South Carolina.

Those words in Article 7, "shall hold and possess perpetually all the lands, regions, islands, colonies, and dominions in the Western Indies under the name of the British King," refer, clearly and expressly, only to what his vassals held and possessed as such occupants, and do not in any manner concede to Great Britain the countries which in his imagination he had granted to his subjects by his patents, both because these patents did not constitute possession, and because the Court of Spain was totally ignorant of them. And it is not possible to imagine that his British Majesty would have given to his vassals possession of territory to which he had no right, and over which the Spaniards had enjoyed full dominion for more than one hundred years previously. . . .

There is no doubt that if Great Britain now has legal rights of ownership over the country under discussion, it would have had the same rights in the past century and in the preceding one, both because the Spaniards have never held possession of any territory that has not been theirs by absolute ownership, and because the English would know when and how they had acquired it. In that case, when these controversies began, which perhaps would not have occurred, they would have been quickly terminated through exhibition by Great Britain of her legal titles, such as would have the necessary force not only to satisfy the world, but also to set aside the true right of the Crown of Spain by obscuring the deeds of her subjects and proving false the original discoveries of the Spaniards as far as 36° 30′ made by Juan Ponce de León, by the elder of his two sons, by Lucas Vásquez de Ayllón, by Pámphilo de Narváez, by Hernando de Soto, and by Don Tristán de Luna. In such a view the Spanish conquests, which were made with so many hardships, such effusion of blood, and the expenditure of great fortunes, by Pedro Menéndez Marqués and his successors, of all the lands as far as Santa Elena, with the settlements and forts which they built, on the coasts as well as in the interior, were mere inventions. The physical and actual possession by the Spaniards of Santa Elena and Santa Catharina from the year 1566 up to 1686 and of the province of Guale up to 1702 was but a dream. The evident and well-established plots of the

English of Carolina against their Spanish neighbors, practiced by themselves and the Indians, their allies, were chimeras; and, the treaties of Madrid made in 1670 and 1721, and that of Utrecht in 1713, being useless, it would have been nonsensical of the Court of Spain to give orders to its governors for the recovery and conservation of its dominions, by force or by good will, and to its ministers for the official communications that they were to present in the Court of London in regard to these matters. All the documents, occurrences, and acts which fully justify the right of the Crown of Spain would be null, imaginary, and suppositious. On the other hand, that of the British Crown would be established and legitimate, solely because upon its word, without other authority, power or justification than that of *Sic volo sic iubeo,* the decree of gift by Don Carlos II would be true, regardless of the fact that if England had legal right she would not need it, and that if it existed it would not be hidden. It would be true that up to the year 1702 the Spaniards inhabited the district of Guale, now contained in Georgia, and that the English were in possession of it at the same time, even though in the year 1724 it was only forty years since they had begun to trade with the Indians of Tamaja River. It would be true that the predecessors of his British Majesty had granted to his subjects the regions as far as 29° before the treaty of 1670, notwithstanding that those of his Catholic Majesty were inhabiting them. The doubts of the British ministry in regard to the matter would become certainties, notwithstanding its need of a report from Nicholson and from the Council of Carolina for its information. The right acquired through the imaginary exploration of Cabot, sustained ninety years afterwards by Drake, would be unassailable, solely because the former came in sight of land at 60° and farther north, and because the latter, for different purposes and other reasons, went to America, sacked Santo Domingo and Cartagena, burned San Agustín, and returned to England with 60,000 pounds sterling in spoils. It would be clear that in the treaty of 1670 there is no description of boundaries touching upon the rights of his Catholic Majesty, while there is such regarding those of his British Majesty, for the British ministry extends its power to the impossible, reconciling two self-contradictory facts. Injustice would be equity. The violation of the sanctity of laws and the rights of peoples would be friendship. And, finally, the proved usurpation of his dominions would be a wish on the part of the British King to please his Catholic Majesty.

DOCUMENT 6

INTRODUCTION TO THE REPORT ON GENERAL OGLETHORPE'S EXPEDITION TO ST. AUGUSTINE, 1741

The clash of rival claims and the establishment of settlements by England and Spain in the Florida-Georgia region resulted in almost uninterrupted warfare. When a committee investigated the failure of General James Oglethorpe to lead troops from Georgia and South Carolina to defeat the Spanish at St. Augustine, the report was prefaced by an account of these eruptions. It states the English claim, condemns Spanish acts of aggression, and brands St. Augustine as a den of iniquity.

St. Augustine, in Possession of the Crown of Spain, is well known to be situated but little distant from hence, in the Latitude of 30 Degrees, 00 minutes N. in Florida, the next Territory to us. It is maintained by his Catholick Majesty, partly in order to preserve his Claim to Florida, and partly that it may be of Service to the Plate-Fleets, when coming through the Gulf, by showing Lights to them along the Coast, and by being ready to give Assistance when any of them are cast away thereabout. The Castle, by the largest Account, doth not cover more than One Acre of Ground, but is allowed on all Hands to be a Place of great Strength. . . .

In April, 1670, Peace then subsisting between the Crowns, the Ship which the Lords Proprietors of this Province sent over with the first Settlers arrived in Ashley-River, and, having landed them, went away to Virginia to fetch a Supply of Provisions, etc., for them; the Spaniards at St. Augustine hearing thereof, in the mean Time sent a Party in a Vessel from thence immediately to attack them. Accordingly they landed at Stono Inlet on their Backs; but those Settlers having by that Time enforted themselves, and the Ship returning timely to their Relief, they made the best of their Way Home again.

In 1686, Peace still subsisting, the Lord Cardross who had obtained from the Lords Proprietors a Grant of a large Tract of Land in Granville County, having just before came over and settled at Beaufort on Port-Royal with a Number of North-Britons, the Spaniards coming in Three Galleys from Augustine landed upon them, killed and whipped a great many, after taken, in a most cruel and barbarous Manner; plundered them all, and broke up that Settlement. The same Galleys going from thence run up next to Bear-Bluff on North-Edisto-River, where those Spaniards again landed, burnt the Houses, plundered the Settlers, and took Landgrave Morton's Brother Prisoner. Their further Progress was happily prevented by a Hurricane, which drove two of the Galleys up so high on the Land that not being able to get one of them off again, and the Country being by that Time sufficiently Alarmed, they thought proper to make a Retreat; but first set Fire to that Galley on board which Mr. Morton was actually then in Chains, and most inhumanly burnt in her.

In 1702, before Queen Anne's Declaration of War was known in these Parts, the Spaniards formed another Design to fall upon our Settlements by Land, at the Head of Nine Hundred Apalatchee Indians from thence. The Creek Indians, in Friendship with this Province, coming at a Knowledge of it, and sensible of the Dangers approaching, acquainted our Traders, then in the Nation with it, when this Army was actually on their March coming down that Way. The Traders having thereupon encouraged the Creeks to get together an Army of Five Hundred Men, headed the same, and went out to meet the other. Both Armies met in an Evening on the Side of Flint-River, a Branch of the Chatabooche. In the Morning, just before Break of Day (when Indians are accustomed to make their Attacks), the

Creeks stirring up their Fires drew back at a Little Distance leaving their Blankets by the Fires in the very same Order as they had slept. Immediately after the Spaniards and Apalatchees (as was expected) coming on to attack them, fired and run in upon the Blankets. Thereupon the Creeks rushing forth fell on them, killed and took the greatest Part, and entirely routed them. To this Stratagem was owing the Defeat of the then intended Design.

In the latter End of the same Year, Queen Anne's War being commenced, Col. Moore then Governor of this Province, with Reason expected a Visit from the Spaniards, and it having been suggested to him, that St. Augustine might be easily taken, if surprized, he judged it best to give them the first Blow. Accordingly he undertook an Expedition against it with about Five Hundred Whites, and Five Hundred Indians. He himself with Four Hundred of the Whites proceeded in the Vessels directly to the Bar of St. Augustine Harbour, whilst Col. Daniel landing at St. Juan's marched directly from thence with the other Hundred and the Indians, and entered the Town with them only, the same Day as the Vessels appeared in Sight. This little Army kept the Castle close besieged above Three Months; and repelled several Sallies with the Loss of very few Men. Yet having no Bombs with them, and a Spanish Man of War coming to its Relief from the Havanna with a considerable Number of Men, on Board Four large Transports, which landed on Anastatia, they were obliged to retreat: *But not without First Burning the Town.*

In 1704, Col. Moore was commissioned as Lieutenant General by Sir Nathaniel Johnson, who succeeded him in the Government, to make an Expedition against the Spaniards and Indians at Apalatchee, about Eighty Miles to the West of St. Augustine, on the same Motives that the preceding Expedition had been undertaken. . . .

In 1706, the Spaniards at St. Augustine joined the French from Martinico, in making up a Fleet of Ten Sail, with Eight Hundred Men, Whites, Mustees, and Negroes, and Two Hundred Indians, to invade this Province. . . .

In 1715, Peace having been some Time concluded between the Crowns, the Yamasee Indians (who before the Settlement of this Province had lived in Amity with the Government at St. Augustine, but afterwards removed and settled on a Body of Land opposite to Port-Royal Island) living contiguous to, and in the most intimate Manner with the Settlers in those Parts, having been ill used by some of the Traders amongst them, were so far disgusted, that they broke out war with this Province, by massacring on the Fifteenth Day of April above Eighty of the Inhabitants of Granville County. But it was manifest that they were prompted to severe Resentment of their Usage, whatever it was, by the Spaniards at St. Augustine. For tho' those Yamasees had, during all Queen Anne's War, been the greatest Instruments in distressing and harassing them, killing and bringing away Numbers of them, insomuch that not a Man dared for a long Time to go out of Sight of the Castle, and destroying even the Cattle; yet, on the very Day this War broke out, the Yamasees shewed so much Confidence in the Spaniards that they sent away their Women and Children in their own Boats by water to Augustine. And having ravaged the Country, killing many more and doing all the Mischief they could, so that all the Southern Parts were broke up, to about the Distance of Twenty Miles from Charles-Town, they themselves soon after retreated to St. Augustine also. There they were received, protected and encouraged to make frequent Incursions from thence into the Settlements of this Province; and being often-times headed by Spaniards, they cut off several of the Settlers, and carried off their Slaves. The Slaves themselves at length, taking Advantage of those Things, deserted of their own Accord to St. Augustine, and upon being demanded back by this Government they were not returned, but such Rates paid for those that could not be concealed as that Government was pleased to set upon them. The Evil encreasing, altho' Col. Barnwell who was sent from hence to St. Augustine, immediately after the Conclusion of Queen Anne's Peace, had in Behalf of this Government then entered into a stipulation with that, mutually to return any Slaves that should for the future desert either Government; Col. Hall was sent to St. Augustine in 1725, with whom that Government confirmed the said Stipulation. Notwithstanding which, the very year following:

In 1727, Peace between the Crowns continuing, fresh Depradations were committed on this Province from Augustine, both by Land and Water; which created the Expense of Two Expeditions to prevent the Progress of them. . . .

In the latter End of 1737, still Peace subsisting, great Preparations were made to invade openly this Province and Georgia. For that Purpose a great Body of Men arrived at St. Augustine, in Galleys from the Havana; which put this Province to a very large Expense to provide against. But happily they were countermanded just as they were ready to set off.

In 1738, altho' Peace subsisted, and Governor Johnson after his Arrival here had, in 1733, renewed the before mentioned Stipulation, another Method was taken by the Spaniards to answer their Ends. Hitherto the Government of St. Augustine had not dared to acknowledge, much less to justify, the little Villainies and Violences offered to our Properties: But now an Edict of his Catholic Majesty himself, bearing Date in November 1733, was published by Beat of Drum round the Town of St. Augustine (where many Negroes belonging to English Vessels that carried thither Supplies of Provisions, etc., had the Opportunity of hearing it) promising Liberty and Protection to all Slaves that should desert thither from any of the English Colonies, but more especially from this. And, lest that should not prove sufficient of itself, secret Measures were taken to make it known to our Slaves in general. In Consequence of which Numbers of Slaves did, from Time to Time, by Land and Water desert to St. Augustine; And, the better to facilitate their Escape, carried off their Master's Horses, Boats, etc., some of them first commiting Murder; and were accordingly received and declared free. . . .

In September 1739, our Slaves made an Insurrection at Stono, in the Heart of our Settlements not Twenty Miles from Charles-Town; in which they massacred Twenty-Three Whites, after the most cruel and barbarous Manner to be conceived; and having got Arms and Ammunition out of a Store, they bent their Course to the Southward, burning all the Houses on the Road. But they marched so slow, in full Confidence of their own Strength from their first Success, that they gave Time to a Party of our Militia to come up with them. The Number was in a Manner equal on both sides; and an Engagement ensued, such as may be supposed in such a Case. But by the Blessing of God the Negroes were defeated, the greatest Part being killed on the Spot or taken; and those that then escaped were so closely pursued, and hunted Day after Day, that in the End all but Two or Three were killed or taken and executed. That the Negroes would not have made this Insurrection had they not depended on St. Augustine for a Place of Reception afterwards, was very certain; and that the Spaniards had a Hand in prompting them to this particular Action, there was but little room to doubt. For in July preceding, Don Piedro, Captain of the Horse at St. Augustine, came to Charles-Town in a Launch, with Twenty or Thirty Men (one of which was a Negro that spoke English very well) under Pretence of delivering a Letter to General Oglethorpe, altho' he could not possibly be ignorant that the General resided at Frederica, not Half the Distance from St. Augustine. And in his Return he was seen, at Times, to put into every one of our Inlets on the Coast. And in the very Month in which the above Insurrection was made, the General acquainted our Lieutenant Governor, by Letter, that the Magistrates at Savannah in Georgia had seized a Spaniard whom he took to be a Priest, and that they thought, from what he had discovered, that he was employed by the Spaniards to procure a general Insurrection of the Negroes.

On this Occasion every Breast was filled with Concern. Evil brought home to us, within our very Doors, awakened the Attention of the most Unthinking. Every one that had any Relation any Tie of Nature; every one that had a Life to lose, were in the most sensible Manner shocked at such Danger daily hanging over their Heads. With Regret we bewailed our peculiar Case, that we could not enjoy the Benefits of Peace like the rest of Mankind; and that our own Industry should be the Means of taking from us all the Sweets of Life, and of rendering us liable to the Loss of our Lives and Fortunes. With Indignation we looked at St. Augustine (like another Sallee!) That Den of Thieves and Ruffians! Receptacle of Debtors, Servants and Slaves! Bane

of Industry and Society! And revolved in our Minds all the
Injuries this Province had received from thence, ever since
its first Settlement: That they had, from first to last, in
Times of profoundest Peace, both publickly and privately,
by Themselves, Indians and Negroes, in every Shape molested us, not without some Instances of uncommon Cruelty.
And what aggravated the same was, that this Government
(on the contrary) had never been wanting in its good Offices with our Indians in their Behalf: And even during
Queen Anne's War had exercised so much Humanity towards them that, in order to prevent those Indians from
scalping them, according to their Custom; when they should
take any of them Prisoners, a Law was passed to give them
Five Pounds Proclamation Money for every one they
should bring in alive; and accordingly a great Number of
the Spaniards, by that Means, were brought in alive, and
the Reward paid for them.

DOCUMENT 7

THE DUKE OF NEWCASTLE ADDRESSES THE HOUSE OF LORDS ON THE SPANISH QUESTION, 1738

*Warlike skirmishes continued to occur where English
and Spanish territories in America were contiguous,
and many Englishmen in Parliament called for a war
declaration against Spain. But the most perceptive
English leaders kept the broader diplomatic issues in
the forefront to maintain equilibrium and peace so
as not to disturb the growth of the English economy
or wage war at the expense of growth. The Duke
of Newcastle, Secretary of State, was one of the most
powerful of those who realized how much was to be
lost and how little to be gained by confronting Spain
at this time.*

My Lords, I do not mention this with any design of
vindicating the Spaniards in their depredations, which I

am sensible have been unjust in themselves, as well as attended with many aggravating circumstances. I do it only to shew to your lordships, that, though the king of Spain is disposed to redress the injuries that have been done us, and which, as I have shewn to your lordships, our ministers have complained of in the strongest terms, there may arise certain points worthy of being discussed in an amicable manner, and in which perhaps it may be necessary as well as prudent in both parties, to recede a little from the rigour of their demands. But, my Lords, when I say this, I have not the most distant thought, that we ought to give up the least point of our right to a free navigation in the American seas. This, I am unalterably for asserting at all events; but I think the most proper way to secure it, is by shewing the world that we will as little support unwarrantable practices in our merchants, as we will suffer them in others. And this manner of proceeding will convince the other powers of Europe, that we have right as well as power on our side.

But should we precipitately enter into a war with Spain upon any doubtful points that may remain undecided betwixt us, or should we attack them without giving them an opportunity of making us reparation in an amicable way, the other powers of Europe would immediately take the alarm; they might look on our proceeding as the effect of a design, either to seize upon some part of the Spanish dominions in America, and to annex it to our own crown; or as an attempt to force the Spaniards to allow us a free trade and commerce with their settlements in America. Did any of our European neighbours, my Lords, suspect that we had formed a design to dismember any part of the Spanish monarchy from that crown, there is not the least doubt but they would look upon us with a very jealous eye; because, as your lordships know, the further alienation of any part of that monarchy is strictly guarded against in a separate article of the treaty of Utrecht, and for the observance of this article both we and the French are guarantees. If it were suspected, that we designed to force the Spaniards to allow us a free trade in all its branches to their settlements in America, the French would not fail to oppose us in such a design, the king of Spain, in the same treaty of Utrecht, having laid himself under an engagement, not to grant it to the subjects of any nation of Europe except his own: and the French monarch, by the same treaty, was obliged to give up all claim to the exercise of any commerce to the Spanish settlements there. This, my Lords, has always been looked upon as a necessary step towards preventing any one nation in Europe from becoming too rich and too powerful for the rest: and the preserving the sole right of navigation and commerce to and from the Spanish settlements in America, to the Spaniards themselves, was not the effect so much of the Spanish policy, as of the jealousy which the powers of Europe entertained among themselves, lest any other should acquire too great a property in that valuable branch of commerce. They knew that while the treasures of the Indies were the property of the Spaniards, or at least while they centred in Spain, that, sooner or later, their subjects must have a proportionable share; because that monarchy is destitute of many of the advantages, which the other nations of Europe enjoy, from their manufactures and the industry of their inhabitants; and that consequently it was not in the power of the Spaniards, let them have never such an aspiring and politic prince at their head, to monopolize these treasures.

Whereas, should too large a share of them come into the hands of any other nation in Europe, whose situation, power or trade, render them perhaps already formidable to their neighbours, they might be employed to purposes inconsistent with the peace of Europe, and which might one day prove fatal to the balance of power, that ought to subsist amongst her several princes. In such a case there is no doubt but that a formidable alliance would be made against the power thus aspiring; and should the differences at last come to be made up by a treaty, it would be found that the most probable way to secure the general peace, is to suffer the Spaniards to remain in the same situation, as to their American settlements, they are now in. I know, my Lords, that in the same year in which the treaty of Utrecht was concluded, some stipulations were made in our favour as to the American trade, particularly the contract for importation of slaves into the Spanish Indies, which was made in consequence of the 12th article of the treaty of commerce at Utrecht. Three years after, we likewise ob-

tained a treaty of declaration in regard to the said slave
trade; which treaty was confirmed by the treaty of Madrid,
which was concluded five years after. But, my Lords, the
privileges which we gained by these treaties, and the execution of them, have put both our government and our merchants to great expence and trouble in their solicitations at
that court; and the obstructions our interests met with
there, no doubt, were secretly promoted and encouraged by
some of our neighbours, who, I believe, might otherwise
wish us very well, but could not, for the reasons I have
already given, bear to see any alteration made in the American commerce, that might endanger the balance of power,
which the princes of Europe have always thought so necessary to her quiet.

From these considerations, my Lords, were there no
other, I think it evidently appears, that to plunge ourselves
into a war with Spain, before we left them inexcusable in
their conduct towards us, would be a very impolitic step.
For, if we meet with success in such a war, the greater the
success, the greater will be the jealousy of our neighbours,
and the stronger their endeavours, either secretly or openly,
to deprive us of the advantages our arms may have acquired.
If the war is unsuccessful on our side, it will confirm the
Spaniards in their refusal to do us justice, and gratify their
pride and insolence. Besides, my Lords, let our success in
a war with Spain be as great as the best friend to Britain
could wish; I am afraid, even in that case, our other merchants would have as much cause to complain of our courage, as our West India merchants affect to do of our forbearance. Your lordships are to consider, that the French,
by observing an appearance of an exact neutrality, may run
away with the most gainful branches of our commerce,
which are those to Portugal, and to Turkey; our trade to
Old Spain must be entirely in their hands, and our trade
to all other places rendered precarious by their privateering.
Thus, in the end, we may find ourselves losers by our conquests. So that, my Lords, there is no occasion for any one
to be surprised, that no violent or precipitate measures have
been yet entered into against Spain, and that our ministry
has hitherto endeavoured rather to persuade than to compel. I say, my Lords, to persuade; for I think it is no hard

matter to convince a Spaniard, who knows any thing of the differences betwixt us and that court, that it is for the advantage of his nation, that the matters of dispute betwixt us should be adjusted in an amicable way. For, should the Spaniards obstinately refuse to come into reasonable terms, our cause would become the cause of all Europe; every power in it would look upon the injustice they do to us, as a prelude to what they themselves are one day to expect. This conduct will convince all our neighbours, my Lords, that we have no design to engross any part of the Spanish monarchy to ourselves, with a view of disturbing the peace of Europe, or of making them more dependent upon us; for hereby they must see that we are forced into a war, in which we are supported by justice; and that we are acting from no principle either of ambition or avarice, but solely from the motives by which every people who understands or regards their own interest must necessarily be determined. It will likewise give the king of Spain time to reflect both on his own danger, in case of a refusal, and to see his own interest in case of a compliance; and if he has been imposed upon by false representations from his own ministers, it may open his eyes, and make him less susceptible of such impressions in time to come, and consequently a more firm ally to Great Britain.

What I have said, my Lords, I think is sufficient to prove, that frequent applications have been made to the court of Spain on the part of his Majesty, "in a manner the most agreeable to treaties, and to the peace and friendship subsisting between the two crowns." I hope your lordships are convinced, that our ministers both at home and abroad have acted for the honour and interest of this nation: and if any of your lordships will take the pains to compare the remonstrances given into the court of Spain by our minister there, with the resolutions that are now under our consideration, I believe it will be found that it was not owing to any defect of application from the ministry, that we have not long since had a full and ample restitution in every point. It was owing to the obstinacy of the Spanish court, and that prince's being misinformed and imposed upon as to the subject of our difference, that they refused us satisfaction; and it was owing to a tender regard for the interest of this nation, that his Majesty did not employ force in order to obtain it. The noble lord who spoke last, was pleased to give your lordships an account of the situation in which things were in betwixt us and Spain, when the treaty of the 20th of King Charles II, was granted. But I believe his lordship is of opinion, that our conduct at that time was a proof rather of the power than of the justice, or soundness of politics of our nation. The Spaniards, it is true, were not then in a condition to make head against the power of England: but the other powers of Europe interfered; they grew jealous, lest, if the Spanish settlements should be ruined in America by means of our depredations, they might be deprived of the advantages they drew from their commerce with Old Spain; and though at that time, there was no good understanding betwixt the French and Spanish courts, yet the French thought it much more for their interest, that the Spanish settlements in America should remain annexed to that crown, than that any of them should fall into our hands: and it appears, that the Dutch, those rivals of our trade, have always been of the same opinion.

Therefore, my Lords, it was not from any inclination, or any pecuniary consideration, that we had to accommodate differences with, or to prevent depredations upon the Spaniards in America, that we agreed to a treaty which they thought so advantageous to themselves; but because we were sensible, that if we delayed any longer to do them justice, the other powers of Europe would interpose and exert themselves in favour of the Spaniards. This, my Lords, was the true reason why we granted them the American treaty; and this must be the case at all times, when we or any other power in Europe shall, by the superiority of a naval force, endanger any part of the Spanish acquisitions in America. I believe, as the noble lord observed, the Spaniards at the same time remitted to us the payment of a considerable sum; but, my Lords, had there been no other reason to oblige us, we could easily have found a pretence for refusing the payment of that sum; and the same force that protected us against their resentment in our depredations, would have protected us in our refusal to pay what was owing to them. Their giving up so considerable a demand might indeed have great influence over a court, which stood so much in need of money as that of King Charles II generally did; but it is plain our principal motive was, the apprehensions we were under, lest our neighbours should make the Spanish quarrel their own. . . .

DOCUMENT 8

GOVERNOR GLEN, THE ROLE OF THE INDIANS IN THE RIVALRY BETWEEN FRANCE, SPAIN, AND ENGLAND, 1761

The powerful Indian nations entrenched on the ridge of the Appalachian Mountains held the balance among the colonial powers on the North American continent. The Six Nations of the Iroquois are best known, but the great tribes southward along the ridge were almost as influential—the Cherokees, the Choctaws, and the Chickasaws. The Cherokees were generally more friendly with the English, but the other two Indian nations were dominated by the Spanish and French. Governor Glen of South Carolina recognized the role of the Indian nations in the contest among the outposts of Spanish, French, and English dominions. He believed that a strong English alliance with the Cherokees in this instance would insure tranquility for Carolina.

The Situation, Strength, and Connections of the several Nations of Neighbouring Indians; the Hostilities they have committed on British Subjects, at the Instigation of the French, and lately upon those Instigators themselves; some Particulars relating to the French Forts, Forces and Proceedings in Louisiana and Mississippi.

The concerns of this Country are so closely connected and interwoven with Indian Affairs, and not only a great branch of our trade, but even the Safety of this Province, do so much depend upon our continuing in Friendship with the Indians, that I thought it highly necessary to gain all the knowledge I could of them; and I hope that the accounts which I have from time to time transmitted of Indian affairs will shew, that I am pretty well acquainted with the subject.

However I think it expedient upon the present Occasion to give a general Account of the several Tribes and Nations of Indians with whom the Inhabitants of this Province are or may be connected in Interest: which is the more necessary as all we have to apprehend from the French in this part of the world, will much more depend upon the Indians than upon any Strength of their own; for that is so inconsiderable in itself, and so far distant from us, that without Indian Assistance, it cannot if exerted, do us much harm.

There are among our Settlements several small Tribes of Indians, consisting only of some few families each: but those Tribes of Indians which we, on account of their being numerous and having lands of their own, call Nations, are all of them situated on the Western Side of this Province, and at various distances as I have already mentioned.

The Catawbaw Nation of Indians hath about Three hundred Fighting Men; brave fellows as any on the Continent of America and our firm friends; their Country is about two hundred miles from Charles-Town.

The Cherokees live at the distance of about Three hundred miles from Charles-Town, though indeed their hunting grounds stretch much nearer to us—They have about Three thousand Gun men, and are in Alliance with this Government.

I lately made a considerable purchase from that Indian Nation, of some of those hunting grounds, which are now become the property of the British Crown, at the Charge of this Province: I had the deeds of conveyance formally executed in their own Country, by their head men, in the name of the whole people, and with their universal approbation and good will.

They inhabit a Tract of Country about Two hundred miles in Extent, and form a good barrier, which is naturally strengthened by a Country hilly and mountainous, but said to be interspersed with pleasant and fruitful vallies, and watered by many limpid and wholsome Brooks and rivulets, which run among the Hills, and give those real pleasures which we in the lower Lands have only in imagination.

The Creek Indians are situated about Five hundred miles from Charles-Town; their number of fighting men is about two thousand five hundred, and they are in Friendship with us.

The Chickesaws live at the distance of near Eight hundred miles from Charles-Town: they have bravely stood their ground against the repeated attacks of the French and their Indians: but are now reduced to Two or Three hundred men.

The Chactaw Nation of Indians is situated at a somewhat greater distance from us, and have till within this year or two been in the Interest of the French, by whom they were reckoned to be the most numerous of any nation of Indians in America, and said to consist of many Thousand Men.

The people of most experience in the affairs of this Country, have always dreaded a French war; from an apprehension that an Indian war would be the consequence of it; for which reasons, I have ever since the first breaking out of the war with France, redoubled my Attention to Indian Affairs: and I hope, not without Success.

For notwithstanding all the intrigues of the French, they have not been able to get the least footing among our Nations of Indians; as very plainly appears by those Nations still continuing to give fresh proofs of their attachment to us: and I have had the happiness to bring over and fix the Friendship of the Chactaw Nation of Indians in the British Interest.

This powerful Engine, which the French for many years past, played against us and our Indians, even in times of Peace, is now happily turned against themselves, and I believe they feel the force of it.

For according to last accounts, which I have received from thence, by the Captain of a Sloop that touched at Mobile about two months ago, the Chactaw Indians had driven into the Town of Mobile all the French Planters who were settled either upon the river bearing the same name or in the Neighbouring Country, and there kept them in a manner besieged, so that a few of the French who ventured out of the Town to hunt up Cattle were immediately scalped.

Monsieur Vaudreuille the Governor of Louisiana was then in Mobile endeavoring to support his people, and trying to recover the friendship of those Indians. At the same time there were some head men with about Twenty of their People in Charles-Town.

I have been the fuller in my Relation of this matter, because I humbly conceive it to be a very delicate Affair, for these Chactaw Indians, have formerly and even so lately as I have been in this Province, at the instigation of the French and assisted and headed by them, in time of Peace, murdered our Traders in their Way to the Chickesaw Indians, and Robbed them of their goods: but I hope the French Governors will never have it in their power to charge us with such unfair Practises.

I shall be particularly cautious of doing any thing inconsistent with the peace so lately concluded: but I think it incumbent on me to say, that it will be impossible to retain those Indians, or any other, in his Majesty's interest unless we continue to trade with them.

And since war and hunting are the business of their lives, both Arms and Ammunition as well as Cloaths and other necessaries, are the goods for which there is the greatest demand among them—I therefore hope to receive instructions in this particular, as a rule of my conduct.

There are a pretty many Indians among the Kays, about the cape of Florida, who might be easily secured to the British Interest: but as they have little communication with any others on the main Land, and have not any goods to trade for, they could not be of any advantage either in peace or war.

There are also a few Yamasees, about twenty men, near St. Augustine: and these are all the Indians in this part of the world that are in the Interest of the Crown of Spain.

The French have the Friendship of some few of the

Creek Indians, such as inhabit near the Holbama Fort: and some of the Chactaw Indians have not as yet declared against them: They have also some tribes upon Mississippi River, and Ouabash, and in other parts: but most of these and all other Indians whatsoever, inhabit above a Thousand miles from Charles-Town; and yet it may be proper to give attention even to what happens among those who are so far from us; for to an Indian, a thousand miles is as one mile their Provisions being in the Woods, and they are never out of the way: they are slow, saying the Sun will rise again to-morrow, but they are steddy.

We have little intercourse with the French; but unless there have been alterations lately, the Accounts I have formerly sent may be relied on, there are not above six hundred men (Soldiers) in what they call Louisiana, and those thinly spread over a widely extended Country: some at New Orleans some at Mobile, and some as far up as the Ilinois.

They had a Fort at the Mouth of the Mississippi river called the Balise, but they found it was not of any service, and therefore they have built another farther up, where it commands the passage: their Forts Holbama, Chactawhatche, Notche, Notchitosh, and another on Ouabash are all inconsiderable stockadoed Forts, garrisoned by 40 and some by only 20 men each. If ever the French settlements on the Missippi grow great, they may have pernicious effects upon South Carolina, because they produce the same sorts of Commodities as are produced there, viz., Rice and Indigo: but hitherto, the only Inconvenience that I know of, is, their attempting to withdraw our Indians from us, and attacking those who are most attached to our interest.

I beg Leave to assure you that I shall never do any thing inconsistent with that good faith which is the basis of all his Majesty's Measures, but it is easy for me at present to divert the French in their own way, and to find them business for double the number of men they have in that Country.

However, this, and even the Tranquility of South Carolina will depend upon preserving our Interest with the Indians, which it will be very difficult to do, unless the presents are continued to them, and those Forts built which I have formerly proposed, or at least, one of them, and that to be in the Country of the Cherokees. . . .

DOCUMENT 9

MEMOIR ON ENGLISH AGGRESSION,
OCTOBER 1750

In 1744, a war broke out in Europe and in America between the Great Powers. In 1748, a peace was concluded, albeit an uneasy one. During the 1750s, the English became increasingly suspicious of the French, particularly of their carefully directed effort to establish forts and settlements from the Great Lakes southward to the headwaters of the Ohio, near present-day Pittsburgh, and down the Ohio River to the Mississippi River in order to link the anchor of Canada with that of Louisiana.

The French view was quite different: The English were the aggressors and the French were merely acting to protect their rights and territory. In this memoir, a translation of a document from the Paris archives whose authorship is uncertain, the French made their case.

The restoration of peace has in no wise diverted the English from their constant design to get possession of all the commerce of America. It is only necessary to consider their actual conduct to be convinced of this truth.

No doubt Spain has good proof on its side. France's is but too certain, both from the publicly professed plans of the English and from the difficulties their commissaries are daily making in the settlement of the disputes of the two nations in America.

England, not content with having already encroached on the lands of France on the side of Hudson Bay, and with pushing its settlements in Acadia on the mainland of New France at the Bay of Fundy, despite the boundaries assigned that country by the Treaty of Utrecht, now plans the invasion of Florida and Louisiana.

It is true the English have already encroached on those provinces, but they have not hitherto pushed their claims to the extravagant extent revealed by the map just published at London, on which, under pretence of correcting one of our recent geographers, they extend their boundaries into Spanish Florida in such fashion as to seat themselves on waters flowing into the Gulf of Mexico.

As to Louisiana, they claim to extend their boundaries over all the lands of the Indians friendly to France as far as the Alabamas; they partially recompense Spain for what they took from Florida at the expense of Louisiana. Although this map is not made by express order of the government, it is well known to be by authority.

However there is no doubt that the English have no justification for such enterprises which have long been no secret. They wish to be in a position to invade Florida, and by that conquest, along with their possession of the Isle of Providence in the Bahamas, to make themselves masters of the outlet of the Bahama Channel, and as a result of the treasure of Europe.

To carry out this plan more easily they seek to put it out of the power of the French of Louisiana to give aid to the Spanish as formerly, and as they will never fail to do in all attempts of the English to work their hurt. In this they can best succeed by seeking to cut the communication of the French of Louisiana with New France and Florida; but is not the common danger resulting to France and Spain a warning to the two powers to concert measures as soon as possible that will insure the failure of this pernicious design? The king on his side is ready to enter into all the measures His Catholic Majesty may think most proper to protect himself from the ambitious projects of a nation with no other aim than to subjugate all the others by seizing on their colonies and their commerce, and which terms that the "balance of Europe."

DOCUMENT 10

MARQUIS DE LA GALISSONIERE, *MEMOIR ON THE FRENCH COLONIES IN NORTH AMERICA,*
DECEMBER 1750

By no means were the French in North America defenseless. They began to prepare for what they considered an inevitable confrontation with the British colonies. In a section of the memoir entitled "The Importance and Necessity of Preserving Canada and Louisiana," Galissoniere set the tone and direction for the French effort. His views were heeded by the French authorities, and orders soon arrived to prepare the line of fortifications. Indeed, the memoir concludes: "In fine, nothing must be spared to strengthen these colonies, since they may, and are to be considered as the bulwark of America. . . . Since they [Canada and Louisiana] cannot be abandoned to their actual strength alone, without being delivered over in some sort to the English, who, by the wealth they would draw thence, to the exclusion of other Nations, would most certainly acquire the superiority in Europe."

Motives of honor, glory and religion forbid the abandonment of an established Colony; the surrender to themselves, or rather to a nation inimical by taste, education and religious principle, of the French who have emigrated thither at the persuasion of the Government with the expectation of its protection, and who eminently deserve it on account of their fidelity and attachment; in fine, the giving up of so salutary a work as that of the conversion of the heathen who inhabit that vast Continent.

Yet we shall not insist on these motives; and how great soever may be the inconveniences set forth in the preceding article, neither will we object to them, the future and uncertain revenues both of Canada and of Louisiana, although, nevertheless, these are extremely probable, since they have for basis an immense country, a numerous people, fertile lands, forests of mulberry trees, mines already discovered, etc.

We shall confine ourselves to regarding Canada as a barren frontier, such as the Alps are to Piedmont, as Luxembourg would be to France, and as it, perhaps, is to the Queen of Hungary. We ask if a country can be abandoned, no matter how bad it may be, or what the amount of expense necessary to sustain it, when by its position it affords a great advantage over its neighbors.

This is precisely the case of Canada: it cannot be denied that this Colony has been always a burthen to France, and it is probable that such will be the case for a long while; but it constitutes, at the same time, the strongest barrier that can be opposed to the ambition of the English.

We may dispense with giving any other proofs of this than the constant efforts they have made, for more than a century, against that Colony.

We will add, however, that it alone is in a position to wage war against them in all their possessions on the Continent of America; possessions which are as dear to them as they are precious in fact, whose power is daily increasing, and which, if means be not found to prevent it, will soon absorb not only all the Colonies located in the neighboring islands of the Tropic, but even all those of the Continent of America.

Long experience has proved that the preservation of the major portion of the settlements in the Tropical islands is not owing so much to their intrinsic strength, as to the difficulty of conveying troops thither from Europe in sufficient numbers to subjugate or keep them, and of supporting such troops there; but if the rapid progress of the English Colonies on the Continent be not arrested, or what amounts to the same thing, if a counterpoise capable of confining them within their limits, and of forcing them to the defensive, be not formed, they will possess, in a short time, such great facilities to construct formidable armaments on the Continent of America, and will require so little time to convey a large force either to St. Domingo or to the Island of Cuba, or to our Windward islands, that it will not be possible to hope to preserve these except at an enormous expense.

This will not be the case if we make a more energetic and generous effort to increase and strengthen Canada and Louisiana, than the English are making in favor of their Colonies; since the French Colonies, despite their destitute condition, have always waged war against the English of the Continent with some advantage, though the latter are, and always have been, more numerous; it is necessary to explain here the causes to which this has been owing.

The first is the great number of alliances that the French keep up with the Indian Nations. These people, who hardly act except from instinct, love us hitherto a little, and fear us a great deal, more than they do the English; but their interest, which some among them begin to understand, is that the strength of the English and French remain nearly equal, so that through the jealousy of these two nations those tribes may live independent of, and draw presents from, both.

The second reason of our superiority over the English is, the number of French Canadians who are accustomed to live in the woods like the Indians, and become thereby not only qualified to lead them to fight the English, but to wage war even against these same Indians when necessity obliges.

Hence 'twill be seen that this superiority of the French in America is in some sort accidental, and if they neglect to maintain it, whilst the English are making every effort to destroy it, 'twill pass into the hands of the latter. There is no doubt but such an event would be followed by the entire destruction of our settlements in that part of the Globe.

This, however serious it may seem, would not be our only loss; it would drag after it that of the superiority which France must claim over England.

If anything can, in fact, destroy the superiority of France in Europe, it is the Naval force of the English; this alone sustained the house of Austria at the commencement of the war of the Spanish succession, as it caused France to lose, at the close of the last war, the fruit of the entire conquest of the Austrian Lower Countries.

We must not flatter ourselves with being able long to

sustain an expenditure equal to theirs; no other resource remains then but to attack them in their possessions; that cannot be effected by forces sent from Europe except with little hope of success, and at vast expense, whilst by fortifying ourselves in America and husbanding means in the Colonies themselves, the advantages we possess can be preserved, and even increased at a very trifling expense, in comparison with the cost of expeditions fitted out in Europe.

The utility of Canada is not confined to the preservation of the French Colonies, and to rendering the English apprehensive for theirs; that Colony is not less essential for the conservation of the Spanish possessions in America, especially of Mexico.

So long as that barrier is well secured; so long as the English will be unable to penetrate it; so long as efforts will be made to increase its strength, 'twill serve as a rampart to Louisiana, which hitherto sustains itself only under the shadow of the forces of Canada, and by the connection of the Canadians with the Indians.

Should any unforeseen revolution disturb the intimate union now existing between the two Crowns, we should even be able, by means of Louisiana, to share with the Spaniards the profit of the rich settlements they possess in America; but this event appears so distant, that it is the opinion that France, for its own interest, and in order to remove every jealousy, must not seek to extend its possessions Westward, that is to say, towards the Spaniards, but apply all its resources to strengthen itself at the East, that is, in the direction of the English.

In fine, Canada, the fertility whereof is wonderful, can serve as the granary of the Tropical Colonies, which, in consequence of the men they destroy, sell their rich products very dear. It is proved that the number of Canadians who die in these Colonies that are admitted to be the most unhealthy, is much less than that of European French.

All that precedes sufficiently demonstrates that it is of the utmost importance and of absolute necessity not to omit any means, nor spare any expense to secure Canada, inasmuch as that is the only way to wrest America from the ambition of the English, and as the progress of their empire in that quarter of the globe is what is most capable of contributing to their superiority in Europe.

DOCUMENT 11

GEORGE WASHINGTON'S *JOURNAL OF A TOUR OVER THE ALLEGHENY MOUNTAINS,* 1753–1754

The French planted lead plates along the Ohio River to reaffirm their sovereignty over the territory and erected forts on the Great Lakes and along the Ohio as far east as present-day Pittsburgh. These actions alarmed the English at home and in the colonies for they considered this territory to be British. An English settlement composed largely of traders and numbering in the hundreds was established near the center of what is now the state of Ohio; but the French marched down and destroyed it. Governor Dinwiddie was instructed by the king to warn the French that their actions were regarded as a direct aggression against England. If the French continued these encroachments on allegedly English soil, the English would be forced to respond.

The man chosen to deliver this message to the French was George Washington, a major in the Virginia militia. Washington kept a journal of this tedious and dangerous trip, which began in November 1753 and ended in January 1754. A biased version of the Journal was published in France; a more accurate version, bringing Washington renown, was published in England.

I was commissioned and appointed by the Honorable Robert Dinwiddie, Esquire, Governor of Virginia, to visit and deliver a letter to the commandant of the French forces on the Ohio, and set out on the intended journey on the same day; the next, I arrived at Fredericksburg, and engaged Mr. Jacob Vanbraam to be my French interpreter, and proceeded with him to Alexandria, where we provided necessaries. From thence we went to Winchester, and got baggage, horses, etc., and from thence we pursued the new road to Will's Creek, where we arrived on the 14th of November.

Here I engaged Mr. Gist to pilot us out, and also hired four others as servitors, Barnaby Currin and John McQuire, Indian traders, Henry Steward, and William Jenkins; and in company with those persons left the inhabitants the next day.

The excessive rains and vast quantity of snow, which had fallen, prevented our reaching Mr. Frazier's, an Indian trader, at the mouth of Turtle Creek, on Monongahela River, until Thursday the 22d. We were informed here, that expresses had been sent a few days before to the traders down the river, to acquaint them with the French general's death, and the return of the major part of the French army into winter-quarters. . . .

According to the best observations I could make, Mr. Gist's new settlement (which we passed by) bears about west northwest seventy miles from Will's Creek; Shannopins, or the Fork, north by west, or north northwest, about fifty miles from that; and from thence to the Logstown, the course is nearly west about eighteen or twenty miles; so that the whole distance, as we went and computed it, is at least one hundred and thirty-five or one hundred and forty miles from our back inhabitants.

25th.—Came to town four of ten Frenchmen, who had deserted from a company at the Kuskuskas, which lies at the mouth of this river. I got the following account from them. They were sent from New Orleans with a hundred men and eight canoe-loads of provisions to this place, where they expected to have met the same number of men, from the forts on this side of Lake Erie, to convoy them and the stores up, who were not arrived when they ran off.

I inquired into the situation of the French on the Mississippi, their numbers, and what forts they had built. They informed me, that there were four small forts between New Orleans and the Black Islands, garrisoned with about thirty or forty men, and a few small pieces in each.

That at New Orleans, which is near the mouth of the Mississippi, there are thirty-five companies of forty men each, with a pretty strong fort mounting eight carriage-guns; and at the Black Islands there are several companies and a fort with six guns. The Black Islands are about a hundred and thirty leagues above the mouth of the Ohio, which is about three hundred and fifty above New Orleans. They also acquainted me, that there was a small palisadoed fort on the Ohio, at the mouth of the Obaish, about sixty leagues from the Mississippi. The Obaish heads near the west end of Lake Erie, and affords the communication between the French on the Mississippi and those on the lakes. These deserters came up from the lower Shannoah town with one Brown, an Indian trader, and were going to Philadelphia.

About three o'clock this evening the Half-King came to town. I went up and invited him with Davidson, privately, to my tent, and desired him to relate some of the particulars of his journey to the French commandant, and of his reception there; also, to give me an account of the ways and distance. He told me, that the nearest and levelest way was now impassable, by reason of many large, miry savannas; that we must be obliged to go by Venango, and should not get to the near fort in less than five or six nights' sleep, good travelling. When he went to the fort, he said he was received in a very stern manner by the late commander, who asked him very abruptly what he had come about, and to declare his business, which he said he did in the following speech.

"Fathers, I am come to tell you your own speeches, what your own mouths have declared. Fathers, you, in former days, set a silver basin before us, wherein there was the leg of a beaver, and desired all the nations to come and eat of it, to eat in peace and plenty, and not to be churlish to one another; and that if any such person should be found to be a disturber, I here lay down by the edge of the dish a rod, which you must scourge them with; and if your father should get foolish, in my old days, I desire you may use it upon me as well as others.

"Now, fathers, it is you who are the disturbers in this

land, by coming and building your towns, and taking it away unknown to us, and by force.

"Fathers, we kindled a fire a long time ago, at a place called Montreal, where we desired you to stay, and not to come and intrude upon our land. I now desire you may despatch to that place; for be it known to you, fathers, that this is our land and not yours.

"Fathers, I desire you may hear me in civilness; if not, we must handle that rod which was laid down for the use of the obstreperous. If you had come in a peaceable manner, like our brothers the English, we would not have been against your trading with us as they do; but to come, fathers, and build houses upon our land, and to take it by force, is what we cannot submit to.

"Fathers, both you and the English are white, we live in a country between; therefore, the land belongs to neither one nor the other. But the Great Being above allowed it to be a place of residence for us; so, fathers, I desire you to withdraw, as I have done our brothers the English; for I will keep you at arm's length. I lay this down as a trial for both, to see which will have the greatest regard to it, and that side we will stand by, and make equal sharers with us. Our brothers, the English, have heard this, and I come now to tell it to you; for I am not afraid to discharge you off this land. . . ."

26*th*.—We met in council at the long-house about nine o'clock, where I spoke to them as follows.

"Brothers, I have called you together in council, by order of your brother, the Governor of Virginia, to acquaint you, that I am sent with all possible despatch, to visit and deliver a letter to the French commandant, of very great importance to your brothers, the English; and I dare say to you, their friends and allies.

"I was desired, brothers, by your brother, the Governor, to call upon you, the sachems of the nations, to inform you of it, and to ask your advice and assistance to proceed the nearest and best road to the French. You see, brothers, I have gotten thus far on my journey.

"His Honor likewise desired me to apply to you for some of your young men to conduct and provide provisions for us on our way, and be a safeguard against those French Indians, who have taken up the hatchet against us. I have spoken thus particularly to you, brothers, because his Honor our Governor treats you as good friends and allies, and holds you in great esteem. To confirm what I have said, I give you this string of wampum."

After they had considered for some time on the above discourse, the Half-King got up and spoke.

"Now, my brother, in regard to what my brother, the Governor, had desired of me, I return you this answer.

"I rely upon you as a brother ought to do, as you say we are brothers, and one people. We shall put heart in hand and speak to our fathers, the French, concerning the speech they made to me; and you may depend that we will endeavour to be your guard.

"Brother, as you have asked my advice, I hope you will be ruled by it, and stay until I can provide a company to go with you. The French speech-belt is not here; I have to go for it to my hunting-cabin. Likewise, the people whom I have ordered in are not yet come, and cannot until the third night from this; until which time, brother, I must beg you to stay.

"I intend to send the guard of Mingoes, Shannoahs, and Delawares, that our brothers may see the love and loyalty we bear them. . . ."

30*th*.—Last night, the great men assembled at their council house, to consult further about this journey, and who were to go; the result of which was, that only three of their chiefs, with one of their best hunters, should be our convoy. The reason they gave for not sending more, after what had been proposed at council the 26th, was, that a greater number might give the French suspicions of some bad design, and cause them to be treated rudely; but I rather think they could not get their hunters in.

We set out about nine o'clock with the Half-King, Jeskakake, White Thunder, and the Hunter; and travelled on the road to Venango, where we arrived the 4th of December, without any thing remarkable happening but a continued series of bad weather.

This is an old Indian town, situated at the mouth of French Creek, on the Ohio; and lies near north about sixty miles from the Logstown, but more than seventy the way we were obliged to go.

We found the French colors hoisted at a house from which they had driven Mr. John Frazier, an English subject. I immediately repaired to it, to know where the commander resided. There were three officers, one of whom, Captain Joncaire, informed me that he had the command of the Ohio; but that there was a general officer at the near fort, where he advised me to apply for an answer. He invited us to sup with them, and treated us with the greatest complaisance.

The wine, as they dosed themselves pretty plentifully with it, soon banished the restraint which at first appeared in their conversation, and gave a license to their tongues to reveal their sentiments more freely.

They told me, that it was their absolute design to take possession of the Ohio, and by G—— they would do it; for that, although they were sensible the English could raise two men for their one, yet they knew their motions were too slow and dilatory to prevent any undertaking of theirs. They pretend to have an undoubted right to the river from a discovery made by one La Salle, sixty years ago; and the rise of this expedition is, to prevent our settling on the river or waters of it, as they heard of some families moving out in order thereto. From the best intelligence I could get, there have been fifteen hundred men on this side Ontario Lake. But upon the death of the general, all were recalled to about six or seven hundred, who were left to garrison four forts, one hundred and fifty or thereabout in each. The first of them is on French Creek, near a small lake, about sixty miles from Venango, near north northwest; the next lies on Lake Erie, where the greater part of their stores are kept, about fifteen miles from the other; from this it is one hundred and twenty miles to the carrying-place, at the Falls of Lake Erie, where there is a small fort, at which they lodge their goods in bringing them from Montreal, the place from whence all their stores are brought. The next fort lies about twenty miles from this, on Ontario Lake. Between this fort and Montreal, there are three others, the first of which is nearly opposite to the English fort Oswego. From the fort on

Lake Erie to Montreal is about six hundred miles, which, they say, requires no more (if good weather) than four weeks' voyage, if they go in barks or large vessels, so that they may cross the lake; but if they come in canoes, it will require five or six weeks, for they are obliged to keep under the shore. . . .

7*th.*—Monsieur La Force, commissary of the French stores, and three other soldiers, came over to accompany us up. We found it extremely difficult to get the Indians off to-day, as every stratagem had been used to prevent their going up with me. I had last night left John Davidson (the Indian interpreter), whom I brought with me from town, and strictly charged him not to be out of their company, as I could not get them over to my tent; for they had some business with Kustalogo, chiefly to know why he did not deliver up the French speech-belt which he had in keeping; but I was obliged to send Mr. Gist over to-day to fetch them, which he did with great persuasion.

At twelve o'clock, we set out for the fort, and were prevented arriving there until the 11th by excessive rains, snows, and bad travelling through many mires and swamps; these we were obliged to pass to avoid crossing the creek, which was impassable, either by fording or rafting, the water was so high and rapid.

We passed over much good land since we left Venango, and through several extensive and very rich meadows, one of which, I believe, was nearly four miles in length, and considerably wide in some places.

12*th.*—I prepared early to wait upon the commander, and was received and conducted to him by the second officer in command. I acquainted him with my business, and offered my commission and letter; both of which he desired me to keep until the arrival of Monsieur Reparti, captain at the next fort, who was sent for and expected every hour.

This commander is a knight of the military order of St. Louis, and named Legardeur de St. Pierre. He is an elderly gentleman, and has much the air of a soldier. He was sent over to take the command immediately upon the death of the late general, and arrived here about seven days before me.

At two o'clock, the gentleman who was sent for arrived, when I offered the letter, etc., again, which they received, and adjourned into a private apartment for the captain to translate, who understood a little English. After he had done it, the commander desired I would walk in and bring my interpreter to peruse and correct it; which I did.

13th.—The chief officers retired to hold a council of war, which gave me an opportunity of taking the dimensions of the fort, and making what observations I could. . . .

This evening I received an answer to his Honor the Governor's letter from the commandant.

15th.—The commandant ordered a plentiful store of liquor, and provision to be put on board our canoes, and appeared to be extremely complaisant, though he was exerting every artifice, which he could invent, to set our Indians at variance with us, to prevent their going until after our departure; presents, rewards, and every thing, which could be suggested by him or his officers. I cannot say that ever in my life I suffered so much anxiety, as I did in this affair. I saw that every stratagem, which the most fruitful brain could invent, was practised to win the Half-King to their interest; and that leaving him there was giving them the opportunity they aimed at. I went to the Half-King and pressed him in the strongest terms to go; he told me that the commandant would not discharge him until the morning. I then went to the commandant, and desired him to do their business, and complained of ill treatment; for keeping them, as they were part of my company, was detaining me. This he promised not to do, but to forward my journey as much as he could. He protested he did not keep them, but was ignorant of the cause of their stay; though I soon found it out. He had promised them a present of guns, if they would wait until the morning. As I was very much pressed by the Indians to wait this day for them, I consented, on a promise that nothing should hinder them in the morning.

16th.—The French were not slack in their inventions to keep the Indians this day also. But as they were obliged, according to promise, to give the present, they then endeavoured to try the power of liquor, which I doubt not would have prevailed at any other time than this; but I urged and insisted with the King so closely upon his word, that he refrained, and set off with us as he had engaged.

We had a tedious and very fatiguing passage down the creek. Several times we had like to have been staved against rocks; and many times were obliged all hands to get out and remain in the water half an hour or more, getting over the shoals. At one place, the ice had lodged, and made it impassable by water; we were, therefore, obliged to carry our canoe across the neck of land, a quarter of a mile over. We did not reach Venango until the 22d, where we met with our horses. . . .

Our horses were now so weak and feeble, and the baggage so heavy (as we were obliged to provide all the necessaries which the journey would require), that we doubted much their performing it. . . .

Accordingly, I left Mr. Vanbraam in charge of our baggage, with money and directions to provide necessaries from place to place for themselves and horses, and to make the most convenient despatch in travelling.

I took my necessary papers, pulled off my clothes, and tied myself up in a match-coat. Then, with gun in hand, and pack on my back, in which were my papers and provisions, I set out with Mr. Gist, fitted in the same manner, on Wednesday the 26th. The day following, just after we had passed a place called Murdering Town (where we intended to quit the path and steer across the country for Shannopin's Town), we fell in with a party of French Indians, who had lain in wait for us. One of them fired at Mr. Gist or me, not fifteen steps off, but fortunately missed. We took this fellow into custody, and kept him until about nine o'clock at night, then let him go, and walked all the remaining part of the night without making any stop, that we might get the start so far, as to be out of the reach of their pursuit the next day, since we were well assured they would follow our track as soon as it was light. The next day we continued travelling until quite dark, and got to the river about two miles above Shannopin's. We expected to have found the river frozen, but it was not, only about fifty yards from each shore. The ice,

I suppose, had broken up above, for it was driving in vast quantities.

There was no way for getting over but on a raft, which we set about, with but one poor hatchet, and finished just after sun-setting. This was a whole day's work; we next got it launched, then went on board of it, and set off; but before we were half way over, we were jammed in the ice in such a manner, that we expected every moment our raft to sink, and ourselves to perish. I put out my setting-pole to try to stop the raft, that the ice might pass by, when the rapidity of the stream threw it with so much violence against the pole, that it jerked me out into ten feet water; but I fortunately saved myself by catching hold of one of the raft-logs. Notwithstanding all our efforts, we could not get to either shore, but were obliged, as we were near an island, to quit our raft and make to it.

The cold was so extremely severe, that Mr. Gist had all his fingers and some of his toes frozen, and the water was shut up so hard, that we found no difficulty in getting off the island on the ice in the morning, and went to Mr. Frazier's. . . .

Tuesday, the 1st of January, we left Mr. Frazier's house, and arrived at Mr. Gist's, at Monongahela, the 2d, where I bought a horse and saddle. The 6th, we met seventeen horses loaded with materials and stores for a fort at the Fork of the Ohio, and the day after, some families going out to settle. This day, we arrived at Will's Creek, after as fatiguing a journey as it is possible to conceive, rendered so by excessive bad weather. From the 1st day of December to the 15th, there was but one day on which it did not rain or snow incessantly; and throughout the whole journey, we met with nothing but one continued series of cold, wet weather, which occasioned very uncomfortable lodgings, especially after we had quitted our tent, which was some screen from the inclemency of it.

On the 11th, I got to Belvoir, where I stopped one day to take necessary rest; and then set out and arrived in Williamsburg the 16th, when I waited upon his Honor the Governor, with the letter I had brought from the French commandant, and to give an account of the success of my proceedings. This I beg leave to do by offering the foregoing narrative, as it contains the most remarkable occurrences, which happened in my journey.

I hope what has been said will be sufficient to make your Honor satisfied with my conduct; for that was my aim in undertaking the journey, and chief study throughout the prosecution of it.

DOCUMENT 12

REMARKS OF THE BRITISH MINISTRY ON THE LETTER OF THE KING OF FRANCE, JANUARY 1756

There was, of course, the official side to the dispute between the Great Powers. King Louis XV of France wrote the British sovereign, George II, on October 21, 1755: "The King is able to demonstrate to the whole universe by authentic proofs, that it is not owing to his Majesty that the differences relating to America have not been amicably accommodated." After listing events that he considered hostile to France, especially the orders given General Braddock in November 1754 to prepare to move against the French forts at the headwaters of the Ohio River and to Admiral Boscawen in April 1755 to prepare the English fleet to attack the French forces, the French king concluded: "But if, contrary to all hopes, the King of England shall refuse what the King demands, his Majesty will regard this denial of justice as the most authentic declaration of war, and as a formed design in the court of London to disturb the peace of Europe." In the following document King George II of England replies.

Whatever may have been or are now the sentiments of the most Christian King, with regard to the differences concerning North America, it is unfortunate that the conduct of the Court of Versailles towards Great Britain should so ill correspond to the dispositions which M.

Rouillé's Memoir ascribes to his Majesty, and to the professions of good faith and unreserved confidence with which, it was pretended, the negotiation on the affairs of America was, on his part, carried on.

If it be from the course of this negotiation that the authentic proofs are to be drawn by which the most Christian King is able to demonstrate to the whole world that it is not owing to him that the differences in question have not been amicably arranged, it will not be improper to touch briefly upon some parts thereof. All the facts will bear witness in favor of his Britannic Majesty's moderation.

In the month of January, one thousand seven hundred and fifty-five, the French Ambassador returned to London and made great protestations of the sincere desire felt by his Court to adjust all disputes between the two Crowns, concerning America, in a final and prompt manner, and, notwithstanding the extraordinary preparations which were at that time and are at present making in the ports of France, her Ambassador proposed:

"That before the ground and circumstances of the quarrel be inquired into, positive orders should be immediately sent to our respective governments, forbidding them thereafter to undertake any new enterprise or to proceed to any act of hostility; enjoining them, on the contrary, to put things without delay, with regard the lands on the Ohio, on the same footing that they were, or ought to have been, before the last war; and that the respective claims be amicably referred to the Commission established at Paris, so that the two Courts might terminate the difference by a speedy accommodation."

England at once declared its readiness to the proposed cessation of hostilities, and that *all the points* in dispute might be discussed and terminated *by the Ministers of the two Crowns,* but on condition that all the possessions in America shall previously be put on the footing of the Treaty of Aix-la-Chapelle. Wherefore his Majesty proposed:

"That the possession of the lands on the Ohio, or Beautiful river, should be restored to the footing it was on at the conclusion of the Treaty of Utrecht, and agree-

ably to the stipulations of the said treaty, which was renewed by that of Aix-la-Chapelle; and, moreover, that
the other possessions in North America should be restored
to the same condition in which they actually were, at the
signing of the said Treaty of Utrecht, and agreeably to
the cessions and stipulations therein expressed; and then
the method of instructing the respective Governors and
forbidding them to undertake thenceforth any new enterprises and acts of hostility might be treated of, and the
claims of both parties reserved to be speedily and finally
discussed and adjusted in an amicable manner between
the two Courts, that is to say, France should repair the
injury done by open force before the parties should enter
into treaty, even about that right, after which the possessions of both parties might be settled on the footing of a
definitive treaty."

The French Ambassador thereupon drew up a kind
of reply which at bottom was only a repetition of his first
proposal. But to soften the matter, he produced, at the
same time, full powers from his Court, couched in very
specious and polite terms.

The effect was, however, as little correspondent thereto
as before, and France soon after delivered a draft of a
preliminary convention, which was nothing more than the
first proposal somewhat enlarged. This, added to what
was doing in the ports of France, was too plain to deceive,
and England took care not to lend herself to a convention
that would leave to France the fruits of her violences and
usurpations, which constituted precisely the grievances
England was complaining of; for after its expiration all
would have to be begun over again.

A draft of a counter convention was afterwards delivered to the Ambassador, containing an offer of the most
moderate terms, confined simply to those points which
were an indispensable right, and essential to the security
of the King's Colonies.

To this France did not vouchsafe any answer, and
her Ambassador was authorized thereupon *only to hear,
but not to make any propositions.*

In fine, after a long series of singular evasions, in
which the cessation of hostilities continually recurred, the

Ambassador, instead of receiving instructions to enter into
negotiations upon the counter convention above mentioned,
was ordered to demand, as a previous condition, that England should desist from three points which formed a large
portion of the matter in dispute.

    I. The south part of the River St. Lawrence and the
        lakes whose waters flow into that river.

    II. The twenty leagues of country demanded along
        the Bay of Fundy.

    III. The territory between the Ohio and the Ouabache.

The discussions by which this extraordinary piece was
followed, and during which France tergiversated at every
step, concluded with a Memoir presented by the Ambassador wherein were treated the affairs of the Islands
as well as those of North America. This also was answered by a very ample piece which refuted the Ambassador's Memoir article by article, and fully justified
the terms of the English counter convention. In consequence of the Ambassador's unexpected retreat, this piece
has remained without any reply.

The assurances France received of his Majesty's pacific disposition were as honest and sincere as they were
formal and precise; but he should have reproached himself had he carried them so far as to endanger the possessions of his Crown and the safety of his people.

It is to no purpose that France applies the epithet of
hostile to the orders given to General Braddock and Admiral Boscawen. She would be very glad to draw a veil
over all the hostilities committed on her part in America
since the peace of Aix-la-Chapelle to the date of those
orders. From the very instant, as it were, of the signing
that treaty, and even at the opening of the commission
which, in consequence of it, was established at Paris for
the affairs of America, France, distrusting beforehand her
right, and setting herself up as judge and party in her own
case, caused the Province of Nova Scotia to be invaded,
and after a series of open hostilities against the inhabitants,
the King's subjects, had erected three forts in the heart of
that Province, and had she not been prevented, was on
her way to destroy the new settlement of Halifax. Like

hostilities were committed, at the same time, against his Majesty's territories and subjects on the Ohio and the Indian lakes, where France, without any shadow of right, forbid the English to trade, seized them by force and sent them prisoners to France, invaded the territories of Virginia, attacked a fort which covered its frontier, and to secure these usurpations, erected, with an armed force, a chain of forts on the lands she had invaded. If his Majesty could have supposed that the Governors of Canada had so acted by orders from their Court, he would have been justified to repel these hostilities at once with the vigor which the case deserved.

He confined himself to complaining thereof to the Court of France, but with so little effect that that Court, not content with not vouchsafing any answer, gave, on this occasion, a very singular instance of its honesty; for, in despite of these complaints made by the late Earl of Albemarle, in consequence of an order from the King, particularly by a Memoir delivered in the month of February, one thousand seven hundred and fifty-two, on those usurpations in America, France had, afterwards, the modesty to allege, that England had never complained of those proceedings, and consequently had nothing to find fault with.

At last, the King's patience being worn out by the continuance of these violences, he found himself obliged to provide for the security and defence of his subjects. Yet, notwithstanding the just reasons he had for proceeding to extremities, he added to his many years' forbearance a signal proof of his moderation in the very smallness of the succors he sent to America, which consisted only of two battalions of 500 men each, escorted by two frigates, and in the orders given to the commanding officer, which were to dislodge the invaders of the King's territories. In these facts there is nothing irreconcilable with the assurances given of his Majesty's pacific dispositions. It is the invasion on the part of France and all the violences which have attended it, that are hostile, and it can never be unlawful to repel an aggressor.

In order to make out the pretended insult to the flag of the most Christian King, France is obliged to invert the order of things. She affects to take the consequence and effect for the cause, and, pretexting the small succors General Braddock carried to America, alleges, as the principal affair, what are only its result and accessory, as if the sending of that succor had given rise to the troubles. France equips a fleet of a very alarming force, and the King is, in consequence, obliged to make proportionable armaments. France dispatches that fleet to America with three times the number of troops carried to the same continent by General Braddock, intending, thereby, to support her previous acts of violence and to superadd new ones.

Now, the same law, the same principle of defence which authorizes the resistance of an invader, authorizes equally the preventing him overwhelming the party attacked by so formidable a reinforcement. It was, therefore, very natural to expect that the King would provide eventually for the protection of his subjects, by preventing the landing of so powerful an armament in America, and by endeavoring to preserve his American Provinces from total ruin.

For the rest, it is hard to imagine why an English fort and English Provinces in America should be less entitled to respect by an aggressor, than a ship of war on the Banks of Newfoundland, by an officer acting under the authority of a Prince, who defends himself and protects his subjects.

The same motive of defence hath forced the King to seize the ships and sailors belonging to the French Nation, in order to deprive the Court of France of the means of making a descent, with which her Ministers in all the Courts of Europe have incessantly threatened England. Menaces, the more significative to England, inasmuch as they have been preceded or accompanied by the precipitate recall of the Ministers of France from London and Hanover; by the march and cantonment of large bodies of troops on the coasts of Flanders and of the Channel, and by the publicly avowed reestablishment of the port of Dunkirk.

For the rest, it cannot be conceived why the French should imagine that the King ought to disavow the conduct of his officers, who have acted by his orders, or why they should wonder at his Majesty's demanding of his subjects the supplies necessary to enable him to frustrate the views equally ambitious and violent of France.

How can that Court pretend to be surprised at the acts of violence it complains of, after the Court of Great Britain had, during the whole course of the negotiation, constantly rejected the proposal made by France for a suspension of hostilities, unless it were preceded by the restitution of the possessions taken by open force from England; a condition to which the Court of Versailles would never agree. This was a broad hint to that Court, of the course the King proposed to follow in the prosecution of his just rights.

It was for such just and valid reasons that the King has rejected the peremptory demand contained in the Memoir signed by M. Rouillé. To avoid all occasion of taking notice of the terms made use of in that paper, which shock common decency, his Majesty caused Mr. Fox, his Secretary of State, to write a brief and negative answer to it, in the form of a letter. And he is the more determined not to admit what France demands, as a preliminary condition, prior to any negotiation, as it appears from that very Memoir that, after granting it, the King would be as far as ever from obtaining an equitable and solid accommodation with respect to the injuries he has to complain of for several years. And it does not appear how his Majesty's resolution to defend his American dominions and hinder France from insulting his Kingdoms, can be construed into a denial of justice, and a design formed by the King to disturb the repose of Europe.

January, 1756.

DOCUMENT 13

DUC DE CHOISEUL, SECRET MEMORANDUM ON A PEACE SETTLEMENT, 17 JUNE 1761

The French lost the war. A French report in the final campaign stated: "The people of Canada must naturally be quite tired of the war. Many have perished in it. They are burthened with the most harassing works, have not time to increase their property nor even to repair their houses; a portion of their subsistence has been wrested from them, many have been without bread for three months. . . . They are told that the English will allow them freedom of religion, furnish them goods at a cheaper rate and pay liberally for the smallest service. These ideas are spreading. . . . It is natural for the people to murmur and allow themselves to be seduced; the inhabitants of the cities will be the most easily debauched."

In this document, the French foreign minister set down in a few sentences, the essentials that were to become the terms of the Peace of Paris of 1763 ending the Great War for Empire between Britain and France.

June 17, 1761

Monsieur le Duc de Choiseul makes the following proposals to Monsieur Stanley: he asks the return of Guadeloupe and Mariegalante as well as Goree for the island of Minorca; he proposes the cession of all Canada except Cape Breton Island, where there shall be no fortifications; and for that cession France asks the preservation of the codfishery as provided by the Treaty of Utrecht, and the fixing the boundaries of Canada in the region of the Ohio by the watershed, to be so clearly stated by the treaty that no further dispute may arise between the two nations with regard to the boundaries in question. France will give back what her armies have conquered in Germany from the British allies.

DOCUMENT 14

PETER KALM, *TRAVELS INTO NORTH AMERICA,* 1748–1749

The contest between Britain and France and its effect on the American colonies did not end with the Peace of Paris in 1763. After that year the scales of the European balance of power tipped decidedly in favor of the British. The French, eager to restore the balance, hoped to reduce British power by dissolving the unity between Britain and its North American colonies. Peter Kalm, a Swedish observer who traveled in the colonies in the late 1740s, recognized, as did many Britons and others, that the French threat against the English colonies during the eighteenth century had restrained colonial responses to British imperial policies. This translation of Kalm is taken from an account published in 1770.

For it is to be observed, that each English colony in North America is independent of the other, and that each has its proper laws and coin, and may be looked upon in several lights as a state by itself. From hence it happens, that in time of war, things go on very slowly and irregularly here: for not only the sense of one province is sometimes directly opposite to that of another; but frequently the views of the governor, and those of the assembly, of the same province are quite different: so that it is easy to see, that while the people are quarrelling about the best and cheapest manner of carrying on the war, an enemy has it in his power to take one place after another. It has commonly happened, that whilst some provinces have been suffering from their enemies, the neighbouring ones were quiet and inactive, and as if it did not in the least concern them. They have frequently taken up two or three years in considering whether they should give assistance to an oppressed sister colony, and sometimes they have expressly declared themselves against it. There are instances of provinces who were not only neuter in these circumstances, but who even carried on a great trade with the power which at that very time was attacking and laying waste some other provinces.

The French in Canada, who are but an inconsiderable body, in comparison with the English in America, have, by this position of affairs, been able to obtain great advantages in times of war; for if we judge from the number and power of the English, it would seem very easy for them to get the better of the French in America.

It is however of great advantage to the crown of England, that the North American colonies are near a country, under the government of the French, like Canada. There is reason to believe that the king never was earnest in his attempts to expel the French from their possessions there; though it might have been done with little difficulty. For the English colonies in this part of the world have increased so much in their number of inhabitants, and in their riches, that they almost vie with Old England. Now in order to keep up the authority and trade of their mother country, and to answer several other purposes, they are forbid to establish new manufactures, which would turn to the disadvantage of the British commerce: they are not allowed to dig for any gold or silver, unless they send them to England immediately: they have not the liberty of trading to any parts that do not belong to the British dominions, excepting some settled places; and foreign traders are not allowed to send their ships to them. These and some other restrictions, occasion the inhabitants of the English colonies to grow less tender for their mother country. This coldness is kept up by the many foreigners, such as Germans, Dutch, and French, settled here, and living among the English, who commonly have no particular attachment to Old England; add to this likewise, that many people can never be contented with their possessions, though they be ever so great, and will always be desirous of getting more, and of enjoying the pleasure which arises from changing; and their over great liberty, and their luxury, often lead them to licentiousness.

I have been told by Englishmen, and not only by such as were born in America, but even by such as came from Europe, that the English colonies in North America, in the space of thirty or fifty years, would be able to form a state by themselves, entirely independent of Old England. But as the whole country which lies along the sea-shore is unguarded, and on the land side is harrassed by the French in times of war, these dangerous neighbours are sufficient to prevent the connection of the colonies with their mother country from being quite broken off. The English government has therefore sufficient reason to consider the French in North America as the best means of keeping the colonies in their due submission. . . .

DOCUMENT 15

FRENCH DIPLOMATIC CORRESPONDENCE ON THE DEGREE OF DISSATISFACTION OF THE NORTH AMERICAN COLONIES, 1776

The French planted observers in the American colonies after 1763 to report on the American temperament. They believed that the Americans were chafing under imperial rule and would soon separate from England. As early af 1768, one French informant believed that "if things could only go on as they were doing, it was all that France could desire . . . the colonies would learn to do without the aid of the mother country [and] England would be ruined. . . ." Another reported: "Were a man of Cromwell's genius to rise up in New York, he would have a less hard task before him than the one which that 'usurper' successfully accomplished." He further observed that a favorable combination of circumstances might produce such a man and that it was the "business of France and

Spain to bring about such circumstances. All that would be required to secure the independence of the colonies was arms, a leader, and a feeling of self-reliance in the minds of the inhabitants."

The following document is a prescription for French watchful waiting on the eve of the Declaration of Independence, looking for an opportunity to strike decisively against Britain by encouraging the English colonies in North America to seek independence, but masking all French activity under the guise of a pacific but interested third party.

No doubt, if the Kings of France and Spain had martial tendencies—if they obeyed the dictates of their own interest, and, perhaps, the justice of their cause, which was that of humanity, so often outraged by England—if their military resources were in a sufficiently good condition—they would doubtless feel that Providence had evidently chosen that very hour for humiliating England, and revenging on her the wrongs she had inflicted on those who had the misfortune to be her neighbours and rivals, by rendering the resistance of the Americans as desperate as possible. The exhaustion produced by this internecine war would prostrate both England and her colonies, and would afford an opportunity to reduce England to the condition of a second-rate power—to ravish from her the empire she aimed at establishing in the four quarters of the world with so much pride and injustice, and relieve the universe of a tyranny which desires to swallow up both all the power and all the wealth of the world. But, the two crowns not being able to act in this way, they must have recourse to a circumspect policy. This granted, M. de Vergennes lays down four propositions: *First*, care must be taken not to commit themselves, and so bring on the evils they desire to prevent. *Secondly*, it must not be supposed that inaction, however complete, could save France from being an object of suspicion; that the actual policy of France did not escape suspicion even then; that the English, accustomed to think of their own interests, and to judge others by themselves, would necessarily think it unlikely that the

French government would let slip so good an opportunity of injuring them; and even if they did not think so, they would feign it if they wanted to attack France, and Europe would believe it in spite of her denial. *Thirdly,* that the continuation of the war would, for obvious reasons, be advantageous to the two crowns. *Fourthly,* that the best mode of securing this result would be, on the one hand, to keep up the persuasion in the minds of the English ministry that the intentions of France and Spain were pacific, so that they might not hesitate undertaking an active and costly campaign; and, on the other hand, to sustain the courage of the Americans by countenancing them secretly, and by giving them vague hopes which would obstruct any attempts England might make to bring about an amicable accommodation, and would contribute fully to develope that desire for independence which was now beginning to be observed amongst them. The colonists would be rendered furious by the injuries inflicted upon them; the contest would grow fiercer; and, even should the mother-country prove successful, she would for a long while have need of all her disposable force to keep down the spirit of independence, and would not dare to risk the attempts of her colonies to combine with a foreign enemy for the recovery of their liberty. Thence he deduces the following inferences:

First, that they should continue dexterously to keep the English ministry in a state of false security with respect to the intentions of France and Spain.

Secondly, that it would be politic to give the *insurgents* secret assistance in military stores and money; that the admitted utility would justify this little sacrifice, and no loss of dignity or breach of equity would be involved in it.

Thirdly, that it would not be consistent with the King's dignity or interest to make an open contract with the *insurgents* until their independence was achieved.

Fourthly, that in case France and Spain should furnish assistance, they should look for no other return than the success of the political object they had at that moment in view, leaving themselves at liberty to be guided by circumstances as to any future arrangements.

Fifthly, that perhaps a too marked inactivity at the present crisis might be attributed by the English to fear, and might expose France to insults to which it might not be disposed to submit. The English, he adds, respect only those who can make themselves feared.

Sixthly, that the result to which all these considerations led was, that the two crowns should actively prepare means to resist or punish England, more especially as, of all possible issues, the maintenance of peace with that power was the least probable.

PART VII

Revolution and Independence

BY 1763, when the French and Indian War ended, the American colonies had grown to be a strong and thriving part of the British empire, whose people were passionately concerned to manage their own affairs. In the past they had been accustomed to a large measure of regulation of their trade by Parliament. But some of the inconvenient regulations, notably those on the trade with the French West Indies, had been regularly evaded by smugglers, and British officials had dealt very indulgently with violators of the law. Parliament had never taxed the colonists for the sake of revenue. Taxes, in the form of duties, had been imposed in the course of regulating trade, but these taxes were not passed to raise money, and it was understood that they were only incidental to regulation.

After 1763, the successive ministries that set policy in London felt that England could no longer afford to be as easy-going as in the past. The empire was expensive; costly wars had been fought to acquire and defend it; still more money would have to be laid out in the future to garrison it. From the British point of view, much of the outlay had been made in the interests of the colonies, and the home government felt it to be only just that the colonists should share in the immense tax burden borne by British subjects at home. Moreover, when smuggling, which had been tolerated before the war, continued to be carried on during hostilities, it became an act of

treason. Therefore, in 1764 Parliament passed the Sugar
Act, which was intended to end this illegal trade as well
as to produce a revenue, and in 1765 passed the Stamp
Act, which it was hoped would raise £60,000 a year.

For the Americans this new and firmer policy could
hardly have come at a more inauspicious time. The
presence of the French in Canada had always driven the
colonists toward the mother country. Now, with the common enemy expelled, the colonists felt free to assert
themselves. The Sugar Act and the Stamp Act found them
in the midst of a postwar business depression and in a
touchy mood. The colonists had always had to struggle
to improve a currency supply that was inadequate to
their needs; now the new taxes threatened to make this
struggle even harder. Moreover, the illegal West Indies
trade had long been one of the best sources of business
profits and hard money for the northern colonies. Southern planters too, who were continually in debt to their
British merchant creditors, were beginning to feel restive.
And the Stamp Act, which affected all colonies in the
same way, united them around a common grievance. The
devices used to enforce the Sugar Act gave American
merchants a legal issue which shrewd colonial lawyers
were quick to exploit. In the past, colonial smugglers,
when brought to trial, could look forward to almost certain acquittal. American juries would not convict them.
Now violators were to be tried in the vice-admiralty
courts, which had no juries. The Americans felt that by
losing the benefit of jury trials they were deprived of one
of the fundamental rights of Englishmen, acquired over
long centuries of struggle for liberty.

In the decade following 1765, several measures of
Parliament provided the colonists with a wide variety of
grievances. But among all these, none occupied so prominent a place in the literature of American protest as the
question of taxation. Taxation without representation became the central issue, the focal symbol which expressed
the entire American feeling of discontent. One reason
why, among all the matters at issue, taxation was given
such importance was that here the colonists felt sure that
their position was supported by British constitutional doc-

trine and prevailing ideas of natural rights. Since they had never before paid revenue-raising taxes, it was possible for them to feel victimized by a vicious innovation. English lawyers had long agreed that it was a violation of both natural rights and of the British constitution to tax a man without his consent, given directly or through his representatives. This was the position stated in the Resolutions of the Stamp Act Congress of 1765 (Document 1).

A standard British rebuttal of the colonial cry of "taxation without representation" was the doctrine of "virtual representation," exemplified here by the pamphleteer, Soame Jenyns (Document 2). The exponents of virtual representation pointed out that there were many Englishmen living in boroughs unrepresented in Parliament; they argued that these Englishmen, and along with them those who lived in the colonies, were virtually represented by the members of Parliament chosen by other constituents. In effect, those who represented some could represent all. Most American spokesmen, however, agreed with Daniel Dulany in his widely read protest against the Stamp Act (Document 3) that virtual representation had no meaning or value for Americans; and there were many Whig leaders in England—among them the elder Pitt in his famous speech against the Stamp Act (Document 4) —who heartily agreed with them, and celebrated American resistance to illegal taxation as a contribution to the rights of all Englishmen.

English merchants, who suffered from the boycotts by means of which the colonists implemented their protests, combined with English friends of the colonists like Pitt and his followers to force the repeal of the Stamp Act. But they did not succeed, as Pitt hoped, in getting Parliament to disavow the principle of taxation. Subsequent taxation acts were designed to exploit the weaknesses in the colonial argument. That is, if the colonists admitted the legality of taxes imposed to regulate trade but rejected those passed solely and frankly to raise money, why not devise taxes which would in fact raise money but which would look like trade regulations? Such was the reasoning behind the Townshend Acts of 1767, which imposed duties on a variety of colonial imports.

But the colonists really wanted to be exempted from all taxation by Parliament, not merely to have their legalistic distinctions observed. The most famous American statement against the Townshend Acts—John Dickinson's *Letters from a Farmer* (Document 5)—pointed out that these measures were unacceptable because, whatever their form, their *purpose* was to raise revenue. But this was not a dependable solution. How could the colonists decide what purpose governed the mind of Parliament when it passed a law? In the end, they found it better to advance from this position to the unequivocal stand, expressed in the Declaration and Resolves of the First Continental Congress, 1774 (Document 6), that no taxation of any kind was legitimate without their consent.

The repeal in 1770 of the Townshend duties (except for that on tea, maintained to uphold the principle of Parliamentary taxation) led to a relative lull in colonial agitation for a few years—though even this lull was disturbed by the "Boston Massacre" and other incidents. However, the attempt of Parliament to bail the vast East India Company out of its financial difficulties, by giving its tea a privileged position in the American market, reopened old issues that had been set aside but never resolved. Universal resistance to the acceptance of this tea was dramatized by the Boston Tea Party, which provoked the Boston Port Act and the other "Intolerable Acts" of the spring of 1774. The crisis here entered a new phase: now the colonists felt their rights and liberties were being invaded in many ways.

While some of the colonists began to advocate a complete break, the Loyalists in America found effective spokesmen for their side. One of the most eloquent of these, Daniel Leonard, argued that the principles invoked by the patriots would lead to anarchy (Document 7). John Adams, in his answer to Leonard (Document 8), expressed a different conception, one toward which a number of thoughtful Americans, including Thomas Jefferson and James Wilson, were tending. Such men had arrived at the conclusion that the Americans should be united to Britain not through any obligation to Parliament, of which they should be completely independent, but solely through loyalty to the crown. This anticipation of what later came to be Dominion status was too much in advance of its time. British government was too corrupt and irregular to undertake daring and constructive innovations, and there were men in England who shared Samuel Johnson's feeling that "the Americans are a nation of convicts and deserve anything we give them short of hanging." To be sure, there were men like Edmund Burke, who, for expediency's sake, preferred to deal with the colonists in a spirit of magnanimity (Document 9) rather than to stand on abstract assertions of Parliamentary right. There were also men like Adam Smith (Document 10) and Josiah Tucker, who soberly calculated the economic value of colonies and warned of the costs of trying to keep them.

In April 1775, the battles of Lexington and Concord took place. By July, the Second Continental Congress was explaining to the world why the Americans had been driven to take up arms, and was threatening to call in foreign intervention (Document 11). However, when the colonists did begin to fight, it was not to win independence but only to defend their rights. Fighting broke out without their having planned it, much less having decided what end they were fighting for. For well over a year, while both sides were futilely attempting to state acceptable terms of peace, Americans discussed what it was that they were fighting for. As the months went by, the logic of those who looked for a restoration of the imperial relationship grew weaker and less persuasive. The case for complete separation was forcefully stated by Thomas Paine in his *Common Sense* (Document 12). A number of Loyalists leaped into the propaganda struggle with answers to Paine in which the dangers of war and the disadvantages of independence were fully reviewed (Document 13). But in July 1776, the movement for independence prevailed, and the Congress committed American arms to this goal (Document 14).

DOCUMENT 1

RESOLUTIONS OF THE STAMP ACT CONGRESS,
OCTOBER 19, 1765

*On June 6, 1765, the Massachusetts House of Repre-
sentatives, on the motion of James Otis, resolved to
propose an intercolonial meeting to resist the Stamp
Act. On June 8 it sent a circular letter to the assemblies of the other colonies inviting them to meet at
New York the following October "to consider of a
general and united, dutiful, loyal and humble representation of their condition to His Majesty and the
Parliament; and to implore relief." Of the thirteen
colonies which later took part in the Revolution, nine
sent delegates. New Hampshire, Virginia, North Carolina, and Georgia were unrepresented; the last three
were prevented by their governors from electing delegates, but New Hampshire gave its approval to the
Congress after the proceedings were over. These resolutions were the chief accomplishment of the Congress. Two early drafts of the resolutions in the hand
of John Dickinson of Pennsylvania suggest that the
credit for the text should go to him, though some historians have concluded that they were drawn up by
John Cruger, the mayor of New York. The principal
issue that divided the twenty-seven delegates was
whether to modify the rebellious tone of their denial
of Parliament's authority to tax; this could be done
by acknowledging explicitly what authority Parliament did have over the colonies. In the end this
proved impossible because the more radical delegates
were afraid of conceding too much. The extent of
the concession they were willing to make is registered
in the rather vague wording of the first resolution.*

The members of this Congress, sincerely devoted, with
the warmest sentiments of affection and duty to His Majesty's Person and Government, inviolably attached to the

present happy establishment of the Protestant succession, and with minds deeply impressed by a sense of the present and impending misfortunes of the British colonies on this continent; having considered as maturely as time will permit the circumstances of the said colonies, esteem it our indispensable duty to make the following declarations of our humble opinion, respecting the most essential rights and liberties of the colonists, and of the grievances under which they labour, by reason of several late Acts of Parliament.

I. That His Majesty's subjects in these colonies, owe the same allegiance to the Crown of Great–Britain, that is owing from his subjects born within the realm, and all due subordination to that august body the Parliament of Great–Britain.

II. That His Majesty's liege subjects in these colonies, are entitled to all the inherent rights and liberties of his natural born subjects within the kingdom of Great–Britain.

III. That it is inseparably essential to the freedom of a people, and the undoubted right of Englishmen, that no taxes be imposed on them, but with their own consent, given personally, or by their representatives.

IV. That the people of these colonies are not, and from their local circumstances cannot be, represented in the House of Commons in Great–Britain.

V. That the only representatives of the people of these colonies, are persons chosen therein by themselves, and that no taxes ever have been, or can be constitutionally imposed on them, but by their respective legislatures.

VI. That all supplies to the Crown, being free gifts of the people, it is unreasonable and inconsistent with the principles and spirit of the British Constitution, for the people of Great–Britain to grant to His Majesty the property of the colonists.

VII. That trial by jury is the inherent and invaluable right of every British subject in these colonies.

VIII. That the late Act of Parliament, entitled, *An Act for granting and applying certain Stamp Duties, and other Duties, in the British colonies and plantations in America, etc.*, by imposing taxes on the inhabitants of these colonies, and the said Act, and several other Acts, by extending the jurisdiction of the courts of Admiralty beyond its ancient limits, have a manifest tendency to subvert the rights and liberties of the colonists.

IX. That the duties imposed by several late Acts of Parliament, from the peculiar circumstances of these colonies, will be extremely burthensome and grievous; and from the scarcity of specie, the payment of them absolutely impracticable.

X. That as the profits of the trade of these colonies ultimately center in Great–Britain, to pay for the manufactures which they are obliged to take from thence, they eventually contribute very largely to all supplies granted there to the Crown.

XI. That the restrictions imposed by several late Acts of Parliament, on the trade of these colonies, will render them unable to purchase the manufactures of Great–Britain.

XII. That the increase, prosperity, and happiness of these colonies, depend on the full and free enjoyment of their rights and liberties, and an intercourse with Great–Britain mutually affectionate and advantageous.

XIII. That it is the right of the British subjects in these colonies, to petition the King, or either House of Parliament.

Lastly, That it is the indispensable duty of these colonies, to the best of sovereigns, to the mother country, and to themselves, to endeavour by a loyal and dutiful address to his Majesty, and humble applications to both Houses of Parliament, to procure the repeal of the Act for granting and applying certain stamp duties, of all clauses of any other Acts of Parliament, whereby the jurisdiction of the Admiralty is extended as aforesaid, and of the other late Acts for the restriction of American commerce.

DOCUMENT 2

SOAME JENYNS, *THE OBJECTIONS TO THE TAXATION . . . CONSIDER'D,* 1765

Soame Jenyns, a minor poet and a member of Parliament from 1741 to 1780, was a member of the Board of Trade and Plantations when he wrote this pamphlet, the full title of which was The Objections to the Taxation of our American Colonies by the Legislature of Great Britain, briefly consider'd. *In this excerpt he argues the case for Parliament's right to tax the colonies, and states briefly the theory of virtual representation.*

The right of the Legislature of Great–Britain to impose taxes on her American Colonies, and the expediency of exerting that right in the present conjuncture, are propositions so indisputably clear, that I should never have thought it necessary to have undertaken their defence, had not many arguments been lately flung out, both in papers and conversation, which with insolence equal to their absurdity deny them both. As these are usually mixt up with several patriotic and favorite words such as Liberty, Property, Englishmen, etc., which are apt to make strong impressions on that more numerous part of mankind, who have ears but no understanding, it will not, I think, be improper to give them some answers: to this, therefore, I shall singly confine myself, and do it in as few words as possible, being sensible that the fewest will give least trouble to myself and probably most information to my reader.

The great capital argument, which I find on this subject, and which, like an Elephant at the head of a Nobob's army, being once overthrown, must put the whole into confusion, is this; that no Englishman is, or can be taxed, but by his own consent: by which must be meant one of these three propositions; either that no Englishman can be taxed without his own consent as an individual; or that no Englishman can be taxed without the consent of the persons he chuses to represent him; or that no Englishman can be taxed without the consent of the majority of all those, who are elected by himself and others of his fellow-subjects to represent them. Now let us impartially consider, whether any one of these propositions are in fact true: if not, then this wonderful structure which has been erected upon them, falls at once to the ground, and like another Babel, perishes by a confusion of words, which the builders themselves are unable to understand.

First then, that no Englishman is or can be taxed but by his own consent as an individual: this is so far from being true, that it is the very reverse of truth; for no man that I know of is taxed by his own consent; and an Englishman, I believe, is as little likely to be so taxed, as any man in the world.

Secondly, that no Englishman is or can be taxed but by the consent of those persons whom he has chose to represent him; for the truth of this I shall appeal only to the candid representatives of those unfortunate counties which produce cyder, and shall willingly acquiesce under their determination.

Lastly, that no Englishman is, or can be taxed, without the consent of the majority of those, who are elected by himself, and others of his fellow-subjects, to represent them. This is certainly as false as the other two; for every Englishman is taxed, and not one in twenty represented: copyholders, leaseholders, and all men possessed of personal property only, chuse no representatives; Manchester, Birmingham, and many more of our richest and most flourishing trading towns send no members to parliament, consequently cannot consent by their representatives, because they chuse none to represent them; yet are they not Englishmen? or are they not taxed?

I am well aware, that I shall hear Locke, Sidney, Selden, and many other great names quoted to prove that every Englishman, whether he has a right to vote for a representative, or not, is still represented in the British Parliament; in which opinion they all agree: on what principle of common sense this opinion is founded I comprehend not, but on the authority of such respectable names I shall acknowledge its truth; but then I will ask one question, and on that I will rest the whole merits of the cause: Why does not this imaginary representation extend to America, as well as over the whole island of Great–Britain? If it can travel three hundred miles, why not three thousand? if it can jump over rivers and mountains, why cannot it sail over the ocean? If the towns of Manchester and Birmingham sending no representatives to parliament, are notwithstanding there represented, why are not the cities of Albany and Boston equally represented in that assembly? Are they not alike British subjects? are they not Englishmen? or are they only Englishmen when they sollicit for protection, but not Englishmen when taxes are required to enable this country to protect them?

But it is urged, that the Colonies are by their charters placed under distinct Governments, each of which has a legislative power within itself, by which alone it ought to be taxed; that if this privilege is once given up, that liberty which every Englishman has a right to, is torn from them, they are all slaves, and all is lost.

The liberty of an Englishman, is a phrase of so various a signification, having within these few years been used as a synonymous term for blasphemy, bawdry, treason, libels, strong beer, and cyder, that I shall not here presume to define its meaning; but I shall venture to assert what it cannot mean; that is, an exemption from taxes imposed by the authority of the Parliament of Great Britain; nor is there any charter, that ever pretended to grant such a privilege to any colony in America; and had they granted it, it could have had no force; their charters being derived from the Crown, and no charter from the Crown can possibly supersede the right of the whole legislature: their charters are undoubtedly no more than those of all corporations, which impower them to make byelaws, and raise duties for the purposes of their own police, for ever subject to the superior authority of parliament; and in some of their charters, the manner of exercising these powers is specified in these express words, "according to the course of other corporations in Great–Britain": and therefore they can have no more pretence to plead an exemption from this parliamentary authority, than any other corporation in England.

It has been moreover alleged, that, though Parliament may have power to impose taxes on the Colonies, they have no right to use it, because it would be an unjust tax; and no supreme or legislative power can have a right to enact any law in its nature unjust: to this, I shall only make this short reply, that if Parliament can impose no taxes but what are equitable, and the persons taxed are to be the judges of that equity, they will in effect have no power to lay any tax at all. No tax can be imposed exactly equal on all, and if it is not equal, it cannot be just: and if it is not just, no power whatever can impose it; by which short syllogism, all taxation is at an end; but why it should not be used by Englishmen on this side the Atlantic, as well as by those on the other, I do not comprehend. . . .

DOCUMENT 3

DANIEL DULANY, *CONSIDERATIONS*, OCTOBER 1765

Daniel Dulany of Annapolis, Maryland, had studied law in England at the Middle Temple, and was considered, at least by one fellow Marylander, Charles Carroll, to be "indisputably the best lawyer on this continent." He wrote this pamphlet, entitled Considerations on the Propriety of Imposing Taxes in the British Colonies, for the Purpose of raising a Revenue, by Act of Parliament, *in opposition to the Stamp Act. Here he argued that virtual representation was empty and meaningless; that the colonies not only were not but could not be represented in Parliament; and that taxation without representation was a breach of the English common law. His arguments were*

widely read in America, and in England were drawn
upon by William Pitt in his plea for repeal of the
Stamp Act (Document 4).

I shall undertake to disprove the supposed similarity of
situation, whence the same kind of Representation is
deduced of the inhabitants of the colonies, and of the
British non-electors; and, if I succeed, the Notion of a
virtual representation of the colonies must fail, which, in
Truth is a mere cob-web, spread to catch the unwary, and
intangle the weak. I would be understood. I am upon a
question of *propriety,* not of power; and though some may
be inclined to think it is to little purpose to discuss the one,
when the other is irresistible, yet are they different considerations; and, at the same time that I invalidate the
claim upon which it is founded, I may very consistently
recommend a submisssion to the law, whilst it en-
dures. . . .

Lessees for years, copyholders, proprietors of the public funds, inhabitants of Birmingham, Leeds, Halifax and
Manchester, merchants of the City of London, or members of the corporation of the East India Company, are,
as such, under no personal incapacity to be electors; for
they may acquire the right of election, and there are
actually not only a considerable number of electors in
each of the classes of lessees for years etc., but in many
of them, if not all, even members of Parliament. The interests therefore of the non-electors, the electors, and the
representatives, are individually the same; to say nothing
of the connection among neighbours, friends and relations.
The security of the non-electors against oppression, is that
their oppression will fall also upon the electors and the
representatives. The one can't be injured and the other
indemnified.

Further, if the non-electors should not be taxed by
the British Parliament, they would not be taxed *at all;*
and it would be iniquitous, as well as a solecism in the
political system, that they should partake of all the benefits
resulting from the imposition and application of taxes,
and derive an immunity from the circumstances of not

being qualified to vote. Under this Constitution then, a double or virtual representation may be reasonably supposed. . . .

There is not that intimate and inseparable relation between the electors of Great–Britain and the inhabitants of the colonies, which must inevitably involve both in the same taxation; on the contrary, not a single actual elector in England, might be immediately affected by a taxation in America, imposed by a statute which would have a general operation and effect, upon the properties of the inhabitants of the colonies . . . wherefore the relation between the British Americans, and the English electors, is a knot too infirm to be relied on. . . .

It appears to me, that there is a clear and necessary Distinction between an Act imposing a tax for *the single purpose of revenue,* and those Acts which have been made for the *regulation of trade,* and have produced some revenue in consequence of their effect and operation as regulations of trade.

The colonies claim the privileges of British subjects —It has been proved to be inconsistent with those privileges, to tax them without their own consent, and it hath been demonstrated that a tax imposed by Parliament, is a tax without their consent.

The subordination of the colonies, and the authority of Parliament to preserve it, have been fully acknowledged. Not only the welfare, but perhaps the existence of the mother country, as an independent kingdom, may depend upon her trade and navigation, and these so far upon her intercourse with the colonies, that if this should be neglected, there would soon be an end to that commerce, whence her greatest wealth is derived, and upon which her maritime power is principally founded. From these considerations, the right of the *British Parliament* to regulate the trade of the colonies, may be justly deduced; a denial of it would contradict the admission of the subordination, and of the authority to preserve it, resulting from the nature of the relation between the mother country and her colonies. It is a common, and frequently the most proper method to regulate trade by duties on imports and exports. The authority of the mother country to regulate the trade of the colonies being unquestionable, what regulations are the most proper, are to be of course submitted to the determination of the Parliament; and if an *incidental revenue*, should be produced by such regulations; these are not therefore unwarrantable.

A right to impose an internal tax on the colonies, without their consent *for the single purpose of revenue*, is denied, a right to regulate their trade without their consent is admitted. The imposition of a duty may, in some instances, be the proper regulation. If the claims of the mother country and the colonies should seem on such an occasion to interfere, and the point of right to be doubtful (which I take to be otherwise), it is easy to guess that the determination will be on the side of power, and the inferior will be constrained to submit.

DOCUMENT 4

WILLIAM PITT, SPEECH ON THE STAMP ACT, JANUARY 14, 1766

William Pitt the elder, later Earl of Chatham, had won great glory in his first ministry, which had laid the basis of victory in the Seven Years' War. He had resigned in 1761, and was absent from the House of Commons when the Stamp Act was passed. Although he firmly upheld Parliament's right to legislate for the colonies, he agreed with the Americans that this right did not extend to taxation. When the Stamp Act's enforcement or repeal was before the House, Pitt was bedridden with one of his fierce and painful attacks of gout, but he said to a friend: "If I can crawl, or be carried, I will deliver my mind and heart upon the state of America." The powerful speech from which this selection is taken was an answer to Prime Minister George Grenville, his brother-in-law, who persisted in defending the stamp duties. The Marquess of Rockingham wrote to King George III the day after Pitt's speech: "The events of yesterday in the

House of Commons have shown the amazing power and influence which Mr. Pitt has whenever he takes part in debate." The speech added new intensity to the admiration Americans already had for its author. Ships, towns, and babies were named after him, and one rhymester wrote:

I thank thee, Pitt, for all thy glorious strife
Against the foes of LIBERTY and life.

Gentlemen,—Sir [to the speaker], I have been charged with giving birth to sedition in America. They have spoken their sentiments with freedom against this unhappy act, and that freedom has become their crime. Sorry I am to hear the liberty of speech in this house, imputed as a crime. But the imputation shall not discourage me. It is a liberty I mean to exercise. No gentleman ought to be afraid to exercise it. It is a liberty by which the gentleman who calumniates it might have profited, by which he ought to have profited. He ought to have desisted from his project. The gentleman tells us, America is obstinate; America is almost in open rebellion. I rejoice that America has resisted. Three millions of people so dead to all feelings of liberty, as voluntarily to submit to be slaves, would have been fit instruments to make slaves of the rest. I come not here armed at all points, with law cases and acts of parliament, with the statute book doubled down in dogs'-ears, to defend the cause of liberty: if I had, I myself would have cited the two cases of Chester and Durham. I would have cited them, to have shown that even under former arbitrary reigns, parliaments were ashamed of taxing a people without their consent, and allowed them representatives. Why did the gentleman confine himself to Chester and Durham? He might have taken a higher example in Wales; Wales, that never was taxed by parliament till it was incorporated. I would not debate a particular point of law with the gentleman. I know his abilities. I have been obliged to his diligent researches: but, for the defence of liberty, upon a general principle, upon a constitutional principle, it is a ground upon which I stand firm; on which I dare meet any man.

The gentleman tells us of many who are taxed, and are not represented. The India Company, merchants, stockholders, manufacturers. Surely many of these are represented in other capacities, as owners of land, or as freemen of boroughs. It is a misfortune that more are not equally represented: but they are all inhabitants, and as such, are they not virtually represented? . . . they have connections with those that elect, and they have influence over them. The gentleman mentioned the stock-holders: I hope he does not reckon the debts of the nation as a part of the national estate. Since the accession of King William, many ministers, some of great, others of more moderate abilities, have taken the lead of government. (He then went through the list of them, bringing it down till he came to himself, giving a short sketch of the characters of each of them.)

None of these thought, or ever dreamed, of robbing the colonies of their constitutional rights. That was reserved to mark the era of the late administration: not that there were wanting some, when I had the honour to serve his Majesty, to propose to me to burn my fingers with an American stamp-act. With the enemy at their back, with our bayonets at their breasts, in the day of their distress, perhaps the Americans would have submitted to the imposition; but it would have been taking an ungenerous and unjust advantage. The gentleman boasts of his bounties to America. Are not those bounties intended finally for the benefit of this kingdom? If they are not, he has misapplied the national treasures. I am no courtier of America; I stand up for this kingdom. I maintain, that the parliament has a right to bind, to restrain America. Our legislative power over the colonies is sovereign and supreme. When it ceases to be sovereign and supreme, I would advise every gentleman to sell his lands, if he can, and embark for that country. When two countries are connected together, like England and her colonies, without being incorporated, the one must necessarily govern; the greater must rule the less; but so rule it, as not to contradict the fundamental principles that are common to both. If the gentleman does not understand the difference between external and internal taxes, I cannot help it; but there is a plain distinction between taxes levied for the purposes of raising a revenue, and duties imposed for the regulation of trade, for the accommodation of the subject; although, in the consequences, some revenue might incidentally arise from the latter.

The gentleman asks, when were the colonies emancipated? But I desire to know, when were they made slaves. But I dwell not upon words. When I had the honour of serving his Majesty, I availed myself of the means of information which I derived from my office: I speak, therefore, from knowledge. My materials were good; I was at pains to collect, to digest, to consider them; and I will be bold to affirm, that the profits to Great Britain from the trade of the colonies, through all its branches, is two millions a year. This is the fund that carried you triumphantly through the last war. . . . You owe this to America: this is the price that America pays you for her protection. And shall a miserable financier come with a boast, that he can bring a pepper-corn into the exchequer, to the loss of millions to the nation? I dare not say, how much higher these profits may be augmented. Omitting the immense increase of people by natural population, in the northern colonies, and the emigration from every part of Europe, I am convinced the whole commercial system of America may be altered to advantage. You have prohibited where you ought to have encouraged, encouraged where you ought to have prohibited. Improper restraints have been laid on the continent, in favour of the islands. You have but two nations to trade with in America. Would you had twenty! Let acts of parliament in consequence of treaties remain, but let not an English minister become a custom-house officer for Spain, or for any foreign power. Much is wrong; much may be amended for the general good of the whole. . . .

The gentleman must not wonder he was not contradicted, when, as the minister, he asserted the right of parliament to tax America. I know not how it is, but there is a modesty in this House, which does not choose to contradict a minister. I wish gentlemen would get the better of this modesty. Even that chair, Sir, sometimes looks towards St. James's. If they do not, perhaps the collective body may begin to abate of its respect for the representative. . . .

A great deal has been said without doors of the power, of the strength of America. It is a topic that ought to be cautiously meddled with. In a good cause, on a sound bottom, the force of this country can crush America to atoms. I know the valour of your troops. I know the skill of your officers. There is not a company of foot that has served in America out of which you may not pick a man of sufficient knowledge and experience to make a governor of a colony there. But on this ground, on the Stamp Act, when so many here will think a crying injustice, I am one who will lift up my hands against it.

In such a cause, your success would be hazardous. America, if she fell, would fall like the strong man. She would embrace the pillars of the state, and pull down the constitution along with her. Is this your boasted peace? Not to sheathe the sword in its scabbard, but to sheathe it in the bowels of your countrymen? Will you quarrel with yourselves, now the whole House of Bourbon is united against you? . . .

The Americans have not acted in all things with prudence and temper. They have been wronged. They have been driven to madness by injustice. Will you punish them for the madness you have occasioned? Rather let prudence and temper come first from this side. I will undertake for America, that she will follow the example. There are two lines in a ballad of Prior's, of a man's behaviour to his wife, so applicable to you and your colonies, that I cannot help repeating them:—

> Be to her faults a little blind;
> Be to her virtues very kind.

Upon the whole, I will beg leave to tell the House what is really my opinion. It is, that the Stamp-Act be repealed absolutely, totally, and immediately; that the reason for the repeal should be assigned, because it was founded on an erroneous principle. At the same time, let the sovereign authority of this country over the colonies be asserted in as strong terms as can be devised, and be made to extend to every point of legislation whatsoever:

that we may bind their trade, confine their manufactures, and exercise every power whatsoever—except that of taking money out of their pockets without their consent.

DOCUMENT 5

JOHN DICKINSON, LETTERS II AND IV FROM *LETTERS FROM A FARMER*, 1767–1768

John Dickinson, one of the outstanding members of the Philadelphia bar, and a man of moderate views, had been a leader of the opposition to the Stamp Act. In December 1767, he began to publish in the Pennsylvania Chronicle *a series of anonymous letters, subsequently published as a pamphlet entitled* Letters from a Farmer in Pennsylvania to the Inhabitants of the British Colonies *(1768). The letters, evoked by the Townshend Acts, were felt to be a signal statement of the American constitutional position, and they won Dickinson much applause. Influential though it was, Dickinson's argument was soon by-passed. It rested upon his assumption that the purpose of Parliament, when it passed a law, was the basis of that law's legitimacy. He defined a tax as an imposition "for the sole purpose of levying money." If a law was intended to raise money, it could be classified as a tax, and was therefore constitutionally unacceptable, no matter if, like the Townshend Acts, it was put forth in the form of a trade regulation. But the implication that the colonists could determine or define the purposes of Parliament presented too many difficulties for the colonial argument to rest long at this position.*

Letter II

There is another late act of parliament, which appears to me to be unconstitutional, and as destructive to the liberty of these colonies, as that mentioned in my last letter;

that is, the act for granting the duties on paper, glass, etc. [the Townshend Act].

The parliament unquestionably possesses a legal authority to regulate the trade of Great–Britain and all her colonies. Such an authority is essential to the relation between a mother country and her colonies; and necessary for the common good of all. He, who considers these provinces as states distinct from the British empire, has very slender notions of justice, or of their interests. We are but parts of a whole; and therefore there must exist a power somewhere to preside, and preserve the connection in due order. This power is lodged in the parliament; and we are as much dependent on Great–Britain, as a perfectly free people can be on another.

I have looked over every statute relating to these colonies, from their first settlement to this time; and I find every one of them founded on this principle, till the Stamp–Act administration. All before, are calculated to regulate trade, and preserve or promote a mutually beneficial intercourse between the several constituent parts of the empire; and though many of them imposed duties on trade, yet those duties were always imposed with design to restrain the commerce of one part, that was injurious to another, and thus to promote the general welfare. The raising a revenue thereby was never intended . . . Never did the British parliament, till the period above mentioned, think of imposing duties in America, FOR THE PURPOSE OF RAISING A REVENUE. . . .

Here we may observe an authority expressly claimed and exerted to impose duties on these colonies; not for the regulation of trade; not for the preservation or promotion of a mutually beneficial intercourse between the several constituent parts of the empire, heretofore the sole objects of parliamentary institutions; but for the single purpose of levying money upon us.

This I call an innovation; and a most dangerous innovation. It may perhaps be objected, that Great–Britain has a right to lay what duties she pleases upon her exports, and it makes no difference to us, whether they are paid here or there.

To this I answer. These colonies require many things

for their use, which the laws of Great–Britain prohibit them from getting any where but from her. Such are paper and glass.

That we may be legally bound to pay any general duties on these commodities relative to the regulation of trade, is granted; but we being obliged by the laws to take from Great–Britain, any special duties imposed on their exportation to us only, with intention to raise a revenue from us only, are as much taxes, upon us, as those imposed by the Stamp–Act.

What is the difference in substance and right whether the same sum is raised upon us by the rates mentioned in the Stamp–Act, on the use of paper, or by these duties, on the importation of it. It is only the edition of a former book, shifting a sentence from the end to the beginning. . . .

Some persons perhaps may say, that this act lays us under no necessity to pay the duties imposed, because we may ourselves manufacture the articles on which they are laid; whereas by the Stamp–Act no instrument of writing could be good, unless made on British paper, and that too stamped.

I am told there are but two or three glass-houses on this continent, and but very few paper-mills; and suppose more should be erected, a long course of years must elapse, before they can be brought to perfection. This continent is a country of planters, farmers, and fishermen; not of manufacturers. The difficulty of establishing particular manufactures in such a country, is almost insuperable. . . .

Great–Britain has prohibited the manufacturing iron and steel in these colonies, without any objection being made to her right of doing it. The like right she must have to prohibit any other manufacture among us. Thus she is possessed of an undisputed precedent on that point. This authority, she will say, is founded on the original intention of settling these colonies; that is, that we should manufacture for them, and that they should supply her with materials. . . .

Here then, my dear country men ROUSE yourselves, and behold the ruin hanging over your heads. If you ONCE admit, that Great–Britain may lay duties upon her exportations to us, for the purpose of levying money on us only, she then will have nothing to do, but to lay those duties on the articles which she prohibits us to manufacture— and the tragedy of American liberty is finished. . . . If Great–Britain can order us to come to her for necessaries we want, and can order us to pay what taxes she pleases before we take them away, or when we land them here, we are as abject slaves as France and Poland can shew in wooden shoes, and with uncombed hair.

Letter IV

An objection, I hear, has been made against my second letter, which I would willingly clear up before I proceed. "There is," say these objectors, "a material difference between the Stamp–Act and the late Act for laying a duty on paper, etc., that justifies the conduct of those who opposed the former, and yet are willing to submit to the latter. The duties imposed by the Stamp–Act were internal taxes; but the present are external, and therefore the parliament may have a right to impose them."

To this I answer, with a total denial of the power of parliament to lay upon these colonies any "tax" whatever.

This point, being so important to this, and to succeeding generations, I wish to be clearly understood.

To the word "tax," I annex that meaning which the constitution and history of England require to be annexed to it; that is—that it is an imposition on the subject, for the sole purpose of levying money. . . .

Whenever we speak of "taxes" among Englishmen, let us therefore speak of them with reference to the principles on which, and the intentions with which they have been established. . . .

In the national, parliamentary sense insisted on, the word "tax" was certainly understood by the congress at New–York, whose resolves may be said to form the American "bill of rights."

The third, fourth, fifth, and sixth resolves are, thus expressed.

[Here Dickinson quoted the resolves of the Stamp Act Congress. See Document 1.]

Here is no distinction made between internal and external taxes. It is evident from the short reasoning thrown into these resolves, that every imposition "to grant to his Majesty the property of the colonies," was thought a "tax"; and that every such imposition, if laid any other way, than "with their consent, given personally, or by their representatives," was not only "unreasonable, and inconsistent with the principles and spirit of the British constitution," but destructive "to the freedom of a people."

Such persons therefore as speak of internal and external "taxes," I pray may pardon me, if I object to that expression, as applied to the privileges and interests of these colonies. There may be internal and external IMPOSITIONS, founded on different principles, and having different tendencies, every "tax" being an imposition, tho' every imposition is not a "tax." But all taxes are founded on the same principles; and have the same tendency.

External impositions, for the regulation of our trade, do not "grant to his Majesty the property of the colonies." They only prevent the colonies acquiring property, in things not necessary, in a manner judged to be injurious to the welfare of the whole empire. But the last statute respecting us, "grants to his Majesty the property of the colonies," by laying duties on the manufactures of Great–Britain which they MUST take, and which she settled on them, on purpose that they SHOULD take.

DOCUMENT 6

FIRST CONTINENTAL CONGRESS, DECLARATION AND RESOLVES,
OCTOBER 14, 1774

The first Continental Congress met at Philadelphia on September 5, 1774, in reaction to the "Intolerable Acts." All the colonies except Georgia were repre-

sented. A committee, which included John Adams, was appointed to draw up a declaration of the rights of the colonies. Adams drew up such a statement, and John Sullivan of New Hampshire prepared a list of cases in which they had been violated. The framers of the Declaration and Resolves were uncertain, according to Adams, as to whether they should "recur to the law of nature, as well as to the British constitution, and our American charters and grants." The radicals, including Adams, wanted to appeal to natural law; the conservatives held that the constitution offered guarantees enough. Adams chose to appeal to both. But, despite the reference to "the immutable laws of nature," the burden of the argument rests mainly on the appeal to constitutional and charter guarantees. The fourth resolution, with its strong repudiation of "every idea of taxation, internal or external," troubled the more conciliatory delegates. Joseph Galloway of Pennsylvania had proposed a plan for an American legislature under a crown-appointed executive, which was rejected by a vote of six colonies to five. In adopting this strong statement instead, the Americans served notice on Parliament that they no longer felt bound by any of its laws beyond those for "the regulation of our external commerce." This too had been much debated, for conservatives and radicals would not agree on "what authority we should concede to Parliament." Note that Parliament's regulation of commerce is something to which the delegates "cheerfully consent" because it is to their mutual advantage, not because it is conceded to be Parliament's rightful prerogative.

Whereas, since the close of the last war, the British parliament, claiming a power of right to bind the people of America, by statute in all cases whatsoever, hath, in some acts expressly imposed taxes on them, and in others, under various pretences, but in fact for the purpose of raising a revenue, hath imposed rates and duties payable in these colonies, established a board of commissioners with unconstitutional powers, and extended the jurisdiction of courts of Admiralty, not only for collecting the said duties, but for the trial of causes merely arising within the body of a county.

And whereas, in consequence of other statutes, judges, who before held only estates at will in their offices, have been made dependent on the Crown alone for their salaries, and standing armies kept in times of peace. And it has lately been resolved in Parliament, that by force of a statute made in the thirty-fifth year of the reign of king Henry the eighth, colonists may be transported to England, and tried there upon accusations for treasons, and misprisions, or concealments of treasons committed in the colonies; and by a late statute, such trials have been directed in cases therein mentioned.

And whereas, in the last session of parliament, three statutes were made . . . [the Boston Port Act, the Massachusetts Government Act, the Administration of Justice Act] And another statute was then made [the Quebec Act] . . . All which statutes are impolitic, unjust, and cruel, as well as unconstitutional, and most dangerous and destructive of American rights.

And whereas, Assemblies have been frequently dissolved, contrary to the rights of the people, when they attempted to deliberate on grievances; and their dutiful, humble, loyal, and reasonable petitions to the crown for redress, have been repeatedly treated with contempt, by his majesty's ministers of state:

The good people of the several Colonies of New-hampshire, Massachusetts-bay, Rhode-Island and Providence plantations, Connecticut, New-York, New-Jersey, Pennsylvania, Newcastle, Kent and Sussex on Delaware, Maryland, Virginia, North-Carolina, and South Carolina, justly alarmed at these arbitrary proceedings of parliament and administration, have severally elected, constituted, and appointed deputies to meet and sit in general congress, in the city of Philadelphia, in order to obtain such establishment, as that their religion, laws, and liberties, may not be subverted:

Whereupon the deputies so appointed being now assembled, in a full and free representation of these Colonies, taking into their most serious consideration, the best means of attaining the ends aforesaid, do, in the first place, as Englishmen, their ancestors in like cases have usually done, for asserting and vindicating their rights and liberties, declare,

That the inhabitants of the English Colonies in North America, by the immutable laws of nature, the principles of the English constitution, and the several charters or compacts, have the following Rights:

Resolved, N. C. D.

1. That they are entitled to life, liberty, and property, and they have never ceded to any sovereign power whatever, a right to dispose of either without their consent.

2. That our ancestors, who first settled these colonies, were at the time of their emigration from the mother country, entitled to all the rights, liberties, and immunities of free and natural-born subjects, within the realm of England.

3. That by such emigration they by no means forfeited, surrendered, or lost any of those rights, but that they were, and their descendants now are, entitled to the exercise and enjoyment of all such of them, as their local and other circumstances enable them to exercise and enjoy.

4. That the foundation of English liberty, and of all free government, is a right in the people to participate in their legislative council: and as the English colonists are not represented, and from their local and other circumstances, cannot properly be represented in the British parliament, they are entitled to a free and exclusive power of legislation in their several provincial legislatures, where their right of representation can alone be preserved, in all cases of taxation and internal polity, subject only to the negative of their sovereign, in such manner as has been heretofore used and accustomed. But, from the necessity of the case, and a regard to the mutual interest of both countries, we cheerfully consent to the operation of such acts of the British parliament, as are bona fide, restrained to the regulation of our external commerce, for the purpose of securing the commercial advantages of the whole empire to the mother country, and the commercial benefits of its respective members; excluding every idea of taxation, internal or external, for raising a revenue on the subjects in America, without their consent.

5. That the respective colonies are entitled to the common law of England, and more especially to the great and inestimable privilege of being tried by their peers of the vicinage, according to the course of that law.

6. That they are entitled to the benefit of such of the English statutes as existed at the time of their colonization; and which they have, by experience, respectively found to be applicable to their several local and other circumstances.

7. That these, his majesty's colonies, are likewise entitled to all the immunities and privileges granted and confirmed to them by royal charters, or secured by their several codes of provincial laws.

8. That they have a right peaceably to assemble, consider of their grievances, and petition the King; and that all prosecutions, prohibitory proclamations, and commitments for the same, are illegal.

9. That the keeping a Standing army in these colonies, in times of peace, without the consent of the legislature of that colony, in which such army is kept, is against law.

10. It is indispensably necessary to good government, and rendered essential by the English constitution, that the constituent branches of the legislature be independent of each other; that, therefore, the exercise of legislative power in several colonies, by a council appointed, during pleasure, by the crown, is unconstitutional, dangerous, and destructive to the freedom of American legislation.

All and each of which the aforesaid deputies, in behalf of themselves and their constituents, do claim, demand, and insist on, as their indubitable rights and liberties; which cannot be legally taken from them, altered or abridged by any power whatever, without their own consent, by their representatives in their several provincial legislatures.

In the course of our inquiry, we find many infringements and violations of the foregoing rights, which, from an ardent desire that harmony and mutual intercourse of affection and interest may be restored, we pass over for the present, and proceed to state such acts and measures as have been adopted since the last war, which demonstrate a system formed to enslave America.

Resolved, That the following acts of Parliament are infringements and violations of the rights of the colonists; and that the repeal of them is essentially necessary in order to restore harmony between Great-Britain and the American colonies, . . . viz.:

The several Acts of 4 Geo. 3, ch. 15, and ch. 34; 5 Geo. 3, ch. 25; 6 Geo. 3, ch. 52; 7 Geo. 3, ch. 41 and 46; 8 Geo. 3, ch. 22; which impose duties for the purpose of raising a revenue in America, extend the powers of the admiralty courts beyond their ancient limits, deprive the American subject of trial by jury, authorize the judges' certificate to indemnify the prosecutor from damages that he might otherwise be liable to, requiring oppressive security from a claimant of ships and goods seized, before he shall be allowed to defend his property, and are subversive of American rights.

Also the 12 Geo. 3, ch. 24, entitled "An act for the better securing his Majesty's dockyards, magazines, ships, ammunition, and stores," which declares a new offense in America, and deprives the American subject of a constitutional trial by jury of the vicinage, by authorizing the trial of any person, charged with the committing any offense described in the said act, out of the realm, to be indicted and tried for the same in any shire or county within the realm.

Also the three acts passed in the last session of parliament, for stopping the port and blocking up the harbour of Boston, for altering the charter and government of the Massachusetts-bay, and that which is entitled "An Act for the better administration of Justice," etc.

Also the act passed the same session for establishing the Roman Catholick Religion in the province of Quebec, abolishing the equitable system of English laws, and erecting a tyranny there, to the great danger, from so total a dissimilarity of Religion, law, and government of the neighbouring British colonies. . . .

Also the act passed the same session for the better providing suitable quarters for officers and soldiers in his Majesty's service in North-America.

Also, that the keeping a standing army in several of

these colonies, in time of peace, without the consent of the legislature of that colony in which the army is kept, is against law.

To these grievous acts and measures Americans cannot submit, but in hopes that their fellow subjects in Great-Britain will, on a revision of them, restore us to that state in which both countries found happiness and prosperity, we have for the present only resolved to pursue the following peaceable measures: . . . 1st. To enter into a non-importation, non-consumption, and non-exportation agreement or association. 2. To prepare an address to the people of Great-Britain, and a memorial to the inhabitants of British America, and 3. To prepare a loyal address to his Majesty; agreeable to resolutions already entered into.

DOCUMENT 7

DANIEL LEONARD, MASSACHUSETTENSIS,
JANUARY 9, 1775

Daniel Leonard, who lived in Taunton, Massachusetts, and practiced law in Boston, was one of the wealthiest and most aristocratic barristers of his day. John Adams marveled at his gold lace and magnificent coach, in which, Adams said, not another lawyer in the entire province could presume to ride. Leonard was thoroughly Tory in his views. In 1774 the patriots, outraged at his espousal of the cause of the crown, drove him from his Taunton home to find refuge in Boston. There, between December 1774 and April 1775, Leonard published a series of weekly "Letters Addressed to the Inhabitants of the Province of Massachusetts Bay" in the Massachusetts Gazette, in which, under the pen name of Massachusettensis, he argued the case for submission to the crown and warned of the dangers of rebellion. These letters constitute one of the ablest statements of the Loyalist case by an American.

January 9, 1775

The security of the people from internal rapacity and violence, and from foreign invasion, is the end and design of government. The simple forms of government are monarchy, aristocracy and democracy, that is, where the authority of the state is vested in one, a few, or the many. Each of these species of government has advantages peculiar to itself, and would answer the ends of government, where the persons intrusted with the authority of the state, always guided themselves by unerring wisdom and public virtue; but rulers are not always exempt from the weakness and depravity which make government necessary to society. Thus monarchy is apt to rush headlong into tyranny, aristocracy to beget faction and multiplied usurpations, and democracy to degenerate into tumult, violence and anarchy. A government formed upon these three principles in due proportion, is the best calculated to answer the ends of government, and to endure. Such a government is the British constitution, consisting of King, Lords and Commons, which at once includes the principal excellencies, and excludes the principal defects of the other kinds of government. It is allowed, both by Englishmen and foreigners to be the most perfect system that the wisdom of ages has produced. The distributions of power are so just, and the proportions so exact, as at once to support and controul each other. An Englishman glories in being subject to, and protected by, such a government. The colonies are a part of the British empire. The best writers upon the law of nations, tell us, that when a nation takes possession of a distant country, and settles there, that country though separated from the principal establishment, or mother country, naturally becomes a part of the state, equal with its ancient possessions. Two supreme or independent authorities cannot exist in the same state. It would be what is called *imperium in imperio,* the height of political absurdity. The analogy between the political and human bodies is great. Two independent authorities in a state would be like two distinct principles of volition and action in the human body, dissenting, opposing and destroying each other. If then we are a part of the British empire, we must be subject to the supreme power of the state which is vested in the estates of parliament, notwithstanding each of the colonies have legislative and executive powers of their own, delegated or granted to them, for the purposes of regulating their own internal police, which are subordinate to, and must necessarily be subject to the checks, controul and regulation of the supreme authority of the state.

This doctrine is not new, but the denial of it is. It is beyond a doubt that it was the sense both of the parent country, and our ancestors, that they were to remain subject to parliament. It is evident from the charter itself, and this authority has been exercised by parliament, from time to time, almost ever since the first settlement of the country, and has been expressly acknowledged by our provincial legislatures. It is not less our interest, than our duty, to continue subject to the authority of parliament, which will be more fully considered hereafter. The principal argument against the authority of parliament, is this, the Americans are entitled to all the privileges of an Englishman, it is the privilege of an Englishman to be exempt from all laws that he does not consent to in person, or by representative; The Americans are not represented in parliament, and therefore are exempt from acts of parliament, or in other words, not subject to its authority. This appears specious; but leads to such absurdities as demonstrate its fallacy. If the colonies are not subject to the authority of parliament, Great-Britain and the colonies must be distinct states, as completely so as England and Scotland were before the union, or as Great-Britain and Hanover are now; The colonies in that case will owe no allegiance to the imperial crown, and perhaps not to the person of the King, as the title of the crown is derived from an act of parliament, made since the settlement of this province, which act respects the imperial crown only. Let us waive this difficulty, and suppose allegiance due from the colonies to the person of the King of Great-Britain, he then appears in a new capacity, of King of America, or rather in several new capacities, of King of Massachusetts, King of Rhode-Island, King of Connecticut, etc., etc. For if our connexion with Great-Britain by the parliament be dissolved, we shall have none among ourselves, but each colony become as distinct from the others, as England was from Scotland, before the union. . . . But let us suppose the same prerogatives inherent in the several American crowns, as are in the imperial crown of Great-Britain, where shall we find the British constitution that we all agree we are entitled to? We shall seek for it in vain in our provincial assemblies. They are but faint sketches of the estates of parliament. The houses of representatives, or Burgesses, have not all the powers of the House of Commons, in the charter governments they have no more than what is expressly granted by their several charters. The first charters granted to this province did not impower the assembly to tax the people at all. Our Council Boards are as destitute of the constitutional authority of the House of Lords, as their several members are of the noble independence and splendid appendages of Peerage. The House of Peers is the bulwark of the British constitution, and through successive ages, has withstood the shocks of monarchy, and the sappings of Democracy, and the constitution gained strength by the conflict. Thus the supposition of our being independent states, or exempt from the authority of parliament, destroys the very idea of our having a British constitution. The provincial constitutions, considered as subordinate, are generally well adapted to those purposes of government, for which they were intended, that is, to regulate the internal police of the several colonies; but have no principle of stability within themselves, they may support themselves in moderate times, but would be merged by the violence of turbulent ones, and the several colonies become wholly monarchial, or wholly republican, were it not for the checks, controuls, regulations, and support of the supreme authority of the empire. Thus the argument that is drawn from their first principle of our being entitled to English liberties, destroys the principle itself, it deprives us of the Bill of Rights, and all the benefits resulting from the revolution of English laws, and of the British constitution.

Our patriots have been so intent upon building up American rights, that they have overlooked the rights of Great-Britain, and our own interest. Instead of proving that we are entitled to privileges that our fathers knew our situation would not admit us to enjoy, they have been arguing away our most essential rights. If there be any grievance, it does not consist in our being subject to the authority of parliament, but in our not having an actual representation in it. Were it possible for the colonies to have an equal representation in parliament, and were refused it upon proper application, I confess I should think it a grievance; but at present it seems to be allowed by all parties, to be impracticable, considering the colonies are distant from Great-Britain a thousand transmarine leagues. If that be the case, the right or privilege, that we complain of being deprived of, is not withheld by Britain, but the first principles of government, and the immutable laws of nature, render it impossible for us to enjoy it. . . . Allegiance and protection are reciprocal. It is our highest interest to continue a part of the British empire; and equally our duty to remain subject to the authority of parliament. Our own internal police may generally be regulated by our provincial legislatures, but in national concerns, or where our own assemblies do not answer the ends of government with respect to ourselves, the ordinance or interposition of the great council of the nation is necessary. In this case, the major must rule the minor. After many more centuries shall have rolled away, long after we, who are now bustling upon the stage of life, shall have been received to the bosom of mother earth, and our names are forgotten, the colonies may be so far increased as to have the balance of wealth, numbers and power, in their favour, the good of the empire make it necessary to fix the seat of government here; and some future George, equally the friend of mankind with him that now sways the British sceptre, may cross the Atlantic, and rule Great-Britain, by an American parliament.

DOCUMENT 8

JOHN ADAMS, NOVANGLUS,
FEBRUARY 6, 1775

*This was part of John Adams' answer to Daniel
Leonard's letters "On my return from Congress,"
Adams recalled, "I found the* Massachusetts *Gazette
teeming with political speculations, and Massachusettensis shining like the moon among the lesser
stars." He set to work at once to answer Leonard in
his own series of letters, signing himself Novanglus.
Adams here provides a forceful statement of the view
many Americans had arrived at—that the authority
of Parliament did not in any respect cross the ocean,
and that the sole bond that united the colonists to
Great Britain was a common loyalty to the crown.
The remarks here quoted by Adams for the sake of
refutation are all those of Daniel Leonard.*

February 6, 1775.

I agree, that "two supreme and independent authorities cannot exist in the same state," any more than two supreme beings in one universe; And, therefore, I contend,
that our provincial legislatures are the only supreme authorities in our colonies. Parliament, notwithstanding this,
may be allowed an authority supreme and sovereign over
the ocean, which may be limited by the banks of the
ocean, or the bounds of our charters; our charters give
us no authority over the high seas. Parliament has our
consent to assume a jurisdiction over them. And here is a
line fairly drawn between the rights of Britain and the
rights of the colonies, namely, the banks of the ocean, or
low-water mark; the line of division between common law,
and civil or maritime law. . . .

"If then, we are a part of the British empire, we must
be subject to the supreme power of the state, which is
vested in the estates in parliament."

Here, again, we are to be conjured out of our senses by the magic in the words "British empire," and "supreme power of the state." But, however it may sound, I say we are not a part of the British empire; because the British government is not an empire. The governments of France, Spain, etc., are not empires, but monarchies, supposed to be governed by fixed fundamental laws, though not really. The British government is still less entitled to the style of *an empire*. It is a limited monarchy. If Aristotle, Livy, and Harrington knew what a republic was, the British constitution is much more like a republic than an empire. They define a republic to be a *government of laws, and not of men*. If this definition is just, the British constitution is nothing more nor less than a republic, in which the king is first magistrate. This office being hereditary, and being possessed of such ample and splendid prerogatives, is no objection to the government's being a republic, as long as it is bound by fixed laws, which the people have a voice in making, and a right to defend. An empire is a despotism, and an emperor a despot, bound by no law or limitation but his own will; it is a stretch of tyranny beyond absolute monarchy. For, although the will of an absolute monarch is law, yet his edicts must be registered by parliaments. Even this formality is not necessary in an empire. . . .

"If the colonies are not subject to the authority of parliament, Great Britain and the colonies must be distinct states, as completely so as England and Scotland were before the union, or as Great Britain and Hanover are now." There is no need of being startled at this consequence. It is very harmless. There is no absurdity at all in it. Distinct states may be united under one king. And those states may be further cemented and united together by a treaty of commerce. This is the case. We have, by our own express consent, contracted to observe the Navigation Act, and by our implied consent, by long usage and uninterrupted acquiescence, have submitted to the other acts of trade, however grievous some of them may be. This may be compared to a treaty of commerce, by which those distinct states are cemented together, in perpetual league and amity. . . .

The only proposition in all this writer's long string of pretended absurdities, which he says follows from the position that we are distinct states, is this: That, "as the king must govern each state by its parliament, those several parliaments would pursue the particular interest of its own state; and however well disposed the king might be to pursue a line of interest that was common to all, the checks and control that he would meet with would render it impossible." Every argument ought to be allowed its full weight; and therefore candor obliges me to acknowledge, that here lies all the difficulty that there is in this whole controversy. There has been, from first to last, on both sides of the Atlantic, an idea, an apprehension that it was necessary there should be some superintending power, to draw together all the wills, and unite all the strength of the subjects in all the dominions, in case of war, and in the case of trade. The necessity of this, in case of trade, has been so apparent, that, as has often been said, we have consented that parliament should exercise such a power. In case of war, it has by some been thought necessary. But, in fact and experience, it has not been found so. . . . The inconveniences of this were small, in comparison of the absolute ruin to the liberties of all which must follow the submission to parliament, in all cases, which would be giving up all the popular limitations upon the government. . . .

But, admitting the proposition in its full force, that it is absolutely necessary there should be a supreme power, coextensive with all the dominions, will it follow that parliament, as now constituted, has a right to assume this supreme jurisdiction? By no means.

A union of the colonies might be projected, and an American legislature; for, if America has 3,000,000 people, and the whole dominions 12,000,000, she ought to send a quarter part of all the members to the house of commons; and instead of holding parliaments always at Westminster, the haughty members for Great Britain must humble themselves, one session in four, to cross the Atlantic, and hold the parliament in America.

There is no avoiding all inconveniences in human

affairs. The greatest possible, or conceivable, would arise from ceding to parliament power over us without a representation in it. . . . The least of all would arise from going on as we began, and fared well for 150 years, by letting parliament regulate trade, and our own assemblies all other matters. . . .

But perhaps it will be said, that we are to enjoy the British constitution in our supreme legislature, the parliament, not in our provincial legislatures. To this I answer, if parliament is to be our supreme legislature, we shall be under a complete oligarchy or aristocracy, not the British constitution, which this writer himself defines a mixture of monarchy, aristocracy, and democracy. For king, lords, and commons, will constitute one great oligarchy, as they will stand related to America, as much as the decemvirs did in Rome; with this difference for the worse, that our rulers are to be three thousand miles off. . . . If our provincial constitutions are in any respect imperfect, and want alteration, they have capacity enough to discern it, and power enough to effect it, without interposition of parliament. . . . America will never allow that parliament has any authority to alter their constitution at all. She is wholly penetrated with a sense of the necessity of resisting it at all hazards. . . . The question we insist on most is, not whether the alteration is for the better or not, but whether parliament has any right to make any alteration at all. And it is the universal sense of America, that it has none. . . .

That a representation in parliament is impracticable, we all agree; but the consequence is, that we must have a representation in our supreme legislatures here. This was the consequence that was drawn by kings, ministers, our ancestors, and the whole nation, more than a century ago, when the colonies were first settled, and continued to be the general sense until the last peace; and it must be the general sense again soon, or Great Britain will lose her colonies. . . .

"It is our highest interest to continue a part of the British empire; and equally our duty to remain subject to the authority of parliament," says Massachusettensis. We are a part of the British dominions, that is, of the

King of Great Britain, and it is our interest and duty to continue so. It is equally our interest and duty to continue subject to the authority of parliament, in the regulation of our trade, as long as she shall leave us to govern our internal policy, and to give and grant our own money, and no longer. . . .

DOCUMENT 9

EDMUND BURKE, SPEECH ON CONCILIATION WITH AMERICA,
MARCH 22, 1775

Edmund Burke had become a Whig leader soon after his first speech in the House of Commons, delivered in January 1766. In October 1774, after he had been invited to stand for Parliament for the city of Bristol, he told his prospective constituents: "To reconcile British superiority with American liberty shall be my great object." Unlike Pitt and so many other contemporaries, Burke professed little interest in the much-argued abstract questions of right and constitutionality. He believed that, while Parliament had a right to tax the colonies, it was impracticable and inexpedient to do so. To attempt to crush American resistance would be disastrous to both British and American liberties, and he hoped not to risk such a disaster by an intransigent stand on the powers of Parliament. His famous speech on conciliation was inspired by Lord North's belated and inadequate conciliatory gesture—the offer to exempt from imperial taxation for revenue any colony that would voluntarily make a satisfactory offer for the support of civil and military government. Because this proposal did not specify the amounts which the various colonies might be expected to deliver, and because in the meantime the colonies were being held in duress with fleets and armies, Burke thought Lord North's gesture was ignominious—"a method of ransom by auction."

To restore order and repose to an empire so great and so distracted as ours is, merely in the attempt, an undertaking that would ennoble the flights of the highest genius, and obtain pardon for the efforts of the meanest understanding. Struggling a good while with these thoughts, by degrees I felt myself more firm. I derived, at length, some confidence from what in other circumstances usually produces timidity. I grew less anxious, even from the idea of my own insignificance. For, judging of what you are by what you ought to be, I persuaded myself that you would not reject a reasonable proposition because it had nothing but its reason to recommend it. . . .

The proposition is peace. Not peace through the medium of war; not peace to be hunted through the labyrinth of intricate and endless negotiations; not peace to arise out of universal discord, fomented from principle, in all parts of the empire; not peace to depend on the juridical determination of perplexing questions, or the precise marking the shadowy boundaries of a complex government. It is simple peace, sought in its natural course and in its ordinary haunts. . . .

Let the colonies always keep the idea of their civil rights associated with your government—they will cling and grapple to you, and no force under heaven will be of power to tear them from their allegiance. But let it be once understood that your government may be one thing and their privileges another, that these two things may exist without any mutual relation—the cement is gone, the cohesion is loosened, and everything hastens to decay and dissolution. As long as you have the wisdom to keep the sovereign authority of this country as the sanctuary of liberty, the sacred temple consecrated to our common faith, whatever the chosen race and sons of England worship freedom, they will turn their faces towards you. The more they multiply, the more friends you will have, the more ardently they love liberty, the more perfect will be their obedience. Slavery they can have anywhere. It is a weed that grows in every soil. They may have it from Spain, they may have it from Prussia. But until you become lost to all feeling of your true interest and your natural dignity, freedom they can have from none but you. This is the commodity of price, of which you have the monopoly. This is the true Act of Navigation, which binds to you the commerce of the colonies, and through them secures to you the wealth of the world. Deny them this participation of freedom, and you break that sole bond which originally made, and must still preserve, the unity of the empire. Do not entertain so weak an imagination as that your registers and your bonds, your affidavits and your sufferances, your cockets and your clearances, are what form the great securities of your commerce. Do not dream that your letters of office, and your instructions, and your suspending clauses are the things that hold together the great contexture of this mysterious whole. These things do not make your government. Dead instruments, passive tools as they are, it is the spirit of the English communion that gives all their life and efficacy to them. It is the spirit of the English constitution which, infused through the mighty mass, pervades, feeds, unites, invigorates, vivifies every part of the empire, even down to the minutest member.

Is it not the same virtue which does every thing for us here in England? Do you imagine, then, that it is the Land-Tax Act which raises your revenue? that it is the annual vote in the Committee of Supply, which gives you your army? or that it is the Mutiny Bill which inspires it with bravery and discipline? No! surely, no! It is the love of the people; it is their attachment to their government, from the sense of the deep stake they have in such a glorious institution, which gives you your army and your navy, and infuses into both that liberal obedience without which your army would be a base rabble and your navy nothing but rotten timber.

All this, I know well enough, will sound wild and chimerical to the profane herd of those vulgar and mechanical politicians who have no place among us: a sort of people who think that nothing exists but what is gross and material, and who, therefore, far from being qualified to be directors of the great movement of empire, are not fit to turn a wheel in the machine. But to men truly initiated and rightly taught, these ruling and master principles, which in the opinion of such men as I have mentioned have no substantial existence, are in truth everything, and all in all. Magnanimity in politics is not seldom the truest wisdom; and a great empire and little minds go ill together. If we are conscious of our situation, and glow with zeal to fill our places as becomes our station and ourselves, we ought to auspicate all our public proceedings on America with the old warning of the Church, *Sursum corda!* We ought to elevate our minds to the greatness of that trust to which the order of Providence has called us. By adverting to the dignity of this high calling, our ancestors have turned a savage wilderness into a glorious empire, and have made the most extensive and the only honorable conquests, not by destroying, but by promoting the wealth, the number, the happiness of the human race. Let us get an American revenue as we have got an American empire. English privileges have made it all that it is; English privileges alone will make it all it can be.

DOCUMENT 10

ADAM SMITH, THE COST OF EMPIRE, 1776

Adam Smith had retired from a professorship at Glasgow University and was living in France in 1764–5 when he began his great work, The Wealth of Nations. *The book was being written all during the years of strife between Britain and her colonies, but it was not published until 1776. In the passages which follow, Smith points to the impossibility of monopolizing the benefits of colonies, and pessimistically calculates the cost of empire, but the book appeared too late to have any effect upon British policy. Because the Declaration of Independence and* The Wealth of Nations, *the political and economic repudiations of empire and mercantilism, appeared in the same year, historians have often designated 1776 as one of the turning points in modern history. The end of this selection, the eloquent exhortation to the rulers of Britain to awaken from their grandiose dreams of empire, is the closing passage of Smith's book.*

The countries which possess the colonies of America, and which trade directly to the East Indies, enjoy, indeed, the whole show and splendour of this great commerce. Other countries, however, notwithstanding all the invidious restraints by which it is meant to exclude them, frequently enjoy a greater share of the real benefit of it. The colonies of Spain and Portugal, for example, give more real encouragement to the industry of other countries than to that of Spain and Portugal. . . .

After all the unjust attempts, therefore, of every country in Europe to engross to itself the whole advantage of the trade of its own colonies, no country has yet been able to engross to itself anything but the expense of supporting in time of peace, and of defending in time of war, the oppressive authority which it assumes over them. The inconveniencies resulting from the possession of its colonies, every country has engrossed to itself completely. The advantages resulting from their trade it has been obliged to share with many other countries.

At first sight, no doubt, the monopoly of the great commerce of America naturally seems to be an acquisition of the highest value. To the undiscerning eye of giddy ambition, it naturally presents itself amidst the confused scramble of politics and war, as a very dazzling object to fight for. The dazzling splendour of the object, however, the immense greatness of the commerce, is the very quality which renders the monopoly of it hurtful, or which makes one employment, in its own nature necessarily less advantageous to the country than the greater part of other employments, absorb a much greater proportion of the capital of the country than what would otherwise have gone to it. . . .

It is not contrary to justice that . . . America should contribute towards the discharge of the public debt of Great Britain. . . . a government to which several of the colonies of America owe their present charters, and consequently their present constitution; and to which all the colonies of America owe the liberty, security, and property which they have ever since enjoyed. That public debt has been contracted in the defence, not of Great Britain alone, but of all the different provinces of the empire; the immense debt contracted in the late war in particular, and a great part of that contracted in the war before, were both properly contracted in defence of America. . . .

If it should be found impracticable for Great Britain to draw any considerable augmentation of revenue from any of the resources above mentioned; the only resource which can remain to her is a diminution of her expense. In the mode of collecting, and in that of expending the public revenue; though in both there may be still room for improvement; Great Britain seems to be at least as economical as any of her neighbours. The military establishment which she maintains for her own defence in time of peace, is more moderate than that of any European state which can pretend to rival her either in wealth or in power. None of those articles, therefore, seem to admit of any considerable reduction of expense. The expense of the peace establishment of the colonies was, before the commencement of the present disturbances, very considerable, and is an expense which may, and if no revenue can be drawn from them ought certainly to be saved altogether. This constant expense in time of peace, though very great, is insignificant in comparison with what the defence of the colonies has cost us in time of war. The last war, which was undertaken altogether on account of the colonies, cost Great Britain . . . upwards of ninety millions. The Spanish war of 1739 was principally undertaken on their account; in which, and in the French war that was the consequence of it, Great Britain spent upwards of forty millions, a great part of which ought justly to be charged to the colonies. In those two wars the colonies cost Great Britain much more than double the sum which the national debt amounted to before the commencement of the first of them. Had it not been for those wars that debt might, and probably would by this time, have been completely paid; and had it not been for the colonies, the former of those wars might not, and the latter certainly would not have been undertaken. It was because the colonies were supposed to be provinces of the British empire, that this expense was laid out upon them. But countries which contribute neither revenue nor military force towards the support of the empire, cannot be considered as provinces.

They may perhaps be considered as appendages, as a sort of splendid and showy equipage of the empire. But if the empire can no longer support the expense of keeping up this equipage, it ought certainly to lay it down; and if it cannot raise its revenue in proportion to its expense, it ought at least, to accommodate its expense to its revenue. If the colonies, notwithstanding their refusal to submit to British taxes, are still to be considered as provinces of the British empire, their defence in some future war may cost Great Britain as great an expense as it ever has done in any former war. The rulers of Great Britain have, for more than a century past, amused the people with the imagination that they possessed a great empire on the west side of the Atlantic. This empire, however, has hitherto existed in imagination only. It has hitherto been, not an empire, but the project of an empire; not a gold mine, but the project of a gold mine; a project which has cost, which continues to cost, and which, if pursued in the same way as it has been hitherto, is likely to cost, immense expense, without being likely to bring any profit; for the effects of the monopoly of the colony trade, it has been shown, are, to the great body of the people, mere loss instead of profit. It is surely now time that our rulers should either realise this golden dream, in which they have been indulging themselves, perhaps, as well as the people; or, that they should awake from it themselves, and endeavour to awaken the people. If the project cannot be completed, it ought to be given up. If any of the provinces of the British empire cannot be made to contribute towards the support of the whole empire, it is surely time that Great Britain should free herself from the expense of defending those provinces in time of war, and of supporting any part of their civil or military establishments in time of peace, and endeavour to accommodate her future views and designs to the real mediocrity of her circumstances.

DOCUMENT 11

SECOND CONTINENTAL CONGRESS, DECLARATION OF THE CAUSES AND NECESSITY OF TAKING UP ARMS, JULY 6, 1775

When the second Continental Congress convened in May 1775, the battles of Lexington and Concord had already been fought, and an informally organized American army was besieging General Gage's troops in Boston. It now became imperative either to plan and justify further operations or to give in. The Americans chose continued resistance. This statement of their case as it stood after the beginning of hostilities was assigned to a seven-man committee, but was chiefly the work of Thomas Jefferson and John Dickinson.

If it was possible for men, who exercise their reason to believe, that the Divine Author of our existence intended a part of the human race to hold an absolute property in, and an unbounded power over others, marked out by his infinite goodness and wisdom, as the objects of a legal domination never rightfully resistible, however severe and oppressive, the Inhabitants of these Colonies might at least require from the parliament of Great Britain some evidence, that this dreadful authority over them, has been granted to that body. But a reverence for our great Creator, principles of humanity, and the dictates of common sense, must convince all those who reflect upon the subject, that government was instituted to promote the welfare of mankind, and ought to be administered for the attainment of that end. The legislature of Great Britain, however, stimulated by an inordinate passion for a power, not only unjustifiable, but which they know to be peculiarly reprobated by the very constitution of that kingdom, and deperate of success in any mode of contest, where regard should be had to truth, law, or right, have at length, deserting those, attempted to effect their cruel and impolitic purpose of enslaving these Colonies by violence, and have thereby rendered it necessary for us to close with their last appeal from Reason to Arms.——Yet, however blinded that assembly may be, by their intemperate rage for un-limited domination, so to slight justice and the opinion of mankind, we esteem ourselves bound, by obligations of respect to the rest of the world, to make known the justice of our cause.

Our forefathers, inhabitants of the island of Great Britain, left their native land, to seek on these shores a residence for civil and religious freedom. At the expense of their blood, at the hazard of their fortunes, without the least charge to the country from which they removed, by unceasing labour, and an unconquerable spirit, they ef-fected settlements in the distant and inhospitable wilds of America, then filled with numerous and warlike nations of barbarians. Societies or governments, vested with per-fect legislatures, were formed under charters from the crown, and an harmonious intercourse was established be-tween the colonies and the kingdom from which they de-rived their origin. The mutual benefits of this union became in a short time so extraordinary, as to excite aston-ishment. It is universally confessed, that the amazing in-crease of the wealth, strength, and navigation of the realm, arose from this source; and the minister, who so wisely and successfully directed the measures of Great Britain in the late war, publicly declared, that these colonies en-abled her to triumph over her enemies.——Towards the con-clusion of that war, it pleased our sovereign to make a change in his counsels.——From that fatal moment, the affairs of the British empire began to fall into confusion, and gradually sliding from the summit of glorious pros-perity, to which they had been advanced by the virtues and abilities of one man, are at length distracted by the convulsions, that now shake it to its deepest foundations. The new ministry finding the brave foes of Britain, though frequently defeated, yet still contending, took up the un-fortunate idea of granting them a hasty peace, and of then subduing her faithful friends.

These devoted colonies were judged to be in such a

state, as to present victories without bloodshed, and all
the easy emoluments of statuteable plunder.—The uninterrupted tenor of their peaceable and respectful behaviour
from the beginning of colonization, their dutiful, zealous,
and useful services during the war, though so recently and
amply acknowledged in the most honourable manner by
his majesty, by the late king, and by Parliament, could not
save them from the meditated innovations.—Parliament
was influenced to adopt the pernicious project, and assuming a new power over them, have, in the course of eleven
years, given such decisive specimens of the spirit and consequences attending this power, as to leave no doubt concerning the effects of acquiescence under it. They have
undertaken to give and grant our money without our consent, though we have ever exercised an exclusive right to
dispose of our own property; statutes have been passed
for extending the jurisdiction of courts of Admiralty and
Vice-Admiralty beyond their ancient limits; for depriving
us of the accustomed and inestimable privilege of trial by
jury, in cases affecting both life and property; for suspending the legislature of one of the colonies; for interdicting
all commerce to the capital of another; and for altering
fundamentally the form of government established by
charter, and secured by acts of its own legislature solemnly
confirmed by the crown; for exempting the "murderers"
of colonists from legal trial, and in effect, from punishment; for erecting in a neighbouring province, acquired by
the joint arms of Great Britain and America, a despotism
dangerous to our very existence; and for quartering soldiers
upon the colonists in time of profound peace. It has also
been resolved in parliament, that colonists charged with
committing certain offences, shall be transported to England to be tried.

But why should we enumerate our injuries in detail?
By one statute it is declared, that parliament can "of right
make laws to bind us IN ALL CASES WHATSOEVER." What is
to defend us against so enormous, so unlimited a power?
Not a single man of those who assume it, is chosen by us;
or is subject to our controul or influence; but, on the contrary, they are all of them exempt from the operation of
such laws, and an American revenue, if not diverted from

the ostensible purposes for which it is raised, would actually lighten their own burdens in proportion as they increase ours. We saw the misery to which such despotism would reduce us. We for ten years incessantly and ineffectually besieged the Throne as supplicants; we reasoned, we remonstrated with parliament, in the most mild and decent language. But Administration, sensible that we should regard these oppressive measures as freemen ought to do, sent over fleets and armies to enforce them. The indignation of the Americans was roused, it is true; but it was the indignation of a virtuous, loyal, and affectionate people. A Congress of Delegates from the United Colonies was assembled at Philadelphia, on the fifth day of last September. We resolved again to offer an humble and dutiful petition to the King, and also addressed our fellow-subjects of Great Britain. We have pursued every temperate, every respectful measure: we have even proceeded to break off our commercial intercourse with our fellow-subjects, as the last peaceable admonition, that our attachment to no nation upon earth should supplant our attachment to liberty.—This, we flattered ourselves, was the ultimate step of the controversy: But subsequent events have shewn, how vain was this hope of finding moderation in our enemies. . . .

Fruitless were all the entreaties, arguments, and eloquence of an illustrious band of the most distinguished Peers, and Commoners, who nobly and strenuously asserted the justice of our cause, to stay, or even to mitigate the heedless fury with which these accumulated and unexampled outrages were hurried on. . . .

General Gage . . . on the 19th day of April, sent out from that place a large detachment of his army, who made an unprovoked assault on the inhabitants of the said province [Massachusetts], at the town of Lexington, as appears by the affidavits of a great number of persons, some of whom were officers and soldiers of that detachment, murdered eight of the inhabitants, and wounded many others. From thence the troops proceeded in warlike array to the town of Concord, where they set upon another party of the inhabitants of the same province, killing several and wounding more, until compelled to retreat by the country people suddenly assembled to repel this cruel aggression. Hostilities, thus commenced by the British troops, have been since prosecuted by them without regard to faith or reputation.—The inhabitants of Boston being confined within that town by the General their Governor, and having, in order to procure their dismission, entered into a treaty with him, it was stipulated that the said inhabitants having deposited their arms with their own magistrates, should have liberty to depart, taking with them their other effects. They accordingly delivered up their arms, but in open violation of honour, in defiance of the obligation of treaties, which even savage nations esteemed sacred, the Governor ordered the arms deposited as aforesaid, that they might be preserved for their owners, to be seized by a body of soldiers; detained the greatest part of the inhabitants in the town, and compelled the few who were permitted to retire, to leave their most valuable effects behind. . . .

The General, further emulating his ministerial masters, by a proclamation bearing date on the 12th day of June, after venting the grossest falsehoods and calumnies against the good people of these colonies, proceeds to "declare them all, either by name or description, to be rebels and traitors, to supersede the course of the common law, and instead thereof to publish and order the use and exercise of the law martial."—His troops have butchered our countrymen, have wantonly burnt Charlestown, besides a considerable number of houses in other places; our ships and vessels are seized; the necessary supplies of provisions are intercepted, and he is exerting his utmost power to spread destruction and devastation around him.

We have received certain intelligence, that General Carleton, the Governor of Canada, is instigating the people of that province and the Indians to fall upon us; and we have but too much reason to apprehend, that schemes have been formed to excite domestic enemies against us. In brief, a part of these colonies now feels and all of them are sure of feeling, as far as the vengeance of administration can inflict them, the complicated calamities of fire, sword, and famine.—We are reduced to the alternative of chusing an unconditional submission to the tyranny of irritated ministers, or resistance by force.— The latter is our choice.—We have counted the cost of this contest, and find nothing so dreadful as voluntary slavery.—Honor, justice, and humanity, forbid us tamely to surrender that freedom which we received from our gallant ancestors, and which our innocent posterity have a right to receive from us. We cannot endure the infamy and guilt of resigning succeeding generations to that wretchedness which inevitably awaits them, if we basely entail hereditary bondage upon them.

Our cause is just. Our union is perfect. Our internal resources are great, and, if necessary, foreign assistance is undoubtedly attainable.—We gratefully acknowledge, as signal instances of the Divine favour towards us, that his Providence would not permit us to be called into this severe controversy, until we were grown up to our present strength, had been previously exercised in warlike operation, and possessed of the means of defending ourselves.— With hearts fortified with these animating reflections, we most solemnly, before God and the world, declare, that, exerting the utmost energy of those powers, which our beneficent Creator hath graciously bestowed upon us, the arms we have been compelled by our enemies to assume, we will, in defiance of every hazard, with unabating firmness and perseverance, employ for the preservation of our liberties; being with our [one] mind resolved to die freemen rather than to live Slaves.

Lest this declaration should disquiet the minds of our friends and fellow-subjects in any part of the empire, we assure them that we mean not to dissolve that Union which has so long and so happily subsisted between us, and, which we sincerely wish to see restored.—Necessity has not yet driven us into that desperate measure, or induced us to excite any other nation to war against them.—We have not raised armies with ambitious designs of separating from Great Britain, and establishing independent states. We fight not for glory or for conquest. We exhibit to mankind the remarkable spectacle of a people attacked by unprovoked enemies, without any imputation or even suspicion of offence. They boast of their privileges and civilization, and yet proffer no milder conditions than servitude or death.

In our own native land, in defence of the freedom that is our birth-right, and which we ever enjoyed till the late violation of it—for the protection of our property, acquired solely by the honest industry of our fore-fathers and ourselves, against violence actually offered, we have taken up arms. We shall lay them down when hostilities shall cease on the part of the aggressors, and all danger of their being renewed shall be removed, and not before.

With an humble confidence in the mercies of the supreme and impartial Judge and Ruler of the universe, we most devoutly implore his divine goodness to protect us happily through this great conflict, to dispose our adversaries to reconciliation on reasonable terms, and thereby to relieve the empire from the calamities of civil war.

By order of Congress
JOHN HANCOCK
President.

DOCUMENT 12

THOMAS PAINE, *COMMON SENSE*, 1776

Many men were talking about independence and a few wrote about it before Thomas Paine's Common Sense *appeared early in 1776. But no appeal for independence had an influence remotely comparable to that of this document, which quickly sold about 150,000 copies. Paine, by his own account, was half finished with the work in October 1775, when Benjamin Franklin offered Paine some of his own materials on the struggle then raging. ". . . as I supposed the doctor's design in getting out a history was to open the new year with a new system, I expected to surprise him with a production on that subject much earlier than he thought of; and without informing him of what I was doing, got it ready for the press as fast as I conveniently could, and sent him the first pamphlet that was printed off." Two republican scientists and fellow members of the American Philosophical Society, Benjamin Rush and David Rittenhouse, seem to have been among the very few contemporaries who knew of the work during its composition. Paine had read each part to Rush as he composed it. Rush claimed that he suggested the title and arranged publication. In the* Crisis, *a pamphlet published the following year, Paine summed up his own argument as follows: "The principal arguments in support of independence may be comprehended under the four following heads: 1st, The natural right of the continent to independence; 2d, Her interest in being independent; 3d, The necessity;—and 4th, The moral advantages arising therefrom." The sections excerpted here deal not with Paine's general political theory but with his application of it to the events of the hour.*

Volumes have been written on the subject of the struggle between England and America. Men of all ranks have embarked in the controversy, from different motives, and with various designs: but all have been ineffectual, and the period of debate is closed. Arms as a last resource decide the contest; the appeal was the choice of the king, and the continent has accepted the challenge. . . .

As much has been said of the advantages of reconciliation, which, like an agreeable dream, has passed away and left us as we were, it is but right that we should examine the contrary side of the argument, and inquire into some of them any material injuries which these colonies sustain, and always will sustain, by being connected with and dependent on Great Britain. To examine that connection and dependence on the principles of nature and common sense; to see what we have to trust to, if separated, and what we are to expect, if dependent.

I have heard it asserted by some, that as America hath flourished under her former connection with Great Britain, the same connection is necessary towards her future happiness, and will always have the same effect. Nothing can be more fallacious than this kind of argument. We may as well assert that because a child has thriven upon milk, that it is never to have meat, or that the first twenty years of our lives is to become a precedent for the next twenty. But even this is admitting more than is true; for I answer roundly, that America would have flourished as much, and probably much more, had no European power taken any notice of her. The commerce by which she hath enriched herself are the necessaries of life, and will always have a market while eating is the custom of Europe.

But she has protected us, say some. That she hath engrossed us is true, and defended the continent at our expense as well as her own is admitted; and she would have defended Turkey from the same motive, viz., for the sake of trade and dominion.

Alas! we have been long led away by ancient prejudices, and made large sacrifices to superstition. We have boasted the protection of Great Britain without considering that her motive was *interest,* not *attachment;* and that she did not protect us from *our enemies* on *our account,* but from her enemies on her own account, from those who had no quarrel with us on any *other account,* but who will always be our enemies on the *same account.* Let Britain waive her pretensions to the continent, or the continent throw off the dependence, and we should be at peace with France and Spain were they at war with Britain. The miseries of Hanover's last war ought to warn us against connections.

It hath lately been asserted in parliament, that the colonies have no relation to each other but through the parent country, *i.e.,* that Pennsylvania and the Jerseys, and so on for the rest, are sister colonies by way of England; this is certainly a very roundabout way of proving relationship, but it is the nearest and only true way of proving enmity (or enemyship, if I may so call it). France and Spain never were, nor perhaps ever will be our enemies as *Americans,* but as our being the *subjects of Great Britain.*

But Britain is the parent country, say some. Then the more shame upon her conduct. Even brutes do not devour their young, nor savages make war upon their families; wherefore, the assertion, if true, turns to her reproach; but it happens not to be true, or only partly so, and the phrase *parent* or *mother country* hath been jesuitically adopted by the king and his parasites, with a low papistical design of gaining an unfair bias on the credulous weakness of our minds. Europe, and not England, is the parent country of America. This new world hath been the asylum for the persecuted lovers of civil and religious liberty from *every part* of Europe. Hither have they fled, not from the tender embraces of a mother, but from the cruelty of the monster; and it is so far true of England, that the same tyranny which drove the first emigrants from home, pursues their descendants still.

In this extensive quarter of the globe, we forget the narrow limits of three hundred and sixty miles (the extent of England) and carry our friendship on a larger scale; we claim brotherhood with every European Christian, and triumph in the generosity of the sentiment. . . .

I challenge the warmest advocate for reconciliation to show a single advantage that this continent can reap, by being connected with Great Britain. I repeat the challenge, not a single advantage is derived. Our corn will fetch its price in any market in Europe, and our imported goods must be paid for, buy them where we will.

But the injuries and disadvantages we sustain by that connection are without number; and our duty to mankind at large, as well as to ourselves, instructs us to renounce the alliance: because any submission to, or dependence on, Great Britain, tends directly to involve this continent in European wars and quarrels, and sets us at variance with nations who would otherwise seek our friendship, and against whom we have neither anger nor complaint. As Europe is our market for trade, we ought to form no partial connection with any part of it. 'Tis the true interest of America to steer clear of European contentions, which she never can do while by her dependence on Britain she is made the makeweight in the scale of British politics.

Europe is too thickly planted with kingdoms to be long at peace, and whenever a war breaks out between

England and any foreign power, the trade of America goes to ruin, *because of her connection with Britain*. The next war may not turn out like the last, and should it not, the advocates for reconciliation now will be wishing for separation then, because neutrality in that case would be a safer convoy than a man of war. Everything that is right or natural pleads for separation. The blood of the slain, the weeping voice of nature cries, 'TIS TIME TO PART. Even the distance at which the Almighty hath placed England and America is a strong and natural proof that the authority of the one over the other, was never the design of heaven. The time likewise at which the continent was discovered, adds weight to the argument, and the manner in which it was peopled, increases the force of it. The Reformation was preceded by the discovery of America, as if the Almighty graciously meant to open a sanctuary to the persecuted in future years, when home should afford neither friendship nor safety.

The authority of Great Britain over this continent is a form of government which sooner or later must have an end. And a serious mind can draw no true pleasure by looking forward, under the painful and positive conviction that what he calls "the present constitution" is merely temporary. . . .

Though I would carefully avoid giving unnecessary offense, yet I am inclined to believe, that all those who espouse the doctrine of reconciliation may be included within the following descriptions: Interested men, who are not to be trusted, weak men who *cannot* see, prejudiced men, who *will not* see, and a certain set of moderate men who think better of the European world than it deserves; and this last class, by an ill-judged deliberation, will be the cause of more calamities to this continent than all of the other three.

It is the good fortune of many to live distant from the scene of present sorrow; the evil is not sufficiently brought to *their* doors to make *them* feel the precariousness with which all American property is possessed. But let our imaginations transport us for a few moments to Boston; that seat of wretchedness will teach us wisdom, and instruct us forever to renounce a power in whom we can have no trust. The inhabitants of that unfortunate city, who but a few months ago were in ease and affluence, have now no other alternative than to stay and starve, or turn out to beg. Endangered by the fire of their friends if they continue within the city, and plundered by the soldiery if they leave it, in their present situation they are prisoners without the hope of redemption, and in a general attack for their relief they would be exposed to the fury of both armies. . . .

But if you say, you can still pass the violations over, then I ask, Hath your house been burnt? Hath your property been destroyed before your face? Are your wife and children destitute of a bed to lie on, or bread to live on? Have you lost a parent or a child by their hands, and yourself the ruined and wretched survivor? If you have not, then you are not a judge of those who have. But if you have, and can still shake hands with the murderers, then you are unworthy the name of husband, father, friend, or lover; and whatever may be your rank or title in life, you have the heart of a coward, and the spirit of a sycophant.

This is not inflaming or exaggerating matters, but trying them by those feelings and affections which nature justifies, and without which we should be incapable of discharging the social duties of life, or enjoying the felicities of it. I mean not to exhibit horror for the purpose of provoking revenge, but to awaken us from fatal and unmanly slumbers, that we may pursue determinately some fixed object. 'Tis not in the power of England or of Europe to conquer America, if she does not conquer herself by *delay* and *timidity*. The present winter is worth an age if rightly employed, but if lost or neglected the whole continent will partake of the misfortune; and there is no punishment which that man doth not deserve, be he who, or what, or where he will, that may be the means of sacrificing a season so precious and useful. . . .

Every quiet method for peace hath been ineffectual. Our prayers have been rejected with disdain; and have tended to convince us that nothing flatters vanity or confirms obstinacy in kings more than repeated petitioning—and nothing hath contributed more than that very measure to make the kings of Europe absolute. Witness Denmark and Sweden. Wherefore, since nothing but blows will do, for God's sake let us come to a final separation, and not leave the next generation to be cutting throats under the violated unmeaning names of parent and child.

To say they will never attempt it again is idle and visionary; we thought so at the repeal of the stamp act, yet a year or two undeceived us; as well may we suppose that nations which have been once defeated will never renew the quarrel.

As to government matters, it is not in the power of Britain to do this continent justice: the business of it will soon be too weighty and intricate to be managed with any tolerable degree of convenience, by a power so distant from us, and so very ignorant of us; for if they cannot conquer us, they cannot govern us. To be always running three or four thousand miles with a tale or a petition, waiting four or five months for an answer, which, when obtained, requires five or six more to explain it in, will in a few years be looked upon as folly and childishness. There was a time when it was proper, and there is a proper time for it to cease.

Small islands not capable of protecting themselves are the proper objects for kingdoms to take under their care; but there is something very absurd in supposing a continent to be perpetually governed by an island. In no instance hath nature made the satellite larger than its primary planet; and as England and America, with respect to each other, reverse the common order of nature, it is evident that they belong to different systems. England to Europe: America to itself. . . .

But admitting that matters were now made up, what would be the event? I answer, the ruin of the continent. And that for several reasons.

First. The powers of governing still remaining in the hands of the king, he will have a negative over the whole legislation of the continent. And as he hath shown himself such an inveterate enemy to liberty, and discovered such a thirst for arbitrary power, is he, or is he not, a proper person to say to these colonies, *You shall make no laws but what I please!* And is there any inhabitant in America so ignorant as not to know, that according to what is called the *present constitution,* this continent can make no laws but what the King gives leave to; and is there any man so unwise as not to see, that (considering what has happened) he will suffer no law to be made here but such as suits *his* purpose? We may be as effectually enslaved by the want of laws in America, as by submitting to laws made for us in England. After matters are made up (as it is called), can there be any doubt but the whole power of the Crown will be exerted to keep this continent as low and humble as possible? Instead of going forward we shall go backward, or be perpetually quarreling, or ridiculously petitioning. We are already greater than the King wishes us to be, and will he not hereafter endeavor to make us less? To bring the matter to one point, Is the power who is jealous of our prosperity, a proper power to govern us? Whoever says *No* to this question is an *independent,* for independency means no more than this, whether we shall make our own laws, or whether the king, the greatest enemy which this continent hath, or can have, shall tell us, *There shall be no laws but such as I like.*

But the King, you'll say, has a negative in England; the people there can make no laws without his consent. In point of right and good order, it is something very ridiculous that a youth of twenty-one (which hath often happened) shall say to several millions of people, older and wiser than himself, "I forbid this or that act of yours to be law." But in this place I decline this sort of reply, though I will never cease to expose the absurdity of it, and only answer that England being the king's residence and America not so, makes quite another case. The king's negative here is ten times more dangerous and fatal than it can be in England; for *there* he will scarcely refuse his consent to a bill for putting England into as strong a state of defense as possible, and in America he would never suffer such a bill to be passed. . . .

Secondly. That as even the best terms which we can expect to obtain can amount to no more than a temporary expedient, or a kind of government by guardianship, which can last no longer than till the colonies come of age, so the general face and state of things in the interim will be unsettled and unpromising. Emigrants of property will not choose to come to a country whose form of government hangs but by a thread, and who is every day tottering on the brink of commotion and disturbance; and numbers of the present inhabitants would lay hold of the interval to dispose of their effects, and quit the continent.

But the most powerful of all arguments is, that nothing but independence, *i.e.* a continental form of government, can keep the peace of the continent and preserve it inviolate from civil wars. I dread the event of a reconciliation with Britain *now,* as it is more than probable that it will be followed by a revolt somewhere or other, the consequences of which may be far more fatal than all the malice of Britain.

Thousands are already ruined by British barbarity; (thousands more will probably suffer the same fate). Those men have other feelings than us who have nothing suffered. All they *now* possess is liberty; what they before enjoyed is sacrificed to its service, and having nothing more to lose, they disdain submission. . . .

But where, say some, is the king of America? I'll tell you, friend, he reigns above, and doth not make havoc of mankind like the Royal Brute of Great Britain. Yet that we may not appear to be defective even in earthly honors, let a day be solemnly set apart for proclaiming the charter; let it be brought forth placed on the divine law, the Word of God; let a crown be placed thereon, by which the world may know, that so far as we approve of monarchy, that in America THE LAW IS KING. For as in absolute governments the king is law, so in free countries the law *ought* to BE king, and there ought to be no other. But lest any ill use should afterwards arise, let the crown at the conclusion of the ceremony be demolished, and scattered among the people whose right it is.

A government of our own is our natural right; and when a man seriously reflects on the precariousness of human affairs, he will become convinced, that it is infinitely wiser and safer to form a constitution of our own in a cool deliberate manner, while we have it in our power, than to trust such an interesting event to time and chance. . . .

Ye that tell us of harmony and reconciliation, can ye restore to us the time that is passed? Can ye give to prostitution its former innocence? Neither can ye reconcile Britain and America. The last cord now is broken; the people of England are presenting addresses against us. There are injuries which nature cannot forgive; she would cease to be nature if she did. As well can the lover forgive the ravisher of his mistress, as the continent forgive the murders of Britain. The Almighty hath implanted in us these unextinguishable feelings for good and wise purposes. They are the guardians of his image in our hearts. They distinguish us from the herd of common animals. The social compact would dissolve, and justice be extirpated from the earth, or have only a casual existence, were we callous to the touches of affection. The robber and the murderer would often escape unpunished, did not the injuries which our tempers sustain, provoke us into justice.

O ye that love mankind! Ye that dare oppose not only the tyranny but the tyrant, stand forth! Every spot of the old world is overrun with oppression. Freedom hath been hunted round the globe. Asia and Africa have long expelled her. Europe regards her like a stranger, and England hath given her warning to depart. O receive the fugitive, and prepare in time an asylum for mankind.

DOCUMENT 13

CHARLES INGLIS, *THE TRUE INTEREST OF AMERICA IMPARTIALLY STATED*, 1776

One of the best evidences of the power of Paine's Common Sense *is the number of Loyalists who leaped to the counterattack. Some of these are better known to history than the Anglican clergyman Charles Inglis, but none made a more succinct statement of the fore-bodings of Loyalists. His anonymous counterblast against Paine was entitled,* The True Interest of America Impartially Stated in Certain Strictures on a Pamphlet Intitled Common Sense. *Inglis had come to live in America in 1755 and, at the outbreak of hostilities, was attached to Trinity Church in New York City. Throughout the war he kept writing essays intended to convince the patriots that they were on the wrong track. But in 1783, when he was about to sail for exile in England, he declared: "I do not leave behind me an individual, against whom I have the smallest degree of resentment or ill-will."*

I think it no difficult matter to point out many advantages which will certainly attend our reconciliation and connection with Great-Britain, on a firm, constitutional plan. I shall select a few of these; and that their importance may be more clearly discerned, I shall afterwards point out some of the evils which inevitably must attend our separating from Britain, and declaring for independency. On each article I shall study brevity.

1. By a reconciliation with Britain, a period would be put to the present calamitous war, by which so many lives have been lost, and so many more must be lost, if it continues. This alone is an advantage devoutly to be wished for. This author [Paine] says—"The blood of the slain, the weeping voice of nature cries, 'Tis time to part." I think they cry just the reverse. The blood of the slain, the weeping voice of nature cries—It is time to be reconciled; it is time to lay aside those animosities which have pushed on Britons to shed the blood of Britons; it is high time that those who are connected by the endearing ties of religion, kindred and country, should resume their former friendship, and be united in the bond of mutual affection, as their interests are inseparably united.

2. By a Reconciliation with Great-Britain, Peace—that fairest offspring and gift of Heaven—will be restored. In one respect Peace is like health; we do not sufficiently know its value but by its absence. What uneasiness and anxiety, what evils, has this short interruption of peace

with the parent-state, brought on the whole British empire! Let every man only consult his feelings—I except my antagonist—and it will require no great force of rhetoric to convince him, that a removal of those evils, and a restoration of peace, would be a singular advantage and blessing.

3. Agriculture, commerce, and industry would resume their wonted vigor. At present, they languish and droop, both here and in Britain; and must continue to do so, while this unhappy contest remains unsettled.

4. By a connection with Great-Britain, our trade would still have the protection of the greatest naval power in the world. England has the advantage, in this respect, of every other state, whether of ancient or modern times. Her insular situation, her nurseries for seamen, the superiority of those seamen above others—these circumstances to mention no other, combine to make her the first maritime power in the universe—such exactly is the power whose protection we want for our commerce. To suppose, with our author, that we should have no war, were we to revolt from England, is too absurd to deserve a confutation. I could just as soon set about refuting the reveries of some brain-sick enthusiast. Past experience shews that Britain is able to defend our commerce, and our coasts; and we have no reason to doubt of her being able to do so for the future.

5. The protection of our trade, while connected with Britain, will not cost us a *fiftieth* part of what it must cost, were we ourselves to raise a naval force sufficient for this purpose.

6. Whilst connected with Great-Britain, we have a bounty on almost every article of exportation; and we may be better supplied with goods by her, than we could elsewhere. What our author says is true—"that our imported goods must be paid for, buy them where we will"; but we may buy them dearer, and of worse quality, in one place than another. The manufactures of Great-Britain confessedly surpass any in the world—particularly those in every kind of metal, which we want most; and no country can afford linens and woollens, of equal quality cheaper.

7. When a Reconciliation is effected, and things re-

turn into the old channel, a few years of peace will restore everything to its pristine state. Emigrants will flow in as usual from the different parts of Europe. Population will advance with the same rapid progress as formerly, and our lands will rise in value.

These advantages are not imaginary but real. They are such as we have already experienced; and such as we may derive from a connection with Great Britain for ages to come. Each of these might easily be enlarged on, and others added to them; but I only mean to suggest a few hints to the reader.

Let us now, if you please, take a view of the other side of the question. Suppose we were to revolt from Great-Britain, declare ourselves Independent, and set up a Republic of our own—what would be the consequence? —I stand aghast at the prospect—my blood runs chill when I think of the calamities, the complicated evils that must ensue, and may be clearly foreseen—it is impossible for any man to foresee them all. . . .

1. All our property throughout the continent would be unhinged; the greatest confusion, and most violent convulsions would take place. It would not be here, as it was in England at the Revolution in 1688. That revolution was not brought about by an defeazance or disannulling the right of succession. James II, by abdicating the throne, left it vacant for the next in succession; accordingly his eldest daughter and her husband stept in. Every other matter went on in the usual, regular way; and the constitution, instead of being dissolved, was strengthened. But in case of our revolt, the old constitution would be totally subverted. The common bond that tied us together, and by which our property was secured, would be snapt asunder. It is not to be doubted but our Congress would endeavor to apply some remedy for those evils; but with all deference to that respectable body, I do not apprehend that any remedy in their power would be adequate, at least for some time. I do not chuse to be more explicit; but I am able to support my opinion.

2. What a horrid situation would thousands be reduced to who have taken the oath of allegiance to the King; yet contrary to their oath, as well as inclination,

must be compelled to renounce that allegiance, or abandon all their property in America! How many thousands more would be reduced to a similar situation; who, although they took not that oath, yet would think it inconsistent with their duty and a good conscience to renounce their Sovereign; I dare say these will appear trifling difficulties to our author; but whatever he may think, there are thousands and thousands who would sooner lose all they had in the world, nay life itself, than thus wound their conscience. A Declaration of Independency would infallibly disunite and divide the colonists.

3. By a Declaration for Independency, every avenue to an accommodation with Great-Britain would be closed; the sword only could then decide the quarrel; and the sword would not be sheathed till one had conquered the other.

The importance of these colonies to Britain need not be enlarged on, it is a thing so universally known. The greater their importance is to her, so much the more obstinate will her struggle be not to lose them. The independency of America would, in the end, deprive her of the West-Indies, shake her empire to the foundation, and reduce her to a state of the most mortifying insignificance. Great-Britain therefore must, for her own preservation, risk every thing, and exert her whole strength, to prevent such an event from taking place. This being the case—

4. Devastation and ruin must mark the progress of this war along the sea coast of America. Hitherto, Britain has not exerted her power. Her number of troops and ships of war here at present, is very little more than she judged expedient in time of peace—the former does not amount to 12,000 men—nor the latter to 40 ships, including frigates. Both she, and the colonies, hoped for and expected an accommodation; neither of them has lost sight of that desirable object. The seas have been open to our ships; and although some skirmishes have unfortunately happened, yet a ray of hope still cheered both sides that, peace was not distant. But as soon as we declare for independency, every prospect of this kind must vanish. Ruthless war, with all its aggravated horrors, will ravage our

once happy land—our seacoasts and ports will be ruined, and our ships taken. Torrents of blood will be spilt, and thousands reduced to beggary and wretchedness.

This melancholy contest would last till one side conquered. Supposing Britain to be victorious; however high my opinion is of British Generosity, I should be exceedingly sorry to receive terms from her in the haughty tone of a conqueror. Or supposing such a failure of her manufactures, commerce and strength, that victory should incline to the side of America; yet who can say in that case, what extremities her sense of resentment and self-preservation will drive Great-Britain to? For my part, I should not in the least be surprized, if on such a prospect as the Independency of America, she would parcel out this continent to the different European Powers. Canada might be restored to France, Florida to Spain, with additions to each—other states also might come in for a portion. Let no man think this chimerical or improbable. The independency of America would be so fatal to Britain, that she would leave nothing in her power undone to prevent it. I believe as firmly as I do my own existence, that if every other method failed, she would try some such expedient as this, to disconcert our scheme of independency; and let any man figure to himself the situation of these British colonies, if only Canada were restored to France!

5. But supposing once more that we were able to cut off every regiment that Britain can spare or hire, and to destroy every ship she can send—that we could beat off any other European power that would presume to intrude upon this continent: Yet, a republican form of government would neither suit the genius of the people, nor the extent of America.

In nothing is the wisdom of a legislator more conspicuous than in adapting his government to the genius, manners, disposition and other circumstances of the people with whom he is concerned. If this important point is overlooked, confusion will ensue; his system will sink into neglect and ruin. Whatever check or barriers may be interposed, nature will always surmount them, and finally prevail. It was chiefly by attention to this circumstance, that Lycurgus and Solon were so much celebrated; and that their respective republics rose afterwards to such eminence, and acquired such stability.

The Americans are properly Britons. They have the manners, habits, and ideas of Britons; and have been accustomed to a similar form of government. But Britons never could bear the extremes, either of monarchy or republicanism. Some of their Kings have aimed at despotism; but always failed. Repeated efforts have been made towards democracy, and they equally failed. Once indeed republicanism triumphed over the constitution; the despotism of one person ensued; both were finally expelled. The inhabitants of Great-Britain were quite anxious for the restoration of *royalty* in 1660, as they were for its expulsion in 1642, and for some succeeding years. If we may judge of future events by past transactions, in similar circumstances, this would most probably be the case of America, were a republican form of government adopted in our present ferment. After much blood was shed, those confusions would terminate in the despotism of some one successful adventurer; and should the Americans be so fortunate as to emancipate themselves from that thraldom, perhaps the whole would end in a limited monarchy, after shedding as much more blood. Limited monarchy is the form of government which is most favourable to liberty —which is best adapted to the genius and temper of Britons; although here and there among us a crack-brained zealot for democracy or absolute monarchy, may be sometimes found.

Besides the unsuitableness of the republican form to the genius of the people, America is too extensive for it. That form may do well enough for a single city, or small territory; but would be utterly improper for such a continent as this. America is too unwieldy for the feeble, dilatory administration of democracy. Rome had the most extensive dominions of any ancient republic. But it should be remembered, that very soon after the spirit of conquest carried the Romans beyond the limits that were proportioned to their constitution, they fell under a despotic yoke. A very few years had elapsed from the time of their conquering Greece and first entering Asia, till the battle of Pharsalia, where Julius Caesar put an end to the liberties of his country. . . .

But here it may be said—*That all the evils above specified, are more to'erable than slavery.* With this sentiment I sincerely agree—any hardships, however great, are preferable to slavery. But then I ask, is there no other alternative in the present case? Is there no choice left us but slavery, or those evils? I am confident there is; and that both may be equally avoided. Let us only shew a disposition to treat or negociate in earnest—let us fall upon some method to set a treaty or negociation with Great Britain on foot; and if once properly begun, there is moral certainty that this unhappy dispute will be settled to the mutual satisfaction and interest of both countries. For my part, I have not the least doubt about it. . . .

But a Declaration for Independency on the part of America, would preclude treaty intirely; and could answer no good purpose. We actually have already every advantage of Independency, without its inconveniences. By a Declaration of Independency, we should instantly lose all assistance from our friends in England. It would stop their mouths; for were they to say any thing in our favour, they would be deemed rebels, and treated accordingly.

Our author is much elated with the prospect of foreign succour, if we once declare ourselves Independent; and from thence promiseth us mighty matters. This, no doubt, is intended to spirit up the desponding—all who might shrink at the thought of America encountering, singly and unsupported, the whole strength of Great-Britain. I believe in my conscience, that he is as much mistaken in this, as in any thing else; and that this expectation is delusive, vain and fallacious. My reasons are these, and I submit them to the reader's judgment.

The only European power from which we can possibly receive assistance, is France. But France is now at peace with Great-Britain; and is it possible that France would interrupt that peace, and hazard a war with the power which lately reduced her so low, from a *disinterested* motive of aiding and protecting these Colonies? . . .

It is well known that some of the French and Spanish

Colonists, not long since, offered to put themselves under the protection of England, and declare themselves Independent of France and Spain; but England rejected both offers. The example would be rather dangerous to states that have colonies—to none could it be more so than to France and Spain, who have so many and such extensive colonies. "The practice of courts are as much against us" in this, as in the instance our author mentions. Can any one imagine, that because we declared ourselves Independent of England, France would *therefore* consider us as really Independent! And before England had acquiesced, or made any effort worth mentioning to reduce us? Or can any one be so weak as to think, that France would run the risque of a war with England, unless she (France) were sure of some extraordinary advantage by it, in having the colonies under her *immediate jurisdiction?* If England will not protect us for our trade, surely France will not. . . .

America is far from being yet in a desperate situation. I am confident she may obtain honourable and advantageous terms from Great-Britain. A few years of peace will soon retrieve all her losses. She will rapidly advance to a state of maturity, whereby she may not only repay the parent state amply for all past benefits; but also lay under the greatest obligations. . . .

However distant humanity may wish the period; yet, in the rotation of human affairs, a period may arrive, when (both countries being prepared for it) some terrible disaster, some dreadful convulsion in Great-Britain, may transfer the seat of empire to this western hemisphere—where the British constitution, like the Phoenix from its parent's ashes, shall rise with youthful vigour and shine with redoubled splendor.

DOCUMENT 14

THE DECLARATION OF INDEPENDENCE,
JULY 4, 1776

On June 7, Richard Henry Lee introduced into Congress a resolution (adopted on July 2), which asserted that "these United Colonies are, and of right ought to be, free and independent States." While this resolution was being discussed, a committee, consisting of John Adams, Benjamin Franklin, Thomas Jefferson, Robert R. Livingston, and Roger Sherman was appointed to draft a Declaration of Independence. The members of the committee asked Jefferson to prepare a first draft, and this was accepted by the committee, with some alterations suggested by Adams and Franklin. The committee's draft was adopted by Congress on July 4, after a number of changes had been made. The most important of these was the excision of a passage indicting the slave trade. This, Jefferson wrote at the time, "was struck out in complaisance to South Carolina and Georgia, who had never attempted to restrain the importation of slaves, and who on the contrary still wished to continue it. Our Northern brethren also I believe felt a little tender under those censures, for tho' their people have very few slaves themselves yet they had been pretty considerable carriers of them to others." A formal parchment copy of the Declaration was available for signing on August 2, and most of the 55 signatures were inscribed upon it on that date. As late as November, Matthew Thornton of New Hampshire, recently elected to Congress, became the last to sign. The intention of the Declaration, Jefferson later wrote, was not to say something new, but "to place before mankind the common sense of the subject, in terms so plain and firm as to command their assent. . . . Neither aiming at originality of principles or sentiments, nor yet copied from any particular and previous writing, it was intended to be an expression of the American mind." The Declaration of Independence is here taken, as an example of formal eighteenth-century styling, from the parchment copy version.

THE DECLARATION OF INDEPENDENCE

The Unanimous Declaration of the Thirteen United States of America

When in the Course of human events, it becomes necessary for one people to dissolve the political bands, which have connected them with another, and to assume among the powers of the earth, the separate and equal station to which the Laws of Nature and of Nature's God entitle them, a decent respect to the opinions of mankind requires that they should declare the causes which impel them to the separation.—We hold these truths to be self-evident, that all men are created equal, that they are endowed by their Creator with certain unalienable Rights, that among these are Life, Liberty and the pursuit of Happiness.—That to secure these rights, Governments are instituted among Men, deriving their just powers from the consent of the governed,—That whenever any Form of Government becomes destructive of these ends, it is the Right of the People to alter or to abolish it, and to institute new Government, laying its foundation on such principles and organizing its powers in such form, as to them shall seem most likely to effect their Safety and Happiness. Prudence, indeed, will dictate that Governments long established should not be changed for light and transient causes; and accordingly all experience hath shewn, that mankind are more disposed to suffer, while evils are sufferable, than to right themselves by abolishing the forms to which they are accustomed. But when a long train of abuses and usurpations, pursuing invariably the same Object evinces a design to reduce them under absolute Despotism, it is their right, it is their duty, to throw off such Government, and to provide new Guards for their future security.—Such has been the patient sufferance of these Colonies; and such is now the necessity which constrains them to alter their former Systems of Government. The history of the present King of Great Britain is a history of repeated injuries and usurpations, all having in direct object the establishment of an absolute Tyranny over these States. To prove this, let Facts be submitted to a candid world.—He has refused his Assent to Laws, the most wholesome and necessary for the public good.—He has forbidden his Governors to pass Laws of immediate and pressing importance, unless suspended in their operation till his Assent should be obtained; and when so suspended, he has utterly neglected to attend to them.—He has refused to pass other Laws for the accommodation of large districts of people, unless those people would relinquish the right of Representation in the Legislature, a right inestimable to them and formidable to tyrants only.—He has called together legislative bodies at places unusual, uncomfortable, and distant from the depository of their public Records, for the sole purpose of fatiguing them into compliance with his measures.—He has dissolved Representative Houses repeatedly, for opposing with manly firmness his invasions on the rights of the people.—He has refused for a long time, after such dissolutions, to cause others to be elected; whereby the Legislative powers, incapable of Annihilation, have returned to the People at large for their exercise; the State remaining in the meantime exposed to all the dangers of invasion from without, and convulsions within. —He has endeavoured to prevent the population of these States; for that purpose obstructing the Laws for Naturalization of Foreigners; refusing to pass others to encourage their migrations hither, and raising the conditions of new Appropriations of Lands.—He has obstructed the Administration of Justice, by refusing his Assent to Laws for establishing Judiciary powers.—He has made Judges dependent on his Will alone, for the tenure of their offices, and the amount and payment of their salaries.—He has erected a multitude of New Offices, and sent hither swarms of Officers to harrass our people, and eat out their substance.—He has kept among us, in times of peace, Standing Armies without the Consent of our legislatures.—He has affected to render the Military independent of and superior to the Civil power.—He has combined with others to subject us to a jurisdiction foreign to our constitution, and unacknowledged by our laws; giving his Assent to their Acts of pretended Legislation.—For quartering large bodies of armed troops among us:—For protecting them, by a mock Trial, from punishment for any Murders which they should commit on the Inhabitants of these States:—For cutting off our Trade with all parts of the world:—For imposing Taxes on us without our Consent:—For depriving us in many cases, of the benefits of Trial by Jury:—For transporting us beyond Seas to be tried for pretended offenses:—For abolishing the free System of English Laws in a neighboring Province, establishing therein an Arbitrary government, and enlarging its Boundaries so as to render it at once an example and fit instrument for introducing the same absolute rule into these colonies:—For taking away our Charters, abolishing our most valuable Laws, and altering fundamentally the Forms of our Governments:—For suspending our own Legislatures, and declaring themselves invested with power to legislate for us in all cases whatsoever.—He has abdicated Government here, by declaring us out of his Protection and Waging War against us.—He has plundered our seas, ravaged our Coasts, burnt our towns, and destroyed the lives of our people.—He is at this time transporting large Armies of foreign Mercenaries to compleat the works of death, desolation and tyranny, already begun with circumstances of Cruelty and perfidy scarcely paralleled in the most barbarous ages, and totally unworthy the Head of a civilized nation.—He has constrained our fellow Citizens taken Captive on the high Seas to bear Arms against their Country, to become the executioners of their friends and Brethren, or to fall themselves by their Hands.—He has excited domestic insurrections amongst us, and has endeavoured to bring on the inhabitants of our frontiers, the merciless Indian Savages, whose known rule of warfare, is an undistinguished destruction of all ages, sexes and conditions. In every stage of these Oppressions We have Petitioned for Redress in the most humble terms: Our repeated Petitions have been answered only by repeated injury. A Prince whose character is thus marked by every act which may define a Tyrant, is unfit to be the ruler of a free people. Nor have We been wanting in attentions to our Brittish brethren. We have warned them from time to time of attempts by their legislature to extend an unwarrantable jurisdiction over us. We have reminded them of the circumstances of our emigration and settlement here. We have appealed to their native justice and magnanimity, and we have conjured them by the ties of our common kindred to disavow these usurpations, which would inevitably interrupt our connections and correspondence. They too have been deaf to the voice of justice and of consanguinity. We must, therefore, acquiesce in the necessity, which denounces our Separation, and hold them, as we hold the rest of mankind, Enemies in War, in Peace Friends.—

We, therefore, the Representatives of the united States of America, in General Congress, Assembled, appealing to the Supreme Judge of the world for the rectitude of our intentions do, in the Name, and by Authority of the good People of these Colonies, solemnly publish and declare, That these United Colonies are, and of Right ought to be Free and Independent States; that they are Absolved from all Allegiance to the British Crown, and that all political connection between them and the State of Great Britain, is and ought to be totally dissolved; and that as Free and Independent States, they have full Power to levy War, conclude Peace, contract Alliances, establish Commerce, and to do all other Acts and Things which Independent States may of right do.—And for the support of this Declaration, with a firm reliance on the protection of divine Providence, we mutually pledge to each other our Lives, our Fortunes and our sacred Honor.

[Names omitted]

*

Note on Sources

THE following list locates the source of each item in the text. The references are given in the order in which they occur in the text and are numbered to correspond with document numbers.

PART I. THE COLONIZING IMPULSE. 1. Adam Smith, *An Inquiry into the Nature and Causes of the Wealth of Nations* (Edinburgh and London, 1828), Vol. III, pp. 1–5, 59–61. 2. *Proceedings of the Massachusetts Historical Society* (Boston, 1878), pp. 323–7. 3. Samuel de Champlain, *The Savages, or Voyage of Samuel De Champlain of Brauage, Made in New France in the Year 1603*, C. P. Otis, trans. (Boston, 1880), Vol. I, pp. 1–6. 4. Richard Hakluyt, *The Original Writings and Correspondence of the Two Richard Hakluyts,* Introduction and Notes, E. G. R. Taylor (London, printed for the Hakluyt Society, 1935), Vol. II, pp. 211–3. 5. *Ibid.,* pp. 492–6. 6. Alexander Brown, *The Genesis of the United States* (Cambridge, 1890), Vol. I, pp. 116–24. 7. William Bradford, *Of Plymouth Plantation, 1620–1647,* Samuel E. Morison, ed. (New York, 1952), pp. 23–7. 8. Susan M. Kingsbury, ed., *The Records of the Virginia Company of London* (Washington, 1906–35), Vol. II, pp. 380–6. 9. Peter Force, ed., *Tracts and Other Papers Relating Principally to the Origin, Settlement, and Progress of the Colonies in North America from the Discovery of the Country to the Year 1776* (Washington, 1836–46), Vol. II, Section III. 10. Rev. William Hubbard, *General History of New England from the Discovery to MDCLXXX* (Cambridge, 1815), pp. 151–3, 268–73. 11. William Hand Browne, ed., *Archives of Maryland, Proceedings of the Council of Maryland, 1636–1667* (Baltimore, 1885), pp. 16–23.

PART II. THE ESTABLISHMENT OF SELF-GOVERNMENT. 1. Francis Newton Thorpe, ed., *The Federal and State Constitutions, Colonial Charters, and Other Organic Laws* (Washington, 1909), Vol. VII, pp. 3802–10. 2. William Stith, *The History of the First Discovery and Settlement of Virginia* (New York, 1865), Appendix IV, pp. 32–4. 3. Thorpe, *op. cit.,* III, p. 1841. 4. *Ibid.,* III, pp. 1852–58. 5. *Ibid.,* I, pp. 519–22. 6. William W. Hening, ed., *The Statutes at Large; Being a Collection of All the Laws of Virginia* (New York, 1823), Vol. I, pp. 224, 272,

273; also: Nathaniel B. Shurtleff, ed., *Records of the Govenor and Company of the Massachusetts Bay in New England* (Boston, 1853), Vol. I, 1628–1641, p. 172; also: Henry Hartwell, James Blair, and Edward Chilton, *The Present State of Virginia, and the Colony,* edited with an Introduction by Hunter Dickinson Farish (Williamsburg, Va., 1940), pp. 44–9. 7. Robert Beverley, *The History and Present State of Virginia,* Charles Campbell, ed. (Richmond, Va., 1855), pp. 60–71. 8. *Collections of the Massachusetts Historical Society* (Boston, 1871), Vol. IX, Fourth Series, pp. 178–81. 9. *Ibid.,* pp. 184–7. 10. *The Virginia Magazine of History and Biography* (Richmond, 1907), Vol. XIV, No. 3, pp. 272–7. 11. Shurtleff, *op. cit.* (Boston, 1854), IV, Part II, 1661–1674, pp. 24–6. 12. J. W. Fortescue, ed., *Calendar of State Papers, Colonial Series, America and West Indies, 1681–1685* (London, 1898), pp. 445–6. 13. Peter Force, ed., *Tracts and Other Papers Relating Principally to the Origin, Settlement, and Progress of the Colonies in North America, from the Discovery of the Country to the Year 1776* (Washington, 1846), Vol. IV, Section X, pp. 6–12. 14. John Wise, *A Vindication of the Government of New England Churches* (Boston, 1860), pp. 28–45.

PART III. THE ECONOMIC REGULATION OF THE EMPIRE. 1. Sir Josiah Child, Baronet, *A New Discourse of Trade* (London), Fourth Edition, pp. 121–35. 2. John Bland, *To the Kings Most Excellent Majesty, the Humble Remonstrance of John Blande of London, Merchant, on the behalf of the inhabitants and planters in Virginia and Mariland* . . . (London? 1661?), *Virginia Magazine of History and Biography* (Richmond, 1893), Vol. I, pp. 142–9. 3. (Anonymous), *A Short Answer to an Elaborate Pamphlet, Entitled, The Importance of the Sugar Plantations* (London, 1731). 4. Joshua Gee, *The Trade and Navigation of Great Britain Considered* (London, 1729), pp. 1–7, 70–90. 5. *Annual Report of the American Historical Association from the Year 1892* (Washington, 1893), pp. 64–5. 6. *Ibid.,* pp. 62–3. 7. *Ibid.,* pp. 56–7. 8. *Colonial Currency Reprints, 1682–1751,* Introduction and Notes by Andrew McFarland Davis (Boston, 1911), Vol. II, pp. 336–44. 9. *Ibid.,* III, pp. 308–38. 10. Leo Francis Stock, ed., *Proceedings and Debates of the British Parliaments respecting North America* (Washington, D.C., 1941), Vol. V, 1739–1754, pp. 448–50. 11. Adam Smith, *An Inqiry into the Nature and Causes of the Wealth of Nations,* J. R. McCulloch, ed. (Edinburgh, 1828), Vol. III, pp. 86–9, 114–19.

PART IV. THE POLITICS OF INTERNAL CONTROVERSY. 1. Thomas Hutchinson, *The History of the Colony of Massachu-*

setts-Bay, from the First Settlement Thereof in 1628, Until Its Incorporation with the Colony of Plimouth, Province of Main, etc., By the Charter of King William and Queen Mary, in 1691 (London, 1760), Vol. I, Appendix II, pp. 492–5. 2. *Publications of the Narragansett Club,* First Series (Providence, Rhode Island, 1867), Vol. III, pp. 3–4, 11–13. 3. Peter Force, col., *Tracts and Other Papers, Relating Principally to the Origin, Settlement, and Progress of the Colonies in North America, from the Discovery of the Country to the Year 1776* (Washington, 1844), Vol. III, No. 8. 4. William Hand Browne, ed., *Archives of Maryland. Proceedings and Acts of the General Assembly of Maryland, January 1637/8–September 1664* (Baltimore, 1883), pp. 244–7. 5. William Stevens Perry, ed., *Papers Relating to the History of the Church in Virginia, A.D. 1650–1776* (Privately Printed in 1870), Vol. I, pp. 368–71. 6. Isaac Backus, *History of New England with Particular Reference to the Denomination of Christians Called Baptists* (Newton, Mass., 1871), Vol. II, pp. 44–6. 7. *Annual Report of the American Historical Association for the Year 1892* (Washington, 1893), pp. 45–50. 8. *A Journal of the Votes and Proceedings of the House of Representatives of the Province of Pennsylvania,* Undated, Vol. IV, p. 211. 9. E. B. O'Callaghan, ed., *Documents Relative to the Colonial History of the State of New York; Procured in Holland, England and France, by John Romeyn Brodhead, Esq., Agent* (Albany, 1856), Vol. VII, p. 946. 10. J. H. Easterby, ed., *The Colonial Records of South Carolina: The Journals of the Commons House of Assembly, September 14, 1742–January 27, 1744* (Columbia, South Carolina, 1954), pp. 547–8. 11. *A Brief Statement of the Rise and Progress of the Testimony of the Religious Society of Friends, Against Slavery and the Slave Trade* (Philadelphia, 1843), pp. 17–21. 12. Rev. William Meade, ed., *Sermons Addressed to Masters and Servants, and Published in the Year 1743, by the Rev. Thomas Bacon, Minister of the Protestant Episcopal Church in Maryland* (Winchester, Virginia, 1813), pp. 111–19. 13. J. W. Fortescue, ed., *Calendar of State Papers, Colonial Series, America and West Indies, 1681–1685* (London, 1898), pp. 228–9. 14. R. A. Brock, ed., *The Official Letters of Alexander Spotswood, Lieutenant-Govenor of the Colony of Virginia, 1710–1722* (Richmond, 1885), Vol. II, pp. 48–51. 15. H. R. McIlwaine, ed., *Journals of the House of Burgesses of Virginia, 1727–1734* (Richmond, 1910), pp. 119–20. 16. *Colonial Currency Reprints, 1682–1751,* Introduction and Notes by Andrew McFarland Davis (Boston, 1911), Vol. IV, pp. 68–80. 17. *Ibid.,* pp. 84–108. 18. Leo Francis Stock, ed., *Proceedings and Debates of the British Parliaments Respecting North America* (Washington, D.C., 1941), Vol. V, 1739–1754, pp. 97–8.

PART V. CONSTITUTIONAL CONTEST BETWEEN COLONY AND CROWN. 1. *Journals of the House of Representatives of Massachusetts, 1727–1729*, The Massachusetts Historical Society (Boston, 1927), Vol. VIII, pp. 315–18. 2. *Ibid.*, pp. 324–30. 3. Walter Clark, ed., *The State Records of North Carolina, Laws, 1715–1776* (Goldsboro, North Carolina, 1904), Vol. XXIII, pp. 12–14. 4. William L. Saunders, ed., *The Colonial Records of North Carolina* (Raleigh, 1886), Vol. IV, 1734–1752, pp. 177–8. 5. *Calendar of State Papers, Colonial Series, America and West Indies*, Vol. XLIII, 1737, C.O.5, 365, *fos.* 202–3 d. 6. Nathaniel Bouton, ed., *Documents and Records Relating to the Province of New Hampshire, from 1749 to 1763* (Manchester, 1872), Vol. VI, pp. 74–6. 7. *Ibid., pp.* 86–7. 8. Gertrude MacKinney, ed., *Votes and Proceedings of the House of Representatives of the Province of Pennsylvania Beginning the Fourteenth Day of October, 1726* (Philadelphia, 1931), Pennsylvania Archives, Eighth Series, Vol. III, pp. 2600–03. 9. *Ibid.*, pp. 2605–11. 10. *Statutes at Large of South Carolina; Edited Under Authority of the Legislature by Thomas Cooper* (Columbia, South Carolina, 1838), Vol. III, 1716 to 1756, pp. 556–9. 11. Malachy Postlethwayt, *The National and Private Advantages of the American Trade Considered* (London, 1772), pp. 1–8. 12. John Pendleton Kennedy, ed., *Journals of the House of Burgesses of Virginia, 1761–1765* (Richmond, 1907), pp. 256–7.

PART VI. THE POLITICS OF INTERNATIONAL RIVALRY. 1. E. B. O'Callaghan, ed., *Documents Relative to the Colonial History of the State of New York; Procured in Holland, England, and France by John Romeyn Brodhead, Esq., Agent* (Albany, 1855), Vol. IX, pp. 319–22. 2. William Cobbett, *Parliamentary History of England from the Norman Conquest in 1066, to the Year 1803* (London, 1809), Vol. V, 1688–1702, pp. 1330–31. 3. *The Official Letters of Alexander Spotswood, Lieutenant-Govenor of the Colony of Virginia, 1710–1722*, Introduction and Notes by R. A. Brock, Virginia Historical Society (Richmond, 1882), Vol. II, pp. 295–8. 4. O'Callaghan, *op. cit.*, pp. 899–903. 5. Herbert E. Bolton, ed., *Arredondo's Historical Proof to Spain's Title to Georgia* (Berkeley, 1925), pp. 209–17. 6. B. R. Carroll, ed., *Historical Collections of South Carolina; Embracing Many Rare and Valuable Pamphlets, and Other Documents, Relating to the History of That State, from Its First Discovery to Its Independence, in the Year 1776* (New York, 1836), Vol. II, pp. 348–59. 7. Cobbett, *op. cit.* (London, 1812), Vol. X, A.D. 1737–1739, pp. 770–5. 8. Carroll, *op. cit.*, pp. 242–7. 9. Theodore Calvin Pease, ed., *Anglo-French Boundary Disputes in the West, 1749–1763*, from Collections of the Illinois State Historical Library, Vol. XXVII (Springfield, Ill.,

1936), Vol. III, French Series, pp. 1–4. 10. O'Callaghan, *op. cit.*, Vol. X, pp. 222–4. 11. Jared Sparks, ed., *The Writings of George Washington; Being His Correspondence, Addresses, Messages, and Other Papers, Official and Private* (New York, 1847), Vol. II, pp. 432–47. 12. O'Callaghan, *op. cit.*, Vol. X, pp. 387–91. 13. Pease, *op. cit.*, pp. 306–7. 14. Peter Kalm, *Travels Into North America; Containing Its Natural History and a Circumstantial Account of its Plantations and Agriculture in general, with the Civil, Ecclesiastical and Commercial State of the Country, the Manner of the Inhabitants, and several curious and Important Remarks on Various Subjects,* John Reinhold Forster, trans. (1770), Vol. I, pp. 205–7. 15. Cornélis De Witt, *Jefferson and the American Democracy: An Historical Study.* R. S. H. Church, trans. (London, 1862), pp. 392–4.

PART VII. REVOLUTION AND INDEPENDENCE. 1. E. S. and H. M. Morgan, *The Stamp Act Crisis* (Chapel Hill, N.C., 1953), pp. 106–7. 2. Soame Jenyns, *Miscellaneous Pieces in Verse and Prose* (London, 1770), 3rd. ed., pp. 421–6. 3. Daniel Dulany, *Considerations on the Propriety of Imposing Taxes in the British Colonies for the Purpose of Raising a Revenue by Act of Parliament* (London, 1766), pp. 4 ff. 4. W. S. Taylor and J. H. Pringle, eds., *Correspondence of William Pitt, Earl of Chatham* (London, 1888), Vol. II, pp. 369 ff. 5. P. L. Ford, ed., *The Writings of John Dickinson* (Philadelphia, 1895), Vol. I, pp. 312 ff., 328 ff. 6. W. C. Ford, ed., *Journals of the Continental Congress* (Washington, 1904), Vol. I, pp. 63 ff. 7. Daniel Leonard, *The Present Political State of the Province of Massachusetts Bay in General and the Town of Boston in Particular By a Native of New England* (New York, 1775), pp. 55–61. 8. C. F. Adams, ed., *The Works of John Adams* (Boston, 1851), Vol. IV, pp. 105 ff. 9. A. S. Cook, ed., *Edmund Burke's Speech on Conciliation with America* (New York, 1899), pp. 6 ff. 10. Adam Smith, *An Inquiry into the Nature and Causes of the Wealth of Nations* (London, 1843), Vol. III, pp. 391 ff., Vol. IV, pp. 419 ff. 11. W. C. Ford, ed., *Journals of the Continental Congress,* Vol. II, pp. 140 ff. 12. M. D. Conway, ed., *The Writings of Thomas Paine* (New York, 1894), Vol. I, pp. 84 ff. 13. Charles Inglis, *The True Interest of America Impartially Stated in certain Strictures On a Pamphlet intitled Common Sense, By an American* (Philadelphia, 1776), pp. 3 ff. 14. Carl Becker, *The Declaration of Independence* (New York, 1958), pp. 185 ff.

✳ INDEX ✳

VINTAGE HISTORY—AMERICAN

VINTAGE POLITICAL SCIENCE
AND SOCIAL CRITICISM

VINTAGE WORKS OF SCIENCE
AND PSYCHOLOGY

VINTAGE BIOGRAPHY AND AUTOBIOGRAPHY